IDEAS IN ACTION: ESSAYS ON POLITICS AND LAW IN HONOUR OF PETER RUSSELL

Edited by Joseph F. Fletcher

This collection of essays pays tribute to the manifold career of Peter Russell, a political scientist and an energetic participant in constitutional debate. Based on the proceedings of a conference held in 1996, the book is divided into five parts: Constitutional Politics, Aboriginal Peoples, Security and Intelligence, Law and the Courts, and Rights and Society. The essays themselves discuss important issues throughout Russell's scholarship, including democratic accountability, political deliberation, and cultural diversity.

Joseph Fletcher has brought together a group of contributors, both scholars and practitioners, whose backgrounds reflect Russell's own diverse academic and personal interests. As a result, the work is a successful blend of analysis and reflection.

Few Canadian academics exhibit the level of productivity that Peter Russell has over the years, and this collection celebrates his significant contribution as a scholar and an activist.

JOSEPH F. FLETCHER is a professor of political science at the University of Toronto.

EDITED BY
JOSEPH F. FLETCHER

Ideas in Action: Essays on Politics and Law in Honour of Peter Russell

UNIVERSITY OF TORONTO PRESS
Toronto Buffalo London

Toronto Buffalo London
Printed in Canada

ISBN 0-8020-4497-2 (cloth)
ISBN 0-8020-8271-8 (paper)

Printed on acid-free paper

Canadian Cataloguing in Publication Data

Main entry under title:

Ideas in action : essays on politics and law in honour of Peter Russell

Based on a conference held Nov. 15–16, 1997.
Includes bibliographical references.
ISBN 0-8020-4497-2 (bound) ISBN 0-8020-8271-8 (pbk.)

1. Federal government – Canada – Congresses. 2. Constitutional law – Canada – Congresses. 3. Civil rights – Canada – Congresses. 4. Intelligence service – Canada – Congresses. 5. Justice, Administration of – Canada – Congresses. I. Fletcher, Joseph F., 1949– . II. Russell, Peter H.

KE4219.5.I33 1999 342.71 C99-931257-X
KF4482.I33 1999

University of Toronto Press acknowledges the financial assistance to its publishing program of the Canada Council for the Arts and the Ontario Arts Council.

University of Toronto Press acknowledges the financial support for its publishing activities of the Government of Canada through the Book Publishing Industry Development Program (BPIDP).

Canadä

Contents

Acknowledgments

My greatest thanks go to Bob Matthews who, as chair of the Department of Political Science at the University of Toronto, gave this project its initial impetus and remained a perfect catalyst at every stage of planning and coordination for the conference, as well as taking responsibility for all financial obligations. Thanks also go to his successor, Rob Vipond, who helped carry this project to completion. I must also thank Jennifer Nedelsky for her work in organizing and running the conference on which this volume is based. For conference funding we relied on the Department of Political Science, the Centre of Criminology, the Faculty of Law, and the Office of the Provost, all at the University of Toronto. The Department of Political Science also provided the subsidy required for publication. My thanks also go to Virgil Duff at the University of Toronto Press, whose early and continuing interest in this project was a welcome incentive. John Parry for the Press did an exemplary job as copy editor.

I also owe a special debt to Hyla Levy, without whom virtually nothing connected with the conference would have worked. Hyla played the key organizational and administrative role in setting up and running all aspects of the event. She saw to the many details big and small with astounding thoughtfulness and thoroughness. In addition, she transcribed the question and answer sessions on which my summaries of the discussions are based. John Browne, principal of Innis College, provided the perfect conference venue at Innis, where Peter Russell had also once served as principal. I also want to thank Joey Schwartz, formerly of Innis College, for his technical assistance in producing audio tapes of the sessions. I also am grateful to Jonathan Malloy, who ably assisted during the conference.

Many of Peter Russell's colleagues, friends, and family also deserve special thanks for chairing sessions, toasting and roasting Peter Russell at the meals, and otherwise advising on the many aspects of the conference and on Peter

Russell's professional contacts. They include Kathy Brock, Alan Cairns, Peter Calamai, Marsha Chandler, John Crossley, Ron Daniels, Brian Dickson, Mary Endress, Stuart Farson, Ted Finn, Ian Greene, Richard Hamilton, Storrs McCall, Gordon Peters, Robert Prichard, Alex Russell, Phillip Stenning, Wesley Wark, Mel Watkins, Lorraine Weinrib, and Jacob Zeigel.

I also want to thank each of the contributors to this volume for his or her thoughtful work on the essays that you find here.

To Sue Russell and her family I would like to express my gratitude for all your help in making the conference a success and, most especially, for your willingness to share Peter Russell with us.

And finally to Peter Russell, I deeply appreciate all you and your work have given me over the years.

Joseph F. Fletcher
Toronto, April 1999

IDEAS IN ACTION:
ESSAYS ON POLITICS AND LAW
IN HONOUR OF PETER RUSSELL

General Introduction

JOSEPH F. FLETCHER

A very minor literary genre that for some reason has always held a great deal of fascination for me centres on the exploits of the splendid amateur. Often set in a time of more grace and elegance than our own, the story usually concerns a person of considerable but not exceptional means who, with little more than his or her wits, sets happily about business with an exceptional interest in one of the then-budding sciences. Sherlock Holmes and Indiana Jones capture part of the spirit I'm thinking of, as does Charles Smithson (minus the ennui) in John Fowles's novel *The French Lieutenant's Woman*.

Part of the charm of these characters lies often in the playful, lighthearted part they play in the emergence of the modern world of science and reason. With an intelligence unmarred by the grand schemes of the modern intellectual or the cynical sneer of his postmodern counterpart, the open and engaged character of mind combined with a sense of the very real limits of his own knowledge animates our hero as he lunches on rather dry potatoes and nearly grey peas at a dowdy, though once grand club with some of his fellows.

The splendid amateur is, of course, long gone, perhaps never having been with us at all, except in romantic fantasy. Yet when one comes across Peter Russell in his Tilley hat, recently returned from the antipodes (probably by way of the Arctic) as he bicycles off to the Faculty Club at University of Toronto for lunch, one quickly realizes that perhaps the most splendid amateur of our time is alive and well.

By his own admission, Peter had no training for his career as political scientist. He has no earned Phd, nor even an earned MA. His undergraduate degree at the University of Toronto was in philosophy and history. He then took a year of philosophy, politics, and economics (PPE) at Oxford in 1957 but returned to Canada to become a personnel manager at the Aluminum Company of Canada. After only a year in business, he took up a position at the University of Toronto as a lecturer with teaching interests primarily in modern democratic theory. The then dean of arts and science, Vincent Bladen, advised his young colleague with such minimal credentials that he had better write if he had any wish to remain with the university.

Appropriately enough, it is largely through Peter's writing that we have come to appreciate what a truly splendid amateur he is, and also what a consummate professional. Without benefit or burden of an advanced degree, he has become a professor of the highest rank at the University of Toronto (University Professor, 1994). He has twice received an honorary doctorate of laws (1990, 1993) and served as president of the Canadian Political Science Association (1990) as well as of the Canadian Law and Society Association (1987). He has been elected fellow of the Royal Society of Canada (1988) and an officer of the Order of Canada (1986). He was selected as a Rhodes Scholar (1955–7) and an Edward Blake fellow (1951) from the University of Toronto Schools (UTS). Yet there is not a stuffy bone in his body. Still as much a boy as man in spirit, charm, and curiosity, his conversation is always animated by his next, rather than his previous, adventure.

Throughout his career, Peter Russell has stood at the crossroads of Canadian intellectual life during perhaps its most vigorous period. And through his professional work he has responded to some of the most basic challenges of law and politics in modern democratic states. His influence on government and students of government spans an astonishing range of issues, including constitutional renewal, the aspirations of Aboriginal peoples, security-intelligence operations, the role of courts, and the relations between legislature and judiciary. But perhaps most important, his career offers a model of the truly engaged scholar, forging optimal links between ideas and action.

While it is hardly surprising that he should have turned his talents to the most important issues at the heart of contemporary society, what is most unusual is that as a scholar and an activist he has consistently chosen to work at increasing the democratic aspects of the institutions in which he has lived, worked, and studied. For if intellectual rigour and a gift for sharply honed prose have kept Peter at the centre of Canadian intellectual life, the narrow familiarity of the Canadian intellectual elite in his youth brought him into early contact with many of the same people with whom he would later work. At UTS among the most academically able boys of his day, at Trinity College with some of Canada's most gifted undergraduates, at Oxford among the most able young scholars, and at the University of Toronto, he has always lived among members of the intellectual elite. Through friendships and acquaintances he has had ongoing access to the corridors of power and tradition. Yet he has not shown anything of the common elite preoccupation with maintaining the elite status of the institutions within which he has lived. Instead, he has long worked towards promoting greater inclusiveness at them. His openness to diversity and his commitment to fairness and justice have wedged open the door of Canadian intellectual, political, and judicial institutions enough to permit entry to those ideas and individuals who would transform them.

On the constitutional front, he has persistently pressed for more democratic deliberative elements. He has consistently stood at the side of Aboriginal peoples in their struggle for recognition. In security intelligence, he has directed the light of democratic oversight into some of the darkest corners of modern democratic states. His work in reforming the selection of judges has transformed the complexion and make-up of the judiciary. And his many writings on the law have opened it to those standing outside legal institutions.

In many respects, his personal history has been clearly shaped by happenstance and the longstanding friendships and connection of his personal circle. But what he has done is obviously also the product of deep underlying convictions.

What motivates such a life and career? Although religious beliefs are not immediately evident in his work, when asked, Peter will describe himself simply as a strong Anglican and comment readily on the role of his religion in his life. Perhaps there is a clue here for someone seeking to understand the overall thrust or philosophy of his work, although surely no one thing can thus explain the complexity of this or any person's accomplishments. Still, in whatever he works on he shows little interest in perfecting people or their institutions, preferring an incrementalism over the search for grand solutions. This patience with imperfection in human affairs may well have its source in his most basic religious beliefs, perhaps even traceable to the Anglican notion of original sin. On occasion he repeats a line from Matthew's account of the Sermon on the Mount (6:34) that his mother often used to sum up the limits on human moral progress, 'Sufficient unto the day is the evil thereof.' Yet as a religious man he does not shrink from the evils of the world, preferring to wade in, never expecting perfection, but only to improve things, if ever so slightly. His substantial influence on public life in this country perhaps illustrates the wisdom of this approach.

The essays drawn together here were originally prepared for the 'Ideas in Action' conference held to honour Peter on the occasion of his early retirement from the University of Toronto. The conference was held on 15 and 16 November 1996 at Innis College, where he had once served as principal. The theme of the conference was chosen to reflect the practical influence as well as the scholarly foundations of his work. The papers focus on broad problems at the intersection of law and politics, reflecting some of the breadth and coherence of Peter Russell's endeavours. They illustrate some of the ways in which his scholarship has affected key issues of public policy, shaping dimensions of political life in Canada.

As at the conference, I have organized the essays here into five sections: Constitutional Politics; Aboriginal Peoples; Security Intelligence; Law and the Courts, and Rights and the Charter. Each section begins with a presentation by a practitioner who has worked closely with Peter Russell at some point in his career. These first papers in each section highlight some practical aspect of Peter's engagement with Canadian law, politics, and society. These practical perspectives are complemented by the reflections of distinguished scholars, all experts in their respective fields. Taken together, the papers not only reflect some of the practical and theoretical range of Russell's work but also reveal something of his approach. They offer us close analyses of our basic institutional arrangements, aimed at explaining how to strengthen their democratic core. These contributions thus exemplify not grand schemes of how things ought to be, but rather Peter's own approach of moving us decisively forward in understanding how our institutional life can better reflect our fundamental values.

At many points the concerns raised in these essays intersect one another, both within and across the sections. At the most general level, they all probe connections between institutional design and democratic theory. In focusing sharply on how institutions actually work, the contributors often cross conventional disciplinary lines. And they move beyond the practical political and legal issues at hand to shed light on ideas at the heart of contemporary social theory. Several such ideas stand out, foremost among them notions of deliberation and diversity, identity and inclusion.

Peter Russell's appreciation of the value of democratic deliberation emerges as a core theme in nearly all the essays. The many theoretical and practical dimensions of law and politics discussed throughout the volume converge on the challenge of creating and sustaining the genuine deliberation at the centre of truly democratic institutions. Whether the constitution or the courts is the topic, or Aboriginal, security, or Charter issues are under examination, a core issue is ensuring deliberative procedures adequate to our fundamental democratic values. The specific approaches and recommendations diverge, even clash at many points, but the fundamental concern is nearly always how best to invigorate the deliberative core of Canadian institutions.

One of the pleasures in editing this work is sharing these fine essays with the reader. One of the frustrations is not being able to capture fully the many exchanges and discussions stimulated by the original presentations at the conference. To offer some access to these exchanges, I have summarized the discussion at the end of each part. By summarizing, I hope to avoid much of the awkwardness and redundancy of direct transcription, while retaining some of the dynamic and colour of the original event. I have taken one other editorial liberty as well by rearranging the order of some of the presentations so as to enhance the overall coherence of certain of the parts.

Perhaps less well represented here are the many aspects of humour, love, admiration, and friendship that found expression in the less formal aspects of the conference. There were stories and vignettes, ranging from the division of dishwashing chores among the children of a constitutional scholar, as shared by Peter Russell's son, Alex, though the rigours of 'Russelling up a thesis,' as told by former student Cathy Brock, to the parallels of Peter's career with that of the Aluminum Company of Canada, as pointed out by colleague Martin Friedland. We also learned from Peter Calanai about Peter Russell's insistence on making collect phone calls in response to journalists and about the many years of department and university service outlined by University of Toronto President Robert Pritchard and by Dean Marsha Chandler. Jacob Zeigel reminded us of Peter Russell's passion for social reform, while Wesley Pue paid tribute to his work on behalf of a fledgling Canadian Law and Society Association. Dick Hamilton regaled us with tales of Russell's good fortune in love and bad luck at cards, and Ted Morton lampooned his accomplishments using the infamous case of *Russell v. The Queen* (1882). The admiration of younger colleagues was evident in reminiscences by Jennifer Nedelsky and me. And there were the toasts and much praise from Brian Dickson, Ted Finn, and others. These all must go untold here beyond this brief mention.

Much to Peter Russell's delight, the conference was enriched by the unscheduled intervention of a group of members of the Canadian Union of Postal Workers. Taking advantage of an open microphone during a discussion period, they protested the firing of some of their members, using placards and chants. Although they achieved their immediate purpose by expressing their displeasure to the federal minister on one of the panels, a palpable tension developed between the protesters and the conference participants as part of the resulting stand-off. A troubling exchange came just as the original disruption was nearly quelled by the minister's promise to communicate the workers' concerns to cabinet and to contact them the following week. As one of the conference organizers, I attempted to get things going again, by inappropriately asking in a somewhat jocular fashion if there were any further questions. The obvious discomfort and tension that had built up in the audience during the confrontation erupted into laughter, incensing the protesters and extending the stand-off. The gap separating the minister and the protesters, and more generally that separating the audience and me from the postal workers, was clearly signified by both the laughter and the offence taken. This encounter in many ways symbolizes something of the difficulties that we face in making our institutions more democratic.

Peter Russell's scholarship consistently highlights the fundamental 'democratic deficits' in our institutional arrangements. The people of Canada, he has warned, now demand a more substantial role in their democratic life, but the 'chattering' classes, as he likes to call us, have yet to find effective ways to include them in the deliberations affecting their lives. The legitimacy of our legal, political, and social arrangements depends on our finding a way to set things right. Yet, as Peter Russell has counselled, there probably is no easy solution, no quick fix. In pointing this out, he has put his finger on a vital tension in our society between the need for more democracy and our recognition of our own great diversity. The more we appreciate the one, the more difficult the other becomes. His approach has been neither to theorize nor to seek either a fully democratic or a fully inclusive society. Rather he has prudently nudged us along to be ever more inclusive and ever more democratic, one small step at a time. In doing so he has steadily brought those who have historically been brushed aside ever more closely into the deliberations at the centre of Canadian law and politics. This volume is our tribute to his success.

PART I:
CONSTITUTIONAL POLITICS

Prior to his appointment in 1958 to the University of Toronto's Department of Political Economy, Peter Russell already thought of himself as a very liberal democrat. His studies in philosophy at Toronto and Oxford had alerted him to shortcomings in Hobbes's and Bentham's constitutionalism, most particularly in their emphasis on the need to hem in the majority. To Peter Russell, a more pressing challenge to democracy lay in the abuse of executive power. His nascent views on constitutional politics were soon to emerge within an academic context, where, thanks largely to C.B. Macpherson's withering critiques, liberalism was very much on the defensive. Perhaps not surprisingly given the man and his context, Peter Russell's views on constitutional politics took a strongly democratic cast, emphasizing the need for more democratic institutions and more democratic practices.

Early in the 1960s Peter prepared a paper for a conference at University of Toronto's Hart House on amending the constitution. The now familiar thrust of his argument was that Canada, lacking custody of its constitution, did not have the means to become a fulfilled democracy. Apparently, the audience had some difficulty staying awake. There seemed to be little interest or enthusiasm among academics of the day for what he had to say. In time, this was to change, of course. Pierre Elliott Trudeau was soon to make his way onto the national stage with his agenda for constitutional patriation.

When Trudeau did arrive, Peter Russell was not much impressed by his approach to constitutionalism. Peter thought of constitutional politics as touching on profound issues of fundamental attachments and national identity, whereas Trudeau's approach seemed designed primarily as an ideological weapon to counter the decentralizing demands coming from Quebec and the other provinces. Besides, Russell detected little real commitment to civil liberties behind Trudeau's constitutionalism, but rather a 'take them or leave them' attitude. Discouraged on both counts, he turned his academic attentions elsewhere, even declining an invitation to go to a Queen's University conference, growing out of the Molgat–MacGregor Report, on the making of a new constitution for Canada.

Nevertheless, as Quebec began to press for a more fundamental reworking of the federation following the election of the Parti Québécois government in 1976, Peter came to realize that Canadians would probably face a choice between accepting an independent Quebec and reworking the constitution. He decided to rejoin the game. His own approach has been to resist the search for a big constitutional breakthrough, preferring to adjust Confederation in a more incremental manner, using a one-reform-at-a-time form of constitutional politics.

Peter's *Constitutional Odyssey*, 2nd ed. (Toronto, 1993), approvingly documents a movement in Canadian political life from an elite-centred constitutionalism to a more participatory, democratic process. Extending the trend, he envisions Canada becoming a new kind of nation-state, where unity derives from the accommodation of diversity. He seeks not a final, once-and-for-all contract, but rather an ongoing deliberative activity, perhaps with governments and legislators at its centre, but with a decisive role for the citizenry. In moving towards this end, he counsels a more open and accountable constitutional process, recognizing that the incrementalist approach is not without its problems, for it offers for now only a marginal role for broadly based democratic participation and is too readily assimilated to the conflicts between the provinces and the federal government.

Summary of Papers

Stéphane Dion's paper, 'The Ethic of Federalism' (chapter 1), draws inspiration from Peter Russell's commitment to making the Canadian federation work. Tracing a continuity between Russell's work and that of George-Étienne Cartier, who played a key role in Confederation, Dion raises central issues of diversity and identity, solidarity and autonomy in Canadian politics. He argues that federalism offers a third way between universalism and diversity. In Dion's view, federalism can promote the cohabitation of cultures and inhibit identity-based fragmentation, while retaining flexibility enough to adapt and evolve. By reconciling the need for autonomy with a genuine solidarity, Dion contends, federalism encourages the tolerance necessary for a heterogeneous society to exist and instills in us Canadians the desire to help each other be who we are. The broad themes of identity and diversity introduced here are taken up in the essays in the section on constitutional politics, as well as by the papers on Aboriginal peoples, the courts, and law and society.

Robert C. Vipond's 'Lament for a Notion' (chapter 2) reviews Peter Russell's scepticism regarding rights-based liberalism and its expression in constitutional bills of rights to highlight Russell's concern with devising more democratic institutions and practices. The central notion here is of government by discussion, rooted in the ideal of public deliberation. Vipond urges a rethinking of liberal principles in facing the rights-based arguments advanced by politicians of the new right, who seek to limit the role of the state in the name of individual freedom and equality. Neither dismissing Charter liberalism nor romanticizing its historic competitors, Vipond offers detailed examples of how Peter Russell's brand of liberalism can reinvigorate legislatures caught in the grip of executive power and reconnect citizens to a larger sphere of public life and concerns. Concentrating on the historic roots of reform liberalism Vipond considers how to breathe new life into the ideas from the last century about public deliberation without bringing back the exclusion and state-sanctioned economic privilege.

The elements of diversity and deliberation in Peter Russell's constitutionalism as emphasized in the two previous papers are brought together and explored in the language of contemporary political theory by James Tully's 'Democratic Constitutionalism in a Diverse Federation' (chapter 3). Starting from Russell's notion of popular sovereignty, Tully argues that Canadians must impose constitutional conditions on themselves through public deliberation. Realizing this ideal of participatory constitutionalism is made especially difficult by our differences, which clearly matter. So the constitutional challenge implicit in Russell's vision of Canada, according to Tully, is to discover a means of multisided deliberation encompassing mutual recognition of diversities and expressing them in our political association. While as citizens we may not know how to go about this, our need to do so is clear. Tully draws on Rawls and other contemporary theorists to elaborate Russell's notion of democratic deliberation and argue that the recognition of diversity is indeed compatible with liberal democracy. He details, for example, how the demands of Aboriginals and Quebecers can be articulated and justified through reasoning and discourse that appeals to liberal-democratic ideas of equality. Some of the specifics of that discourse are explored in the essays by Swinton, Erasmus, and Chartrand.

A more nuts-and-bolts approach comes from Katherine Swinton in 'Rebalancing the Canadian Federation' (chapter 4). She reminds us that formal amendment is not the only means of implementing change within the constitutional framework. A substantial rebalancing of the federal system is already under way, she argues, as a result of policy changes brought on by decentralization and cutbacks. In particular she shows how administrative and fiscal arrangements have been used to negotiate and enforce national standards in internal trade, environmental protection, and reform of social policy. Swinton reviews some of the challenges in finding appropriate mechanisms to permit such cooperation, warning that intergovernmental agreements may not be enough for those wanting constitutional guarantees. She is also concerned about the persistent problems of adequate public deliberation entailed in proceeding through intergovernmental negotiation and agreement. On balance, she recommends pursuing an incremental approach to constitutional change, focusing on particular policy areas.

1

The Ethic of Federalism

STÉPHANE DION

No one can appreciate the advantages of a federal system more than I. I hold it to be one of the most powerful combinations favoring human prosperity and freedom. I envy the lot of the nations that have been allowed to adopt it.

Alexis de Tocqueville, *Democracy in America*

They were placed like great families beside each other, and their contact produced a healthy spirit of emulation. It was a benefit rather than otherwise that we had a diversity of races.

George-Étienne Cartier, *Confederation debates*, 7 Feb. 1865

Quebec nationalists cannot push their nationalist projects through to completion ... without abandoning the practice of mutual respect and tolerance that has been the essential condition for whatever the peoples of Canada have achieved together as citizens of a single state.

Peter H. Russell, 'Can Quebeckers Be a Sovereign People?'

Peter Russell's work goes to the heart of the Canadian debate, reaching values beyond the inevitable constitutional squabbling. We Canadians do not want to choose between universal solidarity and respect for cultural diversities. We are strongly attached to both.

'I should regard it as a great misfortune for mankind if liberty were to exist all over the world under the same features,'[1] wrote Alexis de Tocqueville. That is the very misfortune that the Canadian ideal intends to combat. Canadians know that the quest for what is right, just, and good must be plural; they know that it is by drawing on the best part of each culture, each individual, regional, or historical experience, that we come closer to what is best in civilization. Canadians know that equality must not be confused with uniformity. Those who do not yet know that should read and think about Peter Russell's work.

That dual quest for the universal and for cultural diversity has been with us since the birth of our Confederation. We have often strayed from it and committed grave mistakes and injustices, but the net result is this admirable human achievement that is Canada.

One need only compare the thinking of George-Étienne Cartier with that of Peter Russell to gauge the continuity of the Canadian ideal. In his famous address on 7 February 1865 to the Legislative Assembly on the proposed confederation of the provinces of British North America, Cartier set out the principles that still define Canada today. He first stressed respect for cultures, using the terms of his era, those of 'race' or 'nation.' Cartier identified four 'races' which were then very much present in Canada: the French Canadians, the Scots, the English, and the Irish. Had there been others just as present, he would certainly have mentioned them, for there was nothing exclusionary in his thinking. Cartier did, however, commit the grave error of forgetting Aboriginals, an error that Peter Russell has ceaselessly sought to remedy.

Cartier spoke also of the Catholic and Protestant denominations, noted that there are many Catholics who are not French, and called again for tolerance and unity. 'In our own Federation we should have Catholic and Protestant, English, French, Irish and Scotch, and each by his efforts and his success would increase the prosperity and glory of the new Confederacy.'[2]

Cartier ensured that the dominion government would be strong, able to withstand the American threat – which at that time was military – and also able to carry out large-scale common projects. The provinces for their part would be able to express the specific personality of their inhabitants. He predicted that the union with additional provinces would help Canada East, because his province would thus be able to vary alliances rather than being merged into a united province with a rapidly growing Upper Canada. And thus Quebec today allies itself on occasion with Ontario for industrial policy, with the Prairies and the Atlantic provinces for social policy, and with the western provinces for international trade policy.

Finally, Cartier wanted Canada to be a 'political nation' – a nation of solidarity that transcended race, religion, history, and geography, to ensure that the French in Quebec would never want to break their solidarity with other Canadians. If we seek a contract at the birth of our union, it is certainly the one expressed by Cartier, which has inspired all of Peter Russell's work. Quebecers of all origins have helped other Canadians a great deal to achieve that ideal; they must not renounce it.

The Canadian ideal seeks to guarantee the necessary cohabitation of cultures through an ethic of federalism. That is the idea that I develop in the following text. Although I wrote this text as minister of the Crown responsible for advising the prime minister on Canadian unity, I believe that I have closely adhered to the academic rigour embodied by Professor Russell.

The Necessary Cohabitation of Cultures

At a time when identity-driven aspirations are stronger than ever throughout the world, the idea that any population with its own distinctive characteristics should have its own state is completely false. 'To each people its own state' is obviously an impractical idea, but it is also a moral error, because by learning to have their component cultures live together states give their populations the opportunity of elevating themselves. The cohabitation of cultures within the same state helps human beings to become better citizens, by allowing them to experience and practise tolerance.

According to Daniel Elazar, 'There are some 3,000 ethnic or tribal groups in the world conscious of their respective identities. Of the over 180 politically "sovereign" states now in existence, over 160 are multiethnic in composition.'[3] The idea of 'one people, one state' would cause the world to explode.

This comment from a report by the Secretary General of the United Nations is food for thought indeed: 'Yet if every ethnic, religious or linguistic group claimed statehood, there would be no limit to fragmentation, and peace, security and economic well-being for all would become even more difficult to achieve.'[4]

I have met with my South African counterpart, the minister of intergovernmental affairs of that brand new federation. South Africa does not have, as we do in Canada, two official languages – English and French – that are also international; it has eleven, not to mention all sorts that have been accorded some sort of political status. South Africa is coming out of one of the vilest possible experiences ever invented by human beings for human beings – the nightmare of apartheid. Through reconciliation and striving for harmonious cohabitation of cultures, South Africa, with its eleven official languages, will gradually regain the strength it needs to take on the human and socio-economic challenges that face it. The only solution for South Africa is unity, not fragmentation. Surely Canada, a country so blessed by fortune, will not be an example of break-up for South Africa and for the rest of the world.

Trying to ensure that everyone is part of a majority wherever he or she lives would be an exercise in futility. We need to seek the means by which confident, flourishing minorities and cultures can live together within a single political structure. The presence and influence of the Quebec minority within Canada strengthen not only Canadians in the other provinces, but also Quebecers themselves, through the complementarity of their belonging to Quebec and to Canada. Without sticking my nose into other countries' affairs, I believe that this is the same universal value that should be followed for the Scots in Britain or for the Catalans in Spain.

Canada, this country that has become a universal model of openness, tolerance, and generosity, is the last country in the world where identity-based fragmentation should be allowed to triumph. That would be all the more regrettable because the reason that Canada is so open, so tolerant, and so generous today is because the French and English, from the beginning, have striven to get along and to take advantage both of their respective identities and of the complementarity of their two great cultures. It has not always been easy; there have been some dark pages in our history, but the end result is this rich, tolerant society that is Canada.

Our largest urban centres – Montreal, Toronto, and Vancouver – are models of coexistence that have been able to avoid becoming racist cities, of which there are far too many examples in the world, and for that very reason they deserve to stay within the same state, being so close in spirit despite the geographical distance that separates them. In fact, a survey conducted by the Swiss Corporate Resources Group put them among the best metropolitan areas in the world in which to live – Vancouver finished second, Toronto fourth, and Montreal seventh. These Canadian cities were ranked ahead of Brussels, London, Oslo, and Paris and way ahead of the highest-ranked American city, Boston, which came in at number thirty.[5]

My own riding of Saint-Laurent–Cartierville is another example of a pluralistic, harmonious community, a veritable mini–United Nations, with more than fifty different, vibrant nationalities. I always find it an inspiration, because for me that is what Montreal, and Quebec, and Canada, are all about – different cultures living together harmoniously within a single state.

I would like the Spanish to view the flourishing of Catalonia with confidence as a strength for Spain and not a threat to its unity. I would like the British to feel the same way about Scotland. I do not want my country, Canada, to serve as an example to be held up by the anxious majorities of Spain, the United Kingdom, or elsewhere. My dream is that the U.S. Congress, for example, instead of saying, as we have heard it say, 'We don't want to create "Quebecs" within the United States, so we don't want to grant additional rights to our Spanish-speaking minority,' will say instead, 'Let's take inspiration from what is happening in Canada, where Quebecers and other Canadians live together in harmony, because they accept one another with complete confidence.' I would like to hear the European Union stop saying, 'Careful, let's not give our regions too much autonomy.' I would like Canada to be seen as an inspiration for the future, not only for Canadians, but also for other human beings who are experiencing the cohabitation of cultures within a single state.

The Ethic of Federalism

There are many ways to have populations live together, but the one I recommend and am going to discuss here is federalism. Federalism is often described as being efficient. In my society, Quebec, it is often depicted from that angle, in terms of profitability or profitable federalism: 'Stay in Canada because we have a profitable federation,' Quebecers are told. That's quite true, because four of the five richest countries in the world are federations: Canada, the United States, Germany, and Switzerland.[6]

I am sure that many readers will be aware of the UN or World Bank indicators that give Canada top marks in so many areas of human activity. Canada is a remarkable human achievement, a jewel on the planet, which gives its citizens a quality of life that is among the best in the world. Nevertheless, we do have some serious problems, such as too much unemployment and too much poverty, especially among children. We need to rely on our strengths to tackle those problems, rather than turning our backs on them.

Canada's positive achievements are not the result of chance; in all likelihood, they stem from the fact that our federalism is profitable for so many Canadians. Indeed, federalism as a universal ideal is more than profitable; it has an ethic that encourages cultures to live together.

More than ever, we need to reconcile the global and the local aspect of things, which Tom Courchene at Queen's University calls 'glocalization' – in other words, reconciling extensive solidarity and desires for autonomy. Reconciling those two objectives, through federalism, has served humanity well in the past and will be more necessary than ever in the years to come.

As far back as the nineteenth century, Tocqueville, that great liberal thinker and prophet of democracy, expressed that idea well: 'The federal system was created with the intention of combining the different advantages which result from the magnitude and the littleness of nations.'[7]

Isn't that idea still just as true today, at a time of market 'globalization' and pressure for autonomy? Throughout the world, there are conflicting pressures both for larger political organizations and for smaller, more regional ones. The pressure for larger units has been generated by growing awareness of worldwide interdependence and the need for greater influence in international decision-making. A demand for smaller, self-governing political units has arisen from a need to make governments more responsive to citizens and their primary attachments – linguistic and cultural ties, religious affiliations, historical traditions, and social practices. These are the pillars of community.

Federalism helps to reconcile these dual pressures. It allows regional identities to be expressed both at home and abroad. For example, francophone Canadians are represented in the Commonwealth, just as Anglophone Canadians are represented in the Francophonie. By being together, they form a vast, rich country; both groups have access to the G-7, which they would not have if Canada were to break up. People in eastern Canada have as much access to the Asia–Pacific Economic Cooperation Forum (APEC) as western Canadians do to the Northwest Atlantic Fisheries Organization (NAFO).

At the same time, however, Canada is a federation where each province can have its own perspective and solve its problems in its own way. We have experienced a situation where Canada's ten provinces had budget deficits; each of them has found its own way to resolve that situation, and seven of them have now balanced their budget or are showing a surplus. The method used by New Brunswick's premier was not the same as that used by Alberta and will probably be different from the one that Quebec will devise, with its distinct society and its own culture. All provinces look to their own strengths, but that does not prevent them from helping one another through solidarity, which is something that we need now more than ever – mutual assistance through larger entities and innovation through autonomy.

This leads me to some further comments about the ethic of federalism. The work of Alan Cairns, a recognized Canadian writer on federalism, outlines clearly that institutions not only enable us to do things but also encourage moral principles. They contribute to the way in which we view the world and ourselves.

I believe that the two great moral principles that federalism encourages are tolerance and solidarity.

Tolerance

Federalism as a public philosophy encourages tolerance, which is expressed through the ability to understand different ways of doing things. Tolerance also encourages the ability to accept different ways of contributing to the life of a society. Charles Taylor talks about 'deep diversity':[8] citizens recognize their citizenship in a number of different ways. In its most basic form, tolerance gives people the freedom to be themselves, so as to help one another more effectively.

Some people say that we must all be Canadian in the same way, or else our country is in danger. I believe that's a mistake. The Swiss, for example, have the most powerful municipal system in the world, and from that extensive decentralization they derive a source of pride, an additional reason to feel Swiss. It's the same thing in Canada, where we have strong provinces, as has been demonstrated in the comparative studies by Ron Watts of Queen's University.[9] Some Canadians see decentralization as a threat and feel that that is why the country is threatened with break-up. I am convinced that the opposite is true. Canada would never have been able to survive if it had not been a federation that ensures that Newfoundlanders can be Canadian the Newfoundland way, Manitobans can be Canadian in their way, and Quebecers can be Canadian the Quebec way.

As Peter Russell observed, 'The reality of Canadian citizenship is that at the psychic level it is extraordinarily heterogeneous. Aboriginal Canadians, Quebecois Canadians, Canadians who identify with minority language communities or with ethnic or racial minorities as well as Canadians who yearn to identify with a unified Canadian nation have experienced their connection with Canada historically in very different ways.'[10] I'm a kid from Quebec City, now living in Montreal, and I have my own way of being Canadian; I do not have to be Canadian in the same way as someone from Winnipeg. I know instinctively, however, that sharing this same country with that person from Winnipeg makes both of us better human beings.

When I'm in my home riding and I'm talking with older people of Jewish, Italian, or Greek origin, I almost always have to speak in English, because they have not been sufficiently integrated into Quebec society, for all kinds of historical reasons. When I talk to their eighteen- or nineteen-year-old grandchildren, however, I can speak in French; I can speak in English; I can even try Spanish. Those young people can express themselves in French, in English, and often in one or two other languages and are thus wonderfully equipped for the next century. That's what the Montreal and the Quebec and the Canada of today are all about: a pluralistic society that must remain harmonious and tolerant.

It is sometimes said that federalism can work only in a homogeneous society, with the same religion and language. I could not disagree more. Federalism works well in a homogeneous society, but it is necessary in a heterogeneous society, because it promotes tolerance, which a heterogeneous society needs more than anything else. As Professor Russell has noted, 'The practice of mutual respect and tolerance ... has been the essential condition for whatever the peoples of Canada have achieved together.'[11]

This reflects the thinking of George-Étienne Cartier: 'Some parties ... pretended that it was impossible to carry out Federation, on account of the differences of races and religions. Those who took this view of the question were in error. It was just the reverse. It was precisely on account of the variety of races, local interests, that the Federation system ought to be resorted to, and would be found to work well.'[12]

Solidarity

Samuel LaSelva, a professor at the University of British Columbia, writes in a recent book, *The Moral Foundations of Canadian Federalism*, that 'Canadian nationhood presupposes Canadian federalism which in turn rests on a complex form of fraternity that can promote a just society.'[13] I think that what LaSelva is saying is that this institutional structure of federalism is the bearer of a moral principle that I call solidarity. That was the idea of Cartier, who said that our federation had to be founded on 'kindred interest and sympathies' between the different communities.

Solidarity, which I define as a sense of the common good and of compassion for our fellow citizens, enables us to act together, to join forces and pool our resources. Canadian solidarity is expressed admirably in the principle of mutual assistance among wealthier and less wealthy provinces, through federal government transfers. That principle, which is probably carried further in Canada than in any other federation in the world, means that there are currently seven provinces that receive assistance from what are now the three wealthiest provinces – Ontario, Alberta, and British Columbia. In the 1930s, however, Alberta received assistance from the other provinces, including mine. Albertans know that the day may come when they need Quebecers' help. That is what makes Canadian solidarity so great. Quebecers are currently benefiting from assistance from their fellow citizens in the wealthier provinces and will one day be able in turn to give special assistance to their fellow citizens in the less wealthy provinces.

That is the real meaning of Canadian solidarity. It is more than tolerance; we not only tolerate others as they are, we want to help them be what they are. I want to help Newfoundlanders to be what they are. I also know that they are not like British Columbians. As a Quebecer and a Canadian, I want them in their turn to help Quebec to be a majority francophone society in an English-speaking North America.

The vast majority of Quebecers feel that they are Quebecers and Canadians at the same time, but too many of them believe that they have to choose between their identity as Quebecers and their identity as Canadians. Many of them feel more at home in their Quebec environment and are thus inclined to choose their identity as Quebecers. But why do they feel they have to choose? Because they think that other Canadians do not accept their difference. This is a terrible misunderstanding that must be cleared up to guarantee the unity of our country.

In that spirit, the government of Canada tabled a resolution, which was passed by Parliament, on recognizing Quebec as a distinct society within Canada. In that same spirit, the government of Canada intends to forge ahead so that the other provinces can, with complete confidence, recognize Quebec's distinctiveness in the Canadian constitution.

Conclusion: Flexibility, the Road to Renewal

Federalism, wrote Paul Gérin-Lajoie in his former capacity as Quebec's minister of education, has given human beings a vital tool for coordinating the aspirations of individual communities, making them stronger and giving them broader influence. However, he found a precise definition of federalism somewhat elusive. 'What makes federalism so difficult to describe,' he concluded, 'is precisely what makes it so valuable as a political instrument: its flexibility, its versatility, its ability to take any form.'[14]

He was right. Federalism in Canada is not the same as that found in Switzerland or Belgium, because the contexts are completely different, and the challenges for the populations of South Africa or India are not on the same scale as those facing us in the industrialized countries. Nevertheless, federalism is helping human beings all over the world to live together more harmoniously. That is why I am convinced that it is a valuable solution for human societies – a solution that we must preserve for ourselves and our children and as an example to the world.

But the current Canadian federal system is not only different from its counterparts around the globe. It is very different from that of fifty years ago, and fifty years hence our federation will have undergone a great deal more evolution. That is one of the strengths of federal systems: they are flexible enough to adapt and evolve when faced with new challenges and new contexts.

The flexibility of our federation allows it to respond well to the evolving aspirations of its component provinces, regions, and cultures. This adaptability is part of what Carl Friedrich once called the 'federal spirit.' He defined that spirit as the ability to compromise and accommodate, which are also elements of what I alone called solidarity.[15] A renewal of Canada based on this spirit is, as Peter Russell has so aptly put it, 'in keeping with the Canadian political genius and with the forms of political organization which will be the pace-setters in the twenty-first century.' As Professor Russell has suggested, the alternative – breaking ourselves down into homogeneous nation-states – would be to align ourselves with forces that are receding.[16]

I would make one last reference to Cartier's admirable strength of foresight: 'Nations were now formed by the agglomeration of communities having kindred interests and sympathies.'[17]

It is in this spirit that the federal government is working to renew and modernize the federation. Our government is working with its partners to adapt the federation to the evolving needs of the Canadian population, in line with the moral principles that our system encourages: solidarity and tolerance. At present, our federal system is undergoing a great deal of change. However, Canadians have shown creativity at many points during the past decades, constantly renewing their federation according to internal needs and external forces. The federal system, with its flexibility, can be adapted to face the needs of each successive generation of Canadians. The changes that we are making today are part of a continuum, stretching from the early days of Confederation into a future too distant for our imagining. I am convinced that the Canada of the future will inherit certain characteristics from the Canada of today: it will be strong, flexible, dynamic, generous – and united. This is fortunate, given that the cohabitation of cultures is necessary and, indeed, the only viable possibility, since neither cultural assimilation nor cultural separation is practical or morally acceptable.

The government of Canada is focused on the future. Since the Throne Speech in February 1996, it has put forward a plan to reform our federation. It will do so in a way that will strengthen our precious inheritance from the generations who have built this country to date.

NOTES

1 Alexis de Tocqueville, *Democracy in America*, vol. I (New York: Alfred A. Knopf 1987), 330.

2 *Parliamentary Debates on the Subject of the Confederation of the British North American Provinces*, Tuesday, 7 Feb. 1865, 60.

3 Daniel J. Elazar, *Federalism and the Way to Peace*, Reflections Paper No. 13 (Kingston: Queen's University 1994), 23.

4 Boutros Boutros-Ghali, *An Agenda for Peace* (New York: United Nations 1992), 9.

5 *Ottawa Citizen*, Wed. Jan. 1995, A2.

6 United Nations Development Programme, *Human Development Report* 1994 (New York: Oxford University Press 1994), 104, annex table A5.2.

7 Tocqueville, *Democracy in America, I:* 163.

8 Charles Taylor, 'Shared and Divergent Values,' in Ronald L. Watts and Douglas M. Brown, eds, *Options for a New Canada* (Toronto: University of Toronto Press 1991), 75.

9 Ronald L. Watts, unpublished manuscript, 1996.

10 Peter Russell, 'The Constitution, Citizenship and Ethnicity,' in Jean Laponce and William Safran, eds., *Ethnicity and Citizenship: The Canadian Case* (London: Frank Cass 1996), 101.

11 Russell, 'Can Quebeckers Be a Sovereign People?' 38.

12 *Parliamentary Debates on Confederation*, Tuesday, 7 Feb. 1865, 57.

13 Samuel V. LaSelva, *The Moral Foundations of Canadian Federalism: Paradoxes, Achievements, and Tragedies of Nationhood* (Montreal: McGill-Queen's University Press 1996), xiii.

14 Paul Gérin-Lajoie, 'Canadian Federalism and the Future,' in Gordon Hawkins, ed., *Concepts of Federalism: Thirty-Fourth Couchiching Conference* (1965), 62.

15 Carl J. Friedrich, *Trends of Federalism in Theory and Practice* (New York: Praeger 1968), 39.

16 Russell, 'Can the Canadians Be a Sovereign People?' *Canadian Journal of Political Science* 24 no. 4 (Dec. 1991), 708.

17 *Parliamentary Debates on Confederation*, Tuesday, 7 Feb. 1865, 60.

2

Lament for a Notion: The Eclipse of Reform Liberalism

ROBERT C. VIPOND

In my neck of the political science woods, Peter Russell is best known as a charter member of the club of Charter sceptics. His longstanding view that courts are not well-suited to make policy decisions about rights is of course well known. His early prediction that the Charter of Rights and Freedoms would 'judicialize politics and politicize the judiciary' is one of the best-loved aphorisms of exam setters everywhere.[1] And a number of his students have paid him the ultimate compliment of taking his argument further – and farther afield. Indeed, in one form or another, Charter sceptics occupy a prominent position within Canadian political science, a fact that is the result in no small measure of the enormous influence of Peter Russell's scholarship and teaching. What often gets lost in this 'Charter chatter' (as he likes to call it) is that his scepticism about the Charter has always been part of a larger discomfort about what I call rights-based liberalism, of which Charterized judicial review is the institutional expression.

And what is almost completely forgotten (even by those sympathetic to his Charter argument) is that Russell's reluctance to take rights too, too seriously is the other side of his lament for the eclipse of an alternative form of liberalism that has deep roots in the Canadian political tradition. Although I am not sure that he has ever labelled it quite this way, I want to call his liberalism 'reform liberalism' to emphasize its connection to the Reform tradition that dominated liberal politics in this country for close to 150 years but which over the last generation or so has lost its appeal to liberals. And I want to suggest that it is time to brush off this reform liberalism, revive it, and return it to the mainstream where it belongs – and where it is needed more urgently than ever. Hence the title of my essay.

Shortly after Pierre Trudeau announced his government's intention to pursue the goal of establishing a Charter of Rights for Canadians, Peter Russell wrote an article, published in 1969 in the *University of Toronto Law Journal*, entitled 'A Democratic Approach to Civil Liberties.' It began this way: 'In our society the phrase civil liberties is apt to conjure up the image of the great popular majority, the demos, crushing the sacred rights of the individual or the small minority ... For this tradition of civil liberty the most attractive panacea has been the instrument of a bill of rights – a fundamental code of basic rights enforced by a group of wise and independent judges against the illiberal demands of legislative majorities and their executives.' He then applied this idea, in his typically understated way, to Trudeau's proposal. 'Do you feel menaced by the prospect of the great Canadian majority, acting through its elected representatives in Ottawa, steam-rolling over your basic rights and liberties in pursuit of its own interests? Are you comforted by the possibility that soon the Canadian Bill of Rights may be "entrenched" in the Constitution enabling our judiciary to veto these strident majoritarian demands and secure your liberty? If you ask yourself these questions and can honestly answer them in the affirmative, what you surely need is a psychiatrist not a bill of rights.'[2]

I quote Russell's deliberately provocative challenge at length here because he used this article as a vehicle for sketching two rich caricatures of liberalism, around which he organized his critique of the proposed Charter. From this perspective, liberalism in the Anglo-American world comes, roughly speaking, in two forms. The first, which I call rights-based liberalism, is most powerfully represented by the U.S. constitution and is the inspiration, give or take reasonable limitations here and our multicultural heritage there, for the Canadian Charter of Rights. For such a liberalism, the first object of government is to protect individual rights; and although the list of rights that are considered fundamental varies from place to place and epoch to epoch, property rights have historically enjoyed pride of place in liberal theory. The fundamental problem for rights liberals is that rights are difficult to reconcile with democratic government. Democratic majorities will too often be tempted to use their power to violate individual rights. The basic strategy of rights liberals therefore is to limit executive and legislative power and so limit their potential for damaging liberty; in this sense, rights liberals think it necessary to 'organize out' of political life a set of basic issues. And from that stance derives the liberal mantra: liberal government is institutional government is limited government.[3]

Nor is this view simply a matter of theory. In a famous case before the U.S. Supreme Court in the 1940s, Justice Jackson argued vigorously that there are certain questions that are simply too important to be left to the vicissitudes of politics; this, he maintained, is why constitutions and courts equipped with the power of judicial review exist and need to exist. When two decades later Pierre

Trudeau set out to explain why Canadians needed a Charter to protect individual rights, it is not coincidental that he cited Justice Jackson's formulation word for word – without attribution, but word for word.[4]

The alternative version of liberalism, which can be traced in this country back to the struggle for responsible government in the 1830s and 1840s and which came to be associated institutionally with the Reform Liberal party in the late nineteenth century, views the liberal ideal, the liberal problem, and the liberal solution somewhat differently. For Reformers, liberty has consisted first and foremost in the capacity for self-government broadly understood. From their perspective the great threat to liberty consisted not in the power of democratic majorities but in the denial of power to democratic majorities by kings and their courts in the eighteenth century, Family Compacts and Chateau Cliques in the nineteenth, and corporate wealth and the administrative apparatus of the welfare state in the twentieth. And just as the problem was different for reform liberals, so the solution is different. Where rights liberals have always concentrated on limiting legislative action, for reform liberals the objective has always been to devise democratic institutions and democratic practices that are adequate to the job of self-government.

Now, these two versions of liberalism have never been as monochromatic as this caricature suggests. Rights liberals would never deny that self-government is an important liberal ideal, and most Charters or Bills of Rights, including our own, protect free speech, free association, and other rights that are fundamental to the democratic process. By the same token, most reform liberals talked easily and endlessly about protecting and nurturing individual liberty. Indeed, at its height in the late nineteenth century, reform liberals would have found the very distinction between liberty understood as self-government and liberty as individual rights totally baffling. Self-government was a political good in part because 'the people represented in the legislature' were far more likely to be sensitive to individual liberty than kings or modern executives. As long therefore as self-government was posed as an alternative to executive power, there was simply no question for Reformers that individual rights and self-government were mutually reinforcing.

Still and all, there remains a major difference of emphasis between the two liberalisms. For rights liberals, the threat to liberty posed by powerful and intolerant majorities remains the great problem; for those, like Peter Russell, who view the world from the tradition of reform liberalism, the greatest threat to liberty is posed not by democratic excess but by institutions and practices that do not measure up to democratic ideals. 'The fundamental libertarian problem,' Russell concluded in 1969, 'is not too much democracy but too little democracy.'[5]

Peter Russell lost the debate over the Charter. He once told me that the 1969 article from which I quoted above actually produced hate mail, and when a few years later he was invited to the Faculty of Law at the University of Toronto to debate Walter Tarnopolsky about the merits of a Charter, the largely student audience made it quite clear that it had little use for the so-called democratic approach to civil liberties. Now, I would not want to make the mistake of concluding that through law schools and law students we can glimpse the spirit of the age. As I said above, many people, especially in the community of political science, have been persuaded by his argument; some even describe themselves as liberals. Still, I think the reaction that he encountered from liberal lawyers nicely highlights the rhetorical problem that has plagued reform liberalism over the last several decades.

When the movement was in its prime – that is from about the mid-nineteenth to the mid-twentieth century – its adherents could portray themselves as the representatives of progress struggling against what was corrupt and retrogressive. That is no longer the case. To be against the Charter in English Canada in the 1970s and early 1980s was either to be hopelessly conservative and old-fashioned, outside the liberal consensus, or both. Indeed, progressive liberals bet so heavily on the Charter and thought so little of the Reform tradition that it did not trouble them in the least when right-wing populists bent on dismantling significant parts of the liberal welfare state seized the name Reform for themselves.

It seems to me that it is time that progressive liberals reclaimed the language of reform, especially if they want to wrest control of the public agenda away from the right-wing populists who have made such dramatic political gains in this country recently. Numerous commentators have noted that liberals seem unable to make a case against the political right that resonates with the public. My argument, simply put, is that one of the reasons for this weakness is that liberals by and large have wanted to defend liberal politics in rights-based terms. That strategy has not worked. Indeed, in some respects a position that depends so heavily on rights-based arguments may actually play into the hands of the very people whom liberals want to defeat by providing them with a versatile and powerful argument for limiting the scope of the state in the name of individual freedom and formal equality. My suggestion, given this dilemma, is that liberals need to rethink their principles and to consider the possibility that reform liberalism is better suited than rights liberalism to confront the new right. It is time to return reform liberalism to the mainstream, where it belongs.

Let me offer three examples to illustrate how and why reform liberalism is well-suited to our times. First, at the heart of the new right's program lies a fundamental challenge to the established institutions and practices of representative democracy – that is, to legislatures. Take, for instance, the slogan that fuels the Harris government in Ontario – the 'common sense revolution.' If you think that slogan through, you will see that it is hard to find room for what used to be the normal processes of legislation and policy-making – debate, deliberation, and scrutiny. This is not accidental. Common sense, after all, is common in two ways: it is both widely distributed and easily engaged. Its great virtue is that it does not have to deal in paradox, competing principles, hard choices, or unintended consequences. It therefore leaves very little for a legislature to do; the most important things that needed to be said were said – at the polls, in the simple and eloquent language of common sense. Elections used to produce governments, where governing was understood as an ongoing, incremental, and sometimes messy attempt to act in a way that would sustain public confidence and lead to re-election. Understood as an expression of 'common sense,' elections serve quite a different purpose: they produce a popular mandate for the government to rule, a 'contract' between the government and the people that no one, especially those political parties and their supporters who lost the election, have a right to block.

As to the second half of the slogan, if it really is a common sense 'revolution,' then it is absolutely crucial that common sense insights yield decisive results. If that means rushing legislation through the legislature, eliminating time-consuming and temporizing negotiations with organized interests directly affected by legislation, concentrating enormous discretionary power in ministers' hands, or eliminating local boards and municipal councils, then so be it. The Harris government's 'mega initiative' to restructure the delivery of social services in Ontario illustrates powerfully how these two sides of the 'common sense revolution' work together. One of the arguments given by the Harris government for replacing a host of smaller municipalities and school boards with a few large ones is that this would reduce the number of 'politicians' in the province and so combat 'over-government.' And since such amalgamation appears so self-evidently beneficial, the government thought it perfectly appropriate to talk about the initiative as if it were a fait accompli even before legislation was introduced in the House – a sign of contempt for the legislature that the Speaker felt compelled to censure. It is one of those lovely ironies of modern political life that the Harris government, in its determination to make government less intrusive, has had first to make it more heavy-handed and unilateral. But ironies do not bring down governments, and Harris's has made it clear that it does not intend to let this one stand in the way of its revolution.

What's wrong with this assault on the established 'rules of the game,' and how is it best combatted? One possible answer, and one that springs immediately to the mind of rights-based liberals, is that the sort of concentration of executive power undertaken by the Harris government as part of making good on its 'mandate' violates the Charter of Rights. But this is a stretch, or so the courts, which have thus far turned back virtually every Charter challenge to its initiatives, have concluded. The more powerful objection to this mode of governing is that it trivializes representative legislative institutions, and this is a charge that matters because participating, however indirectly, in legislating is a fundamental part of what it means to be free.

The problem with this approach is that, for at least as long as I can remember, Canadian liberalism has had little positive to say about the 'normal' legislative process. Liberals have had much to say about how citizens can and should be protected from legislatures, and they have contributed to the ongoing debate about how the administrative state can be nurtured and democratized so as to work for citizens. But the legislature itself – one of the first and most conspicuous targets of the Harris revolution – has received little attention from liberals, and when it has it has been viewed more often than not as part of the problem rather than of the solution. In short, liberals have been caught flat-footed by the right's attack on the legislature, which is why I believe that it is high time to revisit the reform tradition and resolder the connection between liberty and legislation.

Where the Harris government (and others on the right) view local legislatures as the source and symptom of over-government, nineteenth-century Reformers viewed legislatures, especially local ones, as the first and best guardian of freedom. As Edward Blake once put it, 'The essence of freedom is that the law should be made practically by the people who are ruled and administered by persons who are responsible to those people.'[6] What followed from this basic conviction was a view of politics that offers a powerful rebuke to Harris-style 'revolutionaries.' For if legislatures and representation come first, then one has to worry about the illiberal possibilities inherent in strong and unchecked executive power. As Blake put it: 'In free Constitutions the executive power must be guarded, limited and restrained, and must not be permitted to encroach on the rights of the people and the representatives ... Whether it be King, President or Cabinet which wields the executive power, the constant tendency of those possessed of such power, is to invade the domain of other branches of the Government and enlarge their own jurisdiction.'[7] And one of the chief casualties of this growth in executive power was the sort of government by discussion that, from Blake's perspective, was crucial to democratic politics. 'Unless you insist that measures shall be brought down at such a time that there shall be a full discussion, and an opportunity given for the popular view being obtained before Parliament finally passes upon a measure,' he concluded, 'you practically reduce the House of Commons into a machine for registering the decrees of the Government instead of being a real representative legislative body.'[8] I needn't belabour the obvious connection between Blake's worry and Harris's initiatives.

Did the reform liberals live up to their principles? Not entirely. As committed as they were to maintaining a robust legislature, reform liberalism ultimately evolved into the Liberal party – a well-oiled, disciplined, and executive-driven 'governing party.' To that extent they helped to create the very institution that helped to undermine the dignity of the legislature that they claimed to cherish so deeply. But, in a way, that is beside the point, or at least it is beside my point. For whatever their shortcomings, reform liberals at least were looking at the right place and provided a vocabulary of politics that valued critical debate, real deliberation, and honest persuasion. At a time when the institutions of local democracy are routinely and authoritatively characterized pejoratively as symptoms of 'over-government,' the reform liberal view offers a powerful rejoinder.

The second point bears less on the process of politics and more on its substance. The new right is dedicated to reducing the size and scope of the state's activities, both because mounting public debt has made it difficult to sustain a large public sector and because neo-conservatives believe that the market imposes a discipline that yields more efficient results. So much is clear, and this aspect of the new right's agenda has attracted considerable attention. But what should worry liberals is not simply that governments like those in Alberta and Ontario have become passionate privatizers. The more subtle, but ultimately more insidious problem is that they (and those who share their views) have taken to describing even the most basic 'public' functions as if they were private – that is, in the language of the market. We are no longer citizens who take pride in collective life, but are 'taxpayers,' whose basic connection to political life is distant and grudging. We are no longer patients but are 'health care consumers,' and no longer members of a political community, but 'clients' of public agencies. The new right has even brushed off and popularized the old notion of 'shareholder democracy' – as if political communities were corporations and citizens shareholders, and as if the language of 'public' and 'private' were essentially interchangeable.

The difficulty with privatizing our public life in this way is that it dramatically distorts the real issues and dilemmas that confront our politics. Take, for example, the ongoing and important debate about the future of publicly funded health care in Canada. One of the arguments frequently made these days is that spending on health care is out of control in part because the system is being 'abused.' While in opposition, for instance, Mike Harris maintained that 'hundreds of millions' of dollars was being siphoned out of the health care system through abuse.[9] Once he was in government, his minister of health, Jim Wilson, argued that widespread 'physician and consumer fraud' made it vital to undertake 'a great deal of fundamental restructuring' of the system.

But as Wilson also made clear, the problem extended beyond the fraudulent use of health services. The deeper problem was 'overutilization'[10] of the system, and this refrain has resonated with others who are concerned about the patterns established by certain groups – those well-educated patients who 'shop' around until they find a doctor and diagnosis they like; the 'worried well,' who, encouraged by 'you-can-have-it consumerism,' demand endless tests to reassure themselves that they are not ill;[11] and even expectant mothers, who want ultrasounds performed even though such scans may be medically unnecessary. And then there are those who do not take care of themselves and who, as a result, impose burdens on the rest of us who end up footing the bill. If only they understood the link between overeating and heart disease, the refrain goes, there would be less pressure on the system. 'Putting more and better information in the hands of consumers and encouraging more active consumer participation in the care-delivery process is definitely the way to go.'[12]

It is not that these are insignificant problems. They are important precisely because they engage some of the central issues arising from democratic citizenship – about the nature and extent of our duties to those around us and to our political community and about the balance between the rights that we enjoy as individuals and the obligations that we owe to others whose need for expensive and therefore increasingly scarce public resources may be greater than ours. To structure the debate in terms of consumerism, however, misses what is at the heart of the debate – namely, our collective responsibilities as citizens not to defraud the system, use it frivolously, or forget that we have a responsibility, not just to ourselves but to others, to act in ways that are not costly and self-destructive. This is why the language and idea of consumerism is misplaced here. Consumers may buy too much, they may miss the sales, and what they buy may be out of fashion, but it is the individual consumer who suffers the consequences. We do not usually complain that consumers are forgetting their duties to others or are acting in a selfish and irresponsible way simply because consumerism appeals to and is sustained by self-interest. If abuse means that social duty has failed to outweigh individual desire, then the very notion of abuse by consumers is an oxymoron, for consumerism celebrates the sovereignty of individual desires.

What we need here and in a host of other contemporary debates is not consumerism, but a better and more robust theory of citizenship. The problem, as more than a few critics of liberalism have pointed out, is that rights-based liberalism has a hard time taking citizenship seriously. The charge against liberalism typically takes one of two forms. On the one hand, critics argue that rights-based liberalism is so relentlessly individualistic and so deeply suspicious of public power that it is difficult for liberalism to accommodate a robust notion of citizenship and an expansive understanding of 'public space.' On the other hand, since liberal rights are usually defended in universalistic terms – as human rights – critics note that it goes against the liberal grain to emphasize civic attachment to one more or less arbitrarily defined place. As Ronnie Beiner nicely points out, the ideal liberal citizen seems to be someone like Pierre Trudeau, the arch-cosmopolitan.[13]

In a sense, however, though, I think that anti-liberals are guilty of the very thing of which they accuse liberalism – namely, of universalizing and decontextualizing experience. For whatever the failings of reform liberalism, and there are many, reform liberals took citizenship, and with it the priority of the public good, very seriously indeed. In the great nineteenth-century debate between 'commerce' and 'virtue,' reform liberals came down squarely in the middle – attracted by commerce, devoted to what they unabashedly called 'public virtue,' and sure that they could find a way to have both flourish. Yet when push came to shove, Reformers were not afraid to defend the public good over individual preference, citizenship over individual rights. Edward Blake, Reform premier of Ontario and leader of the dominion Liberal opposition to John A. Macdonald, once summarized the Reform view this way: 'I am a friend to the preservation of the rights of property ... but I believe in the subordination of those rights to the public good. I deny that the people of my Province are insensible to or careless about the true principles of legislation. I believe they are thoroughly alive to them, and I am content that my rights of property ... shall belong to the Legislature of my country to be disposed of subject to the good sense and right feeling of the people of that Province.'[14] Blake is willing not simply to concede, but to celebrate, the existence of a capacious public sphere. Late-nineteenth-century liberals had a taste for public life and for the role of citizenship – our connection, as individuals, to a larger community and set of concerns. The point simply is that reform liberals saw citizenship as neither illiberal nor tyrannical. Our generation of liberals needs to recapture that sensibility and pose it as an alternative to the parsimonious understanding of citizenship that is now dominant.

The third reason to revisit reform liberalism follows from its political economy. Reform liberals were deeply worried about the political consequences of allowing the concentration of wealth in a few hands. As Allan Greer has noted, early Reformers such as William Lyon Mackenzie considered it crucial to democratic governance 'to bring all public authority under the control of the populace' – including banks and other corporations that operated under and with the protection of charters and other legislative enactments. To be sure, 'Mackenzie was extreme in his hostility to banks and would have done away with them altogether if he had had his way.'[15] But even late-century Reformers, who had made their peace with capitalism and who were more inclined to think of 'public' and 'private' as distinct and sharply bounded 'spheres' best kept apart, were deeply troubled by the political effects of concentrated wealth.

No word better captures the Reformers' worry and no word was used to better partisan effect than 'monopoly.' In the Reform lexicon, monopoly referred to a variety of evils, and in its most basic sense to politically created economic privilege. It saw John A. Macdonald's tariff policy as 'a mass of privilege legislation' intended not for the public good but 'solely for the benefit of individuals and classes.'[16] This criticism of tariff policy in particular shaded into and reinforced Reform's disquiet about Macdonald's approach to taxation altogether. 'The land which deliberately adopts a policy of high taxation, and thus forces the poverty of the many to contribute to the opulence of the few, can no longer claim to be a land of liberty, equality, or fraternity.'[17] Indeed, the problem of monopoly struck to the core of what Macdonald's government called its National Policy. David Mills, one of the most understudied and underrated Reformers of the era, stated the Reform position and alternative this way: 'We propose not a sham National policy, which means class legislation, the promotion of the interests of one portion of the community at the expense of the rest, but a real National Policy that will promote the interests of a whole people, given them control over their own affairs and enable them to manage those matters with which they are especially concerned and which they best understand.'[18]

To borrow Brian Beaven's formulation, the issue for late-century Reformers was not wealth but privilege; it was not the economic conditions for creating wealth but the political effects of state-sanctioned economic inequality that worried Reformers. As one Reform editorialist put it: 'How long are the farmers, the artisans, the mechanics and the labourers of this country, the people who create wealth by industry and pay the taxes out of their hard earnings, to endure this systematic and unscrupulous robbery in the name of the law, for the benefit of a half dozen plutocrats whose millions are then fetished from the pockets of the people?' David Mills was less apocalytic, but his concern about the social consequences of economic inequality was essentially the same. 'I think it will always prove true in the end,' he once said, 'that, when, any section of the community undertake to give themselves an advantage at the expense of their countrymen, they have blundered.'

The conditions of Canadian political economy are obviously dramatically different now. But I often wonder if Reform's crisp critique of state-sanctioned economic privilege would not resonate with the many people who, having worked loyally for a large corporation, now find themselves 'downsized' or 'restructured' out of a job, even while the company records large profits and rewards top executives handsomely. Is it simply fantasy to think that the old principles of reform liberalism, appropriately adapted, might yet have some political mileage in them?

In concluding, I want to try to pre-empt two possible misunderstandings of my argument. First, in drawing the broad distinction between reform liberalism and rights-based liberalism I do not mean to suggest that the two are simply mutually exclusive. And I especially do not want to leave readers with the impression that the Charter has paved the way for the creation of a 'jurocracy' in which courts have displaced legislatures as policy-makers in the first resort. In fact, there are many points at which reform liberalism and Charter liberalism converge. To the extent, for instance, that reform liberals worry about the concentration of executive power, they should welcome the Charter's attempt to place limits on executive discretion.

Beyond this, one can understand the reasonable-limits clause of section 1 as creating a structure or a set of standards by which to evaluate legislative judgments about rights. By this interpretation the point of the Charter is not so much to privilege rights against legislatures, but to ensure that when legislatures do limit rights they provide reasoned justification for their actions. This too seems perfectly in keeping with the spirit of reform liberalism and with its antipathy towards the use of blunt, undeliberative political power.

And then there is the override clause. For latter-day reform liberals such as Peter Russell, the Charter's notwithstanding clause is a useful and perfectly legitimate way of balancing rights claims against legislative priorities. Viewed in the context of the larger Canadian liberal tradition of which Reformism is a part, the clause makes some sense – which is precisely Russell's point. Put slightly differently, it would seem odd to use the principles of reform liberalism to 'trash' the Charter first because the Charter itself to some extent integrates principles that can be traced back to reform liberalism.

Second, I appreciate that there is a real risk in advancing this sort of historical argument of idealizing the Reform liberal tradition, of making the Reformers appear more attractive than they actually were. To take only the most obvious example, nineteenth century reform liberals stoutly defended equality against the sense of 'privilege' they associated with Toryism. But the Reformers were themselves quite content to accept unquestioningly a series of privileges themselves – especially those associated with being male and Anglo-Saxon. For all of their talk about being on the side of progress and democracy, it never occurred to most of them to question the prevailing definition of democratic citizenship that excluded women, Aboriginal people, and non–Anglo-Saxons.

My intention here is not to ignore or whitewash those deep imperfections, but it is also just a little too easy, and actually ahistorical, to use our own alleged moral superiority to dismiss reform liberal principles or to consign them to the regressive past. The point simply is that reform liberals, as limited, flawed, and blinkered as their movement may have been, nevertheless set out certain principles that are worth dusting off and re-examining, for they fill a sizeable gap in our own political environment. Creating an active and vigorous democratic politics, refurbishing the idea of citizenship, and opposing the concentration of private wealth are the ideas and sentiments that informed reform liberalism in this country in the late nineteenth century. Let us not allow them to take early retirement in the late twentieth.

NOTES

1 Peter H. Russell, 'The Political Purposes of the Canadian Charter of Rights and Freedoms,' *Canadian Bar Review* 61 (1983), 51–2. In fact, Russell points out that the credit for coining this turn of phrase belongs to his colleague Walter Berns, who taught with him a third-year course in the Department of Political Science on Canadian–American comparative constitutional law. That is also where I first encountered these subjects. To both of these men I owe an enormous amount.
2 Peter H. Russell, 'A Democratic Approach to Civil Liberties,' *University of Toronto Law Journal* 19 (1969), 109–31.
3 On the American example, see especially Jennifer Nedelsky, *Private Property and the Limits of American Constitutionalism: The Madisonian Framework and Its Legacy* (Chicago: University of Chicago Press 1990).
4 Pierre Trudeau, 'A Canadian Charter of Human Rights' (Ottawa, 1968), 11, quoting Jackson J. in *West Virginia State Board of Education v. Barnette* 319 US 624 (1943).
5 Russell, 'Democratic Approach,' 115.
6 Blake Papers, Archives of Ontario, speech at Bowmanville, 26 Aug. 1873 (B-15, box 110, env. 10).
7 Ibid.
8 Ibid.
9 Lynne Sears Williams, 'Fiscal Problems,' *Canadian Medical Association Journal* 148 (1993), 2004.
10 Ontario, Legislative Assembly, Standing Committee on General Government, 18 Dec. 1995, G-243–250.

11 Michael Rynal, 'Welcome to Jurassic Practice,' *Medical Post, 1993 National Survey*, 94.

12 Michael O'Reilly, 'Don't Seek Medical Help for Minor Problems, Ontario Pilot Project Tells Patients,' *Canadian Medical Association Journal* 151 (1994), 202.

13 Ronald Beiner, ed., *Theorizing Citizenship* (Albany: SUNY Press 1995), Introduction.

14 Canada, House of Commons, *Debates*, 14 April 1882, 915.

15 Allan Greer, 'Smile When You Use the Word "Reform," Stranger,' *Globe and Mail*, 5 Sept. 1996.

16 See Brian Beaven, 'A Last Hurrah: Studies in Liberal Party Development and Ideology in Ontario, 1878–1893,' doctoral dissertation, University of Toronto, 1981, 461.

17 Ibid., 464.

18 Ibid., 465.

19 Ibid., 461.

20 Ibid.

3

Democratic Constitutionalism in a Diverse Federation

JAMES TULLY

The Constitutional Odyssey

I would like to present a brief sketch of Peter Russell's understanding of Canadian constitutionalism. I wish to do this in homage to a great scholar and to express my intellectual debt to him, but also because his understanding of Canada is one of the most profound and humane available. I believe that his vision of Canada has the capacity to hold us together as a federation into the foreseeable future.

In his great book, *Constitutional Odyssey: Can Canadians Become a Sovereign People?* (1993), and more recently in the 1996 Stapleford Lecture at the University of Regina, 'Preserving the Canadian Federation: A Two-Track Approach,' Peter Russell has developed an interpretation of Canadians as a sovereign people engaged in the democratic activity of recognizing and accommodating their deep diversities in federal and constitutional arrangements over time. There are three main features of this compelling vision: popular sovereignty, political diversity, and constitutional accommodation. I first describe these features, and then I comment on them.

The Elements of Russell's Vision

Popular Sovereignty and Democratic Constitutionalism

On Russell's view, Canadians are engaged in a deep and intense 'constitutional odyssey' – a voyage of self-discovery in which they are struggling to define their identity as members of a shared political association. This odyssey has covered five rounds of constitutional negotiations and is now into its sixth.

The aim of this long and tortuous journey is for Canadians to try to become a 'sovereign people.'[1] To become 'sovereign' is for the Canadian people to become 'constitutional democrats' – to impose the constitutional conditions of their association on themselves through a process or processes of public deliberation. The quest thus involves the change from an earlier age of elite constitutionalism to an age of democratic or participatory constitutionalism, in which citizens have a say in the formulation and ratification of constitutional change. As Russell puts it, 'The idea that a constitution to be legitimate must be derived from the people – a dreadful heresy to our founding fathers – has become constitutional orthodoxy for most Canadians.'[2]

The Recognition of Diversity

Democratic constitutionalism is difficult because it involves 'reaching agreement on the identity and fundamental principles of the body politic,' and as a result it is 'exceptionally emotional and intense.'[3] Moreover, there is a fundamental characteristic of Canadians that makes the activity doubly difficult – what Russell calls their 'diversity.'[4] He was one of the first people to use the now-common term 'diversity' to describe the non-uniform constitutional character of Canada's political identity.[5] In a uniform political association, the political identity that citizens share is the same for each. They participate in the same institutions in the same way, since they do not have differences that matter publicly. In a diverse association, citizens have differences that matter publicly, in addition to their similarities. Thus, in addition to sharing some institutions in the same way, such as certain basic rights and democratic practices, they either share the same institutions in ways that allow for the recognition of reasonable differences – for example, by speaking French and English in Parliament and some provincial legislatures – or set up different institutions to give due recognition to their reasonable differences, such as provincial governments, Aboriginal governments, and language-based public school boards. As Russell shows in *Constitutional Odyssey*, all three types of case have long been a part of Canadians' constitutional institutions and conventions and of their judicial and parliamentary traditions of interpretation.

Russell argues that diversity makes democratic constitutionalism more difficult. If citizens are culturally homogeneous, then they can see themselves as a 'single people,' allow the majority to 'act for the whole,' and agree on a constitution that treats them all in identical ways.[6] In the course of their odyssey Canadians have discovered that this model of a 'single people,' derived from the theory of John Locke, is unacceptable: 'There is no evidence that either the Québécois or the Aboriginal nations have agreed to be part of a Canadian people sharing a constitution determined by simple majority rule. By the same token, there is no evidence that the Aboriginal and English minorities in Quebec have agreed to be part of a Quebec people whose constitutional destiny lies in the hands of a majority of the people in that province.'[7]

Of course, all Canadians demand constitutional institutions, such as Parliament and individual rights, in which they are treated all the same, as in the case of a 'single people.' But, they also want constitutional institutions that recognize and protect their diversity as well. Indeed, the very reason why Aboriginal peoples, Quebecers, provincialists, members of the two official-language minorities, and many ethnocultural citizens wish to join a political association is not only to share their similarities but also to gain recognition and protection for their reasonable differences.

The constitutional question therefore is not 'whether Canadians can become a single, sovereign people,' as Russell put it in the first edition of *Constitutional Odyssey*, but rather if they can become a sovereign 'people or peoples' in 'all their deep diversity,' as he rephrased it in the second edition.[8] This is just to say that Canadians form not a 'single people' but a 'federal people.' They are 'deeply diverse' – their society is not only multicultural and multilingual but also 'multinational,' and these differences overlap. Again, Russell was one of the first non-Quebecers and non-Aboriginal scholars to acknowledge the multinational character of Canada's diverse peoples: they include the Quebec people, the majority of whom seek recognition as members of a liberal democratic Quebec nation or society with linguistic and cultural minorities, and the Aboriginal peoples, the majority of whom seek recognition as members of First Nations.

If a constitution fails to recognize the reasonable diversity of its citizens the association ceases to be legitimate in their eyes. The citizens whose differences are denied recognition cannot affirm and identify with the constitution, for they see it as an agent of 'misrecognition' – of assimilation and oppression. As Alan Cairns argues, they fall away from the federal association and identify with minority, provincial, or national associations that give them the recognition they fail to find at the constitutional level.[9] The society becomes unstable and prone to disintegration.

The challenge for Canadians thus becomes to discover a process of democratic and multilateral deliberation in which the sovereign people or peoples can reach agreement on the mutual recognition of their deep diversity in a form of political association.

The Accommodation of Deep Diversity

The answer to this difficulty is what Russell calls 'just accommodation.' In the moving opening passages of his Stapleford Lecture, he looks back on the earlier age of elite constitutionalism and points out that the old elites were skilled practitioners at negotiating and accommodating their diversities in an array of constitutional and federal institutions and practices. He writes: 'It is both the destiny and burden of Canadians to be pioneers in building a new kind of nation state, one whose unity does not derive from uniformity but from the accommodation of diversity. This deeply diverse political community has been governed through a federal process that has made it a truly federal society – one whose citizens have divided political allegiances, identifying strongly with provincial or first nation governments, and in varying degrees with the federation's central government.'[10]

When the process of constitutional amendment passed from the old elites to elected representatives in consultation and ratification with citizens in the 1980s, the citizens were inexperienced at exercising the practical skills of negotiation and accommodation of federal diversity. They were better at demanding unilateral recognition of their own differences and denying the reciprocal recognition to others than they were at achieving mutual recognition and accommodation of the differences of each and all. This inexperience, and so the failure to reach agreement in five rounds of negotiations, are hardly surprising, since the skills of accommodation are acquired through practice, and Canadians are just beginning the democratic experiment of exercising them. The exercise, however, is not as difficult as it appears from a superficial reading of our recent failures. For Russell, it consists in two main lessons.

First, if the Quebec people can give good public reasons for their recognition as a predominantly French-speaking liberal-democratic nation or society in an appropriate relationship with the other members of the Canadian federation, then there is no good reason why the Canadian people should not negotiate a form of accommodation of this relationship, either after a 'yes' vote in some future referendum or preferably by initiating negotiations before the next referendum, through a combination of devolution and long term, low-key constitutional change.[11]

Russell reminds us that 'at the time of the FLQ crisis in 1970 we took the position that Quebec secessionists need not resort to violence because they were free to work for their objective through the democratic process. We must not go back on that undertaking. Force is not the Canadian way of adjusting relationships among the societies that constitute our Confederation.'[12]

Diverse popular sovereignty readily explains and accommodates such federal relationships or 'partnerships.' The majority of Quebecers wish to delegate more of their political powers to their National Assembly than to the federal Parliament. Canadians have no reason to deny this longstanding request, subject to two conditions of fairness. First, Quebecers should agree to give up the exercise of powers in the federal Parliament that they wish to transfer to and exercise in their National Assembly. This would preserve the overall equality of powers of the sovereign people in each province, for what it has gained in the provincial assembly it has lost at the federal. Second, in return for their recognition by Canadians, Quebecers should reciprocally recognize the diversity within Quebec – that is, recognize and accommodate the First Nations, the English minority, and the ethnocultural citizens of Quebec.

The recognition and accommodation of a partnership of 'treaty federalism' with the self-governing First Nations is another example of how a federal system can accommodate diversity fairly. The recommendation that Aboriginal peoples be recognized as equal, co-existing, and self-governing nations in the report of the Royal Commission on Aboriginal Peoples is written in Russell's language of popular sovereignty, diversity, and accommodation, and it has been inspired by his writings and advice.[13]

If Russell's first lesson of constitutional accommodation is willingness to listen to and negotiate reasonable demands for change, the second is to realize that the process of accommodation is an ongoing, cautious, democratic activity, or series of processes, of 'democratic deliberation and consultation.'[14] Unlike the Lockean view, which sees the constitution as a contract reached at a particular time in history and designed to last for all time, Russell casts democratic constitutionalism in conditions of deep diversity in more 'Burkean' terms, as a long-term and 'organic' activity of changing and altering the conditions of the association over time from within as circumstances change: 'I would prefer that we continue to adjust the relationships among the constituent elements of our confederation in a more incremental manner and in a less stressful atmosphere than will pertain in the negotiations that follow a referendum win by Quebec sovereignists. The emotional strain and animosity generated by the referendum campaign will undermine the very capacity for accommodating difference that is the hallmark of the Canadian political tradition. By the same token, I remain convinced that it is only that capacity which can save us from the awful consequences of a union secured or a break-up achieved through force rather than consensus.'[15]

From this perspective, the problem with the Meech Lake and Charlottetown accords, the 1995 referendum in Quebec, and the 'final showdown' is that Canadians are still looking for a solution in terms of a definitive contract rather than the establishment of ongoing processes of constitutional dialogue in which all citizens can engage from time to time and through which they can come to respect the differences of others and identify with the federation as a whole. As he writes: 'But if we succeed with or without a referendum in re-adjusting our federal relationships in the Canadian way, we must recognise that our constitutional arrangements can never be perfected – there are no final solutions, in that sense, no sovereign solutions for a constitutional society with a vision of justice that transcends the simple imposition of majority will and nourishes itself through the mutual respect and dialogue among its constituent parts.'[16]

If Canadians could learn these two lessons and so come to embrace Russell's inspiring vision of Canada, then we could find our way out of our devastating predicament and build a future together. This would be a future that embodies the best of Canadian constitutionalism, and it would be a fitting tribute to the scholar who has taught us what the best of Canadian constitutionalism is.

Comment

Russell's justifications for these three features of democratic constitutionalism in the diverse Canadian federation are pragmatic and contextual: they will preserve the Canadian federation, and they are derived from Canada's constitutional and political traditions of toleration, accommodation, and political pluralism. Canadians who disagree with Russell's vision argue that these justifications are insufficient. For Canadian constitutionalism to be legitimate it must meet the more general and universal standards of liberal democracy. However, they roundly conclude, the deliberative recognition and accommodation of diversity that he defends violates the norms of liberal democracy and so must be rejected.[17] But is this true? Let us examine each of the three features in turn.

There are few people who would disagree with Russell's first claim that constitutional change must now be more democratic than before in order to be legitimate. The concept of a 'constitutional' or 'liberal democracy' seems to involve two different aspects, which always exhibit a certain tension. The first, often associated with John Locke, is that a democracy should limit the exercise of political power by means of fundamental laws, charters of rights and freedoms, checks and balances, and procedures. The second, often associated with Jean-Jacques Rousseau, is that these limits, whatever they are, must be self-imposed if they are to be legitimate: the people themselves must agree on the conditions by which they govern themselves through a process of democratic deliberation.

The demand in Canada since the early 1980s that constitutional change rest on democratic deliberation of some kind derives from the Rousseauesque or 'popular sovereignty' side of democracy. It is not, however, unique to Canada. Many other constitutional democracies are undergoing similar demands for the democratization of constitutional change – the European Union being the best-known example – and plans for global governance are framed in terms of these two aspects of constitutional democracy.[18] Furthermore, political philosophers such as John Rawls and Jürgen Habermas have advanced powerful theories of the conditions under which citizens could reach agreement through public deliberation on the constitutional essentials of a democratic society.[19]

Why is this aspect of democracy important? If, for example, you find the Canadian constitutional settlement of 1981 fair and just, why should you care that other citizens – many Quebecers – have not affirmed it through a process of public deliberation and continue to dissent from it? In defending democratic deliberation and affirmation as a necessary condition of the legitimacy of constitutional democracy, Rousseau presented three main arguments to answer this kind of question.[20] First, democratic deliberation is necessary to the justice of a constitution and its amendment. A constitution founded and amended by elites may occasionally embody just principles, but it will not itself be just. The reason for this is that one feature of democratic justice is that constitutional rule 'rests on' or, in Russell's terms, 'derives from' the 'agreement of the people' subject to it – quod omnes tangit ...' (what affects all must be agreed to by all). So it is not sufficient that the government be based on the agreement of the people through elections; the constitution on the basis of which the government exercises political power must also rest on the consent of the populace. This agreement can thus be given only by citizens acting as a 'sovereign people' – that is, deliberating together in some form.

Second, while a constitution derived from others may contain and protect various kinds of freedoms or liberties, as in the Charter of Rights and Freedoms, there is another conception of freedom that is necessary to democratic legitimacy. This is the republican ideal of freedom, recently reaffirmed by Michael Sandel, that citizens are politically free only if they have a say in the formulation and ratification of the constitutional essentials in accordance with which they associate together.[21] Again, this condition of political freedom can be fulfilled only by some form of participation in actual public deliberation on the justice of the constitution. Otherwise, the constitution is experienced as 'alien' and 'imposed,' as a disabling condition of unfreedom rather than an enabling condition of freedom – an experience all too familiar to Canadians across the federation.

Third, members of a political association develop their identity as citizens through the exchange of public reasons in public discussions on the justice or injustice of constitutional proposals. Citizens' identity and solidarity are engendered through participation itself. If they do not have this experience of participation from time to time, or if they have the experience yet fail to reach agreement, they will tend to identify with their partial communities of deliberation more strongly than with their larger political community – that is, with their linguistic, regional, provincial, municipal, ethnic, environmental, national, or gender communities, in which their non-political or provincial identities are shaped through local deliberation, or, in the absence of such deliberative partial communities, on ascriptive identities. As a result, citizens will not identify with the constitutional association as a whole, and it will become unstable, a mere modus vivendi aggregation of individuals and partial groups, depending on a mere 'balance of forces in contingent and possibly fluctuating circumstances,' in the words of John Rawls.[22] Again, this depressing situation is familiar to Canadians. For Rousseau, civic identity, solidarity, and stability are all closely related to being a member of a deliberative community, and he recommended that constitutional discussions take place in different cities every five years or so.

As I mentioned above, both Russell and Cairns appear to agree that the failure to reach agreement on constitutional essentials in the last five rounds of negotiations has left Canadians in this situation of being unable to affirm and identify with the Canadian association as a whole and so falling back on partial associations of various kinds. Therefore if we wish to follow Russell and 'preserve the Canadian federation,' then we should at least entertain Rousseau's arguments that democratic constitutionalism is necessary to the justice, freedom, and identification of the political association we wish to preserve. Moreover, the appropriateness of Rousseau's arguments to Canada is substantiated by the kinds of complaints that Russell catalogues in *Constitutional Odyssey*, such as the injustice of proceeding without the consent of citizens affected, the alienation and unfreedom of those excluded from the process, and the heightened identification with local communities in opposition to the federation as a whole. Consequently, the answer to those who are satisfied with the status quo is that they should not seek to block cautious processes of constitutional dialogue, for such obstinacy leads to disintegration and instability, but rather to present convincing arguments for the status quo in public discussions.

The difficulty in taking up the challenge of democratic constitutionalism is that Canadians, like most contemporary citizens, are not uniform, as Rousseau presumed, but diverse. On this second feature of Russell's analysis, Rousseau is no help whatsoever. Canadians have differences that matter to them and which they need to see recognized in the constitution, public institutions, and traditions of Canadian society if they are to affirm and identify with them. This is, as Russell puts it, our 'destiny and burden' as Canadians – 'to be pioneers in building a new kind of nation state, one whose unity does not derive from uniformity but from the accommodation of diversity.' Yet it is precisely this feature, which Russell sees as the soul of the Canadian identity, that critics say violates the principles of liberal democracy. At the core of this objection is the claim that to treat citizens – or provinces in a federal system – as 'free and equal' or 'impartially' is to screen out their differences. Whatever differences they have should be relegated to the private sphere. This position, I would argue, is a deeply mistaken and destructive view of liberal democracy, for ever since 1981 it has been the major objection to the kind of constitutional changes that alone are capable of preserving the federation. As we have seen, if this view were true it would render most modern constitutional democracies oppressive and unstable straitjackets, as indeed it threatens to do for Canada.

Now, contrary to Russell's adversaries, the public recognition of reasonable diversity is compatible with liberal democracy, and the failure to recognize it constitutes a kind of injustice. These two theses have been defended by Will Kymlicka, Charles Taylor, and me.[23] Rather than presenting these arguments, I sketch a slightly different argument for the compatibility of the recognition of reasonable diversity and liberal democracy, which starts from Russell's premise of democratic deliberation, as I rephrased it above. John Rawls develops such an argument in *Political Liberalism* (1993).

Rawls argues that anyone committed to both the liberal and the deliberative sides of democracy needs to take into account what he calls 'the fact of reasonable pluralism.' That is, the citizens of liberal democracies have differences that matter to them, which figure in their comprehensive doctrines of the good life. There is a plurality of such reasonable conceptions of the good life in any society, and, given the character of moral reasoning, it is reasonable to accept this fact. In Canada, for example, language, Aboriginality, multiculturalism, and so on are the kinds of differences that figure in citizens' comprehensive conceptions of the good and give rise to constitutional demands for recognition. Citizens are deeply attached to and draw their practical identities from their different and comprehensive doctrines of the good. (This is just to say that they are 'goods' for them.)

Now, citizens will agree to and affirm a constitution as just only if it gives due protection to their different goods. They will agree to and identify with the constitution only if they can see that the conception of the justice that it embodies can be related to and derived from their background comprehensive good or goods. So, given this kind of diversity or pluralism, the problem of democratic legitimacy is to find a way in which citizens who hold a plurality of goods can nevertheless reach agreement on a shared conception of constitutional justice. This agreement is an 'overlapping consensus,' in the sense that the different comprehensive doctrines of the good nevertheless overlap on a shared conception of justice.

Citizens work towards agreement on constitutional essentials or constitutional amendments by the exchange of public reasons in public deliberations in which they treat each other as free and equal. In addition, they accept what

Rawls calls the 'burdens of judgment' – they recognize that citizens are approaching the question of constitutional justice and the task of developing a political identity from different yet reasonable comprehensive doctrines. A demand for constitutional recognition will be reasonable and worthy of acceptance just in so far as the reasons advanced for it can be made good to the other citizens generally. A reasoned argument that can be made good to citizens generally is for that reason a 'public' reason.

A citizen cannot therefore present a convincing argument for constitutional recognition that appeals to his or her background conception of the good, for other citizens do not share this good and so will remain unmoved. It is, in this sense, an unreasonable argument, and citizens can ignore the demand. The person who advances such a non-public reason has failed to accept the burdens of judgment. The reasons for a demand must be general ones that can appeal to all other citizens irrespective of their differences. By this kind of exchange of public reasons, citizens become reciprocally aware of the diversity and importance of the goods of their fellows citizens and how their demands can or cannot be justified by reasons that appeal to citizens in general. Citizens gradually see the demands that survive the exchange of public reasons and the ways to accommodate them in a shared conception of constitutional justice.[24]

This approach starts from democratic deliberation but may seem to end up at the same place as the critics of diversity, with a difference-blind constitution, for the condition that constitutional demands must be justified to citizens generally will eliminate demands for recognition of differences. This is not the case. Aboriginal people justify demands for their recognition as equal, coexisting, and self-governing nations, for example, by public reasons that appeal to very general ideas of equality, impartiality, and justice held by Canadian citizens generally.[25] The demand for the recognition of Quebec as a distinct society or nation, in so far as it contains reciprocal recognition of the First Nations, the English language minority, and the ethnocultural people of Quebec, can also be justified by similar public reasons, which appeal to very general ideas of equality implicit in any liberal-democratic culture.[26] This point has been made with great cogency by Anthony Laden in *Constructing Shared Wills: Deliberative Liberalism and the Politics of Identity*.[27] He demonstrates that many of the most pressing demands for constitutional recognition in Canada are compatible with liberal democracy and could in principle be made good to citizens generally through public deliberation.

So the objection that the recognition of reasonable diversity is incompatible with liberal-democratic principles does not withstand careful examination. The objectors tend to argue that liberal democracy stands for a set of substantive principles of blindness to difference, irrespective of what citizens committed to the ideal of public reason might agree to in processes of democratic deliberation. But this defence abandons the commitment to liberal democracy altogether. Liberal democracy is not a matter of working up a conception of citizens' identity from the outside and holding citizens to it. This stance is a variation on the old elite constitutionalism that liberal democracies have left behind. What is required, Laden argues, is for citizens to work up a shared and often diverse conception of citizens' identity through the exchange of public reasons over constitutional proposals in which they treat each other as free and equal and accept the burdens of judgment that reasonable pluralism demands. Citizens engage in this constitutional deliberation not only to determine which demands are worthy of recognition but also to develop, through participation, their identification with, and the stability of, the diverse federation.

Russell argues that if we accept democratic constitutionalism and the recognition of reasonable diversity, then a commitment follows to understand the constitution as a mutable and changeable form of accommodation over time, rather than as a perfect contract or definitive solution. He describes this understanding as 'Burkean.' Be this as it may, the transition from the idea of a constitution as a fixed contract standing behind democracy to the idea of a constitution as itself open to democratic deliberation and amendment over time is accepted by many liberal democratic theorists.[28] A particularly striking argument for this third feature of Russell's analysis is presented by Simone Chambers. She bases her argument not on pragmatic considerations or contextual justifications; quite the contrary, she draws on the political theory of Jürgen Habermas, one of the best-known European liberal-democratic theorists, who defends an uncompromisingly universal and non-contextual form of justification. Nevertheless, she shows that a commitment to universalization as a means of testing demands for constitutional change in public deliberation is compatible with, and indeed provides a justification for, reconceiving the Canadian constitution as an ongoing 'conversation' rather than a 'contract', in terms almost identical to Russell's call for an ongoing dialogue of mutual respect.[29]

Conclusion

Russell's vision of Canadian constitutionalism as the recognition and accommodation of our irreducible diversity over time through cautious processes of public deliberation and consultation finds support from some of the leading theories of liberal democracy. One of the major obstacles to agreement on constitutional change has been the alleged objection that it violates the norms of liberal democracy. With this obstacle removed, it is perhaps possible for Canadians to continue the odyssey to a successful conclusion and so to become a sovereign people or peoples in all their deep diversity. But odysseys, from Homer to Joyce, are unpredictable. And, in any case, it is not up to the scholars to decide, but, as Russell teaches us, the people themselves.

NOTES

1 Peter Russell, *Constitutional Odyssey: Can Canadians Become a Sovereign People?*, 2nd ed. (Toronto 1993), x, 5.
2 Ibid., 5.
3 Ibid., 75.
4 Ibid., vii.
5 For an analysis of the concept of diversity, see Charles Taylor, 'Shared and Divergent Values,' in Guy Laforest, ed., *Reconciling the Solitudes: Essays on Canadian Federalism and Nationalism* (Montreal 1993) 155–86.
6 Russell, *Constitutional Odyssey*, 5.
7 Ibid., 6.
8 Ibid., ix, vii, cf. 235.
9 Alan Cairns, 'The Charlottetown Accord: Multinational Canada v. Federalism,' in Curtis Cook, ed., *Constitutional Predicament: Canada after the Referendum of* 1992 (Montreal 1994), 25–63.
10 Peter Russell, 'Preserving the Canadian Federation: A Two-Track Approach,' The Stapleford Lecture, University of Regina, 18 March 1996, 1.
11 Ibid., 6–19.
12 Ibid., 14.
13 See *Report of the Royal Commission on Aboriginal Peoples*, vol. 1, *Looking Forward, Looking Back* (Ottawa 1996) 675–94.
14 Russell, 'Preserving the Canadian Federation,' 14–19.
15 Ibid., 20, *Constitutional Odyssey*, 234–5,
16 Russell, 'Preserving the Canadian Federation,' 20.
17 This contrary view is often attributed to former Prime Minister Pierre Trudeau. I believe that his view is more complex and profound than this allows, but the popular characterization of his views by some of his followers will serve as an example of the kind of objections to diversity that I have in mind.
18 David Held, *Democracy and Global Order: From the Modern State to Cosmopolitan Governance* (Cambridge, UK, 1995).
19 John Rawls, *Political Liberalism* (New York 1993), Jurgen Habermas, *Between Facts and Norms: Towards a Discourse Theory of Law and Democracy*, trans.

William Rehg (Cambridge, Mass., 1996), Jürgen Habermas, 'Reconciliation through the Public Use of Reason: Remarks on John Rawls,' *Political Liberalism*' and John Rawls, 'Reply to Habermas,' *Journal of Philosophy* 42 no. 3 (March 1995), 109–80.

20 Jean-Jacques Rousseau, *Du contrat social* (Oxford 1972).

21 Michael Sandel, *Democracy's Discontent* (Cambridge, Mass., 1996).

22 John Rawls, 'Reply to Habermas,' 145.

23 Will Kymlicka, *Multicultural Citizenship* (Oxford 1996), Charles Taylor, *Reconciling the Solitudes*; and James Tully, *Strange Multiplicity: Constitutionalism in an Age of Diversity* (Cambridge, UK, 1995).

24 I have discussed this process of 'diversity awareness' in 'Diversity's Gambit Declined,' in Curtis Cook, ed., *Constitutional Predicament: Canada after the Referendum of* 1992 (Montreal 1994), 149–98.

25 See *Report*, vol. 1, *Looking Forward, Looking Back*, 675–94.

26 See, for example, Charles Taylor, 'The Politics of Recognition,' in Amy Gutmann, ed., *Multiculturalism* (Princeton, NJ, 1994), James Tully, 'Let's Talk,' *Canada Watch*, 3, nos. 7 and 8 (May–June and Aug.–Sept. 1995).

27 Tony Laden, Constructing Shared Wills: Deliberative Liberalism and the Politics of Identity' PhD dissertation, Harvard University, July 1996.

28 See Jeremy Webber, *Reimagining Canada: Language, Culture, Community and the Canadian Constitution* (Montreal 1994), and Tully, *Strange Multiplicity*.

29 Simone Chambers, 'Contract or Conversation? Theoretical Lessons from the Canadian Constitutional Crisis,' paper delivered at Harvard University summer 1996. See also her *Reasonable Democracy: Jurgen Habermas and the Politics of Discourse* (Ithaca, NY; 1996), 155–246.

4

Rebalancing the Canadian Federation: The Constitutional Odyssey Continues

KATHERINE SWINTON*

When people are thinking about constitutional reform, they tend often to focus on the changing of constitutional documents through use of the amending formulae. The project may entail fairly discrete provisions, as Canadians have seen recently with respect to the amendment to denominational school rights in Newfoundland and Quebec. Or the project may be a much more ambitious effort at 'mega-constitutional' reform, to use the words of Peter Russell describing the failed attempts to entrench the Meech Lake Accord and the Charlottetown Accord.[1]

But the formal route is not the only way to implement change within the Canadian constitutional framework, nor has it been the most salient with respect to the design of the federation, as our history makes quite clear. Judicial interpretation of constitutional documents, fiscal instruments (especially the federal taxation and spending powers), and cooperative arrangements between federal and provincial governments, among other initiatives, have reshaped the roles and responsibilities of governments over time – often with long-lasting effect.

Following the failure of the 'mega-constitutional' projects captured in the Meech Lake and Charlottetown accords, Russell suggested that Canadians abandon the enterprise and turn to 'ordinary, one-reform-at-a-time, constitutional politics.'[2]

In fact, current constitutional politics is less and less preoccupied by constitutional amendment of any kind and increasingly absorbed by reform of the federal system through less formal mechanisms. Driven partly by demands from many Quebecers for decentralization, but also by the fiscal problems of federal

* The author wrote this paper while she was a professor at the University of Toronto, before she was called to the bench.

and provincial governments struggling with debts, deficits, and global trade competition, the federal government has promised 'rebalanced federalism' and 'flexible federalism,'[3] while the premiers (other than Quebec's) have called for a non-constitutional rebalancing of federal and provincial roles and responsibilities.[4]

Taken at face value, this language might suggest the possibility of a principled reallocation of functions between Ottawa and the provinces based on criteria such as efficiency, competence, equity, national consensus, and 'subsidiarity.' In fact, the process of 'rebalancing' to date has largely taken the form of a diminished federal role in a number of major policy fields, most significantly social and health policy, yet with Ottawa's continued assertion of its power to set national standards in these areas. More recently, attention has turned to mechanisms for harmonizing and coordinating federal and provincial policies in areas such as internal trade and environmental protection.

This paper deals with the current process of realignment of functions. The first part argues that Canadians are in a period of significant constitutional change, achieved through more informal, and therefore more flexible, methods than constitutional amendment. Given that this change is occurring in a period of fiscal restraint and 'rethinking of government,' the trend to smaller government presents a challenge, examined in the second part – how to address the interdependence of functions, in order to eliminate unnecessary overlap, duplication, and conflict, while still achieving policy objectives, including maintenance of those nation-wide standards fundamental to the social and economic union. An examination, in the third part, of the ability of current policy instruments and intergovernmental machinery to address these issues suggests the need for a more cooperative federalism than has existed in recent decades. Although some commentators have proposed the creation of new intergovernmental institutions with broad decision-making powers, I argue that the immediate goal should continue to be 'functional federalism' that not only acknowledges the role of provincial governments in the creation of nation-wide standards, but does so in a manner sensitive to the often-criticized 'democratic deficit' of executive federalism.

The Forces of Change

Quebec: Decentralization as Antidote to Separation?

In October 1995, Quebec voters narrowly rejected a referendum question proposing sovereignty for Quebec. While the debates continue about the ambiguity of the question, the fairness of the proceedings, the errors in federal strategy, and the meaning of a 'yes' vote, one thing remains clear – a majority of French-speaking Quebecers are very dissatisfied with the current state of Canadian federalism. The changes desired by those still wanting to remain in Canada or who can be persuaded of the benefits of doing so are also clear – explicit recognition of Quebec as a distinct society within the Canadian constitution, a veto for Quebec with respect to constitutional amendments affecting its interests, restrictions on the federal spending power, and some devolution of power from the centre to the provinces.

While the agenda seems clear, the dynamics of Canadian constitutional politics have created a dilemma for Ottawa. Two recent attempts at constitutional amendment – from 1987 to 1990, leading to the Meech Lake Accord, and the Charlottetown Accord, worked out in 1991 and 1992 – failed, and opposition continues in the rest of Canada to recognition of 'special status' for Quebec in the form of asymmetric arrangements in the distribution of powers or the amending formula. 'Equality of the provinces' remains a key principle for many Canadians (even if it misstates the truth of historical constitutional arrangements). Moreover, opponents of 'distinct society' language in the constitution see it as a threat to an ideal of equal citizenship, as well as equality of provinces, resulting in vociferous opposition because of the fear that the Charter of Rights might be detrimentally affected.

Recognizing the futility of seeking constitutional reform, the federal government has pursued more informal processes to try to meet the concerns of those dissatisfied Quebecers who might be wooed back to support federalism. A resolution in the House of Commons has recognized Quebec as a distinct society;[5] a federal statute has committed the cabinet not to introduce any constitutional amendment without the approval of the Quebec legislature (along with certain other provinces or combinations of provinces);[6] and federal promises have been made to vacate areas of jurisdiction, such as forestry and labour market training.[7] Finally, the federal government, in its 1996 Speech from the Throne, promised not to use its spending power to create new shared-cost programs in areas of exclusive provincial jurisdiction without the consent of a majority of the provinces. Opting out would be allowed, with compensation, if a province established equivalent or comparable initiatives. Thus, directly or indirectly, a number of key elements of the Charlottetown Accord have been or are being implemented by means other than constitutional amendment.

Government Fiscal Pressures: Downsizing and Rethinking Government

Serious fiscal problems face all levels of government, but those at the federal level have had the most dramatic impact on Canadian federalism. With a debt of close to $600 billion ($578.4 billion in 1995–6 and $602.7 billion in 1996–7) and a deficit still at $32.7 billion in 1995–6, Ottawa has had to cut spending or increase revenues. While tax increases were a feature of many budgets, from the mid-1980s much of the emphasis was on cutting costs rather than on increasing tax revenues, with the result that federal program spending fall dramatically.[8] Inevitably, cutbacks had to affect transfers to the provinces, which still constituted 16 per cent of the federal budget in 1994–5. Nevertheless, it was not until 1990 that the budget significantly reduced major transfers to the provinces.

To understand the operation and significance of fiscal federalism, it is necessary to recall that for many years the federal spending power has been the main instrument of flexibility in the Canadian constitutional structure. While social policy, health care, and education are all matters within exclusive provincial legislative jurisdiction, the provinces' fiscal capacity has often failed to match their legislative responsibility in these areas. Therefore, even though Ottawa lacked jurisdiction to legislate directly in these and some other areas, it took advantage of the fiscal imbalance by providing funds to shape policy in provincial areas of jurisdiction – sometimes on a shared-cost basis, sometimes through direct grants; at times with conditions, but more often without.

The cornerstone of fiscal federalism has been the group of programs known as Established Programs Financing (EPF), which, up until the 1996–7 fiscal year, included federal contributions for post-secondary education and health care (on a block-grant basis) and for social assistance (on a shared-cost basis for most provinces). The amount of cash transferred under EPF in 1995–6 was $18.5 billion.[9] In addition to EPF, equalization provided some redress against the revenue imbalance among the provinces, with grants paid to all but three of the provinces amounting to $8.7 billion in 1995–6. Moreover, federal spending has occurred and continues in many other areas, as well – infrastructure, highway building, training, and legal aid, to name a few.

The courts have essentially taken a 'hands-off' approach to the spending power in the very few cases in which its validity has been questioned. Treating the allocation of funds as an offer of largesse that the provinces can refuse, the courts have ruled that 'watertight compartments' of legislative jurisdiction need not be 'money tight.'[10] They have not seen even the presence of conditions on use of funds as disguised regulatory activity.[11]

As Ottawa came to realize that provincial transfers had to be curtailed if the federal deficit was to be managed, it made the federal spending power a 'dis-spending' one, in the words of Richard Simeon.[12] First, it placed a 'cap on CAP' (Canada Assistance Plan): until 1990, it paid half the costs of social assistance in the provinces, but that year's budget unilaterally announced a 5 per cent ceiling on the annual growth of payments to the three 'have' provinces of Alberta, British Columbia, and Ontario. That, coupled with a recession that increased the numbers on the welfare rolls, hit Ontario particularly hard, since the federal share of payments went from 50 per cent of costs to 28 per cent in 1992–3, with a loss to Ontario of $1.7 billion.[13]

Although the cap was to last for three years, it became clear that the cost of returning to a 50 per cent federal share of welfare was not feasible, given the widening gap between costs in the 'have' provinces and federal contributions. Therefore the 1995 budget transformed federal–provincial fiscal arrangements, with the announcement of the Canada Health and Social Transfer (CHST). This would replace EPF and CAP as of April 1996, with a new global transfer set up to cover post-secondary education, medicare, and social assistance. Gone was the shared-cost philosophy of CAP, although certain conditions on spending were retained from CAP and the health-care sector.[14] Specifically, the provinces are subject to penalties, through the withholding of funds, if they impose residency requirements on newcomers for the receipt of social assistance (section 19) or if they violate the principles formerly found in the Canada Health Act: accessibility ('reasonable access to health care without financial or other barriers'), comprehensiveness (coverage of all medically necessary hospital and medical services), universality (coverage of all residents of a province after three months' residency), portability (coverage when temporarily absent from the province), and public administration.[15]

While the CHST has been defended as promoting 'flexible federalism,' it was clearly motivated by fiscal considerations, for the new transfer is significantly smaller than the transfers under the earlier programs. Cash contributions under the CHST declined by $6 billion over two years from then current spending (dropping from $18.5 billion in 1995–6 to $12.5 billion in 1997–8). A further drop, to $11.1 billion, was announced for 1999–2000; the March 1996 budget made a commitment to stabilize grants at that time and perhaps increase them by 2002–3. During the 1997 election campaign, the Liberals promised to maintain the $12.5-billion level.

Ottawa has continued to assert that it makes a larger contribution to provincial social programs than these numbers suggest, calculating its contributions to take into account the transfer of tax points to the provinces in 1977 as part of the formula for calculating provincial entitlements to EPF grants. In practical terms, those transfers have become irrevocable, and from the provincial perspective the only current federal contribution from Ottawa is the cash transfer. Realistically, that is the only contribution that Ottawa can use to exert pressure on the provinces to comply with national standards such as those set out above. Without the commitment to stabilizing the cash transfer, as promised in the

1996 budget, that cash will evaporate over the next ten to fifteen years. However, the CHST legislation provides that penalties can be imposed through withholding of funds payable under any legislation or federal–provincial arrangement (section 23.2).

Reading the Message: Rebalanced Federalism?

While the direct goal of federal deficit control may not have been decentralization, that has been the inevitable result in a number of policy areas. Some will argue that this is not a bad thing, and not just because it seems to respond to some of Quebec's historic concerns. Other justifications arise from federalism theory – for example, advocates of a competitive model of federalism, such as Albert Breton, should welcome federal withdrawal from various policy areas within provincial jurisdiction, because this leaves room for the provinces to engage in the experimentation and innovation in policy initiatives for which federalism is valued.[16] And there can be no doubt that different approaches to deficit management and program review have emerged across the country, with provinces such as Ontario and Alberta taking strong neoconservative positions that are significantly reducing the size of government, while others, such as Saskatchewan, have tried to take a more humane and still interventionist approach.

Others are less sanguine about the positive effects of federal action for the efficacy of policy-making. Federal withdrawal has imposed a severe financial burden on the provinces, in the form of reduced transfers, in addition to political costs, as the public demands the same or better levels of service and programs, without understanding who is responsible for decreased resources. The ultimate result of federal 'offloading' is inevitably smaller government, as the provinces in turn pass costs on to municipalities, while simultaneously cutting back their own programs, thus shifting functions to the private sector. Many observers are concerned about the ultimate distributional effects of this cascading deficit control, fearing, with reason, that the least powerful and least popular in our society will be hurt the most.[17] In other words, the result of federal downsizing, while theoretically creating greater room for the provinces to act, results practically in their sharply curtailed ability to do so unless they can find new sources of revenue. Therefore the outcome of much so-called devolution is decentralization not to the provinces but to the market and the private sphere. Many on the left see federal cutbacks as magnifying the effects of the North American Free Trade Agreement, with its curtailment not only of federal activity but of that of the provinces as well, in the pursuit of 'market values.'[18] This verdict is an overstatement, since provincial governments were already having to reconsider their programs and roles because of competition from foreign trade, public resistance to further tax increases, rising program costs, and a general ethos that has questioned many of the activities of governments. However, there can be no doubt that federal downsizing, like NAFTA, has expedited the process of 'rethinking government' in Canada.

But is there serendipity here, in that the federal withdrawal from some fields will at least respond to Quebec's demands for greater autonomy? While Ottawa can try to cast a positive light on its actions, they are a second-best response for Quebec federalists, who demand the symbolism and safeguards that come from formal constitutional amendments. Moreover, in the absence of an equivalent transfer of funds to accompany withdrawal from policy areas, the federal action creates ill-will in Quebec, as in the other provinces. And outside Quebec, federal downsizing has caused increased acrimony in federal–provincial relations, as the provinces' efforts to deal with their fiscal problems may threaten the Canadian social union. Recent examples include British Columbia's imposition of a residency requirement for welfare recipients, which triggered federal financial penalties and prompted litigation in response, and Alberta's ongoing dispute with Ottawa about the legality of private medical clinics under the Canada Health Act.

The current climate suggests the need for Canadians to think seriously about the future distribution of functions between federal and provincial governments. One route would emphasize continued disengagement, with policy areas emerging for each that would make clearer the lines of responsibility and accountability, even if this might create new barriers to citizens' mobility or end national social programs. While some commentators fear that this would undermine the federal government, many exclusively federal policy areas remain, including criminal law, defence, air transport, broadcasting, Aboriginal peoples, and international trade.

But obvious problems with disengagement suggest that the national project should be to develop new approaches to cooperative federalism. First, total disengagement is impossible, for there is inevitable interdependence between federal and provincial governments. Sometimes this results from the constitutional division of responsibility – for example, federal jurisdiction over interprovincial and international trucking versus provincial jurisdiction over intraprovincial aspects; federal power to deal with environmental assessment as ancillary to other federal 'heads of power,' such as navigation and shipping or fisheries, interacting with provincial environmental jurisdiction linked to property and civil rights in the province. Moreover, even where the lines of jurisdiction seem to mark out separate spheres, the action of one government within its jurisdiction can affect policies and expenditures of the other level – for example, when unemployment insurance benefits become more difficult to obtain, the needy turn to provincial social assistance; if Ottawa makes bail harder to achieve before-trial, the provinces' costs for the administration of justice increase. Therefore ongoing coordination is needed to deal with interdependence in a world of overlapping and interlocking jurisdiction. The objective of coordinating efforts in some fields may be to reduce overlap and duplication as part of the process of rethinking government, but this exercise of 'carving up' functions requires ongoing interaction by governments. Finally, many will argue that Ottawa and the provinces should consult and cooperate in the interests of preserving national standards in some areas, such as health policy, and in the hope of creating them in others – for example, through establishment of a national regime of securities law.

Realistically, the challenge is to think about national standards and intergovernmental cooperation in these tough times, when the financial lubricant of federal spending is much harder to employ. Three approaches to the creation and enforcement of national standards are open to consideration. An emphasis on *federal* standards requires, first, continuing use of the spending power with conditions (using the CHST model) or, second, federal legislation (for example, a federally enacted national securities regime). A third alternative approach would acknowledge that *national* standards can be established through federal and provincial negotiation and enforced through a mechanism acceptable to both levels of government. My emphasis in the rest of this paper is largely on the third avenue.

Clearly, the first approach – continued use of the federal spending power – remains not only viable, but important for Ottawa. Thus the current CHST is embedded in the structure of the Canada Health Act and the former CAP, with its limited set of national standards ultimately capable of enforcement through the withholding of federal cash contributions, under either the CHST or other federal transfers to a province.

But there are two obvious problems with this approach. First, conditions can be effective only if there is enough cash transferred to give Ottawa real leverage against the province when it is withheld. With the declining cash contribution to the CHST described above, federal leverage will decline seriously within the next decade. Even though Ottawa has the power to withhold funds from other transfers, there is some question about the constitutionality of such action: the cases mentioned above that upheld the federal spending power suggested that spending was permissible as long as it did not constitute disguised regulation within provincial areas of jurisdiction.[19] To the extent that Ottawa tries to influence provincial medical care policy by withholding funds for training, for example, this looks more and more like unauthorized regulatory action.

But beyond the legalities, there is a serious question of legitimacy if the federal government insists on enforcing burdensome conditions in programs to which it contributes less and less. Provincial revenues now provide the main source of funds for social and health care programs, and the provinces can rightly assert that they should be allowed to make the decisions about program design, since they are held accountable to the electorate for the results. Moreover, the intervention of the federal government, when it has neither particular expertise nor accountability, only increases the acrimony already observable in federal–provincial relations.

The second method – federal legislation to create national standards – has been suggested in social policy and regulation of capital markets. Certainly, in the latter field, there is strong indication in the case law that Ottawa might be able to act unilaterally if it has the political will, given the international and interprovincial nature of capital markets and the Supreme Court of Canada's willingness to allow federal jurisdiction not only over interprovincial and international trade and commerce but also over 'the general regulation of trade.'[20] Other commentators have argued that Ottawa should invoke the 'peace, order and good government' clause in section 91 of the Constitution Act, 1867, to legislate with respect to national standards.[21] However, this method looks more difficult, since federal jurisdiction under that clause rests on criteria such as the presence of a matter of national concern, provincial inability to deal with the problem, and the presence of a discrete matter that does not significantly distort the balance within the federal system if allocated to federal jurisdiction.[22] Given the longstanding provincial power to deal with health care, it is most unlikely that the courts would allow the federal government to step in and take over regulation in the health area.

Given Quebec's sensitivity to further encroachments on its jurisdiction, and the limitations on the spending power and federal legislative jurisdiction, the current political climate suggests the need to rethink 'national' standards and to accept that they need not necessarily be federal-government standards. Cynics will argue that provincial governments' engagement in setting national standards is an exercise doomed to fail, given the self-interest with which they go to the federal–provincial negotiating table. Yet there are some positive developments in the recent past. In social policy, the provinces created a Ministerial Council on Social Policy Reform and Renewal, which reported in December 1995. All provincial and territorial governments, except Quebec, reached a consensus on the report, which outlined a set of principles for reform of social policy. The First Ministers' meeting of June 1996 agreed to establish a committee of federal and provincial ministers to examine the issues further and to put into practice the ministerial council's report. More recently, the premiers agreed at their August 1996 meeting in Jasper, Alberta, to a number of recommendations, including development of a 'national framework to guide the reform process in areas of provincial/territorial responsibility, including a mechanism for settling differences.' They noted that 'the current federal unilateral approach to setting and enforcing national standards is neither fair nor sustainable.'[23]

There have been two other important initiatives. In 1994, federal and provincial governments signed the Agreement on Internal Trade, which came into effect 1 July 1995. This massive document, over 200 pages in length, commits both levels of government to reduce barriers to interprovincial trade, through ending of certain forms of discriminatory treatment (for example, in government procurement) and harmonization of standards and practices.[24] A dispute-settlement process involves both mediation and adjudication by an ad-hoc panel selected from a list of individuals nominated by the parties. A further example of federal–provincial cooperation took place in November 1996, when the Canadian Council of Ministers of the Environment approved in principle an accord on environmental harmonization, which states as one of its objectives the use of a cooperative approach across jurisdictions to develop measures to protect the environment.

Instruments and Institutions for a New Climate of Intergovernmental Relations

With the new emphasis on harmonization, cooperation, and provincial participation in the creation and enforcement of national standards, it is important to ask whether existing intergovernmental machinery is capable of devising effective policies, given the instruments and institutions available. André Burelle, for one, has advocated further institutionalization of executive federalism. Rather than the informal, ad-hoc system in place, he suggests creation of a Council of the Federation, a body composed of federal- and provincial-government representatives, with decision-making power to create a new social pact for Canada.[25]

Tom Courchene, in a 1996 paper called 'ACCESS,'[26] is gravely concerned about current threats to the internal social and economic union, yet he also expresses dissatisfaction with the lack of provincial responsibility for its design and governance. Therefore he advocates, at a minimum, what he calls an 'interim Access model,' characterized by federal and provincial monitoring of the conditions for provincial receipt of the CHST, as well as continued devolution in the policy areas under current discussion, such as training and forestry. More ambitious is his 'full Access' model, which is much more strongly 'interprovincial' than the interim version. It calls for a national convention (or accord), achieved through federal and provincial agreement (and, in places, interprovincial agreement), which would address a broad range of economic and social issues: devolution of labour-market training, treaty-making, national standards in social policy, a strengthened common-market clause in the constitution, and fiscal arrangements (including increased transfers of tax points to provinces and harmonization of budgetary processes). The list goes on, but what is noteworthy throughout is the involvement of the provinces in setting national standards and in enforcing them in a wide array of policy areas.

While the intergovernmental agreements described above suggest increased federal–provincial cooperation, we are still far from Courchene's interim model, let alone the 'full Access' proposal. And whether we proceed incrementally or more dramatically towards a convention or pact, the current constitutional framework contains legal obstacles that can complicate the enforcement of current obligations such as the Internal Trade Agreement or future agreements such as Courchene's ambitious Access proposal. Therefore one of the challenges for the federal system is to find the appropriate machinery and instruments to make effective new intergovernmental arrangements.

The most significant problem arises because intergovernmental agreements cannot be made legally binding, if a government decides later to refuse to comply or withdraws its consent. Since the decision of the Supreme Court of Canada in the *CAP Reference* (1991), it has been clear that parliamentary sovereignty trumps federalism, in that Parliament or a legislature can enact laws that change obligations under an intergovernmental agreement.[27] That case dealt with the legality of the unilateral federal decision to legislate the cap on CAP payments for the 'have' provinces, described above, which changed the federal obligation to pay half the costs of social assistance. The court held unanimously that the terms of the federal statute, not the agreement, contained the formula for payment. Since Parliament has the power to amend legislation at any time, it could change the formula unilaterally. Significantly, the court seemed to go beyond the words of the particular statute and agreement to conclude that no Parliament could bind its successors from legislating through the terms of an agreement, given the principle of parliamentary sovereignty. Entering an agreement is an executive action, which cannot bind the legislative process, so that a legislature can enact laws to change such an agreement.

Thus there is an analogy between the status of federal–provincial agreements and international ones: as actions taken by the executive, international agreements (and intergovernmental agreeements) cannot change existing law, without further legislative action aimed at implementation. And even an obligation made legally binding by legislative action can not bind future Parliaments, which can always change laws.[28] Anticipating this response, anchored in principles of parliamentary supremacy, some of the provinces in the CAP case argued unsuccessfully that the federal level continued to be bound by the federal–provincial agreement through the device of 'manner and form' legislation. This is a doctrine associated with the law of parliamentary sovereignty, which allows Parliament to enact procedural devices to curtail the actions of future Parliaments – for example, requiring a special majority to change a specific law or insisting that another law, inconsistent with the law containing a manner-and-form requirement, contain a notwithstanding clause if it is to take priority.[29] However, these devices must not in fact place effective limits on Parliament's ability to change the substance of the law, or they will be invalid. In the CAP case itself, the court held that there was no manner-and-form requirement built into the federal legislation.

The manner-and-form device has had little play in Canadian law, although courts have provided primacy to human rights codes over other legislation, without offering any real discussion of the basis for doing so, except to note that they are 'quasi-constitutional' in nature. Drawing on the example of human rights codes, governments wishing to make certain kinds of intergovernmental arrangements legally binding could enact laws incorporating agreed-on standards and making it clear that these have primacy – that is, that laws inconsistent would be not be operative. For example, provinces could enact a law requiring recognition of occupational qualifications obtained in another province, or they could incorporate some or all of the standards applying to the CHST, such as the prohibition on discrimination against new residents in the provision of social assistance. These could be enforced through the courts or through some special adjudicative body – provided that courts were willing to accord them superior status, rather than seeing them as an attempt to bind future legislatures in an improper manner.

But if a province were unwilling to comply with these obligations, it could repeal the standards or circumscribe its obligations by legislative action. Any attempt to prevent easy repeal through enactment of procedural devices, such as the need for other governments' agreement before repeal or enactment in accordance with a special procedure such as a two-thirds majority, is likely to fail to bind (even if a government were willing to include such procedures in legislation) because of parliamentary sovereignty.

Despite the lack of legal enforcement, intergovernmental agreements are not ineffective. In some cases, political incentives will motivate compliance – for example, where one province's reluctance to comply with an obligation (such as a prohibition on differential education fees for non-residents or a promise of non-discrimination in letting public-service contracts) may hurt its own residents if retaliation occurs in other provinces. However, in some circumstances a government may renege on its obligations because doing so is beneficial – for example, when a province requires stricter professional qualifications that benefit its residents. Therefore the challenge is to devise mechanisms suited to diverse policy areas that will create more effective checks on such action.

The ideal solution would be a mechanism to make intergovernmental agreements binding. The Charlottetown Accord, for example, contained a proposed constitutional amendment that would have allowed legislatures and Parliament to make intergovernmental agreements binding for up to five years through specific legislation. In the absence of such an amendment, there are some situtations where the continued 'stick' of the federal spending power, with the threat to withhold federal grants, may lead to provincial compliance. However, the declining size of federal contributions in areas such as health suggests the need for a greater provincial role in determining whether there is non-compliance before a sanction is threatened, in order to meet the concerns about the legitimacy of unilateral federal action outlined above. Unfortunately for the provinces, they have no equivalent 'stick' to enforce federal obligations, except refusal to enter into shared obligations in other areas when asked to do so by Ottawa.

Despite calls for a grand new intergovernmental council or convention to govern the federation, Canadians are better served in the short run by an incremental approach to a more cooperative climate in intergovernmental relations. A focus on particular areas, such as social policy, the environment, and securities, has the advantage of avoiding 'summit federalism,' which may turn into 'mega-constitutionalism' in another guise. Consider, for example, a proposal for a council of the federation or the negotiation of Courchene's ambitious convention on social and economic policy. With so much at stake, the need for unanimous approval will probably frustrate the process.

The advantage of focusing on particular policy areas is that it moves us more in the direction of the 'functional federalism' that Dupré tells us has been a more effective form of executive federalism.[30] Moreover, such an approach allows implementation and enforcement mechanisms to be tailored to the policy area and in line with the kind of obligations agreed to.[31] Sometimes the cooperative arrangement may lead to delegation of functions to a federal–provincial body or just to the other level of government. Marketing boards for agricultural products are an excellent example of such delegation, which may well be emulated in a future national securities commission. At other times, carrots and sticks in the form of federal transfers may be effective. In other circumstances, as in the Agreement on Internal Trade, retaliatory action is authorized against governments that fail to comply with the agreement, following the decision of an adjudicative body.

Some agreements may result in fairly precise standards that lend themselves to incorporation in legislation – for example, a prohibition on discrimination against non-residents in contracting by the broader public sector. This can be enforced by adjudication, either by courts or by a specialized panel, as with the internal-trade agreement. In still other areas, all that can be expected is an agreement on processes designed to lead to further action – for example, a commitment to continued efforts at harmonization of environmental standards or recognition of occupational qualifications, as in the internal-trade agreement. Such open-ended obligations do not readily lend themselves to adjudicative oversight, but they might be 'enforced' through mechanisms designed to ensure public accountability – for example, by a reporting requirement to document the progress made, perhaps supplemented by monitoring or evaluation by a political or expert body.

Ultimately, success on a variety of fronts may lead to the creation of a more formal set of institutions to oversee the workings of the federation, such as a Council of the Federation. But whether that is the course taken, or whether a more incremental approach continues across various sectors, government actors must not focus so closely on intergovernmental interests that they lose sight of democratic concerns. The democratic deficit of executive federalism has long been a concern in Canada: Donald Smiley's criticisms from two decades ago[32] have found echoes in vociferous critics of closed-door discussions of constitutional reform or the more recent negotiations on the internal-trade agreement. Observers worry about the lack of public understanding and informed debate about the impact of the current federal downsizing on the federal system, especially on social policy. Using the arcane language of budgets and fiscal federalism, we are, some say, changing social policy by stealth.[33] Therefore a more cooperative approach to intergovernmental relations should not emerge at the expense of losing public input into important policy debates.

Conclusion

Some commentators fear that current decentralization, especially in social and health policy, is irreversible, with the result that our constitutional odyssey by non-constitutional means has transformed Canadian federalism. Yet the pessimism seems ill-founded, given the dramatic swings between centralization and decentralization experienced since 1867. One of the great advantages of doing 'constitutional' change through administrative and fiscal arrangements is the flexibility it permits in altering decisions over time. Sadly, while many outside Quebec extol this characteristic of the constitution, the flexibility is anathema to those who demand the security of constitutional language to prevent the return to an interventionist centre. Moreover, the fact that the current changes fail to deliver the symbolic affirmation of Quebec's distinctive nature provided by constitutional language means that at some point dialogue about formal changes to the constitution must continue, even while many significant changes occur by less formal means. And so the Canadian constitutional odyssey continues.

NOTES

1 Peter Russell, *Constitutional Odyssey: Can Canadians Become a Sovereign People?* 2nd ed. (Toronto: University of Toronto Press 1993).
2 Ibid., at 231.
3 House of Commons, *Debates*, 27 Feb. 1996, Speech from the Throne.
4 *Communiqué*, 37th Annual Premiers' Conference, Jasper, Alberta, 23 Aug. 1996.
5 The resolution reocognizes that 'Quebec's is a distinct society within Canada' and that the distinct society 'includes its French-speaking majority, unique culture and civil law tradition'; resolution, 6 Dec. 1995, House of Commons, *Debates*, 1st Sess., 35th Parl., 17288.
6 Constitutional Amendments Act, SC 1996, c. 1. In effect, the act prohibits a federal minister from proposing a resolution for amendment, except in situations where a province could exercise a veto to avoid being bound (that is, unanimity items in section 41 of the Constitution Act, 1982; amendments allowing opting out (section 38[3]), and bilateral amendments (section 43) unless there is majority support among provinces and within five regions: Ontario, Quebec, British Columbia, two Atlantic provinces with 50 per cent of the population, and two of the Prairie provinces with 50 per cent of the population.
7 Sections 57(2) and (3) of the Employment Insurance Act, SC 1996, c. 23 commit the federal government to work with the provinces to harmonize employment benefits and support measures and to enter into agreements with the provinces. Section 61(2) prohibits federal employment benefits that help insured individuals upgrade employment skills unless the province agrees. In accordance with these provisions, the first agreement on labour-market development was signed by Alberta and the federal government on 6 December 1996. The Speech from the Throne of 27 February 1996 also announced federal withdrawal from forestry, mining, and recreation, as well as training – all areas of devolution proposed in the Charlottetown Accord.
8 The federal budget of 6 March 1996 announced that program spending had fallen from close to $120 billion in 1993–4 to a planned $105.5 billion in 1998–9, which meant a drop to 12 per cent of gross domestic product from close to 20 per cent.
9 For a recent overview, see Susan D. Phillips, 'The Canada Health and Social Trans-

fer: Fiscal Federalism in Search of a Vision,' in D.M. Brown and J.W. Rose, eds., *Canada: The State of the Federation,* 1995 (Kingston: Queen's Institute of Intergovernmental Relations 1995), 65.

10 The phrase comes from Stefan Dupré and David Cameron, quoted by Dupré himself in 'Section 106A and Federal–Provincial Fiscal Relations,' in K.E. Swinton and C.J. Rogerson, eds., *Competing Constitutional Visions: The Meech Lake Accord* (Toronto: Carswell 1988), 205.

11 The Supreme Court of Canada has given indirect recognition to the federal spending power in *Reference re Canada Assistance Plan* (1991), 83 DLR (4th) 297, and *YMHA Jewish Community Centre of Winnipeg v. Brown*, [1989] 1 SCR 532, while the Alberta Court of Appeal expressly approved its use in W*interhaven Stables Ltd. v. Canada (A.G.)* (1988), 53 DLR (4th) 413.

12 Richard Simeon, 'The Political Context for Renegotiating Fiscal Federalism,' in K. Banting, D. Brown, and T. Courchene, eds., *The Future of Fiscal Federalism* (Kingston: Queen's University School of Policy Studies 1994), 146.

13 David Cameron, 'Post-Modern Ontario and the Laurentian Thesis,' in D.M. Brown and J. Hiebert, eds., *Canada: The State of the Federation,* 1994 (Kingston: Institute of Intergovernmental Relations, 1994), 119.

14 Federal–Provincial Fiscal Arrangements Act, RSC 1985, c. F-8, as amended SC 1995, c. 17, Part V, and in particular sections 13–23.2, deal with the Canada Health and Social Transfer.

15 Canada Health Act, RSC 1985, c. C-6.

16 Albert Breton, 'Supplementary Statement,' in Canada, Royal Commission on the Economic Union and Development Prospects for Canada (Macdonald Commission), *Report*, vol. III (Ottawa: Minister of Supply and Services 1985), 486.

17 See, for example, Phillips, 'The Canada Health and Social Transfer.'

18 See, for example, David Schneiderman, 'Canadian Constitutionaliam and Sovereignty after NAFTA,' *Constitutional Forum* (1994), 93; Ian Robinson, 'The NAFTA, the Side-Deals, and Canadian Federalism: Constitutional Reform by Other Means?' in R. Watts and D. Brown, eds., *Canada: The State of the Federation, 1993* (Kingston: Institute of Intergovernmental Relations 1993), 193.

19 See *Winterhaven* and *YMHA*.

20 This is discussed further in K. Swinton, 'Courting Our Way to Economic Integration: Judicial Review and Canadian Economic Union,' *Canadian Business Law Journal* 25 (1995), 280.

21 Robert Howse, 'New Ways to Secure Our Social Union: New Ways to Enforcing Standards,' *Policy Options* (June 1996) 11.

22 *R. v. Crown Zellerbach Ltd.* (1988), 49 DLR(4th) 161 (SCC) at 184.

23 1996 Annual Premiers' Conference, 'Issues Paper on Social Policy Reform and Renewal: Next Steps,' Aug. 1996, 11. One of the priority areas discussed and agreed

on was development of 'options for intergovernmental mechanisms or processes to develop and promote adherence to national principles and standards.'

24 For a critical description, see M.J. Trebilcock and D. Schwanen, eds., *Getting There: An Assessment of the Agreement on Internal Trade* (Toronto: C.D. Howe Institute 1995). After this paper was written, the federal government and the provincial governments entered into 'A Framework to Improve the Social Union for Canadians' on 4 February 1999.

25 André Burelle, 'A Renewed Canada Should Say Yes,' *Canada Opinion* 4 no. 1 (1996) (Ottawa: Council for Canadian Unity).

26 Thomas J. Courchene, '*A C*onvention on the *C*anadian *E*conomic and *S*ocial *S*ystems', Working Paper prepared for the Ontario Ministry of Intergovernmental Affairs, Toronto, 1996.

27 *Reference re Canada Assistance Plan (B.C.)*, [1991] 2 SCR 525, 83 DLR (4th) 297.

28 There is one exception, in that provinces may not be able to change contractual agreements, if the situs of the contract is outside the province (that is, if the province purports to exercise extraterritorial jurisdiction) (*Reference re Upper Churchill Water Rights Reversion Act*, [1984] 1 SCR 297).

29 This is the technique used to give priority to human rights codes: see, for example, the Ontario Human Rights Code, RSO 1990, c. H.19, as amended, sec.47 (2).

30 J.S. Dupré, 'Reflections on the Workability of Executive Federalism,' in R. Simeon, ed., *Intergovernmental Relations* (Toronto: University of Toronto Press 1985), 1.

31 One of the problems with Courchene's ACCESS proposal is its assumption that there would be one kind of mechanism to enforce it, rather than a variety of mechanisms designed in accordance with particular policies.

32 Donald Smiley, 'An Outsider's Observations of Federal–Provincial Relations Among Consenting Adults,' in R. Simeon, ed., *Confrontation and Collaboration: Intergovernmental Relations in Canada Today* (Toronto: Institute of Public Administration of Canada 1979), 105.

33 Simeon, 'Political Context.'

Summary of Discussion on Constitutional Politics

In responding to questions about the ethic of federalism, M. Dion indicated that government exists to help individuals and that collective identities are important only in so far as they help do so. Thus in his view debates over solutions must be defined from an individual point of view.

James Tully contended that he would phrase the situation rather in terms of diversity, not as debate between individual and collective identity. The concept of diversity breaks down the division between individual and collective identities. The goal is to find a set of institutions and arrangements that allows us to live our identities in an unburdensome way. Yet present arrangements often thwart aspects of some people's identity. Embracing diversity means defining a constitutional arrangement that allows the expression of the various aspects of identity.

Darin Barney (a University of Toronto student) asked how Canadian citizens can define constitutional arrangements in a meaningful way, given a shrinking of government and other public institutions.

James Tully agreed that the public sphere is disappearing, finding it tragic that at the very time that public involvement has become a condition for the legitimacy of democratic society, the federal government is dismantling the public institutions that enable citizens to engage in and develop attachments beyond their immediate localities. In his view the decline of the public sphere is one of the factors contributing to the dissolution of Canada.

Stéphane Dion saw this as a gross exaggeration. The same social trends, he observed, are occurring throughout the world. Separatism is not caused by the decline of the public sphere. In fact, the fiscal constraints of the federal government have in fact saved the country.

Thomas Heuglin asked the panelists for more direction on possible scenarios for the federal system in balancing autonomy and solidarity, particularly since property remains a major obstacle to the accommodation of Aboriginal and other claims on the federation.

In responding, Katherine Swinton said that, despite a general thrust towards privatization, a dialogue will continue, largely at the insistence of the provinces, over what degree of market control is needed to protect social standards. She anticipates considerable variation across policy fields, but in all areas she sees the primary challenge being how to bring citizens into the debate.

Gilles Gilbert of Montreal spoke from the floor, questioning whether politicians are the appropriate people to bring about a constitutional solution. He asked whether we did not need instead something like a constitutional council composed of representatives of various aspects of society to develop a consensus as to what Canadians want for their country.

James Tully agreed that citizens must have some say over their constitution but said that governments insist on seeing themselves in the leading role. Thus while Canada as a society has made a transition to wanting and needing a more democratic constitutionalism, it has not yet developed the institutions through which the necessary deliberations can take place.

Stéphane Dion commented that the government of Canada recognizes from recent rounds of constitutional negotiation that we can no longer have a 'top-down' constitutional solution. At the same time, it does not want to formalize anything like a constitutional council because anyone appointed to such a body will automatically no longer be an ordinary citizen. In keeping with its role as our elected representatives, members of the government are now seeking to encourage ordinary Canadians to talk together in grassroots ways and to suggest solutions.

Katherine Swinton, hitting a very Russellian point, argued that we have been trying to do too much through our constitution and constitutional politics. Policy debates are in her view impoverished by being played out in constitutional terms. Instead of focusing on a more democratic constitutionalism, we need to create a more democratic politics, to start talking about policy areas such as the post office, jobs, health care, and how they affect and are affected by federal–provincial relations. She admits that in doing so we still face the danger of federalism trumping policy concerns and that citizens may not be invited in as much as they want. Nevertheless, she sees in this approach a possibility for a more democratic policy debate.

Walter Berns, alluding to Russell's discussion of the interplay between law and politics in the 1982 patriation reference to the Supreme Court of Canada (2 SCR 793), asked the panelists what to expect of the court when it addresses the Quebec separation reference.

Lorainne Weinrib, a lawyer in the 1982 patriation reference, drew together several of the strands of discussion in commenting that the Supreme Court of Canada, through its reference jurisdiction, has served as a forum for principled discussion in mediating some of our most pressing public questions. She recalled a sense in the courtroom during the reference hearings that the future of Canada hung in the balance. In deciding the case, she thought the court played a key role in keeping us on a path towards participatory constitutionalism by sending Pierre Trudeau back to the provinces to renegotiate the present constitution.

In the build-up to the separation reference case, Weinrib found it tragic that the court is being symbolically undermined as an institution for principled mediation of important public issues by Quebec's refusal to participate. This suggests that we are not effectively making a transition into democratic constitutionalism with our present institutions. Nevertheless, Weinrib saw the separation reference case as an opportunity for the Supreme Court to push us once again along the way to participatory constitutionalism but worried that the court's decision will be seen as a provocation in the inflammatory politics of Quebec.

M. Dion replied that the government of Canada referred the separation case to the Supreme Court not to protect the rest of Canada against Quebec but, first and foremost, to protect the individuals of Quebec from the dangers inherent in any attempt at secession where the state of the law is unclear.

David Milne of Prince Edward Island highlighted one of the tensions that grew out of the foregoing discussion. On the one hand, he agrees that we have moved from elitist, Burkean origins to a set of political requirements that are increasingly democratic. These requirements in turn require that we be much more explicit about who we are as a people and about our differences within more democratic forms of participation and ratification. On the other hand, he sees Peter Russell as being pessimistic about the possibility of our successfully meeting these requirements. Part of the reason for this pessimism, he suspects, is Russell's view that the politics of recognition is treacherous territory, leading to mega-constitutional politics, which have failed. In Milne's estimation, it is typical of Russell's political wisdom not to play the politics of recognition but to proceed more by way of other non-constitutional means that deal with substantive issues, as Katherine Swinton has argued. This leaves open the question of how democratic those means are, for they lead us to the lament about executive federalism – governments run such processes – accompanied by the sense that the people would do so much better if only they had a public space in which to do so. While some of the experience with more public vehicles during the 'Canada Round' leading to the Charlottetown Accord were encouraging, there is no guarantee of a consensus emerging from the process.

James Tully responded to Milne that while the current period of various non-constitutional intergovernmental negotiations is necessary, it does not quite answer the demand for recognition of difference. We can never entirely close the door on the politics of recognition. If we do so, Quebecers may well opt for independence rather than sticking with the status quo.

M. Dion emphasized that Canadian democracy is always in evolution – there is no frozen status quo regarding the distribution of powers, for there have been many changes over the last thirty years, and they have strengthened the provinces. Moreover, it is his view that many of the objections of ordinary Quebecers have less to do with actual grievances over powers than with a sense that Quebec is not recognized and respected within the federation. These perceptions need to be addressed with details about the recognition of the French fact in the federation.

PART II: ABORIGINAL PEOPLES

For Peter Russell, a more fundamental constitutional question than national unity concerns sharing sovereignty with Canada's Aboriginal peoples. Unlike the people of Quebec, Canada's indigenous groups do not have what they need to survive as peoples. They have been denied the means and the opportunity to make laws for the internal ordering of their own societies. Canada has barely begun to move towards any genuinely democratic arrangements, based on mutual consent, with its Aboriginal peoples. Reconciling Canadian sovereignty and constitutionalism to the special needs of indigenous peoples is for Peter Russell the most basic challenge to Canada's democratic capacity.

Peter admits that he too was deaf to Aboriginal concerns until he was galvanized by his involvement with the Berger Inquiry on the Mackenzie Valley pipeline. Through the intercession of Mel Watkins and Kelly Creighton, Russell was invited to the Mackenzie Valley to advise the Dene on constitutional questions. Though often later criticized by officials at the Department of Justice, who suspected that he had put ideas into the mouths of the Dene, it was Peter who was changed by his going north.

Meeting with the Dene, he immediately faced penetrating questions about sovereignty. As one Dene elder woman put it early on, 'Professor, what is sovereignty, and how did the Queen get it over us?' There were many such questions, and a number of more narrowly strategic ones as well, such as whether the Dene should approach constitutional issues as Quebecers had or in some other way. On the pipeline, the Dene were ambivalent, but about their determination to link land claims to the issues of sovereignty they were exceedingly clear from the outset. As another Dene elder expressed it, 'Professor, if we own land, how is it secure if we have no power over it?' What really opened Peter's eyes was the Dene's refusal to be subservient by even considering that the right to decide things for themselves might be something that was delegated from other levels of government.

Deeply changed by his contact with the Dene, Peter has since devoted a major portion of his energies to articulating and advancing the concerns of Aboriginal peoples. Most notably, he joined in forming the Dene Land Claims Southern Support group, serving as its chair from 1974 to 1977. And more recently, he was chair of the Research Advisory Committee for the Royal Commission of Aboriginal Peoples; its final report was inspired in part by his many writings on sovereignty, diversity, and accommodation. Most recently he has taken up an appointment as a facilitator in negotiations between the government of Canada and Deh Cho First Nations of the Northwest Territories.

In his academic work, Peter's primary focus has become the constitutional relationship of indigenous people to the larger societies in which they find themselves, as we can see in 'Aboriginal Nationalism and Quebec Nationalism: Reconciliation through Fourth World Decolonization,' *Constitutional Forum* (1997). A particular interest of his has been in documenting the role of the Supreme Court of Canada in securing symbolic legitimacy for Aboriginal concerns. The judicial interpretation of Aboriginal rights has been inconsistent in advancing the social and political goals of Aboriginal people, with the court's *Sparrow* decision to the good, but its *Van der Pleet* trilogy proving to be a major disappointment. Another recent concern in his writing has been the challenges in transferring any judicial gains into the mainstream of politics. While he views with considerable pleasure the success of Aboriginal peoples in learning to use the majority's own political instruments, the lack of public attention to the report of the Royal Commission of Aboriginal Peoples has been another disappointment.

Peter's writings on Aboriginal questions have also developed a strong comparative component, particularly through his work on the Australian High Court's *Mabo* decision. While Aboriginal concerns in Canada have not progressed nearly as well as they perhaps should, Aborigines have fared less well in Australia, where there has been no constitutional recognition of their rights.

With the views of Native people and those of the government of Canada regarding Native sovereignty miles apart, Peter counsels that there must be accommodation of both sides. Canadians must acknowledge the right of Aboriginal self-government, based on the experience of Native people. Aboriginal peoples must accept the legitimacy of the modern state. Consistent with his approach to constitutionalism generally, to realize both goals, he believes, requires ongoing engagement and discussion.

Consistent with his overall constitutional philosophy, Peter argues that a negotiated decolonization process with individual peoples offers the most promising approach. Rather than seeking 'an across-the-board, all-Canada agreement' he favours 'a more piecemeal, people-by-people basis' for settling constitutional and self-government issues with Aboriginal peoples.

Summary of Papers

Paul Chartrand's 'On the Canadian Aboriginal Rights Dialogue' (chapter 5) depicts Canadian law at a crossroads regarding the legal rights and status of Aboriginal peoples. He begins by questioning the moral legitimacy of the Canadian state exerting power over dispossessed Aboriginal nations, and he rejects the common understanding of Aboriginal peoples as racial minorities that has been used to deny their legitimate aspirations to political autonomy. Chartrand illustrates how recent legal decisions hem in Aboriginal rights, effectively narrowing the sphere of protections and possibilities for Aboriginal peoples. He questions the Supreme Court's narrow vision for the Aboriginal peoples, citing the liberal conception of 'one law for all' as a major obstacle to just accommodation with Aboriginal peoples. He urges instead a reinvigorating of Canada's federalism, through a vision of shared rule in national institutions and self-rule for Aboriginals. He foresees Canada's potential to become a genuinely multinational, North American country drawing on both its Aboriginal and its European foundations. These points are extended and amplified in a recent addendum reviewing events through the summer of 1998.

The second essay on Aboriginal issues (chapter 6) is a transcription of Georges Erasmus's presentation at the University of Toronto just days after the conference and the release of the Report of the Royal Commission on Aboriginal Peoples. Erasmus, co-chair of the commission, came to the Department of Political Science to offer a remarkable first-hand account of the royal commission's work and recommendations. His address summarizes the overarching philosophy and vision of the commission – a dimension not always so readily apparent in a reading of its massive report and hundreds of recommendations. For example, while much of the report deals with economic issues, the focus here is firmly on law and politics, with particular emphasis on matters of political structure. Erasmus's central theme is a call for recognition of Aboriginal peoples as nations that takes into account their various complex circumstances as urban, Metis, status, and non-status peoples. Erasmus examines the question of how to define Aboriginal nations as well as the legislative framework needed to make them a contemporary political reality.

Rejecting all forms of assimilation, Erasmus calls for a process of treaty extension and adjudication. He advocates fundamental changes in the structure of the Canadian federal government, creating a substantial Aboriginal role. He concentrates our attention on the primary goal of providing Aboriginal peoples with the structural means for self-government. His primary concern is not an Aboriginal parliament, which received much of the attention of the press. Taking education, health care, and justice as his focus, he gives practical substance to the idea of a diverse, fragmented citizenship discussed in several of the previous papers. Invoking the notion of cultural identity within a vision of society where nation and state are divided, he envisions the re-emergence of Aboriginal peoples from colonialism and assimilationism, by highlighting the capacity in the Aboriginal spirit for self-healing and community development.

Christine Fletcher's 'An Emasculation of Rights in Government–Aboriginal Relations in Australia' (chapter 7) introduces a comparative perspective. She begins with a brief history of the mistreatment and forced assimilation endured by Australia's indigenous people, noting that constitutional rights and freedoms have offered little protection of indigenous tradition. She shows in detail how the little progress that had previously occurred has been largely erased by the Liberal-National government. Fletcher documents the slashes in funding for Aboriginal organizations, the growing racist rhetoric, and the resulting destabilization of government–Aboriginal relations, as well as the divisive effects on Aboriginal organizations. In concluding, she reflects on the lack of constitutional measures to preserve the culture of Aboriginal people in Australia, connecting this dimension back to larger issues of sovereignty at the core of Peter Russell's work. She insists that neither Australians nor Canadians will become a fully sovereign people until the traditions and culture of Aboriginal peoples inform their basic social and political arrangements.

5

On the Canadian Aboriginal Rights Dialogue

PAUL CHARTRAND

I propose to offer some reflections on certain aspects of law and policy – two of Peter Russell's favourite things. My comments are reflections on Canada, which is another one of his, and my, favourite things. I believe that we also share a fondness for other places, especially Australia, which is an adopted country of mine and a place where Peter Russell, I understand, intends to spend quite some time working after his retirement.

I concentrate below on the development of the rights of Aboriginal peoples and on Aboriginal nationalism; an addendum describes major developments since I gave this address. The significance of the Supreme Court's *Calder* decision in the 1970s – its influence on a federal policy shift to recognizing Aboriginal title and entering into the modern era of treaty negotiations – is well-known; it was just around that time that Peter Russell was writing about Aboriginal nations and their accommodation within Canada.

Development of Aboriginal Rights

I should like to begin by offering some comments on certain apparent trends in the development of Aboriginal rights in the Supreme Court of Canada. Who are the proper claimants of Aboriginal rights? Who makes up these groups in which are vested certain collective rights called Aboriginal rights? It seems that we in Canada are at an embryonic stage in the development of proper answers, and this is certainly so in the judicial response.

If we consider the jurisprudence of the last quarter century or so, there are some unfortunate statements in the court that seem to indicate that Aboriginal peoples are 'races,' rather than social and political communities. I imagine that approach is in part moved by the many shades of meaning adopted for the concept of 'race.' So, although it may be correct to characterize unequal treatment of status Indians under the Indian Act as 'racial discrimination' according to the Canadian Bill of Rights and the Charter of Rights and Freedoms, it would be a serious misunderstanding to propose that the Aboriginal peoples whose rights are recognized and protected in the Constitution Act, 1982, and who claim a right of self-government within Canada, are in the category of 'racial minorities.'[1]

The false notion that Aboriginal peoples are racial minorities is used to deny their aspirations to legitimate political autonomy within Canada. Such arguments take on various forms and have a long history. It is at times proposed that racial minorities require the benevolent attention of the liberal state but are not entitled to rights to different status within Canada. Or the spectre of 'race-based' differences in law may be raised. The easy acceptance of this false notion is probably assisted by the Canadian awareness of the American civil rights movement for racial equality. Few seem to notice that in the United States there are American Indians who are recognized in domestic policy as dependent nations with judicially and legally recognized political autonomy.[2]

There is wide acceptance of affirmative-action policies to remedy the effects of racial discrimination in Canada. The remedy is a temporary expedient that aims to provide justice to individuals. The claims of Aboriginal peoples to collective rights fall into an entirely different category. They are group claims based on a demand that indigenous peoples ought to be accorded equal respect as distinct political societies vis-à-vis other 'peoples.' These claims demand the recognition of group rights that inhere in the relevant social and political community; they are not a temporary expedient. Political autonomy requires the establishment of permanent institutions to deal with the eternal exigencies of community life. No one believes that the institution of Parliament should be regarded as a temporary solution to the problems of Western democracies.

The recent final report of the Royal Commission on Aboriginal Peoples emphasizes the point that Aboriginal peoples comprise political communities, not racial minorities.[3] They are political communities in the sense that subjective elements help define both the groups themselves and their members. Objective factors, such as birth, 'race,' and 'ancestry,' are never a sufficient defining characteristic for a political community. This understanding is grounded in the experience of all societies, where spouses may come from other groups, and children may be adopted from biological parents. No useful social purposes are served by basing group definitions on the objective factor of birth alone. That is all that 'race-based' thinking has to offer, and proper understanding of the legitimate legal and political claims of the Aboriginal peoples of Canada today requires that such notions be tossed into the dustbin of history.

I turn next to the way in which the courts have dealt with the question of identifying the proper group claimant of Aboriginal rights. In the *Baker Lake case*[4] the court canvassed four elements of a test for proof of Aboriginal title at common law, including the requirement to show the existence of an 'organized society.' It did so in an attempt to grapple with the identity test of the claimant group, and here the court was eliminating at least temporary groups assembled for narrow social purposes, such as the crowd at a football game. Unfortunately, the court's attempt to deal with the legal requirements of identifying a proper claimant involved considerations of the social organization of Aboriginal claimant groups – a field ripe with possibilities for misunderstanding and offended sensibilities.

In 1996 the Supreme Court of Canada delivered several landmark decisions on Aboriginal rights that have established what is now called the 'Van der Peet' test for proof of Aboriginal rights at common law.[5] In these cases the court seems to be keeping the identity question open, preferring the broad generic term 'group' in cases where the identity issue is not directly argued. So the identity of a proper claimant group in respect to Aboriginal rights remains an open question to be decided in future cases.

The Constitution Act, 1982, recognized and affirmed the existing Aboriginal and treaty rights of the Aboriginal peoples of Canada[6] and it will be interesting to observe the relationship that develops between the judicial evolution of a test for identifying the proper claimants of common-law Aboriginal rights, and the development of a definition of the 'peoples' whose rights are recognized in the constitution.[7] Even if there are constitutional amendments to elaborate the rights of Aboriginal peoples now recognized in the constitution, it is not likely that there will be easy general agreement about any definitions of 'peoples' or 'nations.'[8]

The general agreement that exists in this area seems to concern the goal of protecting distinct Aboriginal cultural societies, and this is indeed a point that Peter Russell was making as early as the 1970s. The recent cases, too, in their very narrow focus, refer to the goal of protecting those customs, practices, and traditions that are integral to distinctive cultures. It is difficult, however, to reconcile the apparent direction of the court in the development of Aboriginal rights with the aspirations expressed by Aboriginal people.

The law of Canada has always displayed an unseemly uncertainty with respect to the legal status and rights of Aboriginal people. It is a type of uncertainty that other Canadians would not tolerate vis-à-vis their own situation, for they have effective access to the institutions of the courts and Parliament. Not only with respect to arcane constitutional issues, but also with respect to many everyday issues, Aboriginal people can not know whether they are on the right side of the law, simply because the law is not known. In some of the most influential cases on the development of the jurisprudence of Aboriginal rights, the Aboriginal people themselves were not represented in court![9] Would it be contemplated today that the most basic collective rights could be litigated without the presence of representatives of the relevant group? I think not. Canadians might well reflect on the historical process by which the doctrine of Aboriginal rights has been developed, and the consequent need to reconsider the unsavoury origins of its emerging doctrine. A new approach required by the 1982 constitutional recognition and affirmation of Aboriginal and treaty rights requires wise and courageous judges willing to vindicate rights that Parliament and governments have failed to protect.

Developments in the most recent cases suggest prima facie that the court is driving in more stakes to define the perimeter of the iron fence being erected around Aboriginal rights. The sphere of protection is dwindling. It is not gratifying to observe the development of tests to protect distinctive practices centred around economic ways of life long ago destroyed by the activities of those whose interests the courts now represent. By way of illustration, under the evolving tests it would seem that buffalo-hunting, as a pre-contact activity, and other activities centred on the buffalo hunt would receive protection of the common law. But none of these activities remains today. The newcomers who have taken over have killed off the buffalo and the economic base of entire indigenous cultures. So, despite its protestations, the law seems to offer the best protection for metaphorical museum pieces under a frozen rights doctrine, and its contribution to protection of the group interests that might be expected to sustain distinct cultures is suspect.

The courts can hardly be expected to do otherwise. They are, after all, Canada's courts, not the courts of the Aboriginal peoples. The courts, by judicial magic, can rationalize an unconscionable dispossession of Aboriginal peoples because the function of the court is not the usually perceived role of protecting the weak and politically powerless. The court must legally legitimize the exercise of state power, at least to a considerable extent, or risk losing the political confidence of the representatives of the state and the disintegration of the legal order.

Since Aboriginal rights are one of the few power resources available to Aboriginal people, they are at times driven to make arguments in court that are not likely to be accepted. The courts play a limited function with limited tools, and they produce limited decisions. If one uses the courts to make claims that can be advanced only in the other branches of the state's institutions, either executive government or Parliament, one should not be surprised at the court's inability to do justice in respect to a just claim. If you squeeze a cow in the right place you will get milk, because that is what the cow gives; if you make legal arguments to the state's judicial arm, you will get what the courts can give – narrow decisions, not likely to upset the status quo very much. The courts are uniquely incapable of drawing the contours of a broad vision of political liberty for the Aboriginal peoples in Canada.

One of the fundamental puzzles about the nature of Aboriginal rights has been decided in the recent cases.[10] We know now that all Aboriginal rights are not derived from Aboriginal title to land; rather, Aboriginal title to land is but one subset of Aboriginal rights. We are at a crossroads where the doctrinal basis of Aboriginal rights is being re-examined, particularly in the light of their contemporary affirmation and recognition in the constitution.

The judicial development of rights does not always result in an advancement of the social and political goals of Aboriginal people. So far the courts have generally dealt with the development of negative rights – that is, rights to carry on customs, traditions, and practices without interference from the state and its agents. Such rights help protect access to and use of resources but do little to advance goals requiring state assistance. On the basis of the test that Aboriginal rights consist of activities, customs, or traditions that are integral to the distinctive cultures of Aboriginal groups, it would seem that language rights are included, but it is far from clear that these will be developed as positive rights that not only require protection from government interference in establishing autonomous educational systems but also impose obligations on Canadian governments to provide resources to make the rights effective.

Aboriginal Nationalism

I move on now to Aboriginal nationalism. It seems that one link between law and politics is to be found somewhere in the project of finding common ground in defining the public interest. If we view Aboriginal peoples as legitimate political communities, it is then understood that each people will argue its right to define the nature and scope of its public interest. The vision of what consititutes a happy neighbourhood, and what means or institutions are necessary or helpful to build them, will vary from community to community. So the Mic Mac will insist on defining the Mic Mac public interest; the Cree will insist on defining the Cree public interest, and so on.

Moreover, each Aboriginal nation will argue that the definition of the nature and scope of its public interest ought not to take place through the filter of the general Canadian public interest. And this the courts can not ensure. The courts, because they are Canada's courts, must run the elaboration of the nature and scope of the Aboriginal interests through the filter of the Canadian public interest.

And that is why we need activity in both law and policy, the former developed with the participation of Aboriginal peoples. Only in that way can we establish mutual interests, common ground, where the interests of all Canadians too will be filtered through the prism of the public interest of the Aboriginal nations.[11]

Perhaps the true vision of Canada's future lies in the concept of a multinational North American country. Canada would be multinational if it accommodated the existence and flourishing of all of Canada's historic nations. It would be North American if it articulated its corporate identity and vision of the future based on a real appreciation of its North American, or Aboriginal foundations, rather than only on its European origins as a modern nation-state. And since Canada is often regarded as a model of a federal country that combines shared rule in national institutions and self-rule in regional institutions, there is every prospect within our existing constitutional traditions to accommodate such a vision.

One of the great obstacles standing in the way of a just accommodation of the Aboriginal peoples within Canada is the idea that Canada's present boundaries are legitimate borders within which all residents are to be treated alike under law and policy. 'One law for all' is the hue and cry of opponents of Aboriginal self-government on all sides. In reflecting on this liberal conception of a legitimate nation-state, within which no legal differences ought to be tolerated, it is important to go back to the prior question about the legitimacy of drawing those boundaries around previously distinct, independent nations in the first place.[12] In what circumstances were each of the Aboriginal peoples enclosed within the Canadian state? Was this inclusion based on consent, or effective participation, or other norms of public morality that Canadians wish to uphold? Even if all treaties were thought to legitimize Canada's exercise of power over Aboriginal peoples – a doubtful proposition – there are large portions of Canada with respect to which the Aboriginal inhabitants have not entered into treaties or been consulted on their wishes concerning the establishment of Canada, the large and powerful state that now unconscionably asserts and exerts its raw power without justification or need of explanation over the small historic nations that it has dispossessed.

Even where apparent agreements have been entered into, and even entrenched in the constitution of Canada, this country has forgotten that promises ought to be kept, even if they are made to those who are politically weak and despised by those making the promises. In these cases even Canada's courts can not help those who lack power at the ballot box. Canada, by ignoring its most fundamental constitutional obligations, risks being seen as a constitutional outlaw, not only in the eyes of the Aboriginal dispossessed, but by all those who may fear that some day their interest too may rely on constitutional protection from the rule of the majority.

Canada should be seen as politically legitimate in the eyes of all its residents. Its security as an internationally medium-level power and a vast and sparsely populated country, its international reputation, and its moral foundation require that. The Aboriginal peoples constitute but 3 per cent or so of the population, but surely it is not right, as has been proposed, that the legitimacy of a nation-state be established on the backs of a 3 per cent minority?

In order to accept the justice and legitimacy of the political claims of Aboriginal peoples for accommodation of their national institutions within Canada, it is not even essential to accept the Aboriginal peoples' own arguments and ideals; the most cherished ideals and values of Canadians generally can accommodate a measure of just political participation and community rights of Aboriginal peoples within Canada.

Conclusion

I would like to suggest that all Canadians have a stake in the dialogue of rights that has been raised by the claims of Aboriginal peoples, whether they be legal, political, or moral rights. Rights, after all, depend on a broadly accepted moral foundation, do they not? And surely it must be in the interests of all Canadians to see to it that Canada's basic institutions rest on a solid moral foundation. Our common ideals require that the interests of all individuals and communities be accommodated. Canada should be a place where all its historic nations matter, even the very small ones. This is one of the points that was urged by the Métis leader Louis Riel, the anniversary of whose hanging by the Canadian state on 16 November 1885 many Canadians now commemorate.

I have dealt with the dialogue of Aboriginal rights, in the courts and beyond the courts in Canada. I have suggested that we reflect on a vision of Canada as a multinational North American country. Is it not interesting to observe that, in this period of national introspection, the dialogue of Aboriginal rights suggests that it may be Canada's dispossessed and marginalized peoples – the Aboriginal peoples – who are the guardians of our most precious liberties?

And in the fight for a better place for the Aboriginal peoples within Canada, it is heartening to welcome the dedication, skills, and energy of scholars who, like Peter Russell, dare to put ideas into action.

Addendum (August 1998)

A number of significant developments and events in Aboriginal law and policy have occurred since our conference in November 1996 that deserve comment. In the field of policy, the federal government published its response to the recommendations of the Royal Commission on Aboriginal Peoples on 7 January 1998. Entitled 'Gathering Strength: Canada's Aboriginal Action Plan,' the policy statement read formally by the minister of Indian affairs in Ottawa focused on a statement of reconciliation that expressed the government's regret for past actions of the federal government that have contributed to the erosion of the political, economic, and social systems of Aboriginal people and nations.

The minister promised discussions with territorial and provincial colleagues about building a common plan of action 'to make renewed partnerships a reality.' Meetings subsequently took place between federal, provincial, and territorial ministers in Quebec City on 19–20 May 1998, out of which came a joint resolve to set up working groups to discuss the nature, structure, and priorities of an ongoing search for a comprehensive approach to Aboriginal issues and to begin development of a National Aboriginal Youth Strategy. The most immediate and significant aspect of the federal policy initiative was the creation of a $350-million Aboriginal Healing Fund to address the legacy of sexual and physical abuse of Aboriginal students at residential schools.

Although Aboriginal leaders generally welcomed these aspects of the federal response to the royal commission, there was considerable criticism of the federal government as well, especially about the lack of consultation with Aboriginal leaders on what the new policy calls 'a new partnership' with Aboriginal peoples. Ironically, the policy was devised largely without the participation of the proposed new partners, contrary to the strong recommendations of the royal commission that the principle of Aboriginal participation ought to be the key feature of federal Aboriginal policy.

The policy approach of the royal commission – to base federal policy on the recognition of historic Aboriginal nations, in a nation-to-nation process that recognized that Aboriginal rights are vested in 'nations,' not in the 'Indian bands' created by federal statute – received little attention. Ottawa did not adopt the basic recommendations to initiate and sustain a twenty-year plan, as proposed in the final report.

In the Supreme Court of Canada, the landmark decision in *Delgamuukw* was handed down on 11 December 1997 – [1998] 1 CNLR. 14. The decision elaborated the distinctions between Aboriginal title and Aboriginal rights and described the elements of the tests to prove Aboriginal title. In order to make out a claim for Aboriginal title, the Aboriginal group asserting title must satisfy three criteria (page 69): the land must have been occupied prior to Euro-Canadian sovereignty; if present occupation is relied on as proof of occupation before then, there must be a continuity between present and pre-sovereignty occupation; and at sovereignty, that occupation must have been exclusive.

On defining the claimant group in which Aboriginal title is vested, the court reviewed the Canadian jurisprudence and used the terms 'nations' and 'peoples' in general language on Aboriginal title, but it still relied on 'claimant group,' as indicated above. It does not seem profitable to speculate on the relationship the court might anticipate between the terms 'claimant group,' 'peoples,' and 'distinctive cultures,' as used in the discussion on Aboriginal rights. The case has been sent back for trial, and it seems quite possible that the question of defining more precisely the nature of the claimant group, especially in relation to a right of 'self-government' that may be argued there, may arise and be discussed by the courts.

Another interesting recent Supreme Court case raised the question of the meaning of 'peoples': the *Quebec Secession Case – Reference re Secession of Quebec*, 20 August 1998, SCC File No. 25506, not yet reported. One of the questions in the reference was whether international law gives a right to the National Assembly or government of Quebec to effect the secession of Quebec from Canada unilaterally. In its discussion, the court noted that 'the right of a people to self-determination ... is considered a general principle of international law.' In considering the definition of 'peoples,' the Court observed that its precise meaning in international law remains somewhat uncertain. Although the court recognized that 'a people' may include only a portion of the population of an existing state, it stated: 'While much of the Quebec population certainly shares many of the characteristics (such as common language and culture) that would be considered in determining whether a specific group is a 'people,' as do other groups within Quebec and/or Canada, it is not necessary to explore this legal characterization to resolve Question 2 appropriately,' ... 'nor is it necessary to examine the position of the Aboriginal population within Quebec.'

A review of the Aboriginal-rights cases seems to suggest that the courts are developing a doctrine within which particular kinds of rights might well be vested in different kinds of groups. For example, specific traditional activities such as fishing in a specific site might be vested in a relatively small community, whereas a broad-based right of self-government at common law might be vested in a larger group. In this regard, the royal commissions final report (vol. II, part 1, especially 180ff.) proposed that an Aboriginal 'nation,' which is entitled to a common-law right of self-government, be characterized by tests similar to those defining 'peoples' in respect to the international-law right of self-determination. First, the nation must have a collective sense of national identity that is evinced by a common history, language, culture, traditions, political consciousness, laws, governmental structures, spirituality, ancestry, and homeland. Second, it must be of sufficient size and capacity to be able to assume and exercise powers and responsibilities flowing from the right of self-government in an effective manner. Third, it must constitute a majority of the permanent population of a certain territory or collection of territories and, in the future, operate from a defined territorial base.

Finally, the historic Nisga'a Final Agreement in British Columbia was signed by representatives of the Nisga'a people and the federal and provincial governments on 4 August 1998. The document still required ratification by the legislature and Parliament and a Nisga'a referendum but was intended to be a treaty and land-claims agreement within the meaning of the Constitution Act, 1982. It was the first proposed treaty in the province since establishment of the British Columbia Treaty Commission and the decision by the province to participate in treaty negotiations, and it has increased the heated public debate earlier generated by the *Delgamuukw* decision. Much of the controversy involves the basic questions considered in this paper, with opponents of Aboriginal rights raising the false cry of 'one law for all' and denouncing 'special laws for racial minorities.'

It is clear, as exemplified by Aboriginal rights issues, that as we move towards the end of the year 1998 some of the same great questions that reveal the interplay between law and policy continue to be a significant part of the national debate in Canada. If the federal government's policy decisions are based more on political expediency than principle, which they appear to be, then the role of the courts and of academic commentators in elaborating appropriate principles for public action seems to be as significant as ever, if not more so.

NOTES

1 See Paul Chartrand, 'Aboriginal Self-Government: The Two Sides of Legitimacy,' in Susan Phillips, ed., *How Ottawa Spends: A More Democratic Canada ...? 1993–1994* (Ottawa: Carleton University Press 1993), chap. 7, 231–56.

2 See Will Kymlicka, *Liberalism, Community and Culture* (Oxford: Clarendon Press 1991), especially chap. 7.

3 *Report of the Royal Commission on Aboriginal Peoples*, vol. II, *Restructuring the Relationship* (Ottawa: Minister of Supply and Services Canada 1996), part one, chap. 3, 'Governance,' 105ff.

4 The test in *Baker Lake (Hamlet) v. Canada (Minister of Indian Affairs and Northern Development)*, [1979] 3 CNLR 17 (Fed. TD) is the following: 1. That the people of the group claiming the right, as well as their ancestors, existed as an organized society; 2. That the organized society occupied the specific territory over which the claimants assert title; 3. That the occupation was to the exclusion of ohter organized societies; and 4. That the occupation was an established fact at the time sovereignty over the land was asserted by England.'

5 See *R v. Van der Peet*, [1996] 2 SCR 507; *R. v. Gladstone*, [1996] 2 SCR 723; *R. v. N.T.C. Smokehouse Ltd.*, [1996] 2 SCR 672; *R. v. Pamajewon* [1996] 2 SCR 821.

6 Section 35 of the Constitution Act, 1982, part II.

7 Historically, the federal government has administered policy respecting Aboriginal people largely through the authority of the Indian Acts, which defined 'Indians' without reference to the various Aboriginal nations' own preferred self-definitions, and this has certainly helped to disintegrate former group and national social and political bonds. Section 31 of the Manitoba Act, 1870, legislated provision of lands for the benefit of the 'families' of the Métis people in Manitoba towards the extinguishment of their Indian title and thus recognized, in the constitution, a distinct group status for one of the Aboriginal peoples whose rights are not protected by section 35 of the Constitution Act, 1982. See Paul L.A.H. Chartrand, *Manitoba's Metis Settlement Scheme of* 1870 (Saskatoon: University of Saskatchewan Native Law Centre 1991).

8 There are numerous fact situations and preferences for social organization, and no formulation is likely to be acceptable enough to satisfy the requirements of an amendment. Internationally, indigenous peoples oppose introduction of a definition in the Draft Declaration on the Rights of Indigneous Peoples. Recently the final report (vol. II, part one, especially 180ff.) of the Royal Commission on Aboriginal Peoples has proposed that federal policy recognize the existence of Aboriginal nations and has suggested a number of elements of a definition that have been broadly acceptable.

9 *St. Catharine's Case* [*St. Catharine's Milling and Lumber Company v. The Queen* (1899), 14 App. Cas. 46 (JCPC), aff'g. (1887) 12 SCR].

10 *R. v. Cote* (1996), 138 DLR (4th) 385; *R. v. Adams* (1996), 138 DLR (4th) 657.

11 For similar suggestions, see Hon. Douglas Graham, Minister of Justice (New Zealand), 'British Law–Aboriginal Law: Merging Jurisprudence,' a speech delivered at the 15th Annual Conference, Australian Institute of Judicial Administration, Park Royal Hotel. Wellington, New Zealand, Saturday, 21 Sept. 1996.

12 See Will Kymlicka, *Multicultural Citizenship* (Oxford: Clarendon Press 1995), especially 116ff.

6

The Royal Commission on Aboriginal Peoples

GEORGES ERASMUS

When we were appointed to the commission, we began by developing a work plan. Like most commissions we decided to hold hearings. We wanted to hold more than the typical number of hearings, where a commission went to twenty-nine or thirty communities in Canada and somehow got a reflection of the whole country. Some commissions took eighteen months to organize these hearings. Not only did we not have that kind of time, but we wanted to hold more than 100 hearings. We decided to get off the ground quickly, by holding our first set of hearings within six months of being appointed. We operated in three teams so that we could get more hearings done as quickly as possible, with reflective periods in between, because we wanted a dialogue started between the last set of hearings and the next. We developed documents to assist us in the next set of the hearings. Ironically some of the people we interviewed early on had just finished running another Royal Commission hearing, and when we told them that we wanted three teams to reach at least 100 communities, they said we were insane – there's no way we could do it.

But we did it, and the hearings were very important to us. They allowed the commissioners the kind of solid base that really facilitated the debate on solutions rather than reaffirm what the problems were. When we organized the hearings we tried, in every way possible, to encourage people to concentrate on solutions. Being pretty sure what the problems were, we wanted to spend 80 per cent of the time in our hearings on the solutions.

We set up an $8-million dollar intervenor/participation program, headed by David Crombie, to assist organizations to do action-oriented research that would be geared to solutions. We funded people whom we thought would come to the hearings and propose solutions from their research.

We also wanted research to assist our work. We knew a lot of commissions ended up completing their reports while their commissioned research continued for years afterwards. Status Indians had been relatively well researched, but there were gaping holes. The Métis was not as well covered. The urban Aboriginal situation was not known at all. We gathered eminent scholars, both Aboriginal and non-Aboriginal, in two workshops to assist us with planning the research, and in the end most of the research came in on time and actually influenced the final report.

We had originally hoped to have our work done by about the fourth anniversary, and we actually signed off on 24 August 1995. The report then went to translation.

The work that we did showed to us that prior to contact Aboriginal people were nations that had whole societies – institutions of government, social, political, and economic – comprehensive ways of life, with long-standing civilizations. Quality of life was extremely important to them. In their world-view, all life was important, including the environment and the ecosystem.

What happened of course, upon contact, was that there was rough equality. Aboriginal people were very strong and more numerous. Their institutions were still intact, and the early treaties recognized their nationhood and self-government. But as time went on, coexistence broke down, and numerically things changed. We entered a period when the newcomers attempted to assimilate the Aboriginal people. Their belief was that Aboriginal people would disappear, that as societies they were incapable of dealing with modernity and they would just evaporate.

But it was not enough to let Aboriginal people simply disappear; the Indian Act and government policies were put in place to pursue this goal aggressively. This was done to some degree with the notion that this was the best thing that could be done for Aboriginal people. Large nations were broken up into individual communities, individual bands, with the approach being to assimilate individuals into the larger society. Everything connected with the Indian Act was intended to teach Aboriginal people how to fit into the larger society – even down to how to run meetings. It was not good enough to run collective meetings the way Aboriginals had been doing for thousands of years; we were taught how to do it so that we could fit into the larger society. Residential schools were very much a part of that policy. The attempt was to remove the language, to remove the influence of the Aboriginal culture, and to indoctrinate young people – to 'save' them, to deliver them to a new civilization with completely new values.

We of course, at the commission, rejected that concept. It has not worked. It has failed miserably. We recommend to Canada that that approach be completed abandoned. Unfortunately there are many hangover influences from the days of assimilation and the colonial approach to Aboriginal people; the remaining Indian Act, the Department of Indian Affairs, are vestiges of what used to be. We still have a minister who views Aboriginal individuals as clients, individual communities as clients, and we think that this situation must come to an end.

We have come firmly to believe that Aboriginal people can govern themselves. The original nations that existed previously should be recognized in a number of ways, but one way would be through federal legislation that recognizes that Aboriginal people are nations, creating a process where in the immediate future the Indian Act would be bypassed. The nations that had been affected by the Indian Act would be encouraged to bring back the individual communities or bands.

One of the most important nation-building steps we outline is that of developing a citizenship code that goes beyond the Indian Act's definition of membership in bands. The approach that we are suggesting would be to create citizenship codes that would recognize all people who have a link to the nation – whether cultural, by marriage, by adoption, by custom, by residence perhaps, and so forth. The nation that we are talking about is not a racially based approach to the recognition of Aboriginal people. It is a recognition that Aboriginal people are political entities, where cultural bonds and identity are more important than blood. The federal recognition legislation would encourage the nations, whether they are Haida, Nisga'a, Mohawk, or Dene, to bring their people together once again, and to develop a citizenship code that is fair, with an appeal process to ensure that fairness.

A great law or constitution should be drawn up that indicates how the nation's government is going to operate; whether it has a judiciary, an executive, or a legislative body. A number of questions should be answered. What kind of structures are we working under? Are we going back to something that is hereditary? Is it part tradition? Is it part modern? Whatever structure we have decided to use as our government should be clear and appropriate. We want to see indications that the communities accept this process via some kind of demonstration of consent at the beginning, and then work on the constitution can begin. It does not have to be written, it can be oral – the Six Nations for instance, may want to go back to the confederacy and the great law of the peacemaker – it need not be written. But we need some way to demonstrate that communities want this process through either public meetings or votes by councils and then, at the end, when they think that they have a package together, some kind of clear public vote.

Let us say for the sake of discussion that twenty communities are participating in the process of nation building of a particular people. For a nation to be recognized in the process we have outlined, we required two majorities for the final vote – a majority of communities voting and a majority of individual voters in each community. Among the participating communities, we need to carry at least 75 per cent of the communities, and within each community we need a simple majority of individual voters. There is also a requirement for at least 40 per cent of the individuals who are members to participate.

Having done that, we see panels being created that would be set up under another piece of legislation creating an Aboriginal tribunal on lands and treaties. The tribunal would be there primarily to facilitate the specific-claims process and the treaty process. I come back to that later. But this institution would also help in the creation of panels in different parts of the country to assist with the recognition of an Aboriginal nation. If the panel heard the proposals from the nations and accepted it, it would recommend recognition status to the federal government. Ottawa would not be compelled to accept this, but it would virtually have to. If it did not accept this particular nation's application for recognition, it would have to provide the specific reasons why, so that either the panel could relook at it or nations could deal with it.

We are suggesting that these nations, on recognition, immediately be able to exercise a large degree of jurisdiction based upon our approach to the inherent right and to self-determination.

We believe that there are a number of ways for Aboriginal nations to come to the table to negotiate self-government or be recognized as self-determining. The first is through the international norms of self-determination. We have accepted and are firmly convinced that Aboriginal people have the right to self-determination. Because they are living within the nation-state of Canada, there are limits as to what they can do in the way of dismembering Canada. But within Canada it means that Aboriginal nations have the right to freely determine their relationship with Canada and to determine the kind of governmental structure that they will have for themselves. Whether or not Canada recognizes them as sovereign nations, we firmly believe that the nations continue to have that right.

Another way to come to the table is if Canada would become dismembered; than the Aboriginal nations have the right to evolve into whole nations outside of the country of Canada. Or, if once again there was the kind of gross oppression and colonization like that which occurred in the past, then Aboriginal people would have reason to consider moving into the international arena on their own. But our reading of the ways in which the international declaration on Aboriginal peoples is evolving into international law is that the right to self-determination will operate within states. When you find Aboriginal indigenous nations, whether in Canada, the United States, New Zealand, Australia, or anywhere where you have Aboriginal populations, it means that within those countries they have the ability to negotiate terms of union to create their own government structure to exercise internal self-determination in the respective nation-state.

Another way to get to the negotiating table on self-government is the inherent right. We are of the opinion that section 35 of the Constitution Act, 1982, now recognizes Aboriginal jurisdiction, which has survived all the years of Canadian law. The position that the commission took is that the inherent right is still there and can be implemented through treaties, either through documents that were signed and agreed to historically or through modern ones.

The jurisdiction within the inherent right actually has two parts to it – a core and a periphery. An Aboriginal nation can exercise its core jurisdiction over those things that are vital to the survival and welfare of an Aboriginal people – its culture and identity – immediately, without agreement. There is no need for agreement for the nation to exercise these areas of jurisdiction. Nevertheless we encourage the nations to seek agreements, because we could see conflicts arising between nations attempting to implement jurisdiction without agreement from the federal and provincial governments. In the periphery, you need agreement from your surrounding government or governments before you can implement that part of the inherent right.

So getting back then to the first piece of legislation that we encouraged, we want basic recognition legislation. The federal government would vacate the field in relation to 91:24 and recognize that the Aboriginal people of the nation at the moment of being recognized could take over a whole series of heads of jurisdictions that the federal government, through the Ministry of Indian Affairs, has been exercising for many years. This would cover many things, such as education, health, social services, child welfare, and the ability to develop a constitution internally. There would be many areas where the nations would be able to move ahead quickly.

The way in which they would deal with the Indian Act would be this – as they pass their own laws, the federal jurisdiction, or provincial jurisdiction for that matter, in that area would be vacated. It would be bumped out. And so rather than having the minister make changes to the Indian Act, the Aboriginal nations, legislative piece by legislative piece, would be able to determine for themselves the kinds of ways they wanted to replace the Indian Act.

So very quickly you would be able to have nations starting to exercise jurisdiction. They would be able to take over their own schools as they would replace provincial legislation in that area with their own legislation. They would be able to move into health and healing and social issues quickly on their own. The drawback is that they start with the territory that is now recognized, that they now have. If you are a First Nation, you start with the reserve land base; if you're a Métis group (and outside Alberta) you do not have a piece of land to deal with, and then it is much more difficult. What you have there is the ability to govern, but it would only be on a volunteer basis. Métis individuals could choose but would not be compelled to live by the legislation of a Métis government without a land base.

The second stage would be the ability to negotiate treaties. Another piece of federal legislation we are encouraging Ottawa to approve quickly is a treaty-implementation act. This would create a process which implements treaties that have been ignored in some cases since before Canada existed and in other cases were signed not long after the creation of Canada, the numbered treaties in the Prairies, and also the modern treaties. Depending upon the circumstances and the treaty, you would be either resolving something that was disputed or misunderstood in existing treaties, or you would be adding new treaties, and so forth.

In the Prairies, for instance, there are treaties that talk about a medicine chest in some instances and schooling in others. In my case, one of my treaties suggests that I would never have to pay Canadian tax. I have been paying it most of my life, but that is supposed to be one of the rights that I have. That is in addition to not having to go to war unless we want to for Canada, and so forth. These are areas of obvious disagreement between the Dene and Canadian governments.

With regard to the historical treaties then, we recommend that commissions be created – independent commissions somewhat like the BC Treaty Commission – that would facilitate the operation of and implementation of treaties. Appointments would be made by the parties – the provincial and federal government and the Aboriginal people – to these commissions that would facilitate the implementation of treaties.

Another piece of legislation that is very closely linked with this would be the creation of a tribunal for Aboriginal lands and treaties. The tribunal would have a number of areas of responsibility; one of the first would be to implement what is called specific claims, which have been around for a long time now. Most of the specific claims are accusations of fraudulent seizure of land. As for the reserve base that Aboriginal people started with in Canada – two-thirds of it has disappeared over time. In many instances it went for railways, highways, expansion of communities, even things like thousands of acres of land for non-Aboriginal veterans. Ironically, the land was not available to Aboriginal veterans but was given to non-Aboriginal veterans.

There is something in the range of 800 to 1,000 specific claims out there right now, where the federal government is judge, jury, and in many instances client too. It has total control over that process. We propose a tribunal that allows for

Aboriginal people to be able to go to some kind of a neutral body, a court-like situation, to deal with these issues a lot faster and more fairly. In addition, the tribunal would also be able to deal with treaty rights. If in fact rights that have been clearly decided on in a treaty have not been lived up to by one of the parties, then the tribunal would be able to remedy the situation.

If the meaning of particular terminology in a given treaty was disputed by the parties and needed to go for arbitration or to some kind of court-like body, it could go to the tribunal. You could take a small part of the negotiations on treaty implementation that was a sticking point to the tribunal for resolution. It would be up to the parties to say that they should go to the tribunal. Let's say that the two sides cannot agree on what the term 'medicine chest' in a given treaty means. One takes the position that it means very limited health care. The other side takes the position that it means all the modern health care that one can get from a modern society. The tribunal could use oral understandings and also operate in a way in which the traditional spirit and intent of the treaties as understood by Aboriginal people would be given the same weight as the written version. This way we would finally have some equality in the understanding of the treaty. The decision of the tribunal on the issue before it would be binding.

Getting back to the treaty: this, for the Prairies, is crucial because we have not been able to get agreement as to what the original treaties really meant. Aboriginal people have one version, the federal government has another. For instance, education is something that was brought up in all the numbered treaties. Very clearly the elders' – version, as it was told by Aboriginal people and as it was told to me as I was growing up, was that the negotiations were all about the idea that Aboriginal people would share this land, in exchange for Aboriginal youths' being trained in your world and also to be given a clear education in their own world. In the end they would be Dene, but they would also have the benefit of a modern education. They would be able to operate in both worlds. So the traditional interpretation from Aboriginal people is that it means elementary, high school, and post-secondary education. It means the best that the incoming society could provide.

The federal government has always suggested that – yeah, well, okay – we could perhaps agree that it might mean a little schoolhouse or an elementary school. It might even be extended to mean high school, but not post-secondary education. The federal government is providing post-secondary educational funding as part of its policy, not because of treaty rights.

So those kind of historical issues would be able to be resolved, issue by issue. There are also many important issues that were not dealt with at the time of treaty signing. They just never came up. Those things that we propose will also be addressed in two ways. Either these would be an extension to the early treaties, or else these issues could be negotiated in new treaties. There are parts of Canada, the east coast for one, where there were treaties, but most of them were treaties of peace and friendship. There were never really any land treaties among the Mi'kmaq and Maliseet people. So they are still waiting for a land-claim process.

We also suggest a piece of legislation to create an Aboriginal parliament. It has received a fair amount of airplay for some reason. It is important, but not as important as the kind of air time that it has been provided. Our thinking on this was that we now have a time in Canada when it is possible to recognize Aboriginal nations and to provide back into the hands of Aboriginal people clear jurisdictions to govern themselves. With the proper encouragement, something like fifty to eighty nations will evolve over the next couple of decades. But outside of places such as the northern territories and perhaps one or two of the Prairie provinces, where they might have some influence, numerically Aboriginal people are just not going to be able to have much role in either the federal or provincial governments. So given our understanding of the way Canada as a federal state governs itself, it provides through the Senate a role for provinces or the regions of Canada in the governance of the country as a whole. Even before a triple-E Senate, the notion is that there is some kind of representation for each of the entities within the larger whole. Then of course you have the Commons, where you have representation by population, more or less.

So, if in fact Aboriginal people are going to be recognized as a significant portion of the country, then we thought that there should be a role for them within the government of the country. So that is where the notion of a third house came up. The first step would consist of what can be done by way of legislation. This would be setting up an Aboriginal parliament, which would be an advisory institution that deals with legislation that specifically affects Aboriginal peoples. A very good example would be what to do in relation to implementation of this report and its more than four hundred recommendations. Another is the proposed legislative changes to the Indian Act that the Ministry of Indian Affairs contemplated sometime back.

The second stage would be a constitutional amendment, actually creating a third house with First People's assembly. The assembly now empowered by the constitution could have specific jurisdiction and maybe even have some kind of a veto in certain areas. An example would be the parts of the constitution that directly affect Aboriginal peoples and also perhaps certain kinds of legislation that affected Aboriginal nations. Legislation affecting these issues could not be passed without the concurrence of the people's assembly, and so forth. That's down the road.

So much for jurisdiction and the recognition of nations. We also want the federal government to be changed. We are proposing legislation for the creation of an Aboriginal relations department and a smaller department of Indian and Inuit services. The notion would be that you have a minister who over time is more and more responsible for the relationships between governments and between nations. Those Aboriginal peoples that are moving into self-government and being recognized as nations move into a new relationship with the Aboriginal relations minister. Some peoples would continue to live under the Indian Act for some time, perhaps as communities, because their priorities right now are more local and they are more concerned with healing, education, or economic development.

We also took a hard look at the land base that Aboriginal people have. It is very small, south of 60°. In comparison to the United States it is frighteningly small. Even though the Aboriginal population there is numerically about the same as we have here – about a million or so – they still own 3 per cent of the land base there, in a nation of 260 million people. So when you go to my relatives down there – the Dene down there are known as the Navajo – you find that they cover four major large states, with a land base bigger than some of the Atlantic provinces and some of the fifty states themselves. Likewise, if you were to go among the Lakota/Dakota people, you would find big reservations. South of 60° in Canada, we have less than one-half of 1 per cent of the land base, even though we make up between 2 and 3 per cent of the total population.

Modern claims have provided the Inuit in the north, some of the Dene, Yukon Indians, and now the Nisga'a, Cree, and Inuit communities in northern Quebec with a land base. One can argue whether it is sufficient or not, but it is vastly better than the small reserves. In fact, there is no comparison. We are proposing that Aboriginal people be provided with the land, the resources, and the jurisdiction to be able to become over time self-reliant and self-sufficient, so they can 'pay their own way.' We want Aboriginal governments to be able to tax and raise revenue on their own lands. In addition, Aboriginal governments need financial resources similar to the provinces, and in particular similar to the kind of funding received by territorial governments, where need is always considered, in formula funding from the federal government.

The process for providing an adequate land base to Canadian Aboriginal peoples must be open and across the board to all Aboriginal peoples, whether they be the Métis, or those living in Ontario, or nations that have treaties on the Prairies. Where the land negotiation process is based on an existing historical treaty, we want the negotiation done on the basis that the original treaty, even where it included blanket extinguishment, did not extinguish rights to land. The approach in treaty land negotiations in the future would be one of sharing and working at ways to recognize Aboriginal peoples. We see three major categories of land. The first would be the land base for Aboriginal people where the Aboriginal people would more or less have exclusive jurisdiction and ownership. The second would involve joint jurisdiction, joint management, and creation of a joint structure of government. The third would be land under more or less exclusive jurisdiction and ownership of other Canadian governments. But overall we would agree that the extinguishment would not be necessary to address Aboriginal title, and this should go in a treaty that would then be constitutionalized.

The approach that we have taken to our work covers two major areas, and I have been dealing primarily with the first part. We think that it is absolutely fundamental that Aboriginal people be provided with the structural means to be able to govern themselves in the future, but we also know very well that because of their experience – the colonization, the alienation, and the attempt to remove all threads of Aboriginal culture – there is a tremendous need for healing and the development of human capacity.

So we spent as much time and resources on the theme of Aboriginal people re-emerging as strong, healthy individuals, with strong families and strong communities. What we discovered was that whether it was in education, social services, child welfare, or tough issues such as sexual abuse and suicide, Aboriginal people generally have found the answers themselves. Not all communities have done so, and not all communities have all the abilities needed in each area. But what we have found is that generally, somewhere among Aboriginal people, the desperate needs are being addressed. We have highlighted them in our report.

And we have been critical. Why, for instance, do Aboriginal people continue to have something like a 40 per cent rate of high school drop-outs? We have come up with good examples to change that – places that have worked. It is obvious that when Aboriginal people get hold of their education, things get better. Aboriginal people can actively take over their education system and make it culturally inclusive and culturally appropriate, involve the elders, and include the many things that are important to Aboriginal people – their world-view, their traditions, whether spiritual or otherwise. The running of schools by Aboriginal people, even if it is in downtown Winnipeg, works – it really works. The successes are there. We have small, fledgling, post-secondary institutions among Aboriginal people, where there is a much higher success rate than in the larger, more established post-secondary institutions.

There is a desperate need for these institutions to be properly funded. We want nations and governments to give degree-granting authority to these institutions, because at the moment that has not happened. These small institutions are forced to arrange working relations with the larger colleges and universities so their programs are recognized. These new organizations are developing courses that are working for Aboriginal people, but the credit goes to the older institutions, because it is under their auspices that these small Aboriginal institutions present courses. As to the funding of these new centres, I know that funding even to larger institutions is precarious. Well, it is a hundred times more so for Aboriginal colleges that are now just getting off the ground. It is funding based on course by course, year by year, for programs that are really working well, that will bring back young people who dropped out of school. The staff of these institutions, of course, are working under precarious kinds of situations, and if members can find a job somewhere else, they are likely to leave and find a more permanent home.

Because of the extreme shortage of Aboriginal people in the health field, there must be a major effort to try and get as many trained health experts among Aboriginal people as possible – ten thousand professionally trained over the next ten years. And that is just the beginning of what is needed. There are so few Aboriginal medical experts who are recognized who have gone through the normal course of training. When we began, there were only fifty-three Aboriginal medical doctors throughout the country. There were more nurses, but many of them are now doing other things.

To deal with the issue of getting more Aboriginal people through post-secondary education, we have many recommendations on how to make universities friendlier to Aboriginal people. Obviously a lot of them are common sense; hire more Aboriginal people on the staff, create a climate that is friendlier to Aboriginal people. Set up departments that deal with Aboriginal studies, try to get a particular kind of threshold number of Aboriginal people. If you have one Aboriginal student in a class, the success rate is not as good as if you have a group that can sustain itself and provide mutual support. Universities still are a harsh place to be for Aboriginal people. The internal strength in those institutions to help Aboriginal people to succeed extends even to residences. The Métis, in particular, encouraged the commission to consider the idea of a residence for their students where their numbers warranted.

The approach that we took to modifications of existing post-secondary institutions in providing a friendlier place for Aboriginal people is indicative of our general approach to Canadian institutions.

On the one hand we recommend, through Aboriginal self-government, the creation of distinctive Aboriginal institutions in education, justice, and so on. These would normally be operated on an Aboriginal land base. On the other hand, because of the continuing contact that Aboriginal people will have with everyday Canadian institutions, we recommend ways to make them more culturally appropriate for Aboriginal people.

There could be many changes in structure and delivery. Studies have preceded us on how justice should be implemented for Aboriginal people. We also released a special report on justice. The whole system should have more Aboriginal people in it; cultural-sensitivity training should take place for all those who work with Aboriginal people.

We recommend the same kind of approach in a number of other areas, so that in the larger society changes are made, in delivering municipal services for Aboriginal people, medical services, social services, and schooling, post-secondary or elementary or otherwise, so that Aboriginal people will find these institutions more culturally appropriate. The reality is that something like 45 per cent of Aboriginal people are living in urban areas, and they are in contact daily with such facilities and using the same institutions as everyone else. So those places need to do a number of things so that Aboriginal people can survive more easily in the larger society.

This provides you with a very general idea of the approach taken in the final report of the Royal Commission on Aboriginal Peoples.

7

An Emasculation of Rights in Government–Aboriginal Relations in Australia

CHRISTINE FLETCHER

Whenever Peter Russell visits Australia he raises our consciousness about the political morality of relations between indigenous peoples and governments, particularly the question of reconciling sovereignty and constitutionalism with the special needs of indigenous peoples. Writing from the perspective of Australia does have a number of advantages – it means, first, that there was never any question mark over the subject of this chapter. Russell's research in Australia reflects his intense interest in the political and constitutional gains of the Aboriginal peoples – yet another avenue in the enormous field of his research interests. He has followed closely the way in which Australia and Canada are attempting to deal with the impact of colonial settler societies on their Aboriginal populations. Progress towards constitutional recognition and self-government through territorial concessions and autonomy for the first peoples has made Canada a model for Aboriginal people in Australia and elsewhere – in Russell's words, this is what 'mega-constitutionalism' is all about (1993).[1]

If this chapter had been written in late 1995, the tone might have been more optimistic, but since John Howard won government at the federal level on 2 March 1996, Australian indigenous society has not had good fortune. Its progress towards what we in Australia term 'social justice' seems slower than ever. Not only has 'mega-constitutionalism' passed us by, but for the indigenous peoples not even the micro variant has become a reality. Federal budget cuts, the promotion of racial intolerance against Aborigines and Asians, attempts by the new government to undermine the spirit of the Native Title Act of 1993, and government intervention in Aboriginal cultural matters to allow investors to proceed with infrastructures developments have left the Aboriginal community with the feeling that its rights are evaporating.

However, before we can grasp their losses, we first need to understand their gains, and, as Peter Russell so wisely points out, only when there is a change of government and we face hard times can the success and gains of the past be truly measured. In indigenous affairs, when policies are obscured by reforms and when financial support begins to wane, that is when the advances made over the last decade or so will become clear.

The first part of this paper provides a brief historical outline of the political position of Aboriginal people in Australia, in relation not only to governments but also to society more generally. In recent times, this has become a backdrop for the ascendancy of a peculiar form of racism, which seems to have the implicit endorsement of some members of the new federal government. The second section confronts the question of racism in Australia – antithetical to the Russell doctrine of elevating and preserving the sovereign rights of the people. Cultural illusions have influenced the way in which non-Aboriginal society responds to the group known as the Aboriginal and Torres Strait Islander community, so much so that policy myths surrounding the occupation of the Australian continent prior to white settlement were perpetuated in Australian law. For example, in 1971, during Aboriginal land claim hearings, Justice Blackburn declared that prior to 1788 Australia was officially *terra nullius* (unoccupied).[2]

Mistakes and absurdities concerning the nature of Aboriginal occupation have been propped up conveniently alongside dispossession – a negative position that was strengthened by government subscription to the doctrine of terra nullius. It was two decades before the judicial and political assault on the rights of the Aboriginal people was reversed, at least in part, by the findings of the High Court in *Mabo v. Queensland* in 1992.[3] The decision in that case recognized that Native title still existed, and this signalled a reversal of fortunes for the Aboriginal people. At that time, the Aboriginal and Torres Strait Islanders seemed suddenly to be placed in a position from which constitutional reform could be reached, but that was before the federal election in 1996. The results saw events turn against them. Government commitments to advancing equity for the indigenous people began to flicker after March 1996. It became clear that progress, if any, would now be slow and the road made more difficult by the obvious ignorance of the new government. Fortunately, certain institutions are beyond its day-to-day reach. For example, the reversal of constitutional discrimination against Aboriginal people that existed under section 127 of the Australian constitution prior to the 1967 national referendum is secure.[4] And there have been other important gains: the political acumen obtained by the Aboriginal people in their historic quest for a fairer and more responsive system, which cannot easily be removed; nor is it likely that the High Court's decision favouring Eddie Mabo's claim to control over his ancestral lands will be easily reversed. These are real gains for indigenous peoples.

Nevertheless, the Howard government immediately targeted the 1993 Native Title Act.[5] It attempted to cut the advancement of Aboriginal rights back to the bone, by closing off the lines of Aboriginal political participation and by substantially reducing government funding to Aboriginal communities and disabling many Aboriginal organizations – the backbone of community life.

Indigenous Occupation of Australia

Aborigines are a minority in the overall Australian population, but in some areas their numbers are quite substantial, and birth rates are increasing – by the year 2000, the indigenous population will reach approximately 300,000. Currently it numbers around 280,000 in an estimated overall population of eighteen million.[6] Before the arrival of the first British settlers in the 1770s, the Aborigines and Torres Strait Islander people living in Australia numbered between 500,000 and one million. By the 1930s, their population had plunged to 60,000. They lived by their own indigenous law and, according to Bonner, a senior Aboriginal man and former senator, their society bore no resemblance to any European-style system.[7] Some insight into the philosophical values of Aboriginal society can be found in anthropological and historical research[8] and in research produced by Aboriginal people themselves.

On the basis of research and with hindsight we can see that the practical relevance of some Western structures that are supposed to serve Aboriginal society need urgently to be questioned. Even though their existence is a fait accompli, government organizations do not function in a responsive manner. The political ideas that developed following white Australian settlement and the philosophy of indigenous peoples have roots in vastly different cultural settings. The structure of authority for the indigenous community is often at variance with Western values: Indigenous traditions are not derived from Euro–Anglo political theories of the nation-state. Theories of indigenous religious and philosophical institutions emerged from considerably more ancient assumptions than the West knows. Beliefs, local political objectives, and attitudes shape the way in which governments react to indigenous people. Said illustrates this in his interpretations of colonial attitudes in the nineteenth century: 'Bringing civilisation to primitive or barbaric peoples (had) the disturbingly familiar ideas about flogging or death or extended punishment being required when "they" misbehaved or became rebellious, because "they" mainly understood force or violence best; "they" were not like "us," and for that reason deserved to be ruled.'[9]

Such attitudes carry reminders of the past and are reflective of the type of negative policies that governments pursued until quite recently. The most harmful strategy employed in Australia was the policy of assimilation. Assimilation was put into effect in earnest after the Second World War, devastating an already fragile Aboriginal population. Officially, the policy ended in the late 1960s, but its effect remains to haunt Aborigines – particularly those who experienced the policies at first hand or whose relatives were traumatized.[10] Assimilation was designed to control Aboriginal people and integrate them into Australian society so that they would become less visible. Children were forcibly taken away from their homes and placed in institutions – a cruel path for thousands of Aboriginal people who then had to suffer the humiliation of abuse and the cost of being removed from the richness of indigenous society and exposed instead to physical abuse and the senseless culture of government institutions.

Assimilation was followed by self-determination, introduced into the government rhetoric of reform in the late 1960s but never realized. By 1996, the shock waves of the enormity of the assimilation period reverberated around the nation as public hearings into the 'stolen generation' (as it is now known) began travelling the country. The situation was compounded by the federal government's refusal to apologize on behalf of the Australian people. The government's non-response was made worse by politicians – notably the racist rhetoric from newly elected federal parliamentarian Pauline Hanson.[11] The enormity of the situation was at first difficult to comprehend because it was so remarkably inconsistent with the response of previous governments to the demands of Aboriginal people.[12]

Earlier Turning Points

Prior to the current negative turn-around, the general Aboriginal and Torres Strait Islander community had been making slow progress, over three decades, towards national recognition of their indigenous rights. First, there was the commonwealth referendum in 1967, in which Australians voted overwhelmingly to give Aborigines the right to be counted in the national census and to allow the government in Canberra to make laws (concurrent with the states) for Aborigines.[13] The inclusion of Aboriginal and Torres Strait Islander people in the census opened up such issues as citizenship entitlements and international human rights, offered them a degree of protection from discrimination, and, most important, led to establishment of a process aimed at restoration of Aboriginal land rights. Within a decade of the referendum, the commonwealth had passed the Racial Discrimination Act, 1975, and the Aboriginal Land Rights (Northern Territory), 1976 – monumental pieces of legislation containing principles that remain influential.

Between the 1970s and the present, the greatest achievements were the design of special public administrative structures, new government attitudes towards reconciliation and a decision handed down by the High Court of Australia in 1992 that recognized Eddie Koiki Mabo's relationship with his ancestral lands and led, after fierce debate, to passage of the Native Title Act in 1993. Had there been sufficient public momentum to alter the constitution, the *Mabo* decision would probably have led to what Peter Russell terms 'mega-constitutionalism.' It challenged institutionalized prejudices and signalled enormous pressure for change. The Aboriginal and Torres Strait Islander negotiating team found that it could bargain from a position of strength for the first time. Unfortunately, the general population's understanding of the issues was distorted: many of the virtues of native title were buried under the pastoral industry's grab for resources; security of pastoral leases took precedence in a process that was driven almost entirely by state politicians and the industry. Soon after John Howard's election victory, gutting the legislation had become an obsession with the new government. This was one of the points of greatest divergence between Howard and Prime Minister Paul Keating.

Paul Keating was the champion of Aboriginal reconciliation. After the election, he was described as 'the greatest political champion of Mabo and reconciliation'[14] He understood that somewhere in the interpretation of Australian history, and in the judicial recognition of native title, there existed enormous potential for reconciliation between black and white Australians. Social justice was a strategic policy framework that had formed the basis for reform under Prime Minister Bob Hawke during the 1980s and, in a much more focused form, under his successor, Keating. Social justice was abandoned by conservative politicians after the 1996 elections, and in the vacuum a currency of votes was created by the apparent popularity of the new rhetoric of racial intolerance. Officially, indigenous affairs were to be brought into line with the government's restoration of the federal budget's pre-deficit figures.

Despite backing from the Keating government, bi-partisan support for Aboriginal rights was at a low level when the new government was elected in March 1996. The freedoms and rights symbolic of constitutionalism, free association, Western liberal democracy, and tolerance have not contributed to the protection of indigenous traditions. Aborigines in Australia do not have constitutional, political, or civil guarantees. The combination of constitutionalism and civil society that is so fundamental to the Australian system does not appear to be capable of adjusting to, or accepting aspects of, indigenous cultures unless the indigenous people themselves compromise their beliefs on land ownership. Yet Western constitutionalism is so binding that, in Peter Russell's words, its tendency to touch citizens' sense of identity and self-worth' is exceptionally emotional and intense.'[15]

As the new government settled itself into office,[16] it was not long before the relationship between the Aboriginal leadership and the prime minister began to deteriorate. Some Aboriginal members of the Reconciliation Council were so shaken by the turn of events that they wanted to resign. Relationships between governments and the Aboriginal community slid into a negative exchange of resistance by Aborigines to an unimpassioned and strangely defensive government.

Championed by the owner and operator of a fish-and-chips shop – a woman from Queensland who was elected to Parliament on a wave of vicious attacks on Asians and Aborigines – racism is now a blight on the nation's immigration policy.[17] Like others before her, Pauline Hanson targeted the vulnerable and perhaps most visibly different groups in Australian society. After she delivered her maiden parliamentary speech, the federal minister for immigration reluctantly defended Australia's Asian immigration policy, but no one in the government defended the Aboriginal people. Their federal minister was not a defender of even their most basic rights. He appears comfortable in his role as unsympathetic to the historical position of Aborigines in Australia.

Australian governments tend to suffer from 'historical amnesia,'[18] particularly when budgeting global amounts for social welfare–type services to Aboriginal organizations and communities or when negotiating between Aboriginal land owners and the pastoral industry. Aboriginal leaders recently made a concerted effort to introduce the new government to the way in which their communities actually operate – a steep learning curve – with very limited initial success. By late 1996, with evidence of human rights violations against Aborigines beginning to surface alongside outrageous claims about Asian immigration, the issue had become almost passé with the government.[19] Public outbursts against Aborigines and Asians were becoming a form of vote-catching. The prime minister refused every opportunity to intervene and stabilize what the media declared to be a race debate. In one controversial radio interview, Prime Minister Howard said, 'I sympathise fundamentally with Australians who are insulted when they are told that we have a racist bigoted past. And Australians are told that quite regularly. Our children are taught that. Some of the school curricula go close to teaching children that we have a racist bigoted past. Now, of course, we treated Aborigines very, very badly in the past – very, very badly – but to tell children whose parents were no part of that maltreatment, to tell children who themselves have been no part of it, that we're all part of a, sort of, a racist bigoted history, is something that Australians reject.'[20]

In the new rhetoric of racism, special programs and community grants to Aboriginal groups have been reclassified as 'preferential treatment' – an argument that favours the abolition of first peoples' status for Aboriginal peoples. The campaign to marginalize Aboriginal constituents in mainstream public policy programs was led initially by Graham Campbell, independent (but ex–Labor party) member for Kalgoorlie, in Western Australia, and later, and with much more powerful effect, by Pauline Hanson, member for Oxley in Queensland. In the months following, there was a certain amount of public support for Hanson's racist campaign. Some candidates running in state elections in Western Australia attempted to ride on the racist vote: for example, Don Green, an endorsed Liberal candidate for Eyre, asserted that Aborigines should be disqualified from claiming Aboriginality if their father happened to be white. Green was forced by the state branch of the party to apologize to his electorate, many of whom are Aboriginal people.[21]

Politicians from both sides of the federal house have been at best coy and naïve with their response to the new rhetoric of racism. While that in itself is bewildering enough, the government's economic rationalist approach to health and living conditions for Aboriginal and Torres Strait Islanders has left the indigenous community fiscally ravaged.

... and Two Steps Back

At one level, the lashing of racism dished out by Pauline Hanson slipped with ease into place alongside some of the responses received in a national survey conducted earlier in the year by the Council for Aboriginal Reconciliation. In it, there was a clear indication that some people held a negative view of indigenous people. To cite an observation in the report, 'Land rights and Mabo are two issues which come to mind when reconciliation is mentioned. Inherent in the term is some form of concession or "giving back" and reconciliation can often falter here on the response "but I didn't take anything."'[22]

A concerted effort has been made to inform people through campaigns conducted nationwide and funded by the Aboriginal and Torres Strait Islander Commission (ATSIC), which oversees almost all the expenditure earmarked for indigenous affairs. But there is division also within the general Aboriginal community about the value of ATSIC, which has strategic objectives not unlike those of Canada's Department of Indian Affairs and Northern Development or the U.S. Bureau of Indian Affairs, but with the additional function of representing Aboriginal and Torres Strait Islander people through a network of directly elected ATSIC local regional councils. A series of elected regional councils covers Australia within the framework of a relatively strong administrative structure that reports directly to the federal minister.

Some Aboriginal communities, in addition to those in the Torres Strait, and including those in the cities and in remote areas, want ATSIC out of the way. Disputes rage over ATSIC's dominance of community budget decisions, the process of local council representation (with some accusations of nepotism), electoral boundaries, and perceptions that decision-making is captured by ATSIC administrators who have little sympathy for the special needs of local constituents. One associated problem is the predominance of white advisers and white consultants in and around remote communities. Some of these act as the final arbiter in community decision-making, and, since they use the language of Western governance, their interpretations of indigenous life and their influence on critical policies and on the political direction of representation raise all sorts of ethical and moral questions, which have not been adequately addressed.[23]

The fabric of Aboriginal society is shaped by indigenous beliefs and traditions and by indigenous knowledge, but it is held together also by constitutional and political principles that governments are supposed to preserve, on behalf of the people.[24] If the flow of funds to Aboriginal communities is blocked, programs will starve – the rights of the people to participate in the process of governing will then be emasculated. One significant and intentional effect of the reduction in commonwealth expenditure – $430 million over three years – is its general impact on the functions of ATSIC and, because of reductions in its appropriations, its effect on Aboriginal organizations. Aboriginal organizations, long held to be crucial to indigenous life in Australia, are now being denied vital funding and are cracking under pressure.

Aboriginal Organizations

Aboriginal organizations such as ATSIC are a safety net – a type of life-support system – for indigenous societies across the Australian continent. They have been part of the infrastructure of indigenous society ever since people were forced to reorganize themselves and their families, following the dislocation and trauma of assimilation, officially introduced in 1951.

Aboriginal organizations are a product of that period. They offer everything from health services, legal aid, and cultural development, through to incentives for political encounters with government as adversaries. By the mid-1990s, there were between 1,500 and 2,000 Aboriginal and Torres Strait Islander organizations registered across all the states and territories. They range from bodies devoted to the provision of family services through to Aboriginal hostels, resource agencies, town camps, and land councils. With the current federal government, many organizations are now under threat.[25] Most are funded through appropriations to ATSIC, and following intense and sustained auditing, by both ATSIC auditors and consultant auditors, a number were found to have breached the accountability guidelines. Many others will feel the heat through fairly savage cuts to their operating grants.

The emergence of many Aboriginal organizations was prompted by the impoverishing effects of government throughout the twentieth century. A large proportion of the Aboriginal population – over 40 per cent – lives in rural or remote regions in communities that are now registered as corporations but which have a tenuous past, shaped by missions, pastoralists, and governments. The Aboriginal people who lived in the cities organized themselves into political groups, and many organizations, such as the Redfern Aboriginal Legal Service and the Aboriginal Medical Service, provided a basis for uniting to resist pressure from governments and from groups within the wider community. Health, medical, and legal services became pivotal in Aboriginal–government relations. Legal services are at risk, which adds to the pressure between the Aboriginal community and state criminal justice systems. The legal scene that supports indigenous societies is spiralling downward because of commonwealth cutbacks to state and territory legal aid.

All Aboriginal organizations are publicly accountable. Some, such as the Social Justice Commission, are attached to mainstream public agencies such as the Human Rights Commission and thus find their role made more fragile by their vulnerability to the whim of the government of the day. For example, funding formerly sent directly to the Social Justice Commission is now to be rerouted to the Human Rights Commission, and, consistent with the new government's approach, the Social Justice Commission was to disappear at the end of 1997. Over time, many policy relationships between governments and indigenous peoples have become increasingly unstable. This is the case despite attempts to develop Aboriginal organizations as a bridge to government. The nearest that any organization has come to providing this link is the Aboriginal and Torres Strait Islander Commission.

The strongest and most enduring forms of Aboriginal organizations, aside from the power sustained by Aboriginal traditions, came from inside Aboriginal health, legal, and land corporations. Notable among these are the land councils. Land councils across the country have cultural and social currency, but those with the most solid land base are the northern and the central land councils in the Northern Territory, formed under the commonwealth Aboriginal Land Rights (Northern Territory) Act, 1976. Outside of the Northern Territory (and Jarvis Bay), Aboriginal land councils in most states fall under state legislation, although in Western Australia they have virtually no land base, as the statutory basis for almost all land use falls firmly under state jurisdiction.

Aboriginal woman have shaped organizations, particularly in remote regions. The Ngaanyatjarra/Pitjantjatjara/Yunkatajara (NPY) Women's Council, for example, provides a framework for Aboriginal women to organize their issues in central Australia. The council represents people in a vast area of inland Australia – approximately 350,000 square kilometres – covering communities within the Northern Territory, Western Australia, and South Australia.[26] Like many organizations, it takes a holistic approach to issues, dealing not only with individual and community health but the arts, culture, and social policy. Such bodies are interlaced with others across a variety of regions: this group has strong affiliations with the Anungu Pitjantjatjara, Ngaanyatjarra Women's Council, Maralinga Tjarutja, and many others.

The NPY Council was established in 1980 as a lobby organization for Aboriginal land rights in South Australia. It has a constituent base of around 6,000 Anangu (Aboriginal people in the region covered by the council). It supports and promotes traditional Aboriginal law and culture, human services, social justice, and policy development and operates health services that include programs for the disabled and against domestic violence, nutrition support for young mothers and babies, aged care, and emergency relief. It is located, and operates, in one of the most remote regions on earth: the federal budget released in August 1996 cut its funding by over 75 per cent.[27]

Conflict within organizations is so bitter that Aboriginal people in some regions saw their vote in the most recent federal election as either for or against ATSIC.[28] In Kalgoorlie, some people wanted to vote for the candidate who promised to cut funding to ATSIC and actually widen the gap between Aboriginal communities and special program grants. And when the anti-ATSIC candidate was returned as an independent, some communities began directly lobbying the new federal minister – some Aboriginal people and more particularly their community white advisers appeared to have direct access to the minister – in the belief that the new government would ultimately disable ATSIC and strike up a direct relationship with communities.

Attempts to alienate people from their culture and refusal to concede that there are explanations for the indigenous universe that differ from those of Western-style society in Australia have led to disfunctional relationships between indigenous peoples and the modern state. At a policy level, alienation is caused by the confusion resulting from the imposition of modern governance on top of indigenous institutions. The situation seems to have been made worse by a government that does not appear to understand the richness of Aboriginal culture or the importance of reconciliation. When the Aboriginal people of Australia speak of ancient traditions, they refer to a religious timelessness that dates back tens (perhaps hundreds) of thousands of years. When Western society speaks of ancient tradition, it invokes the pre-biblical or biblical traditions, notably the ones that laid the foundations for current systems of beliefs, property values, and grounds for the establishment of today's societies.[29]

These are not simply historical differences; they are paradigmatic – far greater than tribal differences; more significant than cultural, ethnic, or religious difference. They shape how people relate to themselves, their community, and their world. Broadly speaking, the entire concept of property, on which Western society rests, conflicts with property in an indigenous context. In Australia, the Aboriginal peoples belong to their country; they and their country are inseparable. Only the artificial structures that now overlap and intertwine with the two belief systems – associations and social, economic, and political coalitions – seem to bridge the cultural chasm that separate these societies.

Mini-constitutionalism

As Peter Russell argues, 'mega-constitutionalism' takes the relationship between laws, principles, and political arrangements and between governments and the people to a heightened level of civil consciousness. In Australia, no such level has yet been reached. In fact, for Aborigines, government policy has sunk to new depths. There is, of course, a stable liberal constitutional system, but it contains no measures for the cultural preservation of the indigenous people.[30] State constitutions are part of the Australian federal constitution, and the combination provides communities in all of the states with their own autonomy. Currently, none of the Australian territories has its own constitution, although, as part of its attempts to achieve statehood, the Northern Territory produced a draft constitution, tabled in the legislative assembly on 22 August 1996, which is the first serious attempt by any Australian territory to reinforce its autonomy. At the present time, that draft is the only 'state' constitution to mention the Aboriginal peoples as the original peoples and to address Aboriginal customary law, but it makes no mention of indigenous rights, or Native rights. The draft constitution has an addendum containing options for a possible Bill of Rights that does not incorporate Aboriginal rights. It refers to express rights (p. 34) contained in the commonwealth constitution, but this is limited to property rights, trial by jury, and freedom of association and of religion. The relationship between the indigenous population of the Northern Territory and successive territory governments is now uneasy but civil. For the territory to achieve its desired statehood, it must address Aboriginal reconciliation and issues such as equity and access to political and economic autonomy.

Constitutionalism also exists at a local level, but this is essentially a management system for incorporating organizations, community councils, and associations – a form of mini-constitutionalism. In Aboriginal affairs, local communities or organizations comply with the rule that they must have constitutions. Such documents are generic, and they can be legitimized under existing legislation enacted by either the commonwealth or the state or territory. Also, rights associated with community constitutions are minimal. Such documents register the community or the organization as a legitimate entity and, if it complies with the regulations set out by the government and fits the criteria for grants, entitle it to receive monies.

Conclusion

In the literature on Western liberal democratic theory, the chief institution of the state to which people pledge their faith is the constitution. Constitutionalism determines the nature of the state and, within that, the relationship of people to government. That relationship affects freedoms and, within those parameters, the characteristics of civil society. The fundamental principles of constitutionalism can be found in the political fabric of any democracy, but the key to success, most particularly in a federal democracy such as Australia, lies in designing institutions for managing diversity, maintaining unity, and preserving the sovereignty of the peoples, particularly those whose social and cultural assumptions about life and the universe are different from those of the West.

In Australia, rights, self-determination, constitutionalism, and sovereignty are part of the contractual relationship between peoples and the state. Other elements include the quality of governance and the democratic nature of society, which, in Australia, provides for broad representation of the diversity of social values within the community at large. Two of the elements required to balance discordant elements in the governance of system that is as diverse as Australia's can be found in the design of institutions for managing diversity, maintaining unity, and preserving the sovereignty of the people and in the overall nature of civil society.

The new federal government is cutting budgets in almost every area of public policy. Over $8 billion has been slashed from commonwealth expenditures and the commonwealth bureaucracy has been reduced by approximately 27,000 positions (and more cuts are planned). Whether intentionally or not, Australia appears to have entered a period of social, economic, and political destruction. Among those whose society is under pressure is the Aboriginal and Torres Strait Islander people. But because of an unhealthy element creeping into the rhetoric of Australian society, lack of strong leadership, and an aggressive denial of history by some independent politicians, a considerable amount of the pressure for reform is negative. The situation needs to be reversed. As Martin Krygier recently argued on national radio: 'Like any society, ours is not without incivilities, the deepest of which have occurred to the aboriginal population. Genuine efforts to repair the consequences of this tragic encounter have occurred, if somewhat belatedly and with mixed results, and it goes without saying that they must continue for the sake, not only of civility, but also of common decency.'[31]

Peter Russell refers to Canadians as 'founding peoples ... but ... not yet a people' (1991, 94). Australians also are 'founding peoples' – colonials who established their Western institutions on land over which they asserted the authority of the British Crown. They overrode Aborigines and pushed them to the fringe, and post-colonialism gave way to perceptions of a 'new nation.' The white settlers brought their own history, based on the Anglo–European past instead of the ancient religious beliefs of the indigenous inhabitants. But, as Russell has so passionately argued during debates on the future of Canada, founding peoples will never be 'a people' until they unite under a social contract shaped by the traditions of all peoples, including the indigenous.

NOTES

1 Russell 1993a.
2 Blackburn, J. 1971.
3 See Pearson 1993.
4 *The Constitution*, as altered to 31 Oct. 1993.
5 The High Court's *Wik* judgment, delivered on 23 December 1996, upheld an appeal by the Wik people (from Cape York, north Queensland) that Native title can coexist alongside pastoral leases. The judgment caused the prime minister to exhibit outrage and threaten to weaken or suspend the Racial Discrimination Act to allow the Native Title Act to extinguish Aboriginal rights in favour of the pastoral industry (*Australian*, 24 Dec. 1996, 1, 4).
6 ATSIC, 1995.
7 Bonner 1988, 20. Aboriginal people have occupied the Australian continent for thousands, perhaps hundreds of thousands, of years (Lanhupuy 1993). There were hundreds of languages, and tribes inhabited the land from one end of Australia to the other (Berndt and Berndt 1964).
8 Berndt and Berndt 1964; Reynolds 1996; Pearson 1993; Langton 1993; Lanhupuy 1993; Bonner 1989.
9 Edward W. Said, *Culture and Imperialism* (New York: Vintage Books 1993).
10 Dodson 1996a.
11 http://www.adfa.oz.au/~adm/politics/#topical events
12 The Council for Aboriginal Reconciliation established prior to the Howard government has produced an enormous amount of material towards black and white reconciliation. Among the latest is a special edition in the series *Walking Together*, titled *Renewal of the Nation*, Dec. 1996.

13 Bennett 1985.

14 R. Manne, *Australian*, 8 July 1996.

15 Russell 1993.

16 The prime minister ordered Kirribili House – official residence in Sydney – to be refurbished, and the Howard family, instead of following tradition and residing at The Lodge in Canberra, lives in Sydney. That decision was based on minimizing disruption to his teenaged children.

17 Pauline Hanson is member for the seat of Oxley, Queensland.

18 This is a term borrowed from Schecter (1994), who used it to explain the attitude of the English speaking community in Quebec.

19 Dodson 1996b.

20 Transcript, John Laws and the prime minister 24 Oct. 1996, provided by the *Sydney Morning Herald.*

21 *Australian*, 25 Oct. 1996.

22 Sweeney & Associates 1996, 20.

23 Rowse 1992 touches on this issue in chap. 3.

24 See Fletcher 1996.

25 ATSIC 1996.

26 NPY Women's Council 1996.

27 Ibid.

28 Based on conversations with people in Ngaanyatjarra Lands and on anecdotal evidence.

29 Fletcher 1996.

30 See Galligan 1995.

31 Krygier 1996.

REFERENCES

Aboriginal and Torres Strait Islander Commission (ATSIC). 1995. *Recognition, Rights and Reform: Report to Government on Native Title, Social Justice Measures.* Australian Government Publishing Service, Canberra.

– 1996.

Bennett, Scott, 1985. 'The 1967 Referendum.' *Australian Aboriginal Studies* 2, no. 1: 26–31.

Berndt, R.M., and Berndt C.H. 1964. *The World of the First Australians.* Sydney: Ure Smith.

Blackburn, J. 1971. Supreme Court of the Northern Territory, *Milirrpum vs. Nabalco Pty Ltd and the Commonwealth of Australia.* Sydney: Law Book Co.

Bonner, Neville. 1988. *Always Anangu: A Review of the Pitjantjatjara and Yankunytjat-*

jara Aboriginal Communities in Central Australia. Canberra: Department of Aboriginal Affairs.

Brennan, Frank. 1991. *Sharing the Country: The Case for an Agreement between Black and White Australians.* Victoria: Penguin.

– 1995. *One Land, One Nation.* Queensland: Queensland University Press.

Council for Aboriginal Reconciliation. 1996. *Walking Together: Renewal of the Nation.* Special edition, Dec.

Dodson, Mick. 1996a. *Assimilation versus Self-Determination – No Contest.* Discussion Paper No. 1. North Australia Research Unit, Australian National University, Darwin and Canberra.

– 1996b. *Indigenous Deaths in Custody, 1989–1996: A Report Prepared by the Office of Aboriginal and Torres Strait Islander Social Justice Commissioner, for the Aboriginal and Torres Strait Islander Commission (ATSIC).* Oct. 1996.

Fletcher, Christine. 1996. *Trapped in Civil Society: Aborigines and Federalism in Australia.* Discussion Paper No. 4. North Australia Research Unit (Australian National University), Darwin.

– Forthcoming. 'Australia.' In Michael E. Brown, ed., *Ethnic Conflict in the Asia–Pacific Region.* Boston: MIT.

Galligan, Brian. 1995. *A Federal Republic: Australia's Constitutional System of Government.* Cambridge: Cambridge University Press.

Hanson, Pauline. Australian House of Representatives, Hansard for 10 September 1996, Appropriation Bill (No. 1) 1996–97 (First Speech).

Krygier, Martin. 1996. *The Sources of Civil Society.* Second Richard Krygier Memorial Lecture, 29 Aug. Melbourne, Australian Broadcasting Corporation, Radio National Background Briefing, transcripts, 15 Sept. 1996. (http://www.abc.net.au/rn/talks/bbing/index.htm)

Langton, Marcia. 1993. '"Well, I heard it on the radio and I saw it on the television": An Essay on the Politics and Aesthetics of Filmmaking by and about Aboriginal People and Things.' North Sydney: Australian Film Commission.

– 1994. 'Indigenous Self-Government and Self-Determination: Overlapping Jurisdictions at Cape York.' In C. Fletcher, ed., *Aboriginal Self-Determination in Australia.* Canberra: Aboriginal Studies Press.

Lanhupuy, Wes. 1993. 'Marine Management for 40,000 Years: A Yolngu View of Sea Rights.' In *Turning the Tide: Conference on Indigenous Peoples and Sea Rights 14 July–16 July 1993: Selected Papers,* 4–8.

Leger, Marie. 1994. 'Regional Autonomy on Nicaragua's Atlantic Coast.' In M. Leger, ed., *Aboriginal Peoples: Towards Self-Government.* Montreal: Black Rose Books.

Marcus, A., and Ricklefs, M.C., eds., 1985. *Surrender Australia: Essays in the Study and Uses of History.* Sydney: George Allen & Unwin.

Martinez Cob, and Jose R. 1986. *Study of the Problem of Discrimination against Indigenous Populations*. UN Document, E/CN.4/Sub.2/1986/7/Add.4, 1986, paragraphs 378–80.

Mann, R. *Australian*, 8 July 1996.

Ngaanyatjarra, Pitjantjatjara, Yankunytjatjara (NPY) Women's Council Aboriginal Corporation. 1996. *Information Package About How the Commonwealth Government Budget Cutbacks to ATSIC Will Drastically Affect the Work of the Ngaanyatjarra/Pitjantjatjara/Yankunytjatjara (NPY) Women's Council.*

Northern Territory, Draft Constitution, Oct. 1996.

Pearson, Noel. 1993. '204 Years of Invisible Title: From the Most Vehement Denial of a People's Rights to Land to a Most Cautious and Belated Recognition.' In M.A. Stephenson and S. Ratnapala, eds., *Mabo: A Judicial Revolution: The Aboriginal Land Rights Decision and Its Impact on Australian Law*. St Lucia, Brisbane: University of Queensland Press.

Perrone-Moises, Beatriz. 1994. 'The Indians of Brazil: A Fragile Constitutional Recognition.' In M. Leger, ed., *Aboriginal Peoples*.

Reynolds, Henry. 1996. *Aboriginal Sovereignty: Three Nations, One Australia*. Sydney: Allen & Unwin.

Rowse, Tim. 1992. *Remote Possibilities: The Aboriginal Domain and the Administrative Imagination*. Darwin: North Australia Research Unit/ANU.

Royal Commission into Aboriginal Deaths in Custody. 1991. *National Report*, Vol. 1 of 5. Canberra: Australian Government Publishing Service.

Russell, Peter. 1991. 'The Future Process of Canadian Constitutional Politics.' In R. Young, ed., *Confederation in Crisis*. Toronto: James Lorimer.

– 1993a. *Constitutional Odyssey: Can Canadians Become a Sovereign People?*, 2nd ed., Toronto: University of Toronto Press.

– 1993b. 'The End of Mega Constitutional Politics in Canada?' In *Political Science and Politics* 26 no. 1: 33–7

Schecter, Stephen. 1994. *Zen and the Art of Post-Modern Canada: Does the Trans-Canada Highway Always Lead to Charlottetown?* Montreal: Robert Davies.

Sweeney, Brian and Associates. 1996. *A New Beginning: Community Attitudes towards Aboriginal Reconciliation*. Prepared for the Aboriginal Reconciliation Branch, Department of the Prime Minister and Cabinet, Study No. 9413, Jan.

Summary of Discussion on Aboriginal Peoples

At the end of the panel on constitutional politics, Gordon Peters, regional chief for Canada's First Nations, wanted to know where indigenous people fit into the constitutional process. He said that they entered constitutional negotiations in the late 1970s seeking recognition of the sovereign abilities of the first nations. But since that time discussion has turned from recognition of long-suppressed nations entitled to self-government to the recognition of peoples subordinate to the governments within the country. He questioned the exclusion of indigenous people from non-constitutional processes such as the first ministers' conferences, noting that there is no forum within which to address issues of concern to indigenous people. The government pays only lip service to inherent rights and simply assumes that indigenous people are assimilated into the Canadian body politic without their having gone through a process of entering confederation. This leaves indigenous people little recourse but to create situations where the government is forced to negotiate.

James Tully argued that indigenous peoples fit into constitutional arrangements as equal partners, a view developed in the 1996 Report of the Royal Commission on Aboriginal Peoples. This framework takes Aboriginal peoples as equal partners with the federal and provincial governments in confederation. At the sub-constitutional level, he saw some hope in the experience of the Nisga'a in attempting to make the treaty process more participatory.

Katherine Swinton added that going to the courts has sometimes been positive for Aboriginal peoples in gaining recognition of legal rights, which they then use as a catalyst to further action on the political side. For example, while the courts are too cautious to recognize a right to Aboriginal self-government, the court's recognition of hunting and fishing rights has led to recognition of land rights as in the case of the Nisga'a.

Stéphane Dion replied that Aboriginal peoples should be treated as individuals within sovereign Canadian institutions. He told Chief Peters that he is the equal of any other Canadian citizen, deserving of the same rights. While recognizing that the needs of Aboriginal peoples are not the same as those of other Canadians, Dion explicitly rejected both collective rights and nation-to-nation status for indigenous peoples, just as he does in responding to separatist or nationalist demands from Quebec. He concluded by saying that he would work with Chief Peters so long as any cultural diversity is compatible with the universal rights that are the basic definition of Canada.

Gordon Peters had the last word in this exchange, saying that he was not satisfied with any of the responses that he received from the panel. He was very disappointed that there had not been more substantial discussion of how relations with indigenous people are going to be dealt with in the context of the constitution. He thought that this gap was indicative of the overall non-attention paid to indigenous peoples and the issues that concern them. He hoped for a relationship of equality between two peoples.

In commenting on the papers on Aboriginal peoples, Cathy Brock drew attention to controversy in the Aboriginal community over recent arrangements worked out by Phil Fontaine in Manitoba, where jurisdiction was being restored to Aboriginal governments through the transfer of power from the federal Department of Indian Affairs to local Native communities. She noted that the then chief of the Assembly of First Nations, Ovide Mercredi, had criticized these initiatives as not leading to permanent constitutional changes guaranteeing the principle of Aboriginal self-government.

Walter Berns, noting that the U.S. federal government, despite all its failings, has been a greater friend of the American Indians than the various states, asked Paul Chartrand whether Aboriginal peoples here were more likely to achieve what they wanted in Canada as it is now constituted or in the Canada that would exist if Quebec were to leave.

Paul Chartrand replied that relationships with Aboriginal peoples were likely to be better advanced by a larger, more distant government. He commented that people are more likely to be expansive about rights for others a little bit removed from their own backyard. He also noted that a great deal can be learned from Quebec as to how the public responds to actions directed towards emancipation. For example, he thought that an emphasis on civic nationalism seemed to be better received than any notion of ethnic nationalism.

Tom Pangle asked Chartrand to speak more concretely and specifically about those aspects of Aboriginal justice that might contribute to a new and more just North American society.

Chartrand cautioned that he was not suggesting that we jettison European values. Instead he was urging greater inclusion, embracing the Aboriginal foundations of Canada. He indicated that indigenous people placed great value on individual autonomy and freedom and getting people to participate in making decisions that affect them. Moreover, he thought that Aboriginal peoples are generally more suspicious of representation, of the idea that someone has a right to speak for another or to represent the interests of the group. Cathy Brock commented on Benjamin Franklin's observation that parliamentarians could learn valuable lessons from the Haudenosaunee about listening respectfully to each other and engaging in civil discourse. She also noted the Aboriginal roots of federalism, as uncovered in the work of Donald Grinde and Bruce Johansen.

PART III: SECURITY INTELLIGENCE

As is their custom, Peter Russell and his wife, Sue, attended the 1977 St Andrew's Ball at the Royal York Hotel in Toronto. Dancing until dawn, Peter consumed a fair amount of punch along the way. The following morning he met with two old friends from his Oxford days to discuss issues of Canadian security and intelligence. Unbeknown to him, David McDonald and Donald Rickerd were travelling across the country looking for a research director for the Royal Commission of Inquiry on Certain Activities of the Royal Canadian Mounted Police. At their meeting Peter spoke of the standard issues of subversion, espionage, and terrorism, but with his typically nimble tongue perhaps a bit further loosened than usual by lack of sleep and the lingering effects of the punch. Apparently, he talked boldly about the broad issues of security intelligence and waxed on about how a democracy needs to protect itself, while also being concerned about the danger of destroying itself in the process.

To his surprise, he was shortly thereafter asked to become director of research for the McDonald Commission. Before agreeing to serve, he sought the good counsel of John Edwards at the University of Toronto. Together they made a list of issues that needed to be investigated for the commission to succeed. That list became the basis for a discussion paper published by Peter and the commissioners setting out the key policy issues faced by the commission ('Freedom and Security: An Analysis of Policy Issues before the Commission of Inquiry,' Ottawa, 1978). Going public in this way at the outset of the inquiry exemplifies Russell's approach to research – try and generate as much and as varied discussion as possible. This method contributed not only to the quality of the final report of the commission, but also to the development of academic inquiry in this area as well. The commission's three-volume report, *Freedom and Security under the Law* (Ottawa: Queen's Printer, 1981), recommended establishing a new civilian security service with a full range of investigative powers and a variety of controls on the activities of the service, including statutory definition of the threats to Canadian security, judicial approval of all surveillance warrants, full ministerial direction and responsibility, as well as an independent review committee to oversee the activities of the service. Peter's long association with Australia also began with the commission, for he first went there in late 1979 to see how similar issues and problems were handled by the Hope Commission.

In so far as many of its recommendations were put into practice, the McDonald Report was highly influential at the level of public policy. It led, for example, to the creation of the civilian Canadian Security Intelligence Service (CSIS) separate from the RCMP, as well as the Security Intelligence Review Committee (SIRC) to oversee the operations of CSIS. Among academics, the commission's discussion paper and final report became a major spawning ground for research in the emerging field of security-intelligence studies. The field quickly matured with the founding of the Canadian Association of Security Intelligence Studies (CASIS), in which Peter also had a hand.

Summary of Papers

The first of the three papers on security intelligence is by Ronald Atkey, who served as first chairman of SIRC. In his remarks (chapter 8), Atkey recognizes Peter Russell's key role not only in establishing the oversight process for CSIS but also over many subsequent years in encouraging and helping refine the activities of SIRC. Atkey details Peter's early advice to SIRC on how to proceed with its mission. He tells of the finesse with which Peter later discussed the sensitive question of whether Canadians should create an agency to gather foreign intelligence. And he sets out the overall orientation of SIRC's efforts by presenting his own response to the often sharp criticism directed at SIRC by a former senior official of the security establishment. Most notable is Atkey's broad interpretation of SIRC's mandate, a matter pursued in Reg Whitaker's paper below.

With 'Designing a Balance between Freedom and Security' (chapter 9), Reg Whitaker shows how Russell's work on the McDonald Commission relates to deeper themes of democratic accountability and the rule of law at the centre of nearly all of Russell's work. Noting the tension between the public interest in the propriety of CSIS's activities and the state's interest in protecting the details of its operations and methods, Whitaker is particularly critical of the limited and ineffective role played by parliamentary committees. Sensing an overall drift away from effective accountability, he argues that the focus has been too exclusively on overseeing the activities of a specific institution, CSIS, and not on the overall security-intelligence function of government in all its forms.

Jean-Paul Brodeur, in 'The Invention of Outsiders' (chapter 10), offers a cautionary tale regarding the continuing closed nature of CSIS. He moves beyond Whitaker's broader concerns with a telling example of how insular CSIS has remained, directly at odds with the original purposes of creating a civilian security service. Brodeur's case study concentrates on the tension between the academic and the practical progeny of Russell's efforts on behalf of the McDonald Commission. While echoing Whitaker's concern for closer parliamentary supervision of CSIS and related agencies, Brodeur also considers possible drawbacks to simply increasing parliamentary oversight. In concluding, he recalls and endorses the nuanced approach of the commission, aimed at ensuring the democratic accountability of Canada's security-intelligence services.

8

Overseeing Security Intelligence

RONALD G. ATKEY

Let me share with you some historical anecdotes related to my role as the first chairman of the Security Intelligence Review Committee (SIRC). I begin by addressing Phillip Stenning's introductory remarks about my book and his allusion to Jeffrey Archer. Whether *The Chancellor's Fool* is entertaining or not, the real reason why I wrote fiction was the same reason that a fellow called John Starnes wrote fiction and another person who changed his name to Le Carré wrote fiction. It is impossible to write in the field of security intelligence as a political matter without either revealing secrets (which no one wants to do) or hurting your friends and professional colleagues. So there you have it – the book does not have anything to do with CSIS or SIRC. If its entertainment value assists anybody in understanding how people think and function in the mysterious world of security intelligence, then maybe something was accomplished.

When I arrived in Ottawa in the late autumn of 1984, having just been named the first chairman of SIRC, I knew precious little about security intelligence. By that time I had read the legislation. On one occasion some six years previously I had met Mr Justice McDonald at a cocktail party. I found him engaging, intelligent, and committed to his task. I had already asked the staff at the Privy Council Office (PCO) to make available to me all the volumes of the McDonald Report and as many of the background studies as could be located. And of course I had a passing knowledge of what the commission had been all about, what had caused its formation, and how it had made sweeping recommendations, including establishment of a separate civilian security-intelligence service for Canada. I had not met the other two commissioners, one of whom I note is here today, but I had read a bit about Ted Finn and his role within the Department of the Solicitor General in overseeing the transition from the RCMP to a separate civilian body, followed up by his appointment as the first director of CSIS.

But I had been around Toronto long enough, at the University of Toronto, to know Peter Russell as a formidable and powerful intellect, who, as director of Research, made the McDonald Commission. This fact had become readily apparent to me after a few days on the job in Ottawa. After combing through the three volumes of the McDonald Report and then the legislation establishing CSIS, I even had the temerity to go back into the legislative history and review all the committee and parliamentary debates. I guess I was not really surprised when I kept seeing the name Peter Russell coming to the fore. I happened to mention this at one of our first meetings of SIRC. Several colleagues, who had a more extensive parliamentary experience than I and were widely read, said that they had noticed this too in their preliminary preparation and wondered if I knew him. I said that I had come into contact with him while I was teaching at Osgoode Hall Law School of York University. Later, after serving for one term in Parliament I had run into him while teaching a course at the Faculty of Law, University of Toronto – a place where Russell was regarded as a bit of an icon in matters of constitutional politics and the Supreme Court of Canada. One colleague, Saul Cherniack, former treasurer in Ed Schreyer's government in Manitoba, asked me if I would introduce him to Russell. Another colleague, Jean-Jacques Blais, a former solicitor-general in the Trudeau government, suggested that we invite him up for dinner. It was our executive director, Maurice Archdeacon, a former general in the Canadian military and a man of considerably more practical experience in matters of security intelligence, who suggested that SIRC probably owed its existence to Peter Russell, since he had probably conceived of the notion of an independent review body to oversee CSIS in his capacity as research director for the McDonald Commission.

It was in this way that we at SIRC came to the realization that we were really 'Peter's Baby.' We realized of course that there were many other great minds that laboured long and hard over the basis for establishing CSIS and the basis of some kind of review or oversight mechanism. But apparently it was Russell who was there at the conception.

It was not too long before we were grappling with our mandate under the CSIS Act, and some of us on SIRC thought that we ought to get some outside advice as to how we should go about our work. The statute was fairly vague, and the government did not seem to have any preconceived idea about what it wanted SIRC to do, other than ensure that members of CSIS obeyed the law. CSIS had no fully developed concept of what it saw as SIRC's role, although it would always suggest that any doubt or ambiguity in the statute he resolved in favour of doing less rather than more.

Well, we did seek some outside help. I remember actually organizing an academic seminar up at a place called Meech Lake. It was the first time that I had met an impressive young academic from the Université de Montreal, Jean-Paul Brodeur. I remember that there was another articulate long-haired radical from York University, Reg Whitaker, who had all kinds of approaches to suggest. We actually asked these academics how they thought we should go about doing our job. Peter Russell was there and gave some good common-sense advice. We met with him after the formal seminar to follow up on some of our discussions. We were still in our infancy, just learning to walk, and he was very good at nurturing us, and in fact he nursed us along to what he saw as the most important part of our job.

I remember vividly the three points that he made to us at that post-seminar meeting. First, the most important part of your job is the questions you ask to the service; make sure that they are full questions, and do not 'pussy-foot' around. Second, make sure that you get answers to all your questions, full answers; and do not hesitate to seek follow-up answers where they are warranted. And third, when you believe that you have all the answers related to a certain field or issue and decide to act, whether through a report to the solicitor-general or through your annual report to Parliament or through comments to the public, make sure that you do so unanimously; as a review body, you have no power unless you can speak with one voice that reflects a carefully considered view of the bi-partisan membership of the committee.

All three pieces of advice proved very sound. But the last, about speaking with one voice, may have been the most crucial. The nature of our appointments as mandated by the CSIS Act meant that some of our members were in effect nominated by the leaders of the opposition parties in the House. But all appointments were made by the prime minister in consultation with the leaders of the opposition parties. Out of necessity this involved some consultation with members of the various parliamentary caucuses shadowing the solicitor-general and his parliamentary assistant. In the end, we were able to reconcile that consultation with both the confidential and frank discussions that we had at the SIRC meetings and the unanimous positions with which we emerged, which were quite critical of some aspects of CSIS and its operations in the early years. These led to changes in how security clearances were conducted and how targets were assessed and caused the disbanding of the counter-subversion branch of CSIS. Already Peter Russell's advice was having an impact.

Two or three years into our mandate, we were no longer 'Peter's Baby,' but more like 'Peter's Child.' As we learned how to walk, sometimes run, we still stumbled occasionally in our zeal to achieve perfection. It was one of these stumbles on a difficult issue that caused us to call Russell back in for further consultation. This was on an issue that was controversial, sensitive, and potentially divisive among members of SIRC and almost sure to raise hackles within the government no matter what position we took. The question was simple: should Canada establish a foreign intelligence agency?

Now that is a tough subject to ask anyone to address in a public context. It is almost guaranteed to produce a *Globe and Mail* editorial. I know that there are some within the government, if not in academe, who would regard the very subject as somehow 'un-Canadian,' since it suggests a Canadian-style CIA conducting covert operations abroad on instructions from Ottawa.

I identified with remarks today from University of Toronto President Robert Pritchard when he said that when there was a tough job to do in the university one called on Peter Russell. Well, at SIRC we had a tough subject to address, it was not a matter that could be easily ignored, and so we called on Peter Russell. Within a few months, he produced a neat little paper of some twenty-four pages, which I pulled out of my personal archives yesterday. It was presented to SIRC in December 1988, and after almost eight years it stands up well. In fact, I do not think that it was 'classified,' so it should be published.

Now Russell's answer to the question 'Should Canada establish a foreign intelligence agency?' was perhaps what you might expect from a lawyer. He said that his answer was both 'yes' and 'no.' First, he said that Canada should not establish a separate foreign intelligence agency because it was too expensive and the risks of accident were too high, even though some of our allies might actually like us to do so, to help in developing reliable foreign information that could be shared. But he noted that Canada, by not having any such capacity beyond its borders, had given up a bit of its sovereignty as a member of G-7 and made decisions on international matters relying on the intelligence of foreign states – primarily the United States and Britain – without any assurance that it was totally valid and reliable for Canadian purposes. He suggested that this was an infringement if not a diminution of Canadian sovereignty, leaving us hostage to the information provided by foreign intelligence agencies.

So he came up with the answer, providing the basis of his 'yes' response. It was what we use to call the 'two little words' solution. Those familiar with the CSIS Act will know that section 16 empowers the minister for foreign affairs (then the secretary of state for external affairs) to assist him or her in the collection of information 'relating to the capabilities, intentions or activities' of foreign states 'within Canada.' Russell's proposal was simply to remove the words 'within Canada' from section 16, suggesting that if Canada needed to increase its capacity to collect and analyse information about foreign sources of threats to its internal security, it would be better to strengthen the capabilities of CSIS and External Affairs than to establish a new intelligence agency.

Russell's advice on this matter, as on so many others, was both clear and practical. In our case he also dealt with political realities, and I quote: 'There is also some political hazard in putting forward the proposal publicly. Espionage, like sex, is a juicy, titillating subject which journalists love to exploit. The simple suggestion of removing two little words from section 16 would probably raise some eyebrows and inspire some innuendo, but I doubt that the proposal would raise a storm. Many Canadians will appreciate the good sense of removing a self-imposed handcuff on our country's capacity to collect foreign intelligence abroad.' Those were wise words. Only time will tell whether the advice is actually heeded. Nevertheless, Russell has established the benchmark for both reasonableness and progress in this area, and that is what is important

The period SIRC moved towards the end of its first five years and I approached the end of my term in the chair were more aking to our 'teenage years.' Our wise and careful parent was still watching over us. I remember participating in a conference sponsored by the Canadian Association for Security and Intelligence Studies (CASIS) in Ottawa, just a month before my departure. SIRC had come under a stinging indictment from the beloved John Starnes, who had been the first civilian director general of the RCMP Security Service in the 1970s and who had long since retired to write novels and critical articles in the *Ottawa Citizen.* I was jolted by the intensity of Starnes's attack, which alleged that SIRC had gone too far, exceeded its mandate, and effectively changed the intention of the CSIS Act. He wrote that Parliament, in conducting the first five-year review of the act, and the prime minister, in determining who should be appointed or reappointed, should take into account that this first group of five members was 'out of control.'

Now, in defending SIRC against these charges, I had occasion to reflect on the earlier advice given to us by Peter Russell, because a good deal of what Starnes criticized us for was very much what we thought Peter Russell would have wanted us to do. Let me review each of the five charges made by Starnes, to all of which, representing all of my colleagues on SIRC, I pleaded guilty.

First, he accused us of expanding the concept of review and asking questions about the Communications Security Establishment (CSC), the Department of National Defence (DND), the Department of External Affairs (DEA), and the National Security Intelligence Section (NSIS) of the RCMP; we had been brash enough to suggest that there might be some kind of independent supervision of the intelligence activities of these departments and agencies.

Second, he accused us of floating ideas and suggestions on the prickly issue of whether Canada should have an independent office of national assessments, implying certain shortcomings within existing arrangements at the PCO, and on the more controversial issue of whether CSIS should be allowed to gather information on operations abroad under section 16.

Third, Starnes accused us of informing the public. He attacked us for publishing a diagram illustrating the intelligence network in Canada for the purpose of explaining to the public a complex set of institutional relationships that even we had difficulty understanding in our infant years. Our published diagram had removed all national security information.

Fourth, he accused us of examining the CSIS budget, thereby infringing on the territorial preserve of the Treasury Board and the auditor general.

Fifth and finally, he accused us of investigating the policy, operations, and management of the service, particularly regarding its operations in infiltrating organized labour, and therefore had eroded CSIS's credibility with the public and with the foreign security-intelligence agencies with which CSIS must work.

I pleaded guilty at the time to each of these accusations. I referred to the broad language of the CSIS Act and also to the rich legislative history behind it, which owes so much to Peter Russell and which Reg Whitaker has so ably reviewed.

I guess the final satisfaction for my colleagues and me was a post mortem that we conducted following the CASIS conference when we reviewed Starnes's attack, each item of his indictment, and our plea of guilty as to how and why we had gone about our work. Essentially, we felt that all of Starnes's criticisms missed the point. None of us had any confusion over this, because we were able to hark back to those early days when we sought advice as to how to do our job and Peter Russell had so ably pointed the way. And we felt then, as we feel now, that Peter Russell would have been proud of his baby.

9

Designing a Balance between Freedom and Security

REG WHITAKER

Introduction

Peter Russell's scholarly career has been extraordinarily multifaceted. One of the byways that bears his scholarly imprint is the arcane world of security intelligence. His work as research director for the McDonald Commission of Inquiry on the RCMP security service is an important contribution to public policy-making in Canada. This was one commission that had very concrete results, in the passage of the Canadian Security Intelligence Service (CSIS) Act of 1984 and its creation of CSIS. This was not just a Canadian event, but one that has had echoes and repercussions elsewhere as well, not least in the United Kingdom, where the Canadian experience arising out of the commission has been frequently cited as a model to be followed – a historic reversal of the traditional roles of the 'mother of parliaments' and her daughter.

If Russell's interest in a world that I have just described as arcane were of the order of aficionados of spy fiction and of the kind of fiction about espionage that sometimes passes as journalism, this would have represented simply a charming diversion from his scholarly project, not unlike his love of baseball. But his immersion in the spy world relates in a most compelling way to the deeper themes of his political science: the rule of law in a liberal society and the accountability of the state to Parliament and public. Put in this way, the secret world of spies is anything but a diversion; instead it represents a hard case, perhaps the hardest of all, of how to balance the need for liberty with the requirements of security and order in a free society.

Generations of liberal thinkers have passed in silence by the twilight world of secret police, security screening, informers and undercover agents, intercepted communications, surveillance dossiers, and occasional dark deeds done in the night. In some instances this silence was dictated by what one can only call wilful ignorance – out of sight, out of mind. In others, it was a prim, smug silence: one simply does not stir up these matters so as to sully the good name of liberal society. In yet other cases, silence arose from the agenda of a more muscular liberalism: a free society can and should defend itself against its enemies by the most efficient means, but dwelling on the details can only assist those enemies.

These forms of indulgent silence have sometimes nurtured monsters in the shadows. The spectre of J. Edgar Hoover, ruthless intimidator of both the powerless and the otherwise powerful, is a repulsive gargoyle that will be for ever fixed on the edifice of American society.[1] Even in the absence of such grotesques, the existence of the secret state still poses acute problems for the theory and practice of liberalism – problems that demand answers, not silences.

Peter Russell and the McDonald Commission

In Canada in the 1970s, our secret state – one that had functioned with relatively impressive smoothness and efficiency for decades – became, for a variety of reasons, publicly and embarrassingly unstuck.[2] It was no longer possible to pass by in silence, as public accusations and revelations of illegalities and wrongdoing by the security service became rampant. This dilemma led to a number of official inquiries, the most notable being Quebec's Commission d'enquête sur des opérations policières en Térritoire Québécois (Keable Commission) appointed in 1981 by the Quebec government and the federal Commission of Inquiry Concerning Certain Activities of the Royal Canadian Mounted Police (McDonald Commission). Peter Russell was for two years research director of this latter commission. In this paper I purpose to examine the legacy of its mammoth report (some 2,000 pages in its published version), especially the important concept of public accountability that it developed.

One should not confuse the McDonald Report with Russell himself. A research director does not write commission recommendations. Although he or she may have influence over the commissioners, the latter may have their own very different agendas. In the case of the McDonald Commission, we have good reason to believe that Russell went a long way towards defining the program of the commissioners. Very early in the history of the commission, he wrote a brief but very concise analysis of the pertinent policy issues.[3] In this document he set out, with considerable precision, the parameters of the debate with which the Commission would have to wrestle and pinpointed the major institutional and procedural foci for reform. He raised a series of questions addressed to each specific area of study, pointing both towards where more information was required and to the policy and ethical issues involved in each.

In a section called 'Governance of the Security Service' he neatly summed up the underlying dilemma:

> Government direction and control of a security service create dilemmas for democracies. Responsible and democratic government means a government whose activities are directed by Ministers and officials responsible to elected representatives and whose policies are open to informed public discussion. The activities of a security service, typically, are directed against those who use stealth, deception or criminal means to accomplish their ends. Consequently, to be successful these activities must be carried out with a great deal of secrecy. A security service that is truly an 'open book' is a contradiction in terms. But a security service accountable only to itself is incompatible with democracy. Clearly the best arrangements for supervising the work of the security service must be found somewhere between these extremes.
>
> There is another principle at stake in the proper governance of the Security Service. In a democracy it is essential that constitutional competition between contending parties be free from police or other coercive interference by anyone, including the government of the day. Hence it is extremely important that the Security Service is never used for pursuing the partisan advantage (or disadvantage) of the party in power or for attacking (or promoting) its constitutional rivals. In assessing the means of ensuring adequate government direction of the Security Service, the need to guard against this danger must always be kept in mind.[4]

I have quoted these passages at length for two reasons. First, they illustrate nicely Russell's essential contribution to our understanding of the governance of security intelligence in a liberal democracy: the difficult balance that must be struck between the partly contradictory but complementary needs for security and for freedom. Russell is at one neither with those liberals who prefer to pass by the secret state in silence nor with those civil libertarian critics who, for whatever fine motives, ignore the necessity of liberal states' using less than liberal means to protect liberalism itself from extraordinary threats. This nuanced and balanced temper infused the McDonald Commission's overall approach to devising practical ways of dealing with the problem and is caught in the title of the two massive volumes of the commission's second report, the substantive meat of its work: *Freedom and Security under the Law.*

The other reason is found in the second paragraph quoted, citing the dangers of political misuse of a security service, as opposed to the dangers of a security service 'accountable only to itself.' Here there may be a subtle, but important difference between the approaches of Peter Russell and those of the commissioners. Having recently examined both the commission and its time in the light of previously classified documentation, I have somewhat reluctantly concluded that the commission played a political role in the interpretation of the facts that displaced a share of the blame away from the Liberal government of Pierre Trudeau and onto the shoulders of the RCMP security service, which was in effect set up as a lightning rod to divert public displeasure. A close reading at the time of the opaque and sometimes convoluted prose of the commission's third and final report, *Certain RCMP Activities and the Question of Government Knowledge*, should have revealed that the commission's recommendations were not in every instance launched straight down the runway. It was less politically awkward to argue that the government had a security service problem that needed fixing than to argue that it was part of the problem and thus required fixing itself as part of the solution.

To be fair to the commission, it did have a broader vision for reform that involved the 'civilianization' (to use a peculiar Canadianism) of the RCMP security service and the foundation of a new agency on a firm statutory basis with a precise mandate, along with mechanisms to ensure various forms of accountability. All of these laudable goals, the theory and practice of which are the focus of this paper, would not likely have been implemented if the commission had prefaced its policy prescriptions with stern public admonitions about the shortcomings of the very government that was receiving the recommendations. The commissioners were well aware that a predecessor commission in the 1960s had also recommended civilianization of the security service and had seen its ideas trampled by the concerted opposition of the RCMP and its allies within government.[5]

Going easy on the Liberals might have been interpreted as purely partisan in and of itself, but as a political strategy for achieving a more fundamental set of reforms it was not without merit. I am pausing over this aspect of the McDonald Commission, however, for a reason: a notion of accountability that stresses the need to bring the security service under political control, however important this may be (as Russell correctly pointed out) may distract attention from a problem potentially just as dangerous, or perhaps even more so – possible misuse of a security service and its extraordinary powers by a government, or a political party, for its own partisan purposes. The latter possibility has not generally received equivalent attention. Despite Russell's admonition, and despite some passages in the McDonald Report pointing to the general problem, the latter did not receive as much study as it should have. This oversight is rooted in the particular circumstances of reform. This is a point to which I return as we look first at the development of CSIS and its governing legislation and then at its first decade or so of operation.

Striking the Balance

The problem that McDonald grappled with is easy to state but extremely difficult to solve in a practical way. The problem is two-fold. First, how does a liberal-democratic state defend itself against threats to its security that seek to take advantage of its very liberalism to undermine it? Second, how does such a state defend its own liberal practices from being undermined by the extraordinary and illiberal methods necessarily employed to combat such threats? The two elements of the problem are inseparable. Indeed, it is an elementary fallacy – one unfortunately reproduced in countless political and bureaucratic rationalizations over the years – that the second problem is one for public policy discussion, while the first is one best left behind closed doors. To be sure, secrecy is a sine qua non of meeting threats that are themselves secret. Of course, the operational methodology of security services will be protected from outside scrutiny. Obviously security forces will insist on the anonymity of their undercover agents and secret sources. However, stating these truisms does not exhaust the legitimate public interest in the first question.

If the definition of what constitutes a threat to security is effectively left to the executive and/or the agency in question, and if there is no standard to judge the propriety or efficacy of the means employed to counter such threats, no mechanism of public accountability, review, or oversight after the fact can have any effect. Thus central to any workable concept of accountability must be the provision of a legal mandate specifying the terms on which the agency is engaged, the broad definition of the threats about which it is empowered to gather information, and the appropriate and proportionate means that it may employ. This mandate, elaborated by ministerial directions and guidelines, interpreted by the courts, and given flesh and blood in the actual practices of the agency, is the text against which review and oversight bodies can read performance.

Given the inevitable constraints of secrecy surrounding the operations of security services, there is an inescapable tension between the public interest in the legitimacy of both the ends and the means and the state's interest in protecting the details of operations and methods. Designing appropriate mechanisms that keep both these concerns in balance is a complex task of statecraft that involves more than clarity of principle and precision in legislative drafting; it also requires political skill and prudence – qualities notoriously difficult to prescribe.

Propriety and Efficacy

There is a central ambiguity in the concept of accountability, or at least a dualistic element that leads to ambiguity if there is no conceptual clarity. Accountability may refer to propriety or to efficacy. In practice, it invariably refers to both, but the two senses should be distinguished conceptually, since each entails a somewhat different mechanism of accountability. Propriety refers to compliance with law and with ethical norms, in relation both to ends and to means. Are the goals of the security service appropriately framed in relation to the values of the society? Are the methods used ethically acceptable in the light of the goals and of democratic values? Efficacy tends to focus on the relation of means to given ends: are they efficient and giving value for money?

This leads to another dimension of accountability: to whom is the agency accountable? Here we can distinguish four actors to whom forms of accountability may be directed: the executive, judicial, and legislative branches of government and a more diffuse concept of the public. Executive accountability relates mainly to efficacy: is the agency doing what the executive has asked it to do, and how effectively and efficiently? Judicial accountability relates almost exclusively to propriety: is the activity in compliance with law? Legislative accountability is usually more mixed, combining concerns about efficacy and propriety in shifting emphases, depending on the issues and orientation of members. Public accountability is also less predictable but has tended to focus more on propriety than on efficacy, first because there is less information available about the latter, and secondly because the public, especially the media (which mediate the public's perceptions of the secret world), respond to scandal and malfeasance more than to the complicated, arcane, and often rather humdrum details of the institutions and processes at work. Or, if the media/public does perceive an efficacy issue, it does so more often than not through the lens of a scandal: how did the CIA allow Soviet mole Aldrich Ames to get away with his activities for so long?

Not only does the dependence of legislative reform on the appearance of scandals that are irresolvable through normal channels encourage a certain dysfunctional rhythm to the politics of policy-making in security intelligence,[6] but the political nature of the scandal that precipitates legislative reform imparts a particular coloration to the reforms themselves. The McDonald Commission was a response to a set of scandals that had engulfed a government and its security service. The CSIS Act reform that followed both reflected and attempted to camouflage this political coloration.

Once the act was set in legislative mould, the question of what precise form it would take in practice remained to be answered. We are now more than ten years from that legislative innovation, and we have the benefit of the five-year parliamentary review, mandated in the act, as well as a decade of public annual reports from the Security Intelligence Review Committee (SIRC) and any number of other SIRC reports, as well as inspector generals' reports, available in truncated form through Access to Information requests. Taken together with the labyrinthine pre-CSIS findings of the McDonald Commission, and some adhoc government task-force reports and official responses, and a unique survey by the auditor general's office, not to speak of transcripts of parliamentary hearings, they form a comparative wealth of information stamped with various forms of official imprimaturs and made available to researchers and journalists. Add to this the material released under Access requests for internal CSIS documentation, and we have a startling contrast to the near-total silence that embargoed virtually all information about the workings of the secret state before the 1980s. In some ways it may even be considered an embarrassment of riches – only a specialist, whether academic or journalistic, can sufficiently master all this information to make much sense of it all. Unfortunately it would appear that so far as journalism goes – and thus so far as any real public awareness goes – there is no informed continuity of coverage. Instead, discontinuous spurts of attention arise from time to time when real or apprehended scandals or otherwise sexy security stories spur short-term focus on the part of the flighty foxes of the media. It is thus fascinating to note that a policy of information management that relies on relative overflow is just as successful as a policy of stonewalling in deflecting public notice – and a good deal more effective at self-legitimation. But perhaps that was always the point.

However, even if a surfeit of information fails to extend the instant-titillation attention spans of the foxes, it does allow a few hedgehogs in the academy to burrow away at small cottage industries on security intelligence. This paper may be taken as a report from one such industry.[7]

From C-175 to the CSIS Act, via Pitfield and Russell

We do have the benefit of one clear statement of Peter Russell of his views about these matters, both as reflective of and distinct from the McDonald Report. In 1983, he published a critical commentary on the Liberal government's first, ill-fated attempt at a legislative reform, Bill C-175.[8] After this bill met with a veritable storm of criticism, from everyone from the provincial solicitors-general to a broad spectrum of representations from civil society, the cabinet executed an elegant legislative manoeuvre by having the former clerk of the Privy Council and now senator Michael Pitfield chair a Senate Special Committee to receive public representations and to send a revised bill back to the Commons.[9] This proposed revision, largely accepted by the government, was finally enacted as the CSIS Act. Russell's pointed evaluation of C-175 ('not bad,' but 'can do much better') is a useful starting point for assessing not only how much improvement there was in the second draft over the first, but how the accountability system has performed over its first decade.

Russell begins his 1983 article by reflecting on why governments have been so reluctant to draft legislative mandates for their security and intelligence agencies. Finding the right balance between freedom and security will always rouse criticism from one side or the other. Governments have generally tried to evade the responsibility of enacting statutory mandates, preferring the unwritten and informal. Doing the thing at all was thus admirable, but how well was it doing it?

Russell focused on three areas: the range of targets for the agency's surveillance; the methods permitted; and the means of monitoring and controlling the agency's activities.

Defining Threats to Security

C-175 received a low grade on the definition of threats to security. The 'bias' of the bill, Russell wrote, was 'strongly toward ensuring there are no undesirable gaps' in the mandate, rather than towards protecting citizens. In other words, the balance was tipped too far towards security. For instance: 'political violence and terrorism' were not qualified by the term 'serious,' thus suggesting too low a threshold for triggering the agency's attention. The Pitfield Committee did not incorporate this suggestion among its recommendations, but section 2(d) of the CSIS Act does – 'Activities ... directed toward or in support of the threat or use of acts of serious violence against persons or property for the purpose of achieving a political objective.' Thus the demonstrator who throws a tomato at a politician is not automatically a target for CSIS surveillance, unless of course there are other circumstances that would trigger an investigation.

C-175 included a definition of 'subversion.' Russell does not challenge this as such but does note that McDonald had recommended that such a definition be confined to revolutionary subversion and had preferred that 'constitutionally established system of government in Canada' be replaced by 'democratic' system of government. Additionally, 'undermining' should replace 'overthrowing.' McDonald had further recommended that only non-intrusive techniques be employed against subversion – a point never embodied in the legislation, though subsequently a subject of ministerial guidelines. As for the McDonald views about the drafting of the subversion threat, Pitfield rejected them as actually making the definition too elastic, rather than tightening it, as the Senate committee preferred. In the event, the government took neither kind of advice and re-enacted in the CSIS Act the very same wording in section 2(d) as had appeared in C-175.

The legislative mandate is important for placing the security-intelligence agency on a firm legal footing and circumscribing the boundaries of its legitimate activities. Here the CSIS Act is quite exemplary, in that it not only describes what the agency is empowered to investigate but also what it is not to get involved in. This favourably distinguishes its mandate from even the more recent legislative innovations in the United Kingdom – the Security Service Act and the Intelligence Services Act, neither of which offers a definition of what the agencies in question should not do, as opposed to what they might do. The mandate is quite important from the perspective of accountability, in that it does present more than a moral argument against surveillance of 'lawful advocacy, protest and dissent': unless such activities are reasonably believed to be carried on in conjunction with one or more of the defined threats to security, surveillance will be strictly illegal, not just improper. Even today in the United Kingdom, for instance, MI5 or Special Branch intrusive surveillance of peace and ecological groups may provoke some unfavourable public commentary, when known, but does not overstep any legal barriers, even, it would appear, those protected by the European Court of Human Rights at Strasbourg. By contrast, CSIS is quick to affirm that it does not spy on the legal Quebec sovereignist parties, the Parti Québécois and the Bloc Québécois. It is possible, of course, that CSIS is misrepresenting its activities in this regard, but if it were to be caught out in such a misrepresentation, it would find itself in quite serious trouble. This is in itself a deterrent against the agency's casting drift nets across whole stretches of civil society, the way the old RCMP security service once did. Moreover, because the legislative mandate is intimately related to the cabinet's directions and guidelines for the agency, these documents, to the extent that they have been made public, do appear to impress on the agency the gravity of targeting decisions and the requirement that the method of gathering intelligence be consistent with the principles of the mandate.[10]

So far so good. There are, however, some apparent flaws in the fabric of the mandate. Foremost is the so-called definition of 'subversion' referred to above – definition 2(d) of threats to security: 'activities directed toward undermining by covert unlawful acts, or directed toward or intended ultimately to lead to the destruction or overthrow by violence of, the constitutionally established system of government in Canada.' This has been widely criticised as dangerously expansive, not least by SIRC in its submission to the five-year parliamentary review committee, which called for its removal. The failure of the government to remove, or even modify, this definition is all the more reprehensible when the Conservatives, acting on the recommendations of both SIRC and a special task force headed by the respected former senior public servant Gordon Osbaldeston, ordered termination of the Counter-Subversion section of CSIS in 1987 and removal from the agency of most of its files, either by destruction or by transferral to the National Archives.[11] As wise as such an administrative decision undoubtedly was, it should have been matched by a modification of the mandate to reflect the new appreciation of the unsuitability of 'subversion' as a targeting criterion. It still has not been. If the McDonald Commission, and even Peter Russell, thinking within the shadow of the still-threatening Cold War in the early 1980s, were unable or unwilling to go beyond tinkering with the definition of subversion, the time has since passed for any further dalliance with any such definition, however framed.

Methods Permitted

Russell in 1983 looked at the matter of judicial warrants for securing listening devices and wiretaps. He wanted closer ministerial supervision of such intrusive investigative methods than C-175 provided, and the CSIS Act – 21(1) – requires prior approval by the minister before a warrant application is sought. Some other complaints were also addressed. The Pitfield Committee wanted inclusion of the language of the McDonald Report on conditions required to be satisfied before warrants were sought; they were, in 21(2)(b). Time limits were placed on warrants (and shorter limits on any 2[d] investigations), and applications for extensions not only require ministerial approval but must meet specific criteria (21[5] and 22[a] and [b]). Of course, the issuance of judicial warrants is not subject to much public scrutiny, except when something goes very wrong, as it did with the regard to the application that led to the resignation of the first director of CSIS, Ted Finn. Warrants have been the subject of a number of studies undertaken by SIRC, but we have to take that body's word on trust that it has found little amiss in practice. Proposals for a 'devil's advocate' to argue against CSIS applications suggest a feeling in some quarters of a need for internal checks and balances, but more recent changes have been inspired more by a desire to streamline the process and make it faster and less bureaucratically cumbersome; as a result, CSIS claims that the number of warrants sought has been declining as it has applied more rigorous criteria.[12] Again, we do have to take all this more or less on trust.

One provision in C-175 that drew Russell's fire was a 'catch-all' clause that would have had the effect of allowing CSIS agents to break the law with impunity. Section 21, 'certainly the most controversial provision,' according to Pitfield, stated that CSIS employees would be 'justified in taking such reasonable actions as are reasonably necessary to enable them to perform the duties and functions of the Service under the Act.' CSIS, Russell stated flatly, should be required to operate within the law, or – and here he was squeamish – permissible infringements should be specified. The CSIS Act drops the offending clause. Instead, section 20 specifies that CSIS officers have the same protection under the law as peace officers and that any unlawful activity must be reported to the attorney general of Canada, and SIRC informed. The original section 21 was obviously disastrous, and its demise is entirely beneficial.

The McDonald Commission, Russell, and Pitfield were unable to figure out any way to appropriately include the use of human sources – the most intrusive of all methods – under the specified jurisdiction of the mandate. The CSIS Act is silent on the matter. The problem is one that has inevitably tipped the famous balance in the direction of security. However, Russell and McDonald did suggest that this kind of activity is best dealt with by administrative guidelines, and Russell particularly wanted a strong ministerial presence in the process. Human sources have posed possible problems of propriety in a few cases during CSIS's lifetime: the two most prominent are the Boivin affair involving alleged infiltration of the Quebec labour movement[13] and, most recently and most notoriously, the Grant Bristow affair.[14]

As a result of the Bristow affair and various Access to Information requests, we now have a better idea of the broad outline of administrative guidelines and the role of the minister in approving the use of human sources, as well as some idea of how things have worked in practice.[15] Although the Bristow affair leaves some lingering doubts about some aspects of the use and control of human sources, fears about lack of a legislative framework for the use of human sources, while not groundless, have in practice been allayed by the apparent willingness of successive governments and CSIS directors to develop and apply fairly rigorous administrative guidelines. Planting undercover agents and sources in organizations deemed to constitute threats to security will inevitably involve messy and sometimes uncomfortable issues of propriety. From the point of view of efficacy, there is no doubt that human sources are among the most productive. The tension will therefore remain.

The First Decade

Looking back over the first decade of accountability under the CSIS Act model inevitably yields a mixed bag of observations. It would be agreeable to report some grand theoretical conclusions from this experience, that a model of accountability could be either verified or refuted. In fact, the Canadian 'model' is no more than a patchwork of institutional and procedural arrangements, the logic of which lies more in political contingency and historical happenstance than in any conscious attempt to embody an abstract conceptualization of 'accountability.' Of course, this is the way public policy usually gets made; it is only in the academy that the owl of Minerva takes flight. We can, however, break down the elements of accountability institutionalized in and around the CSIS Act to assess how well each has worked. One way of doing this is to address the sixteen 'main elements' that the McDonald Report proposed for 'government direction and independent review of the security intelligence agency.'[16] It broke these elements into two broad groupings – mechanisms of internal control and 'checks and balances from external sources.' In the former, which we might call executive accountability, the two major components are the legislative mandate and the mechanisms of direction and control by cabinet. We examined the former above, but the latter, while less obvious, are also very important.

C-157 was deficient in specifying the ministerial role in responsibility for CSIS. It limited the minister to general policy direction and prevented him or her from overriding the director of CSIS on targeting decisions and assessments of threats. Russell was adamant that this represented a misguided attempt to draw a line between policy supervision and operations that could not stand up in practice. The process, he sharply asserted, suggested an attempt to erect 'plausible deniability' into a statutory principle. This comes close to saying that in their first legislative draft, the Liberals were attempting to devise a mandate expressly to avoid their own responsibility. Security intelligence is not equivalent to criminal law enforcement, where arm's-length autonomy from political interference is an established principle. Russell pointed out that in matters of political policing (my phrase, not his), partisan misuse was a real danger, equal and opposite to that of 'not-so-benign neglect.' The answer, according to Russell, was to insist on full ministerial responsibility and then to put effective external oversight mechanisms in place.

The CSIS Act represents a major improvement over the first draft, in that it is much more decisive in assigning clear responsibility for CSIS operations to the solicitor-general and in specifying the chain of reporting from director to deputy minister to minister. While no institutional arrangement can completely prevent impropriety or inefficacy, ministerial 'deniability' is under the present framework inherently unlikely. If serious instances of impropriety do come to light, a minister pleading ignorance would necessarily be pleading incompetence – hardly a defence.

The McDonald Report stressed the need for structures to ensure cabinet coordination of policy, especially a 'hands-on' role for the prime minister in security intelligence. More than a decade on, bureaucratic coordination remains somewhat murky and opaque to outsiders. But one institutional mechanism specifically mentioned by the report has been discontinued altogether. McDonald recommended that among the prime minister's 'special dimensions' in this area was a responsibility to continue to chair the cabinet committee on security and intelligence and for the cabinet secretary and the PCO to support this committee. This committee appears to have been pretty much a dead letter throughout the two Mulroney governments. When his successor, Kim Campbell, was trimming her cabinet, she abolished the committee. Jean Chrétien has not reactivated it. There is thus no obvious mechanism available for either cabinet-level collective coordination or a specific prime-ministerial hand in the process. This would tend to suggest a greater burden on one minister, the solicitor-general, which the McDonald Report deemed unwise, or loose overall cabinet supervision, which is even more imprudent.

In confronting C-175, Russell noted acutely that if controls were only internal (that is, limited to executive accountability), there was a continuing danger of partisan misuse of the agency; thus review must be also be external, done by persons without ties to the governing party. There is, I believe, a subtext here about which the McDonald Commission was not very open. Much of the blame for the scandals of the 1970s could better be laid at the feet of the Trudeau government than of the RCMP security service. The civilianization thrust of the commission rather deflected attention away from the government to the shortcomings of the RCMP.

The commission did go to some lengths to lay out mechanisms for external review that would in practice, if adopted, act as checks on future partisan misuse of the agency. In this regard, Russell found C-157 wanting. The McDonald Report had called for a small, joint parliamentary committee of members of all parties, who could meet with officials in camera and report confidentially (with expurgated versions for public release). It also proposed an independent Advisory Council on Security and Intelligence (ACSI) and a quasi-judicial Security Appeals Tribunal (SAT), to hear individual complaints about security screening decisions. C-157, and the CSIS Act, made no provision for a permanent parliamentary committee. They merged the ACSI and the SAT into a single body, the Security Intelligence Review Committee (SIRC), which combined some of the features envisaged by the commission for both the parliamentary committee and ACSI/SAT. It further created another office, that of the inspector general (IG), quite unlike anything envisaged by the McDonald Report. Russell expressed particular distaste for the projected role of the IG, which he seems to have misconstrued as holding 'the primary responsibility for the continuous monitoring' of CSIS for compliance. Since this office was an innovation, Russell may be forgiven for mistaking its purpose. In practice, the IG is strictly an internal mechanism, but it acts in tandem with SIRC in 'continuous monitoring' of CSIS. It is worth a closer look.

The IG is a dedicated mechanism for executive accountability, which can serve as the 'eyes and ears' of the solicitor-general. Given the pre-CSIS evidence of, at best, faulty lines of communication between ministers and security bureaucrats or, at worst, either deliberate misleading of ministers or the cynical deployment of 'plausible deniability' by ministers to evade responsibility, a mechanism such as the IG is potentially useful, a tool for the minister and a window for the agency. It is difficult to evaluate the performance of successive IGs and their staffs, since we can only catch glimpses of the office in action through heavily censored Access to Information releases. There are some troubling structural limitations on the office, especially with regard to access to information. We know, for instance, that the government has chosen to interpret the notion of 'cabinet confidences' (excluded, rather than exempted, from the Access to Information Act for twenty years) as applying to cabinet communications to CSIS, to which the IG is denied access in principle (as is SIRC).

Russell was forthright in commenting on this clause in C-175: 'The sheer arrogance of this provision is simply numbing ... A government that is itself so distrustful is not entitled to the trust that this legislation demands from the people it represents.'[17] It is indeed very difficult to understand how the IG can be expected to act as the minister's eyes and ears in checking CSIS compliance with ministerial direction when access to such directives is denied – or how SIRC can properly perform its review functions in the absence of such information. Although we have the word of a former IG that this never proved to be a problem in practice, we have the same official's admission that if he had not known what to ask for, he might have failed to know what was being withheld – the usual Catch-22 in matters of information control.[18] We also know that one IG in the early 1990s, Ursula Menke, strongly criticized what she took to be unreasonable limitations on her access to CSIS documents, specifically records relating to ongoing investigations. The CSIS director rather hotly disputed her request by stating that practice had been to limit access to post-facto review only. Menke failed to make her point with the solicitor-general and left her post after a very short tenure to take a position in the private sector.[19]

If SIRC represents the substitute set up by the government for both the parliamentary and independent review and appeal mechanisms recommended by the McDonald Commission, a heavy burden rests on its shoulders. Indeed, it is SIRC that is the centrepiece of most assessments of the Canadian accountability system. In its form, it does represent a rather striking innovation in a parliamentary system of government. It is an independent body of privy councillors chosen in 'consultation' with the leaders of the official parties in Parliament who make annual reports to Parliament but otherwise report directly, and confidentially, to the solicitor-general. As an appeal board – for immigration and citizenship security cases, as well as public-service screening appeals – it operates as a quasi-judicial body, as well as an investigative and review body in its other guise. SIRC thus both offers the public face of accountability and performs a kind of quasi-executive accountability function as well, sometimes in a rather complex relationship to the office of the IG.

There is not the space here to give an overall evaluation of SIRC's performance since 1984. We can, however, try to assess in a preliminary manner how this unusual body has fulfilled the expectations of the McDonald Commission and Peter Russell for the three separate bodies first recommended. Some limits to the capacities of SIRC to perform its projected role are apparent. One of the most striking is the practical restriction on the access to information that SIRC has claimed to possess. I wrote about the 'cabinet confidences' exclusion, Russell's excoriation of such an omission, and SIRC's apparent unwillingness to challenge CSIS over access to records regarding ongoing investigations, as opposed to access ex post facto – although the commission anticipated this limitation. Recently there has come to light a 'Third Party Access Protocol,' signed by SIRC and CSIS, indicating that CSIS will notify foreign governments if SIRC requests documents that originate from that government and further suggests that CSIS 'will use its best efforts to obtain authority to disclose information provided by third parties when requested to do so by SIRC' – not necessarily a clear guarantee of unrestricted access.[20] Recently, SIRC had cause to complain formally when CSIS failed to provide a crucial document on the grounds that it had been returned to the donor agency.[21] Despite such obstacles, there is no reason to believe that when SIRC is launched on an authorized investigation CSIS deliberately stonewalls it. CSIS is unlikely, of course, to volunteer indications about where to look; the ball is presumably in the court of the SIRC investigators. But with experience and a modus vivendi worked out over the years, a reasonable degree of access to CSIS records can be assumed to exist in practice.

This modus vivendi points to a different kind of problem – a structural tension that will always exist in the functioning of any review agency. A close and generally non-antagonistic working relationship between the reviewer and the reviewed is preferable at one level, but suspect at another. It facilitates the flow of information and avoids destructive confrontations, especially when the much smaller and weaker review body will inevitably be more impaired by permanent hostility. Yet the review body may be lulled, or even 'captured,' by the agency that it is supposed to review. Much of the positive reputation of SIRC was built up by a record of relatively sturdy independence and aggressiveness in the early years. This was largely attributable to the forceful leadership of the first chairman, Ron Atkey, who was willing and able to use his political credentials with a Conservative government to build an independent niche for the fledgling committee. Unusually, Atkey was willing to describe his role as that of being a 'pain in the ass' to CSIS.[22] Few political appointees would welcome such a job description, and not surprisingly none of Atkey's successors have followed in his footsteps. In part, this situation may simply reflect the different requirements for establishing a new committee's credibility and status and for maintaining an already existing status. It also points to a decline in the quality of leadership in SIRC[23] and the Mulroney government's increasing willingness to treat later SIRC appointments as patronage plums with diminished requirements for merit. Finally, a kind of iron law of government affects review or regulatory agencies: sooner or later, usually sooner, they tend to lose some of their initial momentum and become institutionalized, routinized, even somewhat domesticated. Presumably there is nothing that can be done about this by legislative architecture, however skilful or well-intentioned. At best, we can hope that Atkey's energetic and aggressive leadership in the early years had a kind of ratchet effect that later routinization will never completely erase. One SIRC member, while being questioned by the Commons Subcommittee on National Security in 1996, twice within a few minutes spoke of CSIS in terms of 'we';[24] one is not reassured about the degree of independence.

Parliament and SIRC: A Tangled Knot

There is another kind of problem, perhaps more intractable, that arises out of SIRC's displacement of the joint parliamentary committee projected by the McDonald Report. In one sense, this dilemma can be seen as arising from the Trudeau government's desire to depoliticize the security issue, understandably enough in the light of the scandal-ridden 1970s. In another sense, it was a defensive thrust by a government that had rather a lot to hide. Keeping Parliament, and thus opposition parties, at arm's length from security matters could represent both depoliticization and political protection for the governing party. SIRC would have a majority of government appointees and was a more controlled instrument than a committee of potentially hyper-partisan parliamentarians. However, this depoliticization had a price: the 'consultation' with the leaders of the parliamentary parties in SIRC appointments. Later attempts have been made to played down the significance of this consultation, but the initial intention and the early practice seem quite clear. SIRC was to be broadly reflective of the parties in Parliament, thus assuring partisan consent to the limitation of Parliament's role. There was a special significance perhaps to the presence of an NDP member (first Saul Cherniack, later Rosemary Brown, and later yet the former premier of Ontario, Bob Rae) in that the NDP, as a third party, had generally been shut out of participation in the workings of the secret state.[25] An NDP-approved SIRC member thus provided reassurance to the NDP and legitimation for the process.

The CSIS Act was the last legislation of the Trudeau government, and the first nine years of SIRC's life were under Conservative governments. The political cataclysm of the 1993 election, with the removal of official status from both the Conservatives and the NDP and the sudden rise of the Bloc Québécois and the Reform parties, left the representativeness of SIRC in considerable disarray. This might not have been a major problem (although the conundrum of the secessionist BQ demanding representation on a body with access to classified information about national security presents very delicate and thorny dilemmas), were it not for the Bristow affair, with its partisan dimensions in relation to the Reform party, and the consequent first appearance of real antagonism between SIRC and Parliament.

Peter Russell argued in 1983 that an active joint parliamentary committee, as envisaged by the McDonald Report, was 'essential' to achieving effective accountability. Disappointed by the absence of such a body in the proposed legislation, he speculated that 'perhaps' the provision for the referral of SIRC annual reports to the appropriate standing committee of the House 'can be the basis for moving beyond the ineffectual parliamentary review process that has prevailed in the past.'[26] He was in fact partially right in this speculation, but parliamentary review emerged not just from the subcommittee of the standing committee on justice and the solicitor-general, which initially received SIRC reports and questioned SIRC members from time to time, but even more from the special committee on the five-year review of the CSIS Act, which was the sole parliamentary role mandated as such in the CSIS Act. The review committee, which drew most of its membership from the subcommittee, developed a remarkable non-partisan spirit and signed a unanimous report.[27]

This non-partisanship was a tribute to the MPs on the committee, but it perhaps owed something as well to the uncooperative and even confrontational stance adopted by the government.[28] It routinely denied access to information and spent far more money in preparing its response than it provided the committee to prepare its report. Finally, when the committee's recommendations appeared, the government rejected them in toto. This rather contemptuous treatment paradoxically cemented cross-party solidarity, which included government supporters. Then the chair of the five-year committee, former MP Blaine Thacker, led a successful move to constitute a permanent Subcommittee on National Security, drawing on the same membership and the expertise that it had gained in the review exercise. The committee deliberately chose not to request access to classified information, out of aversion to being compromised in its public role by the requirements of secrecy and, more to the point, because

SIRC did have such access: the Thacker subcommittee saw itself as working in tandem with SIRC.

A complementary working relationship between Parliament and SIRC might have provided an additional element in the accountability process not foreseen in the CSIS Act but fulfilling some of the original expectations held by the McDonald Commission and by Peter Russell. Alas, it was not to be. The partisan knot drawn by the 1993 election and the Bristow affair put paid to any tandem or complementary relationship. The subcommittee, shorn of all continuity by the election turnover, save the new chair, Liberal MP Derek Lee, and sporting suspicious and antagonistic BQ and Reform members, soon fell into a hostile confrontation with SIRC, some of it televised. Relations between the predominantly Conservative SIRC membership and the Reform party grew particularly strained when the existence for a short period of a CSIS file under the heading 'PRESTON MANNING' was uncovered, along with SIRC's attempt to pass this off as a simple mistake, with no particular consequences.

The Lee subcommittee set off on its own investigation of the Bristow affair, but came up lame. Riven by partisan divisions and the evident desire of the Liberal government to put the whole affair to bed following SIRC's report, the subcommittee floundered through successive drafts before finally producing, a year and a half after SIRC's relatively definitive report, an ineffectual, if not derisory, report of its own, which featured a few innocuous, if not vapid, recommendations agreed on unanimously, followed by a series of partisan minority reports, including a lengthy Reform dissent that is decidedly idiosyncratic.[29] The Reform MP originally assigned to the subcommittee added further discredit to Parliament's role when she made public a tendentious claim by a former CSIS contract employee that CSIS had been harbouring an alleged Russian 'mole' (claims rejected both by CSIS and by SIRC, which investigated). Worse, she released a statement suggesting that the alleged mole had been protected by a senior CSIS counterintelligence officer, whom she dubbed a 'supermole' – and then inadvertently included the actual name of the officer in the press release. This matter is now the subject of a civil suit for libel against the MP by the CSIS officer, now retired.[30]

When the Liberal government of Jean Chrétien returned to office following the 1997 election, it abruptly terminated the fledgling role of Parliament in security intelligence by simply failing to reactivate the National Security Subcommittee. In the current Parliament, SIRC reports to the Standing Committee on Justice and Human Rights. Some members of the former subcommittee, including Derek Lee, belong to it, and Lee has already asserted a robust interpretation of the information that may be demanded of SIRC by Parliament.[31] However, the disappearance of a subcommittee dedicated to this area alone constitutes a distinct dilution of Parliament's focus. Unfortunately, Parliament contributed to its own chastisement by its less than competent performance from 1993 to 1997.

While Parliament was floundering, SIRC seems to have been getting its act back together. The departure of a mediocre chair, Jacques Courtois, has been followed by the appointment of Paule Gauthier, a respected former member from the Atkey era. She was chosen in consultation with the BQ leader; that party seems to have given its approval to her as, if not a BQ representative, then at least an acceptable representative from Quebec. The Liberals have no obvious partisan representative on the committee; this would appear to suggest a genuine desire to depoliticize SIRC after its brush with partisan Tory identification. Can we conclude then that Parliament has shot itself in the foot and that SIRC can return to its original role as, among other things, a substitute for a parliamentary committee? I think not.

The rationale for a strong parliamentary link in the accountability chain remains just as compelling as when the McDonald Commission and Peter Russell articulated it in the early 1980s – perhaps even more so.[32] If parliamentarians are to act more responsibly, they must be allowed more responsibility. If the government were to bite the bullet and give MPs in a special committee clearance in the same way as the U.S. House and Senate intelligence committees have access to classified information, a more effective and responsible national security committee might indeed be able to act in tandem with SIRC and the IG. Marginalizing MPs only makes them act marginally. There might be a danger that MPs would be drawn into the loop, as it were, and lose their ability to take critical stances. Their present standing as rank outsiders, however, does not help them make effective criticisms. Parliament's role is part of the unfinished business of the accountability system.

From Institutionalism to Functionalism

The last point I wish to make is one that was ignored by McDonald, Pitfield, and Russell – understandably, because the terms of reference of the commission referred only to the RCMP Security Service – but it has become clear in the intervening years. The CSIS Act and all of its accountability features are institutional, not functional. It is CSIS, not the security and intelligence function of government, that falls under the ambit of accountability. This arrangement is not only rather invidious for CSIS but offers it the possibility of making various 'end-runs' around accountability by farming out activities to other agencies or departments of government that escape mandated review or oversight. The RCMP has remained a player in national security – as indeed required by the

Security Offences Act, passed in tandem with the CSIS Act.[33] The Communications Security Establishment (CSE) is active on the international stage in communications intelligence, with both an awesome technological capacity to spy on Canadians and an informal mandate that bars such domestic activity. The five-year review committee recognized these realities by calling for a comprehensive National Security Act and a functional accountability system.

Instead of moving in this direction, the Liberal government has opted for fragmentation of national security along institutional lines. When a series of questions was raised concerning the CSE, and Parliament passed a resolution calling for some form of accountability, the government responded by appointing a judge as a one-person oversight mechanism, without first establishing any statutory mandate for the CSE against which the commissioner can check its performance.[34] It seems to have learned nothing from the CSIS experience and to have missed an opportunity to set up a more comprehensive legislative and accountability framework for security and intelligence. Ironically, Canada, once considered a model for British reformers, could take a lesson from Britain's Intelligence Services Act of 1994, which has brought together under the same accountability umbrella the SIS, the external intelligence agency; MI5, the equivalent of CSIS; and the GCHQ, the CSE's sister electronic eavesdropping agency.[35]

There is one new element of accountability not foreseen by the McDonald Commission or Peter Russell. The office of the auditor general has carried out a survey of security and intelligence in the government of Canada with an eye to accountability and control. Its report, itself unprecedented in scope (the U.S. General Accounting Office has done audits of specific programs, but never of the entire field), offers a critical and useful look at the effectiveness of the structures in place and offers recommendations for tightening and modification.[36] This audit appears to have been initiated by the attorney general's office, which promises that its investigators will return to the area regularly in the future. This development adds an element of financial accountability vis-à-vis Parliament and the public and does not focus narrowly on CSIS but covers the broader field – perhaps a sign to the government that it should move more generally from institutionalism to functionalism.

Conclusion

Neither the hopes nor the fears expressed by Peter Russell and the McDonald Commission in the early 1980s about the legislative blueprint brought forward by the government for balancing freedom and security have been fully borne out. After an initial period of innovation, with some genuine achievements, there has been more recent evidence of drift and inertia. There is nothing very surprising about this situation for any student of Peter Russell's political science. Among the many things that he has taught us is that the art of governance in a free society requires constant adjustment and constant vigilance in order that the delicate balance between freedom and security not be allowed to tip too far in either direction.

NOTES

1 See the grisly portrait drawn by Athan G. Theoharis and John Stuart Cox, *The Boss: J. Edgar Hoover and the Great American Inquisition* (Philadelphia: Temple University Press 1988).
2 See Jeff Sallot, *Nobody Said No* (Toronto: James Lorimer 1979); Edward Mann and John Alan Lee, *The RCMP vs. The People* (Don Mills: General Publishing 1979); Robert Dion, *Les Crimes de la Police montée* (Montreal: Éditions Albert Saint-Martin 1979); John Sawatsky, *Men in the Shadows: The RCMP Security Service* (Toronto: Doubleday 1980); Reg Whitaker, 'Canada: The RCMP Scandals,' in Andrei S. Marcovits and Mark Silverstein, eds., *The Politics of Scandal: Power and Process in Liberal Democracies* (New York: Holmes & Meier 1988), 38–61.
3 Commission of Inquiry Concerning Certain Activities of the Royal Canadian Mounted Police, Peter H. Russell, Director of Research, *Freedom and Security: An Analysis of the Policy Issues before the Commission of Inquiry* (Oct. 1978).
4 Ibid., 17, paras. 45 and 46.
5 Canada, Royal Commission on Security (Mackenzie Commission), *Report (Abridged)* (Ottawa: Supply and Services, June 1969).
6 This is a point that I have made in two articles, 'The Politics of Security Intelligence Policy Making in Canada: I, 1970–1984,' *Intelligence and National Security* 6 no. 4 (Oct. 1991), 649–68; and 'The Politics of Security Intelligence Policy-Making in Canada: II, 1984–91,' ibid., 7 no. 2 (April 1992), 53–76.
7 Two excellent studies by British scholars put the Canadian experience in a wider comparative framework. Peter Gill, *Policing Politics: Security Intelligence and the Liberal Democratic State* (London: Frank Cass, 1994) is particularly strong on the political context, while a more legal examination with rich detail is Laurence Lustgarten and Ian Leigh, *In from the Cold: National Security and Parliamentary Democracy* (Oxford: Clarendon Press 1994).
8 Peter Russell, 'The Proposed Charter for a Civilian Intelligence Agency: An Appraisal,' *Canadian Public Policy* 9 no. 3 (1983) 326–37.
9 Senate of Canada, *Delicate Balance: A Security Intelligence Service in a Democratic*

Society, Report of the Special Committee of the Senate on the Canadian Security Intelligence Service, Nov. 1983.

10 Ministerial guidelines on the handling of human sources issued by the solicitor-general to CSIS in October 1989 reminded the agency to be 'mindful of the fact that its investigative actions can inadvertently have a disquieting effect on legitimate political activity or other forms of lawful advocacy, protest and dissent if it leaves the impression that the Service is investigating such activity itself.' Consequently, they enjoined CSIS to seek senior-level authorization of investigations involving the 'most sensitive institutions ... in the academic, political, religious, media and trade union fields.' Pierre Blais to Reid Morden, 30 Oct. 1989.

11 Security Intelligence Review Committee, *Annual Report, 1986–87* (Ottawa 1987), 33–40; *People and Process in Transition*, Report to the General of the Advisory Team on the Canadian Security Intelligence Service (Oct. 1987); Peter Gill, 'Symbolic or Real? The Impact of the Canadian Security Intelligence Review Committee, 1984–1988,' *Intelligence and National Security* 4 no. 3 (July 1989).

12 SIRC, *Annual Report, 1992/93*, 54; *Annual Report, 1995/96*, 13.

13 SIRC, *Section 54 Report to the Solicitor General of Canada on CSIS' Use of Its Investigative Powers with Respect to the Labour Movement* (25 March 1988).

14 SIRC, *The Heritage Front Affair*, Report to the Solicitor General of Canada (9 Dec. 1994); Reg Whitaker, 'The "Bristow Affair": A Crisis of Accountability in Canadian Security Intelligence,' *Intelligence and National Security* 11 no. 2 (April 1996), 279–305; Maurice Archdeacon, 'The Heritage Front Affair,' ibid., 306–12.

15 See, for instance, IG, 'Human Sources' (April 1993) and 'CSIS Handling of Confidential Sources' (April 1995); Solicitor General Pierre Blais to CSIS Director Reid Morgan, 30 Oct. 1989; Deputy Solicitor General Jean T. Fournier to the Solicitor General, 26 Aug. 1994.

16 McDonald, 2–2, 842–3.

17 Russell, 'Proposed Charter,' 336.

18 Interview with Richard Thompson, 1990.

19 Ursula Menke to Herb Grey, 12 Nov. 1993, and the 1993 Certificate, Nov. 1993; R. Protti to Herb Grey, 24 Feb. 1994; documents released by the solicitor-general under Access to Information requests.

20 Ronald Atkey to Reid Morden, 25 May 1988, with Annex of same date.

21 SIRC, *Annual Report, 1995/96* (Ottawa: Supply and Services 1995), 5–6. SIRC made a formal recommendation to the government that such documents not be withheld in future. The chair of SIRC explained that 'we wanted to tell them and the public we are really serious about getting documents when we ask for documents': Canada, House of Commons, Sub-Committee on National Security, 3 Dec. 1996, *Evidence*, testimony of Paule Gauthier.

22 David Vienneau, 'Retiring Watchdog Atkey Doesn't Regret Being "Pain" to Spies,' *Toronto Star*, 1 Dec. 1989.

23 I am referring directly to John Bassett and Jacques Courtois, neither of whom established very distinguished records.

24 Eddie Goodman, Subcommittee on National Security, Evidence, 15 May 1996.

25 One exception was the appointment of former CCF leader M.J. Coldwell as one of the three members of the Mackenzie Commission, McDonald's predecessor in the 1960s. Coldwell proved to be the most zealous Cold Warrior on a generally conservative commission.

26 Russell, 'Proposed Charter,' 337.

27 *In Flux But not in Crisis*, Report of the Special Committee on the Review of the CSIS Act and the Security Offences Act (Sept. 1990).

28 See the very interesting account by Stuart Farson, the committee's director of research: 'The Noble Lie Revisited: Parliament's Five-Year Review of the CSIS Act: Instrument of Change or Weak Link in the Chain of Accountability?,' in Philip C. Stenning, ed., *Accountability for Criminal Justice: Selected Essays* (Toronto: University of Toronto Press 1995).

29 *The Heritage Front Affair: Our View*, First Report of the Standing Committee on Justice and Legal Affairs (June 1996). The Reform dissent is titled with a line borrowed from the TV series on paranormal conspiracies, *The X-Files*: 'THE TRUTH IS OUT THERE.'

30 The MP is Val Meredith, and the plaintiff in the action is Frank Pratt, one of the best-known and most respected counterintelligence officers in the service. The affair of the alleged mole is recounted, rather credulously, by Quebec journalist Normand Lester in his *Enquêtes sur les Services secets* (Montreal: Éditions de l'Homme 1998), 257–88.

31 Canada, House of Commons, Standing Committee on Justice and Human Rights, *Evidence*, 14 May 1998.

32 The most detailed and compelling case for a more responsible parliamentary role can be found in Stuart Farson, 'In Crisis and in Flux? Politics, Parliament and Canada's Intelligence Policy,' *Journal of Conflict Studies* 16 no. 1 (spring 1966), 30–56.

33 The RCMP currently maintains a Security Offences Component within its Criminal Intelligence Program. This body liaises with CSIS, investigates criminal offences relating to the security of Canada, and maintains a 'threat assessment program.' National Security Investigations Sections are located at ten divisional headquarters across the country.

34 'CSE External Review Mechanism,' Government of Canada news release NR-96.06 1, 19 June 1996. Claude Bisson, assisted by what he himself calls a 'small staff,' has issued two reports, neither of which appears to be critical or particularly informative: see Office of the Communications Security Establishment Commissioner, *Annual*

Report, 1997–1998 (Ottawa: Minister of Public Works and Government Services Canada, May 1998).

35 Peter Gill, 'Reasserting Control: Recent Changes in the Oversight of the UK Intelligence Community,' *Intelligence and National Security* 11 no. 2 (April 1966), 313–31. Gill is rightly sceptical about the quality of accountability in the new British legal regime, but on the institutional scope of the mechanism, Britain is now far ahead of Canada.

36 Canada, *Report of the Auditor General of Canada to the House of Commons*, chap. 27: 'The Canadian Intelligence Community – Control and Accountability' (Ottawa: Minister of Public Works and Government Services Canada, Nov. 1996).

10

The Invention of Outsiders: The Relationship between Operatives and Civilian Experts

JEAN-PAUL BRODEUR

It has often been said that academics cast themselves as defenders of human rights and are generally critical of agencies such as the Canadian Security Intelligence Service (CSIS). Some claim that they have little to say on national security that is positive, either because they are not familiar with the issues or because they refuse to address any issue related to it that does not have a critical edge.

This paper focuses on the relationship between the academic and, more generally, the civilian community and organizations such as CSIS. I addressed this issue by presenting a particular case, which I believe illuminates this relationship. First, I provide historical background for the relationship between intelligence operatives and civilian experts in Canada. Second, I present a case that I believe illustrates the present state of this relationship in Canada. Third, I discuss some of the implications of this case.

Historical Background

In its second report, the Commission of Inquiry Concerning Certain Activities of the Royal Canadian Mounted Police (McDonald Commission) reviewed numerous previous attempts at reforming the Security Service of the Royal Canadian Mounted police (RCMP). More precisely, the McDonald Report (henceforth Canada 1981) discussed four such attempts – namely, a 1955 internal study conducted by a senior civilian member of the RCMP, the 1969 report of the Royal Commission on Security (Mackenzie Report, Canada, 1969), the prime minister's 1969 policy statement to the House of Commons, and a 1973 study by the Bureau of Management Consulting (BMC) (Canada 1981: part VI, chap. 1). The McDonald report stresses that all these attempts to change the RCMP Security Service stemmed from the same basic diagnosis: a police organization such as the RCMP was too rigid to meet the demands of work in security intelligence, which had to be performed by a more open-minded type of individual than is usually found in police organizations (Canada, 1981: 688). The 1955 internal study, the 1969 policy statement, and the 1973 BMC study had advocated that the Security Service receive a significant degree of autonomy within the force; the Mackenzie Report recommended that a civilian security-intelligence service replace the RCMP's Security Service.

As is well known, the McDonald Commission endorsed the position taken by Commissioner Mackenzie and recommended a separate, civilianized security-intelligence service. The Canadian Security Intelligence Service (CSIS) was finally created in 1984. The McDonald Commission came to this position as a result of its effort to understand why previous attempts to reform the RCMP's Security Service had failed. Its analysis of past failures is complex, but its conclusion, based on the testimony of knowledgeable individuals such as Jean-Pierre Goyer, a former solicitor-general, John Starnes, the first civilian director-general of the Security Service, and Robin Bourne, a civilian with major responsibilities in security intelligence, was that the RCMP was similar to a religious order, such as the Jesuits. This kind of organization is characterized by the homogeneous membership, rigorous training that acts as a rite of initiation designed to develop a strong esprit de corps, unstinting loyalty to the force, and strict enforcement of discipline.

These traits coalesce to create a body whose main characteristic is its insularity. A paragraph of the McDonald Report (Canada 1981: 690) deserves to be quoted at length: 'Finally, the R.C.M.P. possesses a definite quality of insularity. It has difficulty accepting and working with "outsiders," as the testimony of Mr. Starnes, Mr. Bourne and Mr. Goyer so amply demonstrates. Accompanying this insularity is a certain self-satisfaction which manifests itself in a variety of assumptions: that the organization is headed in the "right" direction; that the managerial ingredients that have worked so well in the past will continue to work in the future; and that staff members who are not regular members of the Force can, with few exceptions, perform only peripheral roles.' The creation of CSIS was a bumpy process, and the first government bill (C-157) to create a separate security-intelligence agency generated so much criticism that a special committee of the Senate was appointed to examine it and to propose amendments. This committee, headed by P.M. Pitfield, recommended many changes, but it never swerved from the McDonald Report's initial contention that members of the new service had to possess a frame of mind different from police and that the insularity of the RCMP had to give way to a mentality of service to the government and the Canadian people (Canada, Senate, 1983: 7).

After the creation of CSIS, the changes in outlook advocated by the McDonald Commission proved from the first difficult to implement. The majority of the new members of the agency were recruited from former members of the RCMP's Security Service: they brought with them the mentality and the habits of work of the RCMP (Security Intelligence Review Committee [SIRC] 1987: 42). In the years following the publication of its first annual report (1984–5), SIRC constantly reminded CSIS of the necessity of civilianization. For instance, its annual report of 1986–7 read: 'The McDonald Commission, like the MacKenzie a decade or so before, recommended the creation of a civilian security intelligence agency, separate from the RCMP. "Civilianization" became one of the policy objectives underlying the CSIS Act adopted by Parliament in 1984. ... We see a real need to keep prodding CSIS along the civilianization path ... Apart from the fact that, as a good employer, CSIS should continue to make room in the IO (intelligence officer) category for surveillants and other employees with the requisite qualities, we think that the emphasis in recruitment should be on factors other than police experience' (SIRC 1987: 42–3).

A particularly thorny issue was the use of the polygraph for screening applicants. Whereas former members of the RCMP either did not have to undergo a polygraph test or, if they did, were queried only on their loyalty to Canada and CSIS, all applicants not coming from the RCMP had to take a lie-detector test and were questioned on both their loyalty and their life-style. In its annual reports, SIRC was critical of the use of the polygraph, particularly with respect to life-style. The report of the Special Committee on the Review of the CSIS Act and the Security Offences Act, chaired by Blaine Thacker, recommended that 'the polygraph not be used by the Service for employment screening purposes.' (Canada, House of Commons 1990: rec. 33). The Ministry of the Solicitor General rejected this recommendation in the government's response to the Thacker report (Canada, Solicitor General, 1991). We have learned through interviews with CSIS applicants that the polygraph is still widely used.

It finally began to seem that the issue of civilianization might be on its way to resolution. From 1989–90 onward, SIRC's annual reports devoted less space to this issue. None the less, SIRC's proposals in *Amending the CSIS Act* (SIRC 1989a) were preoccupied with this issue to an extent that would suggest that it was still not properly resolved. One section of the proposals reads thus: 'Overcoming Isolation We note that the Independent Advisory Team which investigated the Service in 1987 (the Osbaldeston Committee) recommended that "the career paths of CSIS staff should provide for movement within both the security intelligence community and the public service" [p. 17] ... We believe that the Service's Analysis and Production Branch in particular would profit considerably if public servants from elsewhere in government, academics, or others with special expertise, could work with it. CSIS officers engaged in analysis and assessment would also benefit by their ability to work in related agencies of government or universities [4].'

SIRC goes on to recommend that the CSIS Act be amended to provide for rotation through CSIS by public servants and others with special qualifications, subject to provisions that would safeguard the identity of employees engaged in the covert operational activities of the service (SIRC 1989a: 5).

The general point of this historical review is to stress that insularity influenced the decision to take the Security Service out of the RCMP and to civilianize it in order that it improve the collection and analysis of intelligence and that it serve the government rather than being a fortified island within it. Indeed, the McDonald Commission's final assessment – that no reform stood a chance of being truly implemented in a organization akin to a religious order – tipped the scale in favour of the commission's recommendation that a new civilian security-intelligence service be created, that it be wholly autonomous, and that its members not be peace officers with police powers. Consequently, a retreat of the civilian agency thus created towards old forms of insularity and isolation would defeat one of the main purposes of its creation.

I now present a case study suggesting that compartmentalization, which separates members of CSIS from non-members (who are shackled with the negative identity of 'outsiders,' in the strongest meaning of the word), may be in the process of becoming as rigid as it was in the former RCMP Security Service.

A Case Study

A Description of the Case

In 1994, I was chairman of the Canadian Association for Security and Intelligence Studies, known as CASIS, and also director of the International Centre for Comparative Criminology of the Université de Montréal. This centre was funded, as were other centres of criminology, by the secretariat of the Ministry of the Solicitor General of Canada (henceforth, the ministry). The acceptance of this funding carried certain obligations in research, which varied from year to year as the centres made research proposals to the ministry. These proposals were generally accepted with few modifications. In 1994, the last year of this funding program, the ministry decided that the centres so funded should organize workshops for the benefit of one of the agencies accountable to the solicitor-general – that is, the RCMP, the Correctional Services, the National Parole Board, or CSIS.

While I was chairman of CASIS, we had organized an international conference entitled 'Intelligence Analysis and Assessment: The Producer–Decision

Maker Relationship in a Changing World.' This rather big event – several hundred persons attended the conference – took place in Ottawa on 27–29 October 1994, with invited speakers coming from many countries. Among the people who attended were several members of the Canadian 'intelligence community,' who belonged to agencies such as CSIS and the highly secretive Communication Security Establishment (CSE). The general director of CSIS, Ward Elcock, was the guest speaker at the official dinner held by CASIS during the conference. There can be no doubt of the willingness of CSIS to take an active role in this international event.

While this conference was being organized, I proposed to the ministry that our centre organize a small workshop that would be a follow-up to this conference. Unlike the conference, which addressed very broad international issues, the proposed workshop would be organized exclusively for CSIS and would focus on the Canadian context. Indeed, some criticism had been voiced during the CASIS October conference that it did not allow enough time for the discussion of specifically Canadian issues.

The general theme of the workshop was to be in keeping with the October conference and could be described as 'the security intelligence needs of Canada in the post–Cold War era and their impact on the future role of CSIS.' The secretariat of the ministry accepted this proposal, and CSIS agreed to participate in the workshop. Six members of CSIS and one officer from the Privy Council Office (PCO), who was involved in security intelligence and national security, were to attend. The event was not open to the public. In addition to members of CSIS, we invited several experts to take part in the discussion. They included academics, a former solicitor-general, a member of SIRC, a former member of the PCO, and several field experts on counter-terrorism and right-wing extremism, among them a high-ranking officer from a Canadian police force. The group was kept fairly small – under twenty persons – and all invitees had acknowledged expertise in the issues to be addressed.

In order to structure the discussions, a committee of three persons prepared short position papers. The committee included a former member of the research staff of the parliamentary special committee that conducted the five-year review of the CSIS Act, a British expert who had written on the Canadian intelligence community, and me. Eight position papers were produced and disseminated to the participants. The documents were not long – three to five pages – and were considered only as instruments to generate discussion. They consisted of two parts: a series of some ten to fifteen points summarizing current knowledge in respect to the issue addressed and a shorter list of questions for discussion. The issues to be addressed were: (1) The Future Role of Intelligence; (2) The Intelligence Community and the Canadian Economy; (3) Current Canadian Systems for Intelligence Assessments; (4) The Role of the Political Executive; (5) Training of Analysts and Their Managers; (6) Current Issues in Counter-Terrorism; (7) Media Coverage of Intelligence Issues; and (8) Issues in the Review of the Canadian Intelligence System.

Noticeably, several issues related directly to the main theme of the 1994 CASIS conference on intelligence analysis and assessment in changing times; all these issues dealt exclusively with general policy, and no particular case or event was on the agenda for discussion. Oversight and accountability – the staple topic of academic research on national security agencies – was only one of eight issues to be addressed. The appendix to this paper reproduces the position paper written for session 4 of the workshop, 'The Role of the Political Executive.' This is one of the topics that was to be covered in the CASIS October conference. The topic had been omitted then because of time constraints.

The workshop was initially to take place in Montreal but was moved to Ottawa, in order to make it easier for qualified resource persons to participate. It was scheduled for Monday and Tuesday, 15 and 16 May 1995. By the beginning of the previous week, all travelling arrangements, hotel and restaurant bookings, and meeting room reservations were in place. All invitations had also been sent and accepted. The final agenda was faxed to CSIS during the first week of May, but this fax was apparently not received or not disseminated. The agenda was faxed again on Tuesday 9 May, and its reception was acknowledged. Early in May, the officer from PCO had decided to withdraw from the workshop, without giving specific reasons.

On Friday 12 May – that is, the Friday that preceded the Monday on which the workshop was to be begin – at precisely five o'clock in the afternoon, I was still working in my office at the university. I remember the exact time, because it marked the end of the working week. I received a telephone call from a CSIS officer informing me that the service had just decided to withdraw from the workshop, its members being explicitly forbidden to attend. I then informed my caller that I had no other choice than to cancel the workshop. Since it been organized for the benefit of CSIS, once CSIS decided not to participate, there was no point in holding it.

Naturally, I asked for the reasons for the withdrawal. I was given this answer on the telephone: all the topics that we had selected were quite relevant, but, since CSIS was then discussing these questions internally and had not yet reached final conclusions on what its position was to be concerning them, it was not willing to address them within a forum external to the service and with non-members of CSIS present. This answer, given to me on the phone, was later confirmed in a letter sent on 19 May 1995 by a CSIS officer and disseminated by CSIS to the other participants to explain its withdrawal. A paragraph of this letter, written in French, reads thus: 'La position que j'ai donc dû adopter sur ce, procède, vous vous en doutez bien, de l'ordre du jour retenu pour la conduite de votre atelier. Quelque huit sujets, tous pertinents j'en conviens, mais dont la plupart ne peuvent, dans la perpective de nos obligations et responsabilités, être discutés dans un forum tel que celui que vous nous proposiez, cela étant dit sans la moindre déconsidération. (The position that I had to take [withdrawing CSIS from the workshop] proceeds, as you well suspect, from the agenda developed for the conduct of the workshop. Some eight topics, all relevant, I admit, but most of which cannot be discussed, in view of our obligations and responsibilities, within a forum such as you proposed, this being said without intending to be inconsiderate.)'

I spent the weekend writing the fax that I proposed to send to all non-CSIS participants in the workshop and insisted that its text be approved by CSIS. It was approved by the junior CSIS officer with whom I worked on the text of the fax during the weekend. This text went out by fax to all non-CSIS participants on Saturday, 13 May 1995 and the next day (all had been previously reached by phone, as soon as I decided to cancel the workshop). The higher management of CSIS apparently thought that my fax, though approved by a CSIS officer, put too much responsibility on the service for the cancellation of the workshop. Thus it felt obliged to provide in writing its own explanation to the participants, which they did, as we saw above.

The Significance of the Case

There are, I believe, lessons to be drawn from this case. Within the limits of this paper, I can discuss only a few in some detail. Although it did cause me some aggravation, I do not raise the issue of the belatedness of CSIS's decision to withdraw from the workshop. It would have done so earlier, if the agenda had percolated sooner to senior management. The rashness of the withdrawal only indicates how strongly CSIS did not want its members to participate. There is, however, another point that needs to be stressed. The workshop was prepared over several weeks in partnership with junior and middle-ranking intelligence officers within CSIS. Although they were well aware of the workshop's agenda, they never raised as much as a single question about its content. It was apparently only when the agenda finally reached the upper echelons that the decision to withdraw was taken.

The good news signalled by this incident is that academics and, more generally, outsiders can in fact draw up an agenda of meaningful issues related to national security. The problem here was perhaps that the issues selected were too relevant for CSIS to engage willingly in dialogue on them with non-members. This good news, so to speak, provides some refutation of the often-voiced opinion that no outsider can really understand what is at stake in national security, unless he or she goes through a ritual of initiation performed by insiders who have privileged access to the treasured sources of covert information.

There is, however, a crucial 'downside' to this apparent good news. The dichotomy between members/insiders of the service and non-members/outsiders has no foundation other than institutional, in a purely formal sense. As this example demonstrates, non-members were not cast aside as outsiders because of their lack of expertise, nor were they to be excluded because they were security risks and might have leaked the results of the workshop. All participants in the workshop, from a former solicitor-general, who was also a member of SIRC for several years, to academics who had taught at the CSIS training academy and had in the course of their research interviewed key participants in security intelligence, had been previously exposed to sensitive information and had properly followed the code of confidentiality, whenever it applied. Consequently, it is difficult to explain CSIS's withdrawal from the workshop, convened for its benefit, without considering the staunch persistence of old habits of dividing the world into 'us' and 'them' – 'us' being stringently interpreted as formal members of the agency.

As the good news is not so good, the bad news is truly wretched. CSIS appears to make it a pre-condition for entering into dialogue with outside experts that they raise issues that are irrelevant or at best only marginally significant. Until it is persuaded that it is dealing with blue-blooded academics, stereotyped as long-winded idealists, endlessly chirping under the sun of frivolous matters, the service will not enter into any meaningful exchange that might have the potential for changing its perspective.

For several reasons, this is dispiriting. Let me first declare that I consider it natural for CSIS not to engage in public debates on particular cases in which it is operationally involved, such as the Heritage Front affair. But I want to stress, as I mentioned above, that all the items on our agenda were policy issues, which members of CSIS could meaningfully address without disclosing any confidential cases. I do not dispute that such a topic as 'Current Issues in Counter-terrorism' would be discussed differently among CSIS members, who might illustrate their position with the help of specific cases unknown to the public. But the mere fact that an internal discussion of a policy issue would take a turn different from a discussion involving 'outsiders' is certainly no reason for refusing to engage in any such discussion with non-members of CSIS.

A second reason to be discomfited touches on the lack of candidness in CSIS's exchanges with non-members. What I was told on the telephone was not only that the workshop agenda was not fit to be discussed in an external forum, but also, and perhaps more important, that CSIS had not yet determined its position on most if not all of the items on the agenda. A common-sense reply to this argument would run thus: the fact that CSIS had not yet made its mind up on these issues was all the more reason to consult with outside experts. Then it might decide what its position would be after having heard all the arguments. CSIS apparently thought otherwise and felt that it had to define its position before facing 'outside help.'

The implication of this attitude is that outsiders should not be allowed to have an input in the determination of CSIS policy on the items listed on the agenda. It might be hypothesized that once CSIS had determined its position on all these issues, it would be willing to engage in dialogue with outsiders. But such dialogue can only be manipulative on the part of CSIS, because its policy appears to be to participate only after it has internally cast its position in stone. The mere possibility that these positions might be subject to amendment on the basis of external input must be ruled out for the precise reason that outsiders are completely excluded from the policy-making process until it is concluded internally. If such policy can be made initially only by excluding outsiders, it would be inconsistent to change it, once it has been internally determined, by suddenly discovering the wisdom or the expertise of outsiders.

In these conditions, the reasons for engaging in 'dialogue' (monologue, actually) with outsiders can be only to convert them or just to test the water outside the agency's own pool. Now, if academics and other experts not belonging to the agency were actually told before any exchange that, whatever their ruminations regarding security intelligence policy amounted to, they could not have any impact, it is doubtful that they would be at all interested in participating. Indeed, the least suspicion that the discussion might get serious was enough to send CSIS running from the table.

There are other questions that deserve further analysis. Is the claim that academics and other outsiders have nothing 'positive' to contribute to the debate on national security not a self-fulfilling prophecy? If such people seek to contribute to this debate in broad terms – rather than just by being critical of national security agencies for their actual or potential violations of civil liberties – yet none the less always find themselves excluded from this debate by insiders, they will inevitably conclude that a 'constructive' dialogue with agencies such as CSIS is futile. In other words, since they are always cast as closet civil libertarians, they might as well play the part attributed to them with as much savvy as they can and write off as cant the traditional lament of intelligence agencies that intellectuals are always on their backs. Actually, there may be nowhere else for them to be.

Does the incident that I described not suggest that CSIS is still very much an authoritarian organization? Despite the promises of its first years of operation, it may have just traded its former RCMP police persona for an even more rigid military type of management. What happened on the eve of the cancelled conference was the result of an order given by headquarters to a reconnaissance party to return at once to the base. There was no choice but to comply. This issue is actually much broader than authoritarianism and touches the core of why CSIS was created. We saw above that what spelled doom for the RCMP Security Service was a general perception that it had evolved into something akin to a religious order. Such an order was so strongly wrapped around itself that it was incapable of changing to comply with external demands and, more important, unable to serve the government on terms that it did not itself define, terms that had the government's needs only tangentially in view. Has CSIS regressed to the insular position that its creation was intended to remedy?

Finally, why should all issues that appertain to the redefinition of the role and mandate of a security service in the post–Cold War era be determined solely from within the agency, with possible input from other core government agencies, such as PCO? The question is much broader than merely the participation of external experts in this redefinition. Should all the arguments used in the process of determining policy in security intelligence be barred from public debate – even of a limited kind – in a democracy? If it should be, why?

This issue is quite complex. For instance, it might be argued that with regard to session 2 of the workshop, 'The Intelligence Community and the Canadian Economy,' it would not be advisable to debate publicly whether CSIS should engage in industrial espionage (a positive conclusion to this debate would act as a warning to potential targets). However, since CSIS operates only domestically, at least in theory, its sole mission in this respect would be to counter foreign industrial espionage undertaken on Canadian territory and against Canadian interests. Such a position can be publicly debated and advertised without any difficulty.

All questions cannot be resolved as easily as this one, and perhaps some aspects of the issues on the cancelled workshop agenda cannot usefully be debated outside CSIS or, in any event, outside a very narrow forum. Nevertheless, it does not follow that the whole debate on the redefinition of the role of CSIS should take place exclusively within the agency.

Generalizing the Case

There is an important and much misunderstood question of method that I want to address. It is a methodological truism in social science that one should not draw conclusions that are not based on a significant sample of cases. According to this principle, one should not make any extrapolations from the discussion of a single case. Consequently, I should refrain from making any general statement on the basis of the single instance that I have presented.

And so I do. I would nevertheless like to make the following points. Unless exceptional circumstances occur, such as happens in rare commissions of inquiry, it is doubtful that a researcher will ever be able to rely on a 'statistically meaningful' number of instances in writing about organizations such as security services, traditionally shrouded in secrecy. Hence waiting to attain the magical threshold of a significant number of cases is generally tantamount to remaining silent; methodological purity becomes a convenient way of putting issues deserving of public scrutiny under the rug. Within the hazy realm of security intelligence and national security, we must surely sometimes rely on the significance of the single instance, as measured against a reasonable background of presumptions, to raise questions and make suggestions.

Is there anything that would act as a 'reasonable background of presumptions' allowing me to raise the kinds of questions that I have been asking about the lack of external input into security intelligence matters, on the basis of the case to which I was a privileged witness? I believe that there is. The CSIS Act was submitted to a five-year assessment by the Special Committee on the Review of the CSIS Act and the Security Offences Act. The committee in September 1990 released its report (Canada, House of Commons, 1990), which offered 117 recommendations. The government responded in *On Course: National Security for the 1990s* (Canada, Solicitor General, 1991). Opinions vary as to the real content of the government's response. According to members of the committee itself and of its director of research, the government agreed with at most two or three of the recommendations. According to our own analysis of the government's response, it rejected all but eight. There are government officials who believe that the government's response was favourable. The last report of the auditor general appears to have settled this issue when it declared that the government generally chose not to follow virtually all the recommendations (Canada, Auditor General, 1996: sec. 27.44). The report was, to all practical purposes, ignored.

The special committee was an official body of the House of Commons; its report was based on public hearings conducted over several months by eight MPs. It heard over eighty witnesses and received briefs from sixty-five groups and individuals. The significance of its proceedings reached far beyond the workshop that I helped organize. Yet its work was swept aside, as was the much more modest workshop.

It is against this background that the case that I have presented and discussed gains significance. It allows at least for a critical assessment of the situation that is now prevailing in security intelligence.

Conclusion

Before submitting my conclusion, I want to remind the reader of some of the proposals made by the McDonald Commission and by the Special Committee that relate to the issues discussed in this paper.

As is well known, the McDonald Report proposed an elaborate structure of internal and external controls for the supervision of the civilian agency to be created to replace the Security Service of the RCMP. With respect to internal controls, the report discussed the role of the cabinet, of the Privy Council Office, of interdepartmental committees, and of ministerial direction coming from the prime minister and most specifically from the solicitor-general. It recommended that the latter be appointed as the minister responsible for the security-intelligence agency (Canada 1981: 876).

The judiciary – more especially the Federal Court of Canada, an Advisory Council on Security and Intelligence (ACSI) acting as an oversight body, and Parliament – were the primary institutions responsible for the external control of the security-intelligence agency in the blueprint developed by the McDonald Commission. The judiciary was to give the necessary legal authorizations and warrants for the use of intrusive means of collecting intelligence, and it now performs this function. The ACSI was later re-created as the Security Intelligence Review Committee (SIRC). The recommendations of the McDonald Commission were in the main followed with respect to the creation of an oversight agency, its basic function being to conduct a continuing review of the legality and propriety of the activities of the security intelligence agency (Canada 1981: 887). The McDonald Commission also wanted the role of Parliament in security intelligence enhanced and recommended establishment of a Joint Committee of the Senate and House of Commons to review the activities of the service and of any other government agency involved in similar work (Canada 1981: rec. 182, p. 904), This joint committee, unlike ACSI (later SIRC), was not limited to reviewing the propriety and legality of the operations conducted by the intelligence security agency, but was also to review their effectiveness (Canada 1981: 899).

This was not the only difference. The McDonald Report not only proposed a structure for controlling the new agency, but it also wanted mechanisms set up to encourage public debate on national security and related issues. This latter concern has been overlooked by the government. The joint committee of Parliament was to increase public knowledge of the issues surrounding national security and generate enlightened discussion of them (Canada 1981: 905). It was to hold its sessions in camera in order to preserve the necessary confidentiality, but it was also to publish an expurgated report of all its non-public proceedings (Canada 1981: rec. 185, p. 905). It is of paramount importance that the McDonald Commission conceived the functions of ACSI/SIRC and of the joint committee as different and as complementing each other. Consequently, it recommended establishment of both external mechanisms of control. In his November 1996 report, the auditor general asserts mistakenly that when the government created SIRC as an instrument of external control, it chose to establish this kind of body *rather than* a joint committee (Canada, Auditor General, 1996: sec. 27.61). The McDonald Report had in fact recommended both.

The McDonald Report proposed another device to promote wider public participation in security and intelligence matters. It described this device in the chapter on internal governmental controls and discussed it in the concluding section of the chapter on external controls. This latter section, entitled 'Public Knowledge and Discussion of Security Matters,' bears witness to the fact that the commission saw both control of the intelligence security agency and enlightened public debate on the issues of security intelligence as essential and distinct matters. The primary function of the proposed Bureau of Intelligence Assessments was to produce intelligence assessments in line with the priorities and needs of the government, as determined by cabinet and civil service committees in national security (Canada 1981: 854). The report described the function and workings of this body:

> [It] would provide another opportunity for wider public participation in security and intelligence matters. The Office of National Assessments in Australia [which served as a model for the recommendation] from time to time arranges seminars attended by experts from outside government to discuss subjects on which it is preparing an intelligence assessment. If such a Bureau were established in Canada, we think it too should draw upon the perceptions and knowledge of Canadians outside of the security and intelligence community in collating intelligence on various topics. Indeed, we think that one of the distinct advantages of such a Bureau is to ensure that the intelligence estimates prepared for government combine information and viewpoints obtained from covert sources with insights from a broad range of public sources. (Canada 1981: 905–6)

As we know, neither the joint committee nor the bureau has been created. The special committee chaired by Blaine Thacker also recommended that a new permanent body – a subcommittee of the House Standing Committee on Justice and Solicitor General – deal exclusively with security and intelligence matters (Canada, House of Commons, 1990: rec. 107, p. 193). The government rejected this recommendation, along with most of the recommendations of the special committee. As for the bureau, there is a unit nested in the PCO that deals with intelligence and security, but its ways of operating are unknown to the public.

The case that I discussed above highlights once more the need for closer parliamentary oversight of CSIS and similar Canadian agencies and for better-informed public debate on security intelligence – and also the strong perception of this need. If there is agreement on the problem, the difficulty of answering it adequately has increased as we have become more aware of how complex this question really is. However great the obstacles to parliamentary supervision, only committees appointed by Parliament have the legal clout to bring into an external forum – and eventually into the open, whenever it is advisable – the policy-making process in security intelligence. Given the lack of any effective alternative for introducing public input in policy development, parliamentary oversight, for all its disadvantages, becomes crucial.

There are several drawbacks to parliamentary oversight of security intelligence. It is often alleged that parliamentary oversight increases the risk of security leaks. I would tend to view this more as defensive rhetoric than as a serious objection. Leaks of confidential information occur at all levels of government. However, I see no reason to single out MPs as being more prone to divulge privileged information than other members of the state apparatus. The most notorious moles in the history of espionage have not been elected representatives. Aldrich Ames, a CIA officer, did more effective damage to his agency than all the members of the various House and Senate oversight committees put together.

However, other drawbacks cannot be so easily discounted. First, the oversight committees may be chaired, as was often the case in the United States, by war hawks acting more like cheerleaders of the agencies than as watchdogs. Second, these committees may also be led to compete with non-parliamentary reviewing bodies, such as SIRC in Canada, and to develop antagonistic relationships with them. The problems may be compounded when members of the supervisory bodies (such as SIRC and a parliamentary committee) have conflicting views on the function of the agency. Both forms of supervision become highly vulnerable to manipulation, and they tend to cancel each other out. In this regard, the auditor general had recently to report that relations between SIRC and the Subcommittee on National Security (SCNS)[1] were strained, particularly since the inquiries conducted by SIRC and the SCNS into the Heritage Front affair conflict in their results (Canada, Auditor General, 1996: sec. 27.63).[2]

This situation is disquieting and should serve to caution us against simply calling for more parliamentary supervision of CSIS without considering how it might affect SIRC. SIRC is one external control mechanism widely held to have worked successfully, and its operation should not be hindered. What then to do? I believe that we ought to follow the sound advice of the auditor general and clarify the respective roles and responsibilities of SIRC and of parliamentary committees (Canada, Auditor General, 1996: sec. 27.63). The best way to begin doing that would be to go back to what the McDonald Commission recommended – a joint committee on security intelligence, for which it made detailed proposals. This committee was never created: the former SCNS seemed a far cry from the McDonald Commission's thoughtful proposals. It is conceivable that the SCNS was frustrated because of its limited role in security intelligence, which in turn may help explain bellicose mood.

Just increasing parliamentary review may not be enough in the present complex situation, where the kind of oversight that can be exercised over CSIS and other intelligence agencies such as the CSE is constrained by agreements into which Canada has entered with its partners in security intelligence, and particularly with the United States. The McDonald Commission stressed the need for increasing the quality of the public debate on security intelligence affairs through better public information and through external input. Its recommendations for the creation of a Bureau of Intelligence Assessments that would bring together human resources from different backgrounds and with different kinds of expertise deserves a second reading. I believe that the recommendations are still relevant. Their implementation would complement the work of Parliament in assuring that the policy-making process in the field of security intelligence be better informed, more accountable and more public – as it should be in a democracy.

APPENDIX: Workshop on Intelligence Analysis and Assessment

Session 4: The Role of the Political Executive

4.1 At the October Conference there was no panel covering the issue of the consumers of intelligence. As intended, the Conference covered 'Analysis and Assessment' in detail, but the failure to consider whether any elected officials actually act on the intelligence product is perhaps similar to lawyers assuming that laws simply enforce themselves.

4.2 The one area in which the role of politicians was considered, albeit briefly, was in the first workshop session where, at the apex of national systems, are committees such as the MIS (UK), CCSI (Canada until 1993). Clearly, however, these meet (met) only a few times a year and consider primarily budgets and only the broadest issues of policy. Otherwise assessment systems, whether elite or committee, are run by officials.

4.3 Historically, the two primary characteristics of ministerial involvement in security intelligence matters have been either passivity leading to a lack of control or partisan direction. The former has given rise to the 'rogue elephant' image of agencies in which they enjoy the greatest autonomy from political control. The latter, is reflected in the idea of agencies as 'political police' where they are (ab)used by governing politicians who fail to distinguish between the interests of the 'state' and those of the 'government' ...

4.4 Identifying actually existing minister–agency relations with one or other of these is difficult, not least because of 'plausible deniability' – a politician may actually 'task' an agency to conduct some intelligence operation but in such a way that responsibility for the operation can be denied should it become publicised. On the other hand, by way of a 'law of anticipated reactions' an agency might gather information that it believes a minister would like whether or not she ever actually asks for it.

4.5 Legislation in some countries has set out clearer minister–agency relationships, for example, the requirement for written ministerial directions in the case of both ASIO and CSIS. These must be shared with review bodies but these procedures have not succeeded entirely in removing the issue of partisan direction. This is illustrated by the continuing belief of some Reform MPs that CSIS was being used against them prior to the 1993 federal election, or, at least, that PC Ministers were the beneficiaries of information gathered by CSIS.

4.6 With respect to foreign intelligence, attention is more likely to be focused on the issue of ministers as 'consumers' of the intelligence product. It should be borne in mind that ministers do have sources of policy-relevant information other than intelligence agencies, e.g. official and political staffs, personal experience, etc. ...

Issues for Discussion

4.7 Should intelligence agencies be more or less integrated into policy debates[?] Should analysts be aware of policy concerns so that they can produce intelligence with greater policy relevance (that is more likely to be listened to) or should they 'tell it like it is' regardless of whether this is in line with current policy or not (with the greater likelihood of not being listened to) [?] The former, specifically its adoption in the CIA under Casey/Gates, gave rise to much discussion at the October conference under the heading of 'politicization' ...

4.8 Speaking to the CASIS Conference, the director of CSIS claimed to have found a middle way between these two courses: 'Intelligence has to be better integrated with the decision-making process ... Intelligence must continue to be policy neutral; Intelligence must be policy relevant' ... To put it mildly, this involves treading a very fine line. It again raises the issue of how appropriate it is for agencies with a security intelligence function to extend into the broader field of intelligence. Security intelligence is not 'policy neutral' – it involves targeting on the basis of executive decisions about 'threats.'

4.9 Other questions here include: do ministers make adequate use of intelligence in their formulation of policy, or, rather, do they see the role of intelligence as restricted to 'warning', to preventing nasty surprises?

4.10 Can ministers be 'trained' to make better use of intelligence? They are often in office for relatively short periods of time; can agencies educate ministers to pay greater attention to the product? Is there any way of balancing the politican's demand for brevity with the agencies' preference to explore complexity?

4.11 If ministers know what they want from intelligence, do agencies know and do they try to provide it? If, on the other hand, agencies provide ministers with what they think the ministers 'need to know' then what is the danger that they simply tell ministers what they want to hear?

NOTES

1 The Subcommittee on National Security (SCNS) was a subcommittee of the House Standing Committee on Justice and Legal Affairs. One member of the Bloc Québécois and one member of the Reform party sit on it. In its June 1996 report, the standing committee was critical of the performance of SIRC in the Heritage Front affair. The SCNS no longer exists.

2 For more details on the strained relations between SIRC and SCNS, see Henderson (1996: 17–18). See also also Henderson (1995).

REFERENCES

Canada. 1969. *Report of the Royal Commission on Security* (Mackenzie Report). Ottawa: Government Printer.

– 1981. *Freedom and Security under the Law: Second Report of the Commission of Inquiry Concerning Certain Activities of the Royal Canadian Mounted Police* (McDonald Report). 2 vols., Ottawa: Minister of Supply and Services Canada.

– Auditor General. 1996. *Report of the Auditor General of Canada to the House of Commons*. Ottawa: Minister of Public Works and Government Services Canada.
– House of Commons. 1990. *In Flux But Not in Crisis. Report of the Special Committee on the Review of the CSIS Act and the Security Offences Act* (Thacker Report). Ottawa: Canadian Government Publishing Centre, Supply and Services Canada.
– Senate. 1983. *Report of the Special Committee of the Senate on the Canadian Security Intelligence Service. Delicate Balance: A Security Intelligence Service in a Democratic Society*. Ottawa: Minister of Supply and Services Canada.
– Solicitor General Canada. 1991. *On Course: National Security for the 1990s. The Government's Response to the Report of the House of Commons Special Committee on the Review of the Canadian Security Intelligence Act and the Security Offences Act*. Minister of Supply and Services Canada.

Henderson, Robert D'A., ed. 1995. *CASIS Intelligence Newsletter* no. 21 (winter 1995).

Henderson, Robert D'A. 1996. 'SIRC: A Crisis of Accountability?' *Casis Intelligence Newsletter* no. 27 (fall 1996), 17–18.

Security Intelligence Review Committee (SIRC). Every year, 1985–96. *Annual Report 1984–85* [1985–86, ...] Ottawa: Minister of Supply and Services Canada.
– (1989a). *Amending the CSIS Act: Proposals for the Special Committee of the House of Commons 1989*. Ottawa: Minister of Supply and Services.

Summary of Discussion on Security Intelligence

In a brief historical overview of the papers, Wesley Wark noted that until the end of the 1970s there was no scholarship on security intelligence. One effect of the McDonald Commission was that it created more public knowledge, giving Canadians an opportunity to address this secretive area of state-craft seriously. Wark warned, however, that while other democratic countries are engaging in public debate over the future of security intelligence, Canada has not. He urged Canadians to take more seriously the questions that Peter Russell's work in this area has opened up for us.

The discussion following the presentations focused at first around the difficulties in implementing an accountable security service and a more transparent policy process. There were some examples of the closed nature of CSIS, such as Phillip Stenning's receiving a business card from someone in the service that had no indication of the organization for which the fellow worked.

Carl Baar commented that he has encountered a similar closedness on the part of the Ministry of the Attorney General and wondered whether the insularity of CSIS were not at least in part the result of the service's operating along traditional lines of a closed system of cabinet government that some areas of government have not been able to escape. Baar also asked how we can have parliamentary accountability if one of the basic principles of espionage is that one lies when asked about what one has done?

Jean-Paul Brodeur replied that it is not necessary to lie, it is much easier simply to forget, or be vague and evasive. Nevertheless, his experience suggests that this practical problem can be solved. Sometimes an evasive witness can be led to open up by a committee member's clever use of the documents.

Ted Finn, first director at CSIS, commented that it was absolutely appalling to hear what Brodeur had reported about the reluctance of CSIS to engage with academics so many years after the civilianization of the force. He added that the longstanding assumption that people involved in security intelligence are somehow prone to being dishonest or unable to recognize the truth is simply untrue. He noted, however, that as director of the service he had had times when his conscience did not permit him to answer a question from an investigative body or other public forum. In those instances he would say only, 'I'm sorry, I cannot answer that question.' However, in a private forum such as with SIRC, his response could be different. There, as director of CSIS, he could say that he did not want to go into detail right then and suggest a private meeting with the commissioners so that staff would not be involved in sensitive matters. This provided a mechanism not only within which to tell the truth but also genuinely to inform. He commented further that extending this to a parliamentary context requires parliamentarians' willingness to go in camera and accept information that otherwise cannot, and must be expected not, to go into the public domain.

Ron Atkey confirmed what Finn had said. Moreover, he suggested that neither of the two directors at CSIS with whom he had worked had ever deliberately stonewalled or refused to give information. He did not, however, feel that this was true of the staff at CSIS, who would not want to reveal more than necessary. Atkey was also quick to note that there were not different classes of oversight, because he shared all information given to him as chair of SIRC with his colleagues on committee, but not the staff. He and his colleagues had sometimes been awestruck by the onerous responsibility of possessing the information they received and dealing with it responsibly in the context of their duty to report to the solicitor-general, Parliament, and the public. He added that having been an MP and being aware of the diverse forms of accountability of someone in that position, he is not fully comfortable with entrusting an MP who is not a minister with this responsibility.

Jean-Paul Brodeur commented that keeping information secret may be justified with regard to some specific cases and policies but that CSIS seems often unwilling to discuss even broad policy questions. Ted Finn agreed.

One of only two points at which Peter Russell himself directly intervened in the conference proceedings was at the close of the sessions on security intelligence. He did so to say that the idea of independent review was not his own, but rather grew out of a weekend of discussion at Mt Ste Marie with David McDonald and Don Rickerd. The problem was how to control an agency whose work is vital to a democracy but always endangers it. Their answer was a civilian monitoring committee to oversee the double-edged nature of security-intelligence operations. He emphasized the importance of such operations, noting as an example the serious dangers involved in the covert circulation of the materials for making nuclear weapons. But he also praised the scholars in this field, working with little information yet trying to keep the public intelligently informed about the risks. He closed by thanking the royal commission for resisting when the RCMP at first refused to give him the necessary security clearance to serve as research director.

PART IV: LAW AND THE COURTS

As a new lecturer at the University of Toronto in 1958, Peter Russell was assigned to teach the government of Canada course, using the standard text by McGregor Dawson. Finding that the chapter on the judiciary extended only through 1949, he decided to prepare something on the courts since then for his first paper at the Learned Societies meetings. To his delight, he found that the field was virtually untouched, making it a perfect niche for a young scholar. Inclusion of his paper in Paul Fox's 1962 edition of *Politics: Canada* gave him his first academic publication and an unexpected academic profile. When Pauline Jewitt called from Carleton University wanting him to write a paperback on important constitutional decisions, he was thrilled. And in 1963, when Claude Bissell called to say that the Royal Commission on Bilingualism and Biculturalism (B&B Commission) wanted him to prepare a study of the Supreme Court, he was convinced that there had been a mistake, that it must have had some other Peter Russell in mind. The work in each case produced splendid fruit. His *Leading Constitutional Decisions* (1965), was the first collection of constitutional cases to be assembled for political scientists in Canada. It set the standard for the field, going through multiple editions. In preparing his report for the B&B Commission, he virtually lived at the court for more than a year, making his first use of quantitative methods to describe the court's decision-making procedures. His report, *The Supreme Court of Canada as a Bilingual and Bicultural Institution*, appeared in 1969.

While his early works on the courts were aimed at its highest level, Peter soon came to realize the importance of lower courts and even informal courts when the opportunity came for him to go to Africa. At Harvard on sabbatical in 1967–8, he learned that the Rockefeller Foundation wanted Canadians to go to Africa. Andre Gombay, who had been best man at his wedding, and Storrs McCall, a former Oxford buddy, were already in Uganda teaching philosophy.

So Peter was delighted to accept an appointment as visiting professor at MaKerere University in Kampala. Nominally there to look at law and justice in an oral society as it developed a new legal culture following independence, he spent roughly half his time looking into courts and prisons for the Ugandan attorney general. On his first trip visiting country magistrates he observed little going on in the official courts but noticed a steady stream of people going to the local headman seeking more traditional justice. Looking into these informal courts, Peter came to respect the traditional approach to justice and advised the attorney general's office to build on it.

This experience with traditional African justice drove home for him the notion that a society expresses its genius through its legal system. As a result he became a legal pluralist, rejecting the assumption of the common law's superiority and becoming more open to the critical strain in legal scholarship. Visiting Ugandan prisons gave him a further appreciation of some of the broader social impact of the justice system. He found, for example, that delays in going to trial seriously undermined the domestic economy and ended up unduly burdening women in the society. He also saw at first hand the consequences of making even modest practical reforms, such as clearly identifying those prisoners who had been awaiting trial for more than two years.

Other more brutal lessons were also learned in Africa. The coup in Uganda on 26 January 1971 brought with it hard political lessons, not least of which involved Idi Amin's direct manipulation of Peter and his work. Placing the attorney general, with whom Peter had closely worked for the past eighteen months, under house arrest, Amin demanded that Russell nevertheless complete his report on the justice system. Within twenty-four hours of his delivering *The Administration of Justice in Uganda*, Idi Amin held a press conference using the report to legitimate the imposition of his own harsh methods and to trumpet the advantages of rule by decree over parliamentary democracy. Peter returned to Canada in June 1971 with a new appreciation of why Aristotle says that debate about justice is what differentiates us from brutes.

Peter Russell's conviction that the law as a phenomenon deserved more than the technical study it received in law schools was deepened by contact with the American Law and Society Association, beginning with its meeting in Toronto. He realized more fully now that the study of law could be strengthened by greater input and interaction with the social sciences and humanities, a perspective given a boost some years later by Harry Arthurs's influential report to SSHRCC. He also came to appreciate better how forms of cultural expression shape the substance of our legal institutions, dovetailing neatly with ideas discussed while watching hockey games on TV with his neighbour, Marshall McLuhan.

Peter further recognized that it was a mistake to analyse judicial review without a thorough knowledge of the functioning of the courts below the Supreme Court. His inaugural essay 'Overcoming Legal Formalism' in the *Canadian Journal of Law and Society* (1986) emphasizes the lower courts, for all levels of the justice system can affect public policy and the welfare of Canadians. Moreover, he values the political dimension of the law; *The Judiciary in Canada: The Third Branch of Government* (1987) announces in its subtitle his mission to counter the common view that courts are not significant actors in the political process. Beyond being a pioneer in these areas, Peter has helped to institutionalize research on law and society in Canada, serving as a founding member and later president of the Canadian Law and Society Association.

Beyond writing the standard Canadian text on the judiciary, Peter Russell has had a longstanding interest in the appointment of judges. He had served as research adviser to the Canadian Bar Association Committee on the appointment of judges in the mid-1980s and also wrote a small armload of scholarly articles. Meanwhile, a former fraternity brother at University of Toronto and former chief counsel in the Berger Inquiry, Ian Scott, had become attorney general of Ontario. He asked Peter to put his body where his mouth was in developing a new system for the appointment of judges in Ontario. A major motivation for overhauling the system was to create a buffer between the attorney general and the deluge of advice to which he was subjected regarding whose brother-in-law might make a fine judge. In addition, there was the matter of diversity; of 240 provincial court judges only ten were women. Scott was also concerned about there being no judges from the Black, Italian, and Aboriginal communities. Nor had the government yet delivered on a promise to appoint more French-speaking judges.

Accepting the chair of the Judicial Appointments Advisory Committee of Ontario in 1989, Peter worked for four years to set in place a process that has transformed the province's judiciary. The guiding principle in his efforts was that courts in a democratic society must be sensitive to and reflect the community they serve. Opposed to quotas, he and a committee of non-lawyers devised a system of advertising and outreach that gained multi-party support in the Ontario legislature. Many outstanding judges have been appointed under the auspices of the Russell committee, including the author of one of the papers in this section. Recognizing that something similar had to be done at the federal level, he and Jacob Zeigel have turned their scholarly attention to federal judicial appointments.

Summary of Papers

The papers in this part exemplify some of the themes that have been important in Peter Russell's work on law and the courts. Madame Justice Maryka Omatsu's 'On Judicial Appointments' (chapter 11) briefly reviews the homogeneous demographic profile of the Canadian judiciary and the work of the Russell committee in Ontario in increasing its diversity, including her own appointment. Omatsu focuses on the effects of greater judicial diversity, particularly the inclusion of women. Her primary concern is whether female judges perform differently from males. Although she finds the social scientific data inconclusive, she sees scope for a unique contribution by women in criminal, family, and tort law, where gender and legal considerations coincide. Drawing parallels from her experience representing Aboriginal people before administrative tribunals, Omatsu describes some of the changes needed to reflect women's needs and experiences. She expresses a balance of optimism and realism in detailing some of the ways in which women can come to play an equal role in the Canadian legal system.

Carl Baar's contribution systematically pursues one of Peter Russell's key insights – namely, that courts are part of the political structure of society. 'Courts as State Actors' (chapter 12) uses quantitative methods to assess the role of trial and appellate courts in Canada. Consistent with the idea that courts are agents of the state, his data reveal that on the whole the lower courts reinforce the exercise of state authority in criminal cases. More specifically, he shows how the outcomes of trial and appellate courts define the law-based regime of a society, a theme consistent with Hugh Corder's work on South Africa.

Martin Friedland and Kent Roach pick up on Peter Russell's interest in local legal cultures in 'Borderline Justice: Choosing Juries in the Two Niagaras' (chapter 13). Their primary concern is why there are fewer jury trials on the Ontario side of the Niagara River than on the New York side. Despite limitations of data, they creatively canvass a wide range of possible explanations for the differences between jurisdictions, concluding that the interplay of legal culture, rules, and practices accounts for the distinction.

Hugh Corder's 'South Africa's Constitutional Odyssey' (chapter 14) describes the process by which the rule of law has returned to South Africa. Despite the substantial damage done to public trust in courts and law under apartheid, both the African National Congress and the National party have helped revive the rule of law through their emphasis on rights and legal transition. But Corder also argues that the rule of law could serve as an invaluable lowest common denominator only when the futility of violence was recognized by both parties. In touching on the mechanisms used to maintain momentum throughout a multi-party negotiation process, Corder explains the role of technical committees in handling divisive issues concerning creation of a transitional constitution, achieving a democratic assembly, and establishing a constitutional court. His focus on the participatory aspects of South Africa's constitutionalism offers a much needed perspective on our own constitutional politics, for its achievement in the face of extraordinary division and diversity is a true inspiration.

11

On Judicial Appointments: Does Gender Make a Difference?[1]

JUSTICE MARYKA OMATSU

Towards Greater Diversity

For several years, business has not been as usual in the appointment of Ontario provincial judges. The system of judicial selection, introduced as a pilot project in 1989 by Attorney General Ian Scott, was the first of its kind in Canada. Scott, a legal innovator, declared a moratorium of sorts on the political appointment of provincial judges. Openings were advertised[2] and a twelve-person committee was established to recruit and select candidates for the judiciary.[3] The committee was for a time referred to as the Russell Committee, after its first chair.[4]

The committee's mandate[5] is to winnow applicants, run background audits on aspirants, and then interview a smaller pool. Additional follow-up checks are conducted on successful candidates, whose names are forwarded to the attorney general's office.[6] The names of any 'survivors' are forwarded to cabinet for final consideration and affirmation.

Demographics

The statistics compiled by political scientists Peter McCormick and Ian Greene[7] confirm the perception that the judiciary is homogeneous. They point out that judges as a group are married, overwhelmingly male, of British or French ancestry, in their mid-fifties, Judaeo-Christian, born into the middle or upper-middle classes and had been successful lawyers, with limited trial experience.[8]

By the mid-1990s, there were approximately 2,500 judges in Canada: 1,000 were appointed by Ottawa and 1,500, by the provinces. The subset to which I belong demographically is one of 263 women judges (women make up approximately 12 per cent of the judiciary in Canada)[9] and one of a small percentage (about 2 per cent) of visible-minority judges.

To change these demographics, in 1989 Ontario introduced an employment-equity recruitment policy for provincial judicial appointments, as advocated by Ian Scott, Peter Russell, and others. Prior to the establishment of the Judicial Appointments Advisory Committee, six of the 235 Ontario provincial judges (2.6 per cent) were women. By December 1998, 56 of the 253 judges in Ontario are female (22 per cent).[10] From 1989 to 1995, 1,300 lawyers (about one-third women) applied for the 105 appointments, of whom approximately 30 per cent were women.[11] During this period, of the 111 new appointments, sixty-eight were men (61.2 per cent) and 43 were women (38.7 per cent). In addition, three were Aboriginal (2.7 per cent; one is a woman); ten are from racial minorities (9 per cent; three are women); and eight are francophone (7.2 per cent; three are women). Some milestones are reflected in these recent appointments: in 1991, Terry Vyse became Canada's first Aboriginal woman judge; in 1992 Micheline Rawlins became Ontario's first Black woman judge (second Black Canadian woman judge), and in 1993, I became Canada's first East Asian woman judge.

In the remainder of this paper I address the arguments about increasing the numbers of women judges and whether their presence is significant. I deal only with female judges, because of the paucity of other non-majority appointments to the bench and thus the lack of literature on their impact. Then I turn to discussion of the changes said to be required for women's full participation in the law and what if any unique role female judges can play.

Justification

The report of the Canadian Bar Association (CBA) on gender equality[12] adopts the following rationale for ensuring gender representation on the bench:

> (a) women who are bound by the justice system should be participants in it at all levels; (b) public confidence in the system would be enhanced by the participation of both sexes; (c) female judges are important role models; and (d) female judges can make a unique and important contribution to the adjudication process.[13]

Regarding points a–c, which are largely non-controversial, I have few comments to make. The bulk of the paper addresses point d – 'unique and important contribution' – which is both complex and contested.

Point a: Women who are bound by the justice system should be participants in it at all levels. The mere fact of having a female presiding judge can sometimes make a difference. I recall the experience of a female colleague, Judge Sally Marin, sitting at Metro North court in Toronto. Judge Marin was conducting a hearing involving a man charged with sexually assaulting two girls when they were very young. One child was unable to testify in the presence of men. The courtroom was cleared, save for the accused. As the court staff, defence counsel, crown attorney, and the judge were all women, the trial was able to continue and the child gave her evidence. Such a scenario would have been impossible until recently.

Point b: 'Public confidence in the system would be enhanced by the participation of both sexes.' This principle likewise raises no controversy and appears to be accepted wisdom. There is general support for the notion that justice must not only be done but be seen to be done. One argument for appointing women judges derives from the 'fair reflection' principle – i.e., that the judiciary cannot be composed in total disregard of a diverse society. Australian Professor Sean Cooney wrote that this principle does not entail proportionate representation but means simply that 'in addition to the other criteria for judicial selection, regard be had to the present composition of a court so as to determine whether a particular appointment will enhance the breadth of experience on it.'[14] Even critics such as American academic Michael Solimine, who argues against the appointment of women 'simply because of their gender,' supports the notion of 'more women on the bench based on an intuitive sense of fairness.'[15]

The Canadian Bar Association's justifications for female judicial appointments support the belief that the bench should continue to change in order to reflect society more closely than at present, to maintain public confidence and legitimacy, and to help balance an existing 'tilt' that comes as a result of centuries-old near homogeneity.[16] They also support the idea that increasing public respect for the law requires a judiciary that is more reflective of the people and issues before the court and that proactive measures maintain people's confidence that they can receive justice in a diverse society.

Point c: 'Female judges are important role models.' Again no raised eyebrows. Let me relate a story that took place during my first weeks sitting as a judge at Old City Hall in downtown Toronto. As I was leaving the courtroom in my black robes and red sash, two Black teenage girls approached me. One of the girls asked me, 'How long did it take you to get here?' Slightly confused, I asked, 'Do you mean to become a judge?' She responded, 'Yes.' I replied that I had been a lawyer for sixteen years. 'Gosh,' she exclaimed, 'you mean it's going to take me that long?' I am sure that the many other Canadian women judges can tell similar experiences.

Point d: 'Female jurists can make a unique and important contribution to the adjudication process.' Expectations range from i) the sceptical view that women judges will be mere window dressing, ii) through the more ambitious hope that they will reform and gender-neutralize the law, to iii) the most radical claim that they will bring about structural changes in the legal system.

Point di: Window dressing. The mere presence of women (and minority) judges caused former U.S. Supreme Court Justice Joseph Grodin to write: 'The diversity within our court gave collegiality a special dimension, and it made me realize that the significance of including women and minorities on a tribunal is much more than symbolic. Bird, Broussard, and Reynoso brought to our discussions perspectives that went beyond my own experience, but even apart from anything they said, their very presence tended to heighten my own sensitivity toward those perspectives, and I believe the same was true for other judges as well.'[17]

Point dii: Reform. The 'do women judges make a difference?' question has usually been raised by those who think that women judges have a special perspective on the cases they hear and thus can introduce genuine neutrality and impartiality into the justice system.[18] Several recent studies on judicial decision-making conclude that gender is not a determining factor for predictability of result.[19] By contrast, critics of a diverse judiciary have raised the spectre that a worldview other than the prevailing one might wreak havoc with the sacrosanct concept of judicial impartiality.[20]

The issue at hand comprises at least three separate, if related, questions, which I address in turn: first, do women in general differ from men with respect to their values?; second, does the fact of being a judge make a women judge different from other women?; and third, are women judges different from male judges in the performance of their jobs?

Regarding the first question, noted psychologist Carol Gilligan is often cited to support the view that 'women view the world and what goes on in it from a different perspective from men.' Gilligan believes that the sexes have different worldviews – that women see themselves as members of a community and men view themselves as independent of others.[21]

Some argue that a woman's special commitment to fairness comes not from gender per se but from personal experiences of discrimination. U.S. Federal District Court Judge Fern Smith expressed an opinion that I share when she said that women do not see fairness, justice, right, and wrong differently from men, but that 'ethnicity and race and socioeconomic status change people's perceptions of fairness and justice.'[22]

Second, on women judges being different from others of their sex, social scientists Peter McCormick and Twyla Job speculate that one reason why female judges do not perform along gender lines is because they have learned male behaviour in the context of legal culture and are in a sense no longer 'real' women. As a result, they 'raise the specter that the class and character preferences built into the triple hurdles of university entrance, law school admission, and judicial recruitment, combined with the learned values of the legal "professional project" itself, may seriously limit the immediate impact of women on the bench.'[23] Law professor Christine Boyle writes that a principled feminist 'might experience ethical difficulties in accepting an [judicial] appointment. A feminist might feel herself to be restricted to mere reformism as a judge, or as giving credibility to a morally bankrupt system, and therefore refuse such an appointment.'[24]

I agree with McCormick and Job that education and work help to mould the people we become. I also agree with Boyle that a woman deciding to accept a judgeship considers the impact that the appointment will have on her life and what if any contribution she can make to her field. To my mind, however, McCormick, Job, and Boyle overstate their positions. Although a female judge is a woman with some privileges, outside the courtroom her daily experiences are those of any woman with her demographic characteristics.

On the third question, whether there is a difference between male and female decisions, many commentators are now largely sceptical that gender determines judgments, although the jury is still out.[25] Social scientists have analysed judicial decision-making from various perspectives.[26] In a recent Canadian study, McCormick and Job applied two hypotheses about female behaviour to 6,262 criminal-appeal decisions of the Alberta Court of Appeal from 1985 to 1992, when at least two of the eleven appellate judges were women. First, given that the literature suggests that women are less punitive,[27] more liberal, and more compassionate and conciliatory than men, the writers predicted that there should be fewer convictions and fewer successful sentence appeals by defendants on panels with female judge(s). Second, on the assumption that women view sexual assault and sex-related offences as serious and are more likely to sympathize or identify with the victim, there would be more convictions for these offences.

McCormick and Job's research indicated that the presence of female judges resulted, as predicted, and in slightly fewer successful sentence appeals by defendants and more convictions upheld for sexual assault. However, contrary to their expectations, there was a slightly higher rate of conviction (5 per cent), except for drug-related offences. The authors conclude that 'it does not appear that women judges make a great deal of difference, and certainly not in the directions that might have been expected from related research.'[28]

Commenting on this research, Joan Brockman criticized the assumptions, method, and results. She believes that a more qualitative content analysis of criminal appeal decisions would better reflect 'the reality of what is occurring.'[29] I concur with this criticism and note as well that McCormick and

Job's study is misleading because it is limited solely to appellate decisions. Generally, at that level, the court is concerned primarily with errors in law. An application of their thesis to trial-level decisions might not provide the same results.

A paper on American women judges concluded that 'the empirical studies show only slight if any differences between the overall voting behaviour of male and female judges.'[30] Initially Solimine and Wheatley feared that female judges would ignore statute and common law and decide cases by hormones. However, satisfied to the contrary as a result of their investigations, they concluded that, in regard to handling cases, 'Instinct and experience suggest that in all likelihood, there is not a meaningful difference' (between the sexes). They determined that the appointment of female jurists can do no harm and supported appointing more female judges because of the 'possibility' that 'men and women bring different perspectives to bear in their roles as judges.'[31]

Since data on gender-specific judicial decisions are sparse and inconclusive, I base my own current view on my limited experience on the bench and only with reference to judicial decisions. With those provisos, I have not noted a variance between men and women judges about principles of fairness, justice, and right and wrong. A difference I have observed, and which is in keeping with the comments of Judge Wilson cited below in Lavallee,[32] pertains to the application of general principles, where women judges may make different judgments regarding such matters as what counts as a defence or a mitigating circumstance at least in cases where the experiences of women are germane.

In Lavallee, expert evidence was admitted to assist the court to understand spousal abuse. Judge Wilson commented: 'If it strains credulilty to imagine what the ordinary man would do in the position of a battered spouse, it is probably because men do not typically find themselves in that situation. Some women do, however. The definition of what is reasonable must be adapted to circumstances which are, by and large, foreign to the world inhabited by the hypothetical "reasonable man."'

My conclusion therefore regarding whether women judges will reform the law (Point dii) is that gender, like ethnicity, race, and social class, affects judges' application of basic legal principles. Female judges are sometimes able to draw on experiences specific to women (for example, in sexual assault, child care, abortion, and wife battering cases), to gender-neutralize the law or at least widen the debate.

Point diii: Radical change. Judge Wilson in her paper 'Will Women Judges Really Make a Difference?' opined that contract, real property, and corporate law were gender-neutral but that criminal, family, and tort law had a 'distinctly male perspective,'[33] which has 'resulted in legal principles that are not fundamentally sound.'[34]

Regina Graycar agrees that fundamental changes are needed to transform the male-centredness of law and legal reasoning – which, in her opinion, cannot be addressed 'simply by adding some women to the bench and stirring.'[35] Graycar mentions the institution of the law, with its texts, hierarchy, and method (how judges 'orient' their narratives) as barriers to 'women's stories being heard in courts and if heard, being given credibility and authority.'[36] Graycar believes that the goal of ungendered decisions is a much larger project that requires 'scrutinising the gendered underpinnings of legal stories ... We need to confront the epistemological processes by which legal discourses construct reality and give authority to particular versions of events.'[37] She echoes the view of other feminist legal theorists who have called for basic changes in the principles of legal reasoning,[38] legal procedure, women's participation in the legal process,[39] and alternatives to the adversary system.[40]

During the 1970s and 1980s in response to widespread criticism and pressure, the government, courts, and law schools made significant efforts to address obvious sexism. Governments and the legal system have responded to the demands of women and, pursuant to the Charter, amended laws. Albeit less radically than hoped for by feminist legal theorists.

I am not competent to evaluate the more abstract, epistemological dimensions of their ideas, but I believe that they are right to focus on what Judge Wilson calls 'the traditional reluctance of courts to get too deeply into the circumstances of a case ... to reduce the context of the dispute to its bare bones through a complex system of exclusionary rules.' I also agree with the observations of Carrie Menkel-Meadow that women are more comfortable with mediation and alternative forms of dispute resolution than with the adversarial system.[41]

Nor do I think that the changes advocated are unrealistic to achieve. Many are already daily practice in administrative tribunals, where there is also a higher percentage of women litigators and adjudicators. Court practices are also being altered. Examples are amendments to the hide-bound rules of evidence;[42] to the calling of experts; to the inapplicability of the reasonable-man standard when applied to a battered woman;[43] and to the admission of intervenors in human rights cases to broaden the context of the dispute beyond the parties.[44]

Can female (and male) judges play a role in the challenge thrown up by Judge Wilson to the Canadian judiciary to infuse 'the law with an understanding of what it means to be fully human'?[45] Without being unduly Pollyannaish about it, I believe that the law is transforming itself as we speak due in no small measure to the increased presence of women on the bench.

NOTES

1 I gave an earlier version of this paper on 15–16 November, 1996, at the University of Toronto, at a conference to mark Peter Russell's retirement. Participants at this event made helpful comments; Judge Robert Walmsley and Professors Constance Backhouse, Harry Glasbeek, Regina Graycar, and Mary Jane Mossman provided useful suggestions on an earlier draft.

2 The advertisements appeared in the *Ontario Reports*. They encouraged interested lawyers of ten years' standing and members of 'traditionally under-represented groups in the judiciary, aboriginal peoples, francophones, persons with disabilities, racial minorities and women' to apply.

3 From 1989 to 1995, the committee was composed of six lay persons appointed by the attorney-general, one lawyer appointed by the Canadian Bar Association, one lawyer selected by the Law Society, two lawyers appointed by the attorney general, and two judges (one selected by the Judicial Council and one from the provincial bench).

4 Peter Russell, *The Judiciary in Canada: The Third Branch of Government* (Toronto: McGraw-Hill Ryerson 1987), 164–6, 'Should the Judiciary Be Socially Representative?'; Peter Russell and Jacob Ziegel, 'Federal Judicial Appointments: An Appraisal of the First Mulroney Government's Appointments' (May 1989), draft paper for the Canadian Association of Law Teachers

5 The procedure of judicial selection that I describe has been codified by the Courts of Justice Statute Law Amendment Act, proclaimed 28 February 1995. A major change was in the composition of the committee, which is now composed of seven lay persons appointed by the government, two provincial judges, three lawyers, and one member of the Judicial Council.

6 Section 43(12) of the Courts of Justice Statute Amendment Act provides that 'the Attorney General may reject the Committee's recommendations and require it to provide a fresh list.'

7 Peter McCormick and Ian Green, *Judges and Judging: Inside the Canadian Judicial System* (Toronto: James Lorimer 1990). Harry Glasbeek, Review of *Judges and Judging*, *Ottawa Law Review* 23 no. 2 (1991), 453.

8 McCormick and Green, *Judges and Judging*, 68; Madame Justice Bertha Wilson, *Touchstones for Change: Equality, Diversity, and Accountability* (Ottawa: Canadian Bar Association 1993), 186. Her report stated that 'approximately 12% of the federally appointed judges and 13% of the provincially-appointed judges were women' (61). The authors conclude that minority ethnicities are 'significantly under-represented among the senior judiciary.' The authors cite Peter Russell's observation that visible minorities are 'especially under-represented on the judiciary in all the provinces' (64). The average age of federally appointed judges is fifty-nine and of provincially appointed judges fifty-three. Both groups serve on average ten years on the bench

(66–7). The authors conclude that 'socially, judges come disproportionately from upper-class backgrounds.' George Adams and Paul Cavalluzzo, 'The Supreme Court of Canada: A Biographical Study,' *Ontario Historical Law Journal* 7 (1969), 61, found that only two of the first fifty Supreme Court of Canada judges were born into working-class families (70); Table 3.4 indicates that judges as a group are inclined to be 'high achievers' (69). 'About one-fifth ... considered themselves to be primarily trial lawyers before appointment.'

9 In 1994 there were 263 female judges in Canada – 125 federally appointed and 138 provincially appointed. See Canadian Bar Association, *Touchstones*, 186, which sets the figures at 12 per cent federally appointed and 13 per cent provincially.

10 Statistics for fall 1996 were provided by the Office of the Chief Judge and the Judicial Appointments Advisory Committee. Law Society of Ontario (LSUC), fall 1996 analysis, shows that the percentage of women members of LSUC called to the bar for ten or more years is 15.8 per cent. According to the LSUC's *Transitions Report*, many more female than male lawyers do not remain in practice, or practise part-time. Women are found in family law 62.9 per cent, and in the public and non-profit sector. Sixty-nine per cent of women start in private practice, as compared to 81 per cent of men. Figures are from the LSUC, *Crossing the Bar: A Century of Women's Experience 'Upon the Rough and Troubled Seas of Legal Practice' in Ontario* (Toronto 1993), 29.

11 The Judicial Appointments Advisory Committee, *Annual Report, 1994–95* (Toronto 1995), xiii.

12 The Canadian Bar Association, *Touchstones for Change: Equality, Diversity and Accountability* (Ottawa 1993), 185.

13 Isabel Grant and Lynn Smith, 'Gender Representation in the Canadian Judiciary,' in Law Reform Commission of Ontario, *Appointing Judges: Philosophy, Politics and Practice* (Toronto: Queen's Printer 1991), 57.

14 Sean Cooney, 'Gender and Judicial Selection: Should There Be More Women on the Courts?' *Melbourne University Law Review* 19 (June 1993), 21–3.

15 Michael Solimine and Susan Wheatley, 'Rethinking Feminist Judging,' *Indiana Law Journal* 70 no. 89 (K93), 915–18.

16 Grant and Smith, 'Gender Representation,' note 68.

17 Joseph R. Grodin, *In Pursuit of Justice: Reflections of a Supreme Court Justice*, (Berkeley: University of California Press 1989), 58.

18 Madame Justice Bertha Wilson, 'Will Women Judges Really Make a Difference?' *Osgoode Hall Law Journal* 28 no. 3 (1990), 515, citing Carol Gilligan.

19 Peter McCormick and Twyla Job, 'Do Women Judges Make a Difference? An Analysis of Appeal Court Data,' *Canadian Journal of Law and Society* 8 no. 1 (1993), 135; Solimine and Wheatley, 'Rethinking Feminist Judging.'

20 I discuss this issue in 'The Fiction of Judicial Impartiality,' *Canadian Journal of*

Women and the Law 9 no. 1 (1997). A review of American expungement cases and Canadian judicial-review hearings of administrative tribunals indicates that less homogeneity on the bench and on administrative tribunals may result in women and minority decision-makers being scrutinized more closely for bias for displaying the very characteristics that they are said to bring to the job.

Richard Devlin, '"We Can't Go on Together with Suspicious Minds": Judicial Bias and Racialized Perspective in *R. v. R.D.S.*,' *Dalhousie Law Review* (1995), 408. The author analyses the history of a decision of Corrine Sparks, who is Canada's first Black woman judge and Nova Scotia's only Black judge. Two Nova Scotia appellate courts had found a reasonable apprehension of bias by Judge Sparks. The Supreme Court of Canada overturned the appellate decisions. *RDS* v. *Q.* (1997), 118 CCC (3d) 353.

Bronwyn Naylor, 'Pregnant Tribunals,' *Legal Service Bulletin* 14 (1989), 41, relates an application for review against a pregnant tribunal member, who 'suffered from the well-known medical condition "placidity" which detracts significantly from the intellectual competence of all mothers-to-be'!

Martha Minow, 'Stripped Down like a Runner or Enriched by Experience: Bias and Impartiality of Judges and Jurors,' *William and Mary Law Review* 33 (1992), 1201. In reviewing the appointment of Clarence Thomas as associate justice of the U.S. Supreme Court, Minow considers views of bias and their relationship to the ideal of fair representation in the selection of jurors and judges. Thomas, during the Senate hearings, said that, as a judge, 'You want to be stripped down like a runner and shed the baggage of ideology.'

21 Carol Gilligan, *In a Different Voice: Psychological Theory and Women's Development* (Cambridge, Mass.: Harvard University Press 1982).

22 Panel, 'Different Voices, Different Choices? The Impact of More Women Lawyers and Judges on the Judicial System,' *Judicature* 74 (1990), 138, 145.

23 McCormick and Job, 'Do Women Judges?' 147.

24 Christine Boyle, 'Sexual Assault and the Feminist Judge,' *Canadian Journal of Women and the Law* 1 (1985), 93.

25 David Allen and Diane Wall, 'The Behavior of Women State Supreme Court Justices: Are They Tokens or Outsiders?' *Justice System Journal* 12 no. 2 (1987), 232. In an interesting study, the authors found that women justices tend to be the most pro-woman member of a court; and on both criminal rights and economic liberties they tended to be either the extreme liberal or the extreme conservative.

26 Burton Atkins, Lenore Alpert, and Robert Ziller, 'Personality Theory and Judging,' *Law and Policy Quarterly* 2 no. 2 (1980) 189–220. The authors, decision-making theorists, applied self-esteem psychological models to determine how a judge's personality might affect his or her decisions and sentences.

27 Gilligan, *In a Different Voice*, cited by McCormick and Job, 144 note 28.

28 McCormick and Job, 'Do Women Judges?' 146.

29 Joan Brockman, 'A Difference without a Distinction? A Comment on 'Do Women Judges Make a Difference? An Analysis of Appeal Court Data' by Peter McCormick and Twyla Job,' *Canadian Journal of Law and Society* 8 no. 1 (1993), 149; Peter McCormick and Twyla Job, 'Hypotheses, Statistics, and Women Judges: A Response,' *Canadian Journal of Law and Society* 8 no. 1 (1993), 165; McCormick and Job respond to Brockman's comment.

30 Solimine and Wheatley, supra, 898. The writers oppose the view that judges should be representative (the partiality argument) but mention that political party affililation might play a stronger role than gender in decision-making.

31 Ibid., 919.

32 *R. v. Lavallee*, [1990] 1 SCR, 852. The accused shot her common-law spouse in the back of the head as he was leaving her room after an altercation. Theirs had been a violent and abusive relationship. At trial, the accused was acquitted of murder on the grounds of self-defence. A psychiatrist had testified to the 'battered-wife syndrome' and had concluded that the accused had felt that she must react in a violent way or be killed.

33 The American National Association of Women Judges in 1985 determined that 'residual prejudice against women remained in personal injury damages, criminal sentencing, divorce, child custody and juvenile justice.' 'Gender Bias in Courts,' *Judicial Conference Report* 1 (1985), 7 (New Jersey study), cited by Hon. Patricia Wald, 'The Role of Morality in Judging: A Woman Judge's Perspective,' *Law and Inequality* (1986) Vol. 4 no. 3 (1986) ff 41.

34 Bertha Wilson, 'Will Women Judges Really Make a Difference?' 515; Reg Graycar, 'Hoovering as a Hobby: The Common Law's Approach to Work in the Home *Refractory Girl* 28 (1985), 22. Graycar surveys the damages awarded housewives in tort law.

35 Graycar, 'Hoovering,' 269.

36 Ibid., 268–9; discusses former Justice Wilson's decision in *R. v. Lavallée* [1990] 1 SCR, 852, as a model.

37 Ibid., 281.

38 Mary Jane Mossman, 'Feminism and the Legal Method: The Difference It Makes,' *Wisconsin Women's Law Journal* 3 (1987), 147.

39 Christine Boyle, 93.

40 Regina Graycar and Jenny Morgan, *Hidden Gender of Law* (New South Wales: Federation Press (1990), 410.

41 Carrie Menkel-Meadow, 'Portia in a Different Voice: Speculations on a Women's Lawyering Process,' *Berkeley Women's Law Journal* 1 (1985), 39, and 'The Comparative Sociology of Women Lawyers: The "Feminization" of the Legal Profession' *Osgoode Hall Law Journal* 24 (1986), 897; Bertha Wilson, 'Will Women Judges?' 520; Mossman, 'Feminism'; Graycar, 'Hoovering,' 281.

42 The 'hearsay' exception-rule trilogy of cases: *R. v. Khan* (1990), 59 CCC (3d) 92, SCC; *R. v. Smith* (1992) 75 CCC 257, SCC; and *R. v. B.(K.G.)* (1993) 79 CCC 257, SCC.

43 *R. v. Lavallee* (1990), 55 CCC (3d) 97, SCC. Expert evidence was admitted to assist the court to understand the battered-wife syndrome.

44 Wilson, 'Will Women Judges?' 521.

45 Ibid., 522.

46 The *Lavallee* decision, written by Madame Justice Wilson, for example, illustrates my experience that the presence of women judges increases and does not diminish impartiality.

12

Courts as State Actors: Comparing Appeal and Trial Courts

CARL BAAR

A major development in political science over the past decade has been the rediscovery of political institutions.[1] Yet Peter Russell never lost them. In particular, he has maintained a career-long interest in the courts as political institutions. His interest has been empirical, as shown in one of the earliest analyses of voting behaviour in the Supreme Court of Canada[2] and in the most comprehensive text on the judiciary as 'the third branch.'[3] His interest has also been normative, as reflected in his commitment to understanding and strengthening judicial independence and impartiality and the quality of constitutional judgments. These interests were once again translated into action, most visibly in his chairing of Ontario's first screening committee for judicial appointments.

At the same time, Russell's premise that courts are political institutions has been enough to rankle generations of judges who respect his scholarship and views on specific legal and political issues. If the courts should be independent and impartial, how can they also be political?

The answer has always been obvious to political scientists regardless of their ideological persuasion. Courts articulate authoritative statements of the law. Judges apply their findings and conclusions in making specific, binding orders. Courts and judges are therefore political actors no matter how carefully they separate themselves from politics in the narrow sense of 'partisan politics' or 'interest group politics.' They are state actors, agents of the state, even as they define themselves apart from government – again in the narrow sense of 'the government of the day' rather than the law-based regime that helps define a democratic society.

This paper examines Canadian courts as state actors, as institutions of the state. First, it looks at recent research. Second, it attempts an empirical examination of the work of trial and appeal courts throughout Canada, going beyond the traditional focus on the Supreme Court of Canada alone. Most important, it looks not just at the decisions made by judges but at the processing and outcomes of cases brought to court. The data, the conclusion suggests, indicate that courts, on a regular, routine, and expected basis, act to reinforce state authority even as judges conduct themselves as independent, impartial, and conscientious adjudicators. It may be that the more conscientious, independent, and impartial judges are, the more effectively the courts defend state authority.

Examining both appeal courts and trial courts as political institutions requires application of a common frame of reference to both of those broad categories of judicial bodies. This paper argues that political and social science literature on judicial behaviour has not done that. It has tended to examine appellate courts as collections of diverse, independent decision-makers and typically seen trial courts as components in a larger scheme of social control. In practice, both types of courts and judges – trial and appeal – can be seen, not only theoretically but also empirically, from both perspectives.

This analysis would benefit from broader historical, contextual, qualitative, and comparative analysis than space permits here. But beginning close to home, I hope to provide an additional basis for the broader consideration of courts as political institutions.

Research on Appeal and Trial Courts

While Peter Russell's writings and prescriptions on judges have been egalitarian in character,[4] political science as a discipline has reinforced hierarchical distinctions within the judiciary. It focuses on the Supreme Court of Canada, as American counterparts focus on the U.S. Supreme Court. It leaves to sociologists, criminologists, and law professors all the other courts, which political scientists too often lump together as 'lower courts.' As a result, the way in which higher and lower courts have been studied has made their differences appear sharper than they are in reality and has erased some of the key similarities in case-processing shared by these courts.

Empirical studies of supreme courts began by examining non-unanimous cases decided after a full hearing. Researchers sought to examine the differences among individual judges by finding out when they voted in blocs that may have reflected different approaches (or ideologies or attitudes) towards the issues.[5] Judges could be ranked and classified by their comparative willingness to support the prosecution or the defence in criminal cases, the competing constitutional claims of federal or provincial/state governments, and civil-liberties claimants or public authorities in Charter (or Bill of Rights and Fourteenth Amendment) cases.

These rankings could generate overall scores that could be studied cross-nationally. Thus Tate and Sittiwong ranked justices on the Supreme Court of Canada by their votes over a thirty-six-year period using a personal-attributes analysis and generated striking differences in voting preferences on two scales.[6] Because their main interest was seeing whether and how personal attributes of the individual justices produced variations in voting behaviour, they considered only non-unanimous cases. As a result, it is impossible to find out how frequently the judges were in agreement, or the direction of that agreement – for example, were unanimous judgments more likely to support the crown than the defence, the federal government or the provinces, the civil liberties claim or the public authority? The authors explored the decisions of individual justices but could say nothing comparing individual courts.

Andrew Heard went beyond non-unanimous decisions in his study of the voting behaviour of individual Supreme Court justices in Charter of Rights cases.[7] By choosing Charter cases, however, he drew a sample with twice as high a proportion of non-unanimous decisions as non-Charter litigation.

The biases of existing approaches to the quantitative analysis of the voting behaviour of appellate judges were clear once again in a recent American article, 'The Influence of *Stare Decisis* on the Votes of United States Supreme Court Justices.'[8] Not only did the authors begins with non-unanimous cases, but they rejected the use of unanimous (and frequent) summary disposition cases, over the objections of two sets of critical commentators.[9]

In contrast, research on trial courts has concentrated on the activities of the highest-volume courts. The prototypical studies have examined plea bargaining in criminal intake courts. Empirical studies of trial courts have emphasized how many accused persons are found guilty and rarely focus on the close cases decided by a trial judge or by a jury after a full hearing – cases that most closely resemble the non-unanimous judgments of appellate courts.

In fact, all courts, whether trial or appellate, process a variety of cases using a range of techniques, routines, and officials to do the job. If we studied criminal trial courts with the methods that political scientists have used to study national courts of last resort, trial judges would look much more impartial and even-handed than the popular academic interpretation of those studies suggests. Conversely, using trial-court research techniques to study appellate courts may make those institutions appear less even-handed.

An empirical examination of the courts as political institutions requires this kind of comparison. Two classes of data are needed – all the cases that enter the court (for trial or appeal) and the cases that move through the system to a hearing on the merits, whether that hearing is by a trial or by an appeal court. How large is the gap between the first and second group? And what happens to the cases that enter the system but do not proceed to a hearing on the merits? Are over 90 per cent of those charged with criminal offences found guilty? Examination of trial-court work suggests that past empirical generalizations are oversimplified at best.

To build the analysis, we begin with courts of appeal, looking at the outcome of criminal cases that go to hearing and then enlarging the analysis to include all criminal appeals. The analysis then shifts to the outcome of criminal trials, both before a jury and before a judge alone, expanding once again to include all criminal dispositions in those trial courts. In principle, a similar comparison could be made of civil cases, but Canadian data on criminal trial and appellate courts are richer.

Case Processing by the Courts

Criminal Appeals

While the study of the votes of individual appellate judges in non-unanimous cases continues to dominate in the literature on judicial behaviour, a new perspective has emerged based on case outcomes themselves. Under the label of 'party capability theory,' political scientists have taken Marc Galanter's classic article on trial courts, 'Why the Haves Come out Ahead,'[10] and applied his distinction between repeat players and 'one-shotters' to the parties on appeal. Burt Atkins has used this approach to examine the English Court of Appeal,[11] Songer and Sheehan have examined federal courts of appeal in the United States,[12] and Peter McCormick has looked at Canadian appellate courts.

McCormick's data on who comes out ahead in the Supreme Court of Canada show the crown winning 57 per cent of its 227 appeals and losing 30 per cent of the 739 cases in which defendants appeal.[13] A new study covering the whole range of Canadian appellate courts, directed by political scientist Ian Greene, collected data on the flow and disposition of criminal appeals. Table 12.1, based on the outcomes of conviction appeals heard in nine provincial courts of appeal,[14] shows the crown even further ahead of the accused, winning 63.6 per cent of its appeals following acquittals and losing 25.8 per cent of the cases in which defendants appealed their convictions. Adding together all criminal appeals argued on the merits (i.e., excluding appeals limited to the nature and length of the sentence), the difference expands still further: the crown won 470 (72 per cent) and the accused 187 (28 per cent), or 68 per cent to 27 per cent if one includes the thirty-three cases where the issue was not decided or the appellant won only in part.

Table 12.1
Outcome of conviction appeals after hearing in provincial courts of appeals, by whether accused or crown was appellant

	Appellant	
Outcome	Crown (%)	Accused (%)
Won as appellant	63.6	25.8
Won in part as appellant	0.8	3.8
Issue not decided	3.0	1.3
Lost as appellant	32.6	69.0
Number	(132)	(558)
Total wins by crown	68.1	
Total wins by accused	27.1	
Other dispositions	4.8	
Total cases calculated*	(690)	

Sources: Case file sample, nine provincial courts of appeal, from Ian Greene et al., Canadian Appeal Court Project, York University. See Ian Greene et al., *Final Appeal* (Toronto, 1998), 176 (see Table 8.9).
*From 749: 19 with other appellants; 40 with missing data.

When Greene and his colleagues collected data on criminal cases filed in the provincial appellate courts, they assumed that those cases would normally go to hearing, since such courts provide the first appeal – an appeal available as one of right – from trials for indictable offences. This situation contrasts with that in the Supreme Court of Canada, whose appellate jurisdiction is largely (and increasingly) discretionary, and the U.S. Supreme Court, which is accessible only via a writ of certiorari and has spawned a whole literature on the strategic use of discretionary jurisdiction to set a policy agenda for that court.[15]

In fact, however, almost half the criminal cases that go to provincial courts of appeal are decided before a hearing on the merits. As Table 12.2 shows, a large proportion – 43.5 per cent of Greene's sample – does not even move past the first stage of filing a full set of documents.[16] Table 12.3 breaks down these disposition figures by province. It shows that the largest drop-off occurs in the three largest provinces – Ontario, Quebec, and British Columbia. While almost 60 per cent of Ontario's criminal appeals drop out early, over 70 per cent of Nova Scotia, Manitoba, Saskatchewan, and Prince Edward Island's criminal appeals move through a full hearing before disposition. This suggests that case

Table 12.2
When cases are disposed of in provincial courts of appeal

	Timing of disposition (%)
Before documents are filed	43.5
After documents are filed but before hearing is completed	4.4
After hearing	52.1
Number	(2,874)

Source: As Table 12.1; see *Final Appeal*, 54, Table 3.2.

Table 12.3
Stage when case dispositions occurred in courts of appeal, by province

Province	Before documents (%)	Before hearing (%)	After hearing (%)	Row total (no.)
British Columbia	48.4	9.6	42.0	448
Saskatchewan	27.7	0.4	72.0	271
Manitoba	21.6	2.3	76.1	264
Ontario	58.3	0.4	41.3	808
Quebec	51.6	6.4	42.0	438
New Brunswick	36.6	3.2	60.2	93
Prince Edward Island	20.0	5.0	75.0	60
Nova Scotia	21.8	6.1	72.1	312
Newfoundland	52.5	3.4	44.1	118
Total for Canada				2,812

Source: As Table 12.1; see *Final Appeal*, 56, Table 3.3.

screening processes are likely to vary among provinces, perhaps increasing with caseload pressures.

At the same time, however, the crown's relative advantage is magnified further if we look at filings, rather than at judgments after hearing. Table 12.4 shows that a higher proportion of crown appeals reach the hearing stage than do defence appeals, so that if we place dropped-off matters in the appellant's loss column,[17] the crown's advantage increases to close to four to one.[18]

Table 12.4
Stage when case dispositions occurred in courts of appeal, by whether crown or accused was appellant

	Appellant			
	Crown		Accused	
Stage	No.	(%)	No.	(%)
Before documents		32.4		46.5
Before hearing		5.1		3.6
After hearing		62.5		50.0
Number	552		2,212	
Total 'wins' (from Tables 12.1 and 12.4)				
Crown: 1,028 + 79 + 470 =	1,477	78.9		
Accused: 179 + 28 + 187 =			394	21.1
Number: 1,477 + 394 = 1,871				

Source: As Table 12.1; top half from *Final Appeal*, 57, Table 3.4.

How one interprets these various figures may depend on where one stands within the system: law enforcement, defence, judiciary, or observer (in political science or a theorist of courts). From the perspective of law enforcement, one might be tempted to see in Table 12.1 some indication that the courts of appeal are being softer than the trial courts, overturning convictions 144 times, while overturning acquittals only eighty-four times. And this table does not include appeals only on sentence, in which in the aggregate sentences are probably reduced far more often than they are increased.

From the defence perspective, the appeal courts may appear to be stacked against the accused. Not only is the crown more than twice as likely to win an appeal on the merits (Table 12.1), but it comes out ahead in the preliminary stages, since nearly half of the appeals by the accused never get beyond the documents stage (compared with one-third of crown appeals; see Table 12.4).

From the judges' perspective, any statistical difference between success rates for crown and accused, or overall 'wins' and 'losses,' may reflect the quality of the legal basis of the appeals. To the extent that the crown wins more frequently, this result may reflect greater selectiveness in what the crown decides to appeal. Accused persons are necessarily concerned about the outcome of their individual cases; counsel for the crown may be less likely to contest a single loss at trial for its own sake, preferring to take stronger cases on appeal to increase the likelihood of securing useful precedents for future cases.

From a political scientist's perspective, more data are needed to assess these conflicting interpretations. While defendants appeal more frequently, we need additional data on the outcome of trials for indictable offences to see whether the defendants' appeal rate is also higher. If trials result in convictions three-quarters of the time, we would expect three-quarters of the appeals to come from defendants and only one-fourth from the crown. If that were the case, the judges' hypothesis about crown effectiveness would be undermined, the greater drop-off for defendants (Table 12.4) would be a function of their weaker position in the process, and the higher proportion of hearings lost would reflect a greater likelihood that trial judges would rule on their behalf. Conversely, if the conviction rate at trial is well under three-quarters but defence appeals outnumber crown appeals by three or four to one, the pattern suggests that the crown has filtered out a larger proportion of possible cases for appeal than the defence, increasing the likelihood that a higher proportion of defence appeals would drop out before hearing or fail to persuade the panel at the hearing. If this pattern holds, any differences between individual judges would not have affected the aggregate outcomes in one court or another.

From the perspective of a theory of the courts as state actors, the findings can be interpreted in a number of ways. In one sense, the availability of an appeal in a criminal case assures the accused an additional protection against arbitrary government action; a right to appeal has become fundamental to a democratic system. In another sense, this right adds legitimacy to the exercise of the coercive power of the state, since the normal use of the criminal sanction is appealed in only a tiny percentage of the cases (i.e., appeals occur only in a minority of trials, and trials themselves constitute a small minority of case dispositions in trial courts). While some scholars who view the courts as state actors may attack individual judges for their lack of impartiality, the function that a court performs is a product not of the individual preferences of its members but of the institutional role that it plays.

Criminal Trials

While McCormick's findings and the data on provincial appellate courts show a consistent statistical edge in favour of the crown in criminal appeals, this advantage, even at its most substantial, seems more evenhanded than suggested by popular understanding of criminal trial courts, in which most accused plead guilty rather than go to trial. Yet, since pleading guilty amounts to dropping out

Table 12.5
Outcome of criminal trials, ten section-96 court locations, 1985–8

Outcome	All trials (%)	Jury trials (%)	Judge alone (%)
Guilty	66.2	61.5	69.7
Not guilty	33.83	38.5	30.3
Number	(845)	(369)	(476)

Source: Data collected on SSHRCC grant; adapted from tables submitted in an appendix to affidavit in *R. v. Askov.*
Note: Jury trials made up 43.7 per cent of cases tried in these courts, compared with 56.3 per cent tried by a judge alone.

of the process prior to a full court hearing on the merits of the crown's case, it is analogous to filing an appeal but not carrying it through to a disposition after oral argument. Thus a valid comparison of disposition by trial and by appellate courts requires that we examine comparable groups of cases. To do so, I first construct a table analogous to Table 12.1, limited to the disposition of criminal case carried through to judgment or verdict.

An examination of data collected in 1988–9 on criminal cases in section-96 trial courts in British Columbia, New Brunswick, and Ontario shows that two-thirds of criminal trials result in judgments or verdicts of guilt (66.2 per cent), as against 33.8 per cent acquittals. The table shows that while the crown comes out ahead, conviction in a criminal trial is more problematic than an initial reading of the literature might suggest. In fact, the overall percentages are slightly less favourable to the crown than the overall outcomes of appeals from convictions and acquittals, as shown in Table 12.1.

While the overall pattern of trial and appeal dispositions is similar, the trial data should be disaggregated before conclusions are drawn. First, trial outcomes should separate trials by jury from trials by judge alone. Doing so, as shown in Table 12.5, reveals that judges more frequently find defendants guilty than do juries, even though the conventional wisdom of social scientists would be that the public is more hostile to persons accused of crime than is a law-trained professional skilled in maintaining his or her impartiality, and the conventional wisdom of the criminal defence bar would be that you put your strong cases before the judge alone and your weak cases before less predictable juries.

Second, trial outcomes should be put in the context of all case outcomes. Thus Table 12.6 includes cases that did not end in a judgment or verdict following trial. Here trials make up 28.7 per cent of the dispositions, with guilty pleas

Table 12.6
Dispositions of criminal cases, ten section-96 court locations, 1985–8

Method of disposition	Disposition (%)
Guilty plea	57.8
Withdraw/stay/dismissal	13.5
Jury trial	12.5
Judge-alone trial	16.2
(Number)	(2,942)
Total 'wins' (from Tables 12.5 and 12.6)	
Crown (guilty pleas + convictions at trial)	78.6
1700 + 559 =	(2,259)
Accused (withdraw/stays/dismissals	
plus acquittals at trial)	23.2
397 + 286 =	(683)
(Number)	(2,942)

Source: As Table 12.5.

accounting for double that amount, or 57.8 per cent. The remaining cases were withdrawn or stayed by the crown (a stay allows a change to be reinstituted at a later date) or dismissed by the court, in some instances after the beginning of the trial. Thus the overall won–lost percentage favours the crown by well over three to one – 76.8 per cent to 23.2 per cent. As with appeals, the statistical margin in favour of the crown increases when all dispositions are counted. At the same time, the crown was two percentage points below its overall record on appeals – 78.9 per cent to 21.1 per cent, as shown in Table 12.4.

While guilty pleas make up the bulk of the case dispositions in the sample of criminal-trial courts, as the social science literature has stressed, the number of withdrawals, stays, and dismissals was large enough – more than the total number of jury trials[19] – to generate a larger-than-expected proportion of dispositions that favour defendants.

Table 12.3 showed substantial variations among provinces in the processing of criminal appeals and in the proportion that drop off prior to a formal hearing. Can similar differences be observed among the trial courts? Table 12.7 ranks the courts sampled from the highest to the lowest percentages of guilty pleas. Four out of five Ontario district courts had guilty-plea rates in a narrow range between 62.8 per cent and 67.5 per cent. The two BC county courts and the New Brunswick Court of Queen's Bench[20] were all lower, along with the Peel

Table 12.7
Disposition rates in criminal cases, ten section-96 court locations,1985–8

Court location	Total cases	Guilty pleas (%)	Trials (%)	Other* (%)
London District Court	431	67.5	24.6	7.9
Ottawa District Court	575	66.8	15.8	17.4
Toronto District Court	505	64.8	20.6	14.7
St Catharines District Court	274	62.8	15.3	21.9
Vancouver County Court	302	49.0	39.7	11.3
New Westminster County Court	272	46.7	42.3	11.0
Brampton District Court	426	45.8	42.0	12.2
New Brunswick Queen's Bench (three locations)	87	28.7	56.3	14.9

Source: As Table 12.5.
*Includes withdrawls, stays, and dismissals.

District Court in Brampton, Ontario.[21] Conversely, trial rates are generally over twice as high in the latter four courts as in the four Ontario courts with high rates of guilty pleas. Differences, however, are not uniform; London's trial rate is higher than the next three Ontario locations because it had the lowest proportion of withdrawls, stays, and dismissals.

Table 12.8 shows the breakdown of convictions and acquittals in jury and judge-alone trials. Here I show the courts in the same two groups and the same order as in Table 12.7. Doing so dramatizes the fact that the proportion of convictions at trial is consistently higher in jurisdictions with a lower proportion of guilty pleas. (Jury trials in St Catharines are the only exception.) Acquittals occurred in a majority of criminal jury trials in Toronto and London. In judge-alone trials, convictions were higher in seven out of eight court locations.

The patterns observed in Tables 12.7 and 12.8 support the view of many judges that numbers showing the judiciary supporting the crown more frequently than the accused reflect not judicial bias but the nature of pre-trial screening practices. In courts with a higher percentage of guilty pleas, conviction rates at trial are lower than in courts with a lower percentage of guilty pleas. For example, it is clear that crown attorneys in Brampton take cases to trial that would be handled by guilty pleas in other Ontario courts.[22] The disposition pattern in Brampton more closely approximates the BC pattern.

Interviews with judges, lawyers, and court officials in the three provinces reinforce the relationship between differences in local practices and expectations, on one hand, and disposition patterns, on the other. Queen's Bench jus-

Table 12.8
Dispositions at jury and judge-alone criminal trials, ten section-96 court locations, 1985–8

	Jury Trials			Judge-alone trials		
Court location	Total cases (no.)	Guilty (%)	Not guilty (%)	Total cases (no.)	Guilty (%)	Not guilty (%)
London District Court	69	48.6	51.4	37	58.0	42.0
Ottawa District Court	30	52.5	47.5	61	56.7	43.3
Toronto District Court	74	43.3	56.7	30	64.9	35.1
St Catharines District Court	14	71.4	28.6	28	64.3	35.7
Vancouver County Court	86	64.7	35.3	34	75.6	24.4
New Westminster County Court	66	63.3	36.7	49	75.8	24.2
Brampton District Court	123	64.3	35.7	56	74.0	26.0
New Brunswick Queen's Bench (three locations)	14	68.6	31.4	35	85.7	14.3

Source: As Table 12.5.

tices in New Brunswick have the reputation of being hostile to guilty pleas, which are seen as a manifestation of judge shopping; as a result, it appears that cases go to trial in that province that would be disposed of by guilty pleas in Ontario. BC judges indicate that they are much less involved in guilty-plea discussions than their Ontario counterparts, who conduct pre-trial conferences in criminal cases (not the pattern in British Columbia in the late 1980s) and have been known to ask defence counsel why they are proceeding to trial in a case where evidence is overwhelming.

The one exception to Ontario's tendency is in Brampton. Judges, lawyers, and court administrators from outside Peel Region consistently comment on the unwillingness of Brampton's crown attorneys to engage in plea bargaining. Both the high proportion of trials and the high proportion of convictions suggest that cases are going to trial that, elsewhere in the province, would be disposed of by pleas of guilty – perhaps one of the reasons why Brampton has long complained about having insufficient resources to do its job. The fact that the Brampton court is described by Ontario participants as deviant from practices elsewhere in the province suggests that Ontario has a provincial legal culture – a set of shared expectations about case processing that operates beyond the local level. The facts that New Brunswick's Court of Queen's Bench tends to operate differently from Ontario, but in a similar fashion in its three busiest centres, and that British Columbia's two largest centres share a common pattern of trial and plea rates further suggest the existence of provincial legal cultures in

Table 12.9
Overall dispositions in criminal cases, ten section-96 court locations, 1985–8

Court location	Total cases (no.)	Guilty pleas/verdicts/ judgments (%)	Acquittals/withdrawls/ stays/dismissals (%)
London District Court	431	81.0	19.0
Vancouver County Court	302	77.8	22.2
Toronto District Court	505	76.8	23.2
New Westminster County Court	272	76.5	23.5
Brampton District Court	426	75.6	24.4
Ottawa District Court	575	75.3	24.7
St Catharines District Court	274	73.4	26.6
New Brunswick Queen's Bench (three locations)	87	70.1	29.9

Source: As Table 12.1.

Canada, rather than the local legal cultures that have been identified and emphasized in the United States.[23]

While the data show different patterns of processing of criminal cases in Canadian trial courts, the outcomes are remarkably similar. If we calculate an overall won–lost percentage for each of the courts in Tables 12.7 and 12.8, putting guilty pleas and guilty verdicts in the 'win' column, the large differences observed above narrow sharply to a range between 70 and 81 per cent. It is ironic but entirely consistent with the analysis here that the crown's lowest 'winning percentage' is in New Brunswick, which has the highest conviction rate at trial, but the lowest rate of guilty pleas. See Table 12.9.

Conclusion: Comparing Appeal and Trial Courts

The statistical material shown here points again and again to similarities between trial and appeal courts, between trial judges and appellate judges. At both stages, trial and appeal, judges are more likely to find for the crown than for the accused in criminal cases. At both stages, large proportions of the courts' work are disposed of before trial or hearing. A higher proportion of trial-court cases reach a disposition without trial than the proportion of appeals that reach a disposition without hearing, but in each case the drop-off is disproportionately favourable to the crown. Furthermore, the greater drop-off of cases in trial courts may reflect the use of plea bargaining, which suggests some degree of compromise between the crown and the accused. In court locations that do not practise plea bargaining, or do not do so to the same degree (British Columbia, New Brunswick, and Brampton, Ontario), there is a balance between pleas and trials (as shown in the bottom half of Table 12.7) that more closely approximates the balance between appeals that go to hearing and those that do not (as shown in Table 12.3).

These output patterns suggest that the routine criminal work of trial and appeal courts (even including the criminal caseload of the Supreme Court of Canada[24]) has fundamental similarities, and so do the way in which trial and appeal courts process that work and the way in which trial and appellate judges approach their task as independent and impartial adjudicators.

For the past generation, empirical researchers in political science and in law and society have broadened our view of courts and judges by supplementing the traditional legal framework for analysing judicial decisions. But this research has tended to differentiate the behaviour of trial and appellate courts and of trial and appellate judges in ways that have distorted their similarities. In effect, empirical research has looked at trial courts more than at trial judges and at appellate judges more than at appellate courts. By comparing the outcomes of all appeal hearings, not just those in which the panel or full court is not unanimous, we can see similarities between trial and appellate judges. Statistically speaking, trial judges are no more partial to the state than are appellate judges.

By separating the outputs of trial and appeal courts from the outcomes of trial proceedings and appellate hearings, we can find the extent to which the 'haves' come out further ahead in the former than in the latter. Thus courts generally reinforce the exercise of state authority in criminal cases, even as judges – and juries – often, though not as predominantly, decide in favour of the state.

What emerges is a pattern not of the automatic ratification of the exercise of state authority but of its steady support over time. This is to be expected. Whether it is a reflection of the dominance of state authority or class interests over the courts, or a matter of mutual adjustment between the state as prosecutor and the courts as adjudicator, depends on the theoretical framework chosen by the analyst. At this time, the data do not preclude either explanation.

An examination of disposition patterns in civil litigation may actually show that private plaintiffs in civil cases succeed at a higher rate than the crown in criminal cases.[25] That would seem to support the mutual-adjustment thesis: plaintiffs will not invoke expensive civil-court processes unless they have a strong case, so they win frequently, even though they are not powerful state actors. However, it will be necessary to disaggregate civil plaintiffs to see whether their success is uniformly high or tends to be greater for business and corporate plaintiffs than for individual plaintiffs.[26] If business and corporate plaintiffs fare better, the thesis of dominant class interests would be able to reassert itself.[27] In the process, a definitive answer is unlikely. But an understanding of the functions of courts – and particularly the political meaning of what they do – should emerge more clearly.

NOTES

1 On the new institutionalism in political science, see Michael M. Atkinson, *Governing Canada: Institutions and Public Policy* (Toronto: Harcourt Brace Jovanovich 1993); James G. March and Johan P. Olsen, *Rediscovering Institutions: The Organizational Basis of Politics* (New York: Free Press 1989).

2 Peter H. Russell, *The Supreme Court of Canada as a Bilingual and Bicultural Institution* (Ottawa: Royal Commission on Bilingualism and Biculturalism 1969).

3 Peter H. Russell, *The Judiciary in Canada* (Toronto: McGraw-Hill Ryerson 1987).

4 He has been criticized by some members of the judiciary for de-emphasizing the differences between superior court judges and provincially appointed judges, for saying that 'a judge is a judge is a judge.'

5 Starting with C. Herman Pritchett, *The Roosevelt Court: A Study in Judicial Politics and Values 1937–1947* (New York: Octagon Books 1963 [c. 1948]), and Glendon Schubert, *The Judicial Mind* (Evanston: Northwestern University Press 1965), and including Canadian work by Russell, note 2 above; Sidney R. Peck, 'The Supreme Court of Canada, 1958–1966: A Search for Policy through Scalogram Analysis,' *Canadian Bar Review* 45 (1967), 666–725, and 'A Scalogram Analysis of the Supreme Court of Canada, 1958–1967,' in Glendon Schubert and David J. Danelski, eds., *Comparative Judicial Behavior* (New York: Oxford University Press 1969), 293–334; and Donald E. Fouts, "Policy-Making in the Supreme Court of Canada, 1950–1960," in Schubert and Danelski, eds., *Comparative Judicial Behavior*, 257–91.

6 C. Neal Tate and Panu Sittiwong, 'Decision Making in the Canadian Supreme Court: Extending the Personal Attributes Model across Nations,' *Journal of Politics* 51 no. 4 (Nov. 1989), 900–16.

7 Andrew D. Heard, 'The Charter in the Supreme Court of Canada: The Importance of Which Judges Hear an Appeal,' *Canadian Journal of Political Science* 24 no. 2 (June 1991), 289–307.

8 Jeffrey A. Segal and Harold J. Spaeth, 'The Influence of *Stare Decisis* on the Votes of United States Supreme Court Justices,' *American Journal of Political Science* 40 no. 4 (Nov. 1996), 971–1003.

9 Donald R. Songer and Stefanie A. Lindquist, 'Not the Whole Story: The Impact of Justices' Values on Supreme Court Decision Making,' *American Journal of Political*

Science 40 no. 4 (Nov. 1996), 1055–6, and Saul Brenner and Marc Stier, 'Retesting Segal and Spaeth's *Stare Decisis* Model,' *American Journal of Political Science* 40 no. 4 (Nov. 1996), 1036–48.

10 Marc Galanter, 'Why the Haves Come Out Ahead: Speculations on the Limits of Social Change,' *Law and Society Review* 9 (1974–5), 347.

11 Burton M. Atkins, 'Party Capability Theory as an Explanation for Intervention Behavior in the English Court of Appeal,' *American Journal of Political Science* 35 (1991), 881.

12 Donald R. Songer and Reginald S. Sheehan, 'Who Wins on Appeal? Upperdogs and Underdogs in the United States Courts of Appeal,' *American Journal of Political Science* 36 (1992), 243.

13 Peter McCormick, 'Party Capability Theory and Appellate Success in the Supreme Court of Canada, 1949–1992,' *Canadian Journal of Political Science* 26 no. 3 (Sept. 1993), 523–40.

14 Alberta is the missing province. The number of cases from other provinces is weighted in terms of annual cases, with larger provinces contributing a larger proportion of cases to the database.

15 The best-known works are Doris Marie Provine, *Case Selection in the United States Supreme Court* (Chicago: University of Chicago Press 1980), and H.W. Perry, Jr, *Deciding to Decide: Agenda Setting in the United States Supreme Court* (Cambridge, Mass.: Harvard University Press 1991).

16 A comparison of Tables 12.1 and 12.2 shows that less than half of the cases decided after a hearing (1,498 in Table 12.2) are included in Table 12.1. This is because a majority of provincial criminal appeals concern sentences, and these were excluded from Table 12.1, which is restricted to conviction appeals, on the assumption that reductions and increases in sentence cannot automatically be considered wins or losses for the accused or the crown.

17 This is crude in any legal sense, especially since the crown is obligated in principle to place evidence before the court without regard to which party is helped by the case. At the same time, an appeal that is started and is abandoned before a final decision could be considered a loss for the appealing party, just as the crown's dropping a charge before trial would normally be interpreted as a loss.

18 To obtain a complete figure we would need to factor in the outcomes of sentence appeals, but this would require either considering every sentence reduction a victory for the accused or examining the specific outcome of each request in relation to what change the appellant sought.

19 Partly because Canadian criminal procedure, unlike Australian and English, allows an accused to waive trial by jury in all but a handful of indictable offences.

20 Because of the small number of cases, I combined three Queen's Bench locations, Fredericton, Moncton, and Saint John in Tables 12.7 and 12.8.

21 Site of the case decided in *Regina v. Askov*, [1990] 2 SCR 1199, (1990), 74 DLR (4th) 355.

22 In U.S. jurisdictions, this can result in what American expert Ernie Friesen has called 'slow pleas,' in which the prosecution presents its evidence and the defence does not answer, preferring to let the judge see that the prosecution's case does not justify the penalty that will be sought on conviction.

23 This point is developed in 'Carl Baar, Trial Rates and Plea Rates in Canadian Criminal Cases: Local Legal Culture, Gender Politics and the Comparative Study of Trial Courts,' presented at the World Congress of the International Political Science Association, Buenos Aires, Argentina, 22 July 1991.

24 See McCormick, 'Party Cabability Theory and Appellete Success,' and discussion in text.

25 See John Twohig, Carl Baar, Anna Meyers, and Anne Marie Predko, 'Empirical Analyses of Civil Cases Commenced and Cases Tried in Toronto,' in *Rethinking Civil Justice: Research Studies for the Civil Justice Review* (Toronto: Ontario Law Reform Commission 1996), 77–181, especially 126–9.

26 Ibid., 127–8.

27 In turn, it will be necessary to consider criminal trials conducted in provincial courts, since their jurisdiction overlaps with that of section-96 trial courts shown in Tables 12.5–9 above. If provincial courts dispose of – and provincial court judges try – a substantial proportion of indictable offences (and evidence suggests that the proportion is growing), findings from that court will need to be examined. Most observers would hypothesize a higher proportion of convictions in those courts, both by plea and by trial.

13

Borderline Justice: Choosing Juries in the Two Niagaras

MARTIN L. FRIEDLAND AND KENT ROACH

This paper examines the use of juries in criminal cases in Canada and in the United States. It is part of a larger study of the administration of criminal justice in Niagara County, Ontario, and Niagara County, New York.[1] The study has been influenced in many ways by Peter Russell's work.[2] It seeks to explain why persons accused of serious crimes in the United States usually select a jury, whereas people in similar circumstances in Canada normally select trial by judge alone. Peter Russell has taught us to examine the courts as complex institutions and part of government – its third branch.[3] In both countries a complex interplay of procedural rules affects the decision whether to select juries. For example, the way judges are selected – a topic dear to Russell's heart – also makes a difference, as do the methods of jury selection and other procedural rules. The use of juries in Canada and the United States also reflects political and social culture. The widespread use of juries in the United States is consistent with the more populist, grassroots attitude in American society, which tends to distrust government, compared with the traditional respect for authority, including the authority of judges, in Canada.

It is of course somewhat problematic to draw an inference that what happens in one county also happens in the state or province, let alone the entire country. As we see below, there are wide variations in practice from state to state and, to a lesser extent, because criminal law and procedure is a federal legislative responsibility in Canada, from province to province.[4] There are also variations from county to county in both Ontario and New York, but again less in Ontario, because the administration of justice tends to be more centralized in Canada. We made a similar conclusion in our study of policing in the two Niagaras.[5] Nevertheless, by focusing on the specific, one gains insights that will help to explain the larger picture. This study does not take a position on whether there should be greater use of juries; indeed, the two authors are not in agreement on the matter. We first compare the use of juries on both sides of the Niagara frontier and then examine eight factors that may influence the decision to choose trial by jury.

Ontario v. New York

When Can One Choose a Jury?

The opportunity for choosing to be tried by a jury in Canada occurs in far fewer cases than in the United States. New York state provides for a jury trial for all felonies unless the accused waives a jury.[6] Offences punishable by imprisonment of more than one year are felonies.[7] Moreover, there is the right to a jury in all misdemeanour cases in New York City when the potential penalty is more than six months and in all misdemeanour cases outside New York City, whatever the penalty.[8] The right to a jury trial outside New York City goes further than required by the U.S. Bill of Rights,[9] which has been interpreted to require the right to a jury trial in all cases where the penalty is six months or more.[10] Thus in Niagara County, New York, anyone charged with a felony or a misdemeanour, whether in the higher state court or in the lower city court, can elect trial by jury.

In contrast, the Canadian Charter of Rights and Freedoms of 1982 constitutionally requires the right to a jury trial only when the potential penalty is imprisonment of five years or more.[11] Canadian law gives the right to a jury trial in more cases than are constitutionally required, but in far fewer cases than in the United States. Offences in Canada are broken down not into felonies and misdemeanours but rather into indictable and summary offences. Summary offences are not tried by jury; in general, the maximum penalty for such an offence is six months' imprisonment.[12] There are also hybrid offences, which can be tried either summarily or by indictment, with the prosecutor having the right to choose the procedure.[13] There is a growing trend in Canada to make more and more offences hybrid.[14] This enables the prosecutor to eliminate the right of the accused to a jury trial. A number of serious offences, such as sexual assault[15] and assaulting a peace officer,[16] are hybrid offences. These are often the very offences in which an accused will want a jury but cannot have one if the prosecutor proceeds summarily. Another trend is to increase the penalty for some summary offences beyond the usual six months' maximum. The penalty for a summary-conviction sexual-assault charge has recently been increased from one year to up to eighteen months.[17]

Further, not all indictable offences can be tried by a jury. There is a list of offences that are within the provincial court judges' absolute jurisdiction.[18] Provincial court judges sit without a jury. One major offence that is on this list is 'theft under,' and its definition has been expanding steadily and dramatically in amount over the years. It is now theft under $5,000.[19] The number of indictable offences within the provincial court judges' absolute jurisdiction is now quite substantial.

There is a very small group of offences, such as murder and treason, that require trial by jury.[20] This list was substantially longer in the past than it is now.[21] Moreover, even these offences can be tried without a jury if both the accused and the attorney general agree.[22] Indictable offences that do not fall within the exclusive jurisdiction of a judge and jury or within the absolute jurisdiction of a provincial court judge can be tried by a jury if the accused so elects.[23] This description shows that the number of offences that potentially can be tried by jury is far less in Canada than in the United States. So this is a partial explanation of why there are fewer jury cases in criminal matters in Canada.

As we see below, however, the accused in Canada normally does not elect to be tried by jury when given the opportunity to so choose. In contrast, the accused in New York, given the chance to waive a jury and have what is called a bench trial, normally does not do so. The New York Criminal Procedure Law provides that an accused person tried by indictment – that is, tried in the superior courts – can waive a jury 'with the approval of the court' in any case except one for first-degree murder,[24] and the case law generally requires the court to accept the waiver.[25] Prior to an amendment in 1937,[26] New York's constitution was interpreted as barring a defence waiver of a jury for a felony trial.[27] Thus accused persons had to be tried by a jury in the superior courts. There is therefore no requirement that the prosecutor consent, as there is in the U.S. federal system[28] and most state jurisdictions.[29]

The purpose of this paper is to find out why the Canadian and American accused and their lawyers act as they do. Let us examine some statistics.

Statistics

In Niagara County, New York, there are almost no bench trials for felony cases.[30] In the five-year period from 1991 to 1995 inclusive, there were only four bench trials out of 236 felony trials. In 1995, for example, there were fifty-six jury trials and only two bench trials. Misdemeanours dealt with in the city courts, in contrast, rarely end up with a jury trial, even though, as we saw above, jury trials are permitted for all misdemeanour cases outside New York City (where they are permitted only for offences punishable by over six months). In the three city courts in Niagara County, New York, in 1995, only thirty of the 173 cases that went to trial were jury trials.[31] A similar pattern is found in the neighbouring Erie County. Very few cases tried in its city courts are tried by jury. In the Buffalo City Court, for example, only twenty-seven of the 435 cases that went to trial were tried by a jury. City court judges dislike having to conduct jury trials because of the time they take and may discourage them by imposing harsher sentences on conviction.[32] So there is a significant difference in numbers between jury trials for felonies and misdemeanours.

The Erie County superior court, in contrast, uses bench trials for felonies to a greater extent than does Niagara County. Over the five-year period from 1991 to 1995 inclusive, 324 (32 per cent) of the 1,002 felony trials were bench trials. In 1995, for example, there were 143 superior-court jury trials in Erie County and fifty-six bench trials. In New York state as a whole, the proportion of bench trials in the superior courts is about 14 per cent.[33] Why there is such variation from county to county is discussed below.

It is not easy to compare the rate of bench trials in Canada with that in the United States. In Niagara County, Ontario, there were twenty-four jury trials in 1995. In the same year, the superior court had nine bench trials. But how many indictable cases were tried in the provincial court in cases where the accused could have elected trial by a jury in a superior court? Ontario does not produce such data. Using figures published from other provinces, however, we can estimate the number of trials for which the accused could have elected trial by jury.[34]

For Ontario as a whole, it seems likely that there are about 80,000 persons each year charged with indictable offences who could elect trial by jury. Most of these plead guilty and do not have a trial. Perhaps about 8,000 have a trial, if we assume a trial rate of about 10 per cent of all cases that could be tried by jury.[35] About 6,000 of these are tried in the provincial court, about 1,000 by a superior-court judge without a jury, and about 1,000 by judge and jury.[36] About 12 or 13 per cent of the trials of indictable offences where a jury could have been selected are therefore tried by jury. It is not likely that the percentage will increase substantially in the future because of the cost controls recently imposed by the legal aid system in Ontario and because extensive pre-trial disclosure by the prosecutor is available to the accused even if the trial takes place in provincial court.[37]

Thus, in New York state, bench trials for felonies comprise about 14 per cent of all felony trials, whereas in Ontario jury trials comprise a little less than 14 per cent of all indictable offences that could have been tried by jury. So the situation is roughly the opposite in the two jurisdictions. We now consider eight specific factors that may variously influence the decision to choose trial by jury – chances of acquittal, judicial selection, jury nullification, jury selection, case assignment, rules of evidence, previous convictions, and double jeopardy.

Chances of Acquittal

Could the difference between the two jurisdictions be explained by a greater likelihood of success for the accused with a jury in Niagara, New York, as compared with Niagara, Ontario? It is difficult to compare jury and bench trials in Niagara, New York, because, as we saw above, there are virtually no bench trials in that county. There are, however, a substantial number of bench trials in Erie County and in other New York counties, but the available statistics do not enable one to compare the results of jury and bench trials. So we look at studies in other American jurisdictions.

Kalven and Zeisel's well-known study on the U.S. jury[38] shows that judges indicate that the jury is more lenient than they (the judges) would be if they were trying the case without a jury. But whether they would have acted on their expressed view if they had in fact been trying the case is not, of course, known. In the study, the judge gave an opinion on whether he or she would have decided the case in the same way as the jury. Kalven and Zeisel state that 'the jury is less lenient than the judge in 3 per cent of the cases and more lenient than the judge in 19 per cent of the cases.'[39] There is therefore a net leniency of 16 per cent. The acquittal rate for juries varies from crime to crime, as does the net leniency rate.[40] Among major crimes, the highest net leniency rate was for murder (29 per cent), and the lowest was for drug-law violations (6 per cent). The authors show that jury waiver is directly related to the net leniency rate. Of all the major crimes, murder has the lowest waiver rate, and drug-law violations the highest – at that time 13 per cent for murder and 70 per cent for drugs.[41] Defence counsel therefore tend to know whether their clients will be better off with a jury.

A recent study of crown courts in England[42] asked judges to state whether the jury's verdict was problematic. As in the Kalven and Zeisel study, judges thought juries more lenient. They found 29 per cent of jury acquittals problematic: 25 per cent of them were against the weight of the evidence, and 4 per cent were 'inexplicable.'[43] But again, we do not know whether the judges would have convicted in these cases. There is no way of knowing in England because crown courts hear cases only with a jury. Comparisons with trials in magistrates' courts show a significantly higher conviction rate in magistrates' courts than in the crown courts.[44] In one study, the chance of an acquittal in the crown court was 57 per cent, whereas in the magistrates' courts it was 30 per cent.[45] So there would seem to be an incentive to elect trial in the crown court. As a counterweight to the apparently more favourable result with a jury, however, sentences tend to be higher for comparable cases when the accused elects trial in the crown court.[46] A recent study showed that judges in the crown court 'were three times as likely to impose immediate custody and sentences were on average two and a half time as long' as comparable convictions in the magistrates' courts.[47]

It is not possible to compare conviction rates for cases tried with a jury in Ontario and cases tried by a provincial court judge because available statistics do not permit such a calculation. Statistics in the provincial division relate to charges rather than to individuals, and so a count that is dismissed when a conviction is registered on another count may look like an acquittal, but is in fact very different from an individual being acquitted on all counts.

In spite of Kalven and Zeisel's conclusion, recent statistics concerning trials by the same level of judge with or without the jury do not show that the judge is less lenient than the jury. Statistics from the Administrative Office of the U.S. Federal Courts show that in 1993 there were 5,589 defendants tried by jury in federal criminal cases and 898 tried by a judge alone.[48] Judges acquitted 44 per cent of the defendants, while juries acquitted in only 19 per cent of the cases.

This discrepancy may occur because judges may act differently when they have to make a real decision than they do when they are simply asked for an opinion, as they were in the Kalven and Zeisel study. There may also be a difference in the type of case that is now being tried by a jury because of the present harsh sentencing structures throughout the United States, as compared to when Kalven and Zeisel were writing. There are now significant minimum sentences in New York,[49] which induce most accused persons to plead guilty to a lesser charge rather than risk a conviction for the greater offence. The guilty-plea rate for felonies in New York state in 1995 was about 85 per cent of the cases.[50] It was even higher (91 per cent in 1990 and 92 per cent in 1992) in state courts throughout the United States for the most serious felonies.[51] It was greater outside New York City (90 per cent) than within New York City (83 per cent).[52]

Niagara County had a guilty-plea rate in 1995 of 81 per cent, and Erie County, 85 per cent. There were wide variations among judges. One of the two superior court judges in Niagara County accepted pleas in 88 per cent of the cases, and the other judge, in only 76 per cent. The same variation among judges is evident in Erie County, where guilty pleas range from 75 per cent to 100 per cent. Many of the cases left for trial may well be relatively hopeless ones, in which the prosecutor will not reduce the charge and the accused is hoping for a lucky break from the jury. There will also be a number of jury cases where the accused is innocent. Many of the judge-alone cases may be ones in which the accused has a good legal argument to present or where community sentiment against the accused or the crime is so strong that the accused and his or her counsel believe that a jury could not decide the issue fairly.[53] Canadian defence lawyers say that they tend to avoid jury trials for cases involving the sexual assault of children. Some lawyers say that certain issues, such as identification, and some defences, such as insanity, are more sympathetically dealt with by a judge than by a jury.

In Canada, there are virtually no minimum sentences,[54] and so there is less incentive to seek to plead guilty to a lesser charge than in the United States, although there is still a considerable incentive to seek to have the charge reduced or to agree on a set sentence. The guilty-plea rate is thus not as high in Canada as in the United States, although the actual rate is unclear. One knowledgeable observer recently estimated that it was somewhere between 70 and 95 per cent[55] – a very wide range indeed.

Ontario statistics for trials conducted by superior-court judges with or without a jury in fact show the same acquittal rate for both types of trials.[56] In Ontario as a whole, superior-court judges tried 1,105 cases in 1995 with a jury and 1282 without a jury. In each type of case, the conviction rate was about 50 per cent. In Metropolitan Toronto in 1995, there was actually a higher acquittal rate for trials by superior-court judges without a jury (50 per cent) than for trials with a jury (38 per cent).[57] Similarly, in Niagara County in 1995 there was a higher acquittal rate for cases tried by a superior-court judge alone than for jury cases.[58] Carl Baar collected data from superior-court trials from the period 1985–7 in seven Canadian cities in Ontario and British Columbia.[59] In the cases that he studied, the acquittal rate for jury trials was somewhat higher than that for non-jury trials (38 per cent for jury trials, compared with 32 per cent for non-jury trials).[60] What is particularly striking is the wide variation from offence to offence. The jury, for example, acquitted in 44 per cent of the sexual-assault cases, but only 5 per cent of the narcotics cases.[61]

It is hard to draw firm conclusions based on the inadequate statistics available. Our impression is that the English situation would also be echoed in Ontario: that is, one has a better chance of acquittal when tried by a jury than if tried by a judge in a lower court, but the sentence would be higher if convicted. The statistics that we do have for superior courts in Ontario indicate that the rate of acquittal for bench trials is about the same as or more favourable than jury trials, but much depends on the offence involved.

Judicial Selection

Does the method of selecting judges have an effect on whether a jury is selected? In our view it clearly does. If a judge has to face re-election, there might be a tendency to favour a 'law and order' approach and thus convict in more cases than would a judge who was appointed. This perception might explain why there are so few bench trials in New York, where judges are elected and have to face re-election in partisan elections.[62] One of the authors was present in Niagara County during the last election of one of the two county-court judges and was struck by the high visibility of the election contest for the judgeship. The closer the time for re-election, the greater the tendency there may be to be a law-and-order judge. This would make an interesting research study: does the rate of waiver of jury trials decrease, the closer one gets to the time of re-election? Personnel in the Niagara County jail told us that the jail tends to be fuller before elections, suggesting that sentencing is higher before election. Whether this is so, we do not know. Will the conviction rate by judges sitting without a jury before an election also be higher?

The two superior-court judges in Niagara County trying criminal cases are elected for ten-year terms. Most of the Erie County judges trying criminal cases, in contrast, are supreme court judges, where the term of office is fourteen years.[63] The longer the term, the less likely that the judge will seek re-election, and thus in these cases the more independent the judge may be. This might help explain the greater use of bench trials in Erie County than in Niagara County.

Another factor in the greater use of bench trials in Erie County is that there are some former defence lawyers on the superior-court bench, whereas both county-court judges in Niagara County are former prosecutors. Being a former prosecutor does not of course mean that one is necessarily prosecution-minded, but there will probably be such a tendency – or at least observer will perceive such a tendency – in the majority of former prosecutors. Alan Dershowitz recently wrote in his book on the O.J. Simpson case that 'the prosecution almost always has the judge, who is typically a former prosecutor, on its side.'[64] 'The bench,' he wrote, 'has many former prosecutors (such as Lance Ito), but few former defence attorneys.'[65]

In Canada, judges have greater independence than do New York judges.[66] Both the superior-court and provincial-court judges are appointed, not elected. The appointment lasts until they retire, which in both cases can be up to the age of seventy-five.[67] Appointments to the superior court and the provincial court come from both the prosecution and the defence side. Our impression is that there is a higher proportion of judges that have come from the defence side in the superior courts than in the provincial courts. Many successful defence lawyers are willing to take an appointment only to the better-paid superior court, but many prosecutors will accept an appointment to the less remunerative provincial court, whose judges are still normally paid more than prosecutors. If it is true that there is a higher percentage of former prosecutors than former defence lawyers in the provincial court, this might help to explain the higher conviction rates in the provincial courts.

An annual volume, *Examining the Work of State Courts*, gives the rate of bench trials for twenty-one jurisdictions.[68] Do jurisdictions that elect judges have a lower rate of bench trials than those that appoint judges or choose judges by a merit system?[69] The statistics are not clear-cut enough to permit a definitive statement Many other factors influence whether a bench trial is sought and obtained than whether the judge is elected or appointed. In some jurisdictions, for example, waiver of a jury trial requires the consent of the prosecutor, which might not generally be forthcoming.[70] We ranked all twenty-one states in descending order of percentage of bench trials out of all contested criminal cases.[71] The highest percentage for 1994 was Wyoming, where 76 per cent of all cases were bench trials and where selection of judges was based on a merit plan. The lowest percentage was in California, where there were bench trials in only 2 per cent of contested cases and where selection was based on non-partisan election. Though a number of states do not fit the theory, in general the theory holds. Of the ten states with 50 per cent or more bench trials, seven had appointment or the merit plan. Of the eleven other states with under 50 per cent bench trials, eight chose judges by election and only three by appointment or the merit plan.

The theory also tends to hold when the cases are restricted to felonies.[72] Of the five states with 50 per cent or more bench trials for felonies, four have an appointed judiciary. Similarly, of the six states with under 15 per cent bench trials for felonies, four have elected judges.

Jury Nullification

Might laws on jury nullification explain differences in the use of juries in the United States and Canada? Jury nullification is the term normally applied to a jury's power to disregard the law or the facts in arriving at a verdict. The applicable laws in New York and Ontario are now about the same. The judge does not tell the jury in either jurisdiction that it has the power to acquit in spite of the law. Moreover, in both jurisdictions counsel for the accused cannot urge the jury to acquit and disregard the law. Even though the law is the same, however, one suspects that there are differences in practice. U.S. juries are more aware of their power to acquit than juries in Canada, and this will probably increase the chances of acquittal in certain types of cases.[73] Juries will either ignore the law or, more likely, will tend to find a reasonable doubt on the facts.

The leading Canadian jury-nullification case is the Morgentaler[74] abortion case. In the defence counsel's closing address to the jury, counsel stated that while the jury had to take the law from the judge, 'I submit to you that it is up to you and you alone to apply the law to this evidence and you have a right to say it shouldn't be applied.'[75] Chief Justice Brian Dickson stated for the Supreme Court of Canada that, although the jury has a sovereign right to acquit, it 'was quite simply wrong to say to the jury that if they did not like the law they need not enforce it. He should not have done so.'[76] To do so could therefore be a ground for an appeal by the prosecutor, which is permitted in such a case in Canada.[77]

Early New York cases had taken the opposite approach. The jury was specifically told by counsel and by the judge that it could acquit in spite of the law.[78] There had been a long history of jury nullification in libel trials in pre-revolutionary America and in fugitive-slave trials in the nineteenth century.[79] But the U.S. Supreme Court held in a 1895 case, *Sparf and Hansen v. U.S.*,[80] that the jury had to follow the law set out by the judge. New York state has followed this ruling. In a 1955 case, Justice Fuld stated for the New York Court of Appeals, relying on *Sparf and Hansen*: 'As to the jury's proper function or duty, that consists solely of applying the legal definition of crime, as laid down by the trial court, to the evidence and of convicting of the crime charged, if that is established beyond a reasonable doubt.'[81] The New York Court of Appeals took the same approach in the well-known subway-killing case of Goetz,[82] in which it held that the trial judge did not err in instructing the jury that if it found that the People had proved each of the elements beyond reasonable doubt it 'must' find the accused guilty. The court stated: 'While there is nothing to prevent a petit jury from acquitting although finding that the prosecution has proven its case, this so-called "mercy-dispensing power" ... is not a legally sanctioned function of the jury and should not be encouraged by the court.'[83]

Up until 1994, the New York cases discussed the issue in terms of what the judge should say to the jury. It is likely that there was considerable ambiguity as to what counsel could say. Some judges probably permitted counsel to remind jurors of their power of acquittal; others would attempt to prevent it. In 1994, however, in the case of *People v. Weinberg*,[84] the New York Court of Appeals held that counsel could not urge the jury to nullify the law and acquit. Justice Levine stated for the court: 'Defendant's final argument that he should have been permitted by the trial court to present the concept of jury nullification during summation is foreclosed by our holding in *People v. Goetz* ... Permitting defense counsel instead to encourage the jury to abdicate its primary function would directly contravene the trial court's authority recognized in *Goetz*, to instruct the jury that they must follow and properly apply the law.'[85]

Decisions of their highest courts now discourage defence counsel in both New York and Ontario from urging jurors to employ the power of nullification.

A 1972 case in the District of Columbia Circuit Court of Appeals, *U.S. v.*

Dougherty,[86] had also held that counsel could not urge nullification, although the discussion by the majority centred wholly on what the trial judge should say. Chief Justice Bazelon, dissenting on this point, found merit in the concept of jury nullification: 'The doctrine permits the jury to bring to bear on the criminal process a sense of fairness and particularized justice.'[87] In any event, he would have permitted counsel to raise the issue: ' At the very least, I would require the trial court to permit defendants to argue the question before the jury.'[88]

Despite the law, American jurors will probably have a greater understanding of their right to disregard the law than a Canadian jury. There is now even an organization, the Fully Informed Jury Association (FIJA), operating in New York, that advises citizens and prospective jurors of their power of nullification.[89] Canadians tend to show greater deference to authority,[90]and if the judge tells juries that they should take the law only from the judge, they will probably do so. Apart from the abortion cases,[91] there is not a long tradition in Canada of jury nullification. Juries in Canada are much more under the control of the judge than U.S. juries. Canadian judges, unlike their American counterparts, give the jury guidance with the facts as well as the law.[92]

Moreover, defence counsel in the United States probably approach the issue with less fear of consequences than would a Canadian lawyer. If counsel makes the suggestion of nullification in a closing address, the prosecutor cannot appeal an acquittal that may result.[93] This gives U.S. defence counsel more scope for introducing the concept. The judge could declare a mistrial but would normally be reluctant to do so. In the O.J. Simpson case, defence counsel Johnnie Cochran stated: 'Stop this cover-up ... Both prosecutors have now agreed that ... there's a lying, perjuring, genocidal racist and he's testified wilfully false in this case on a number of scores ... You are empowered to say we're not going to take that anymore ... When a witness lies in a material part of his testimony, you can wipe out all of his testimony as a judge of the facts ... You're the ones who send the message.'[94] Prosecutor Marcia Clark later commented to the judge: 'I have never had a defense attorney make an argument like Mr. Cochran made, nor have I ever seen a defense attorney get up and ask for jury nullification in this way.' Judge Ito replied: 'It was very artfully phrased.'[95] At that stage of the case, Judge Ito was certainly not going to declare a mistrial and start again!

It may be that in the future Canadian juries will be more aware of the power to nullify a law and more willing to use it. And perhaps the *Weinberg* case in New York will cut down on the use of nullification in that state, at least. But at the present time one seems to have a better chance of such an acquittal in New York than in Ontario.

Jury Selection

The accused's ability to shape the jury will obviously influence the extent to which defendants choose trial by jury. The more the jury is sympathetic to the accused, the greater the chance of an acquittal. The ability to create an apparently favourable jury is clearly greater in New York than in Ontario, and this factor has probably affected use of juries in the two jurisdictions. A defence counsel in Ontario fearing a jury with unknown attitudes and sympathies may prefer to elect trial by judge alone.

The pool from which juries are selected is broader in New York than that in Ontario. Jury lists from which juries are selected in New York state include a number of categories of persons not included in Ontario. In Ontario, jury lists come from those people on municipal or county election rolls who are Canadian citizens and reside in the municipality or locality.[96] The system potentially covers most residents, but many people eligible to vote are probably not in fact enumerated for municipal elections.[97]

New York has been widening its lists over the years beyond voters' registration rolls. In the early 1980s, the source lists included also drivers' licences and state income-tax rolls.[98] It was estimated in 1984 that about 90 per cent of eligible jurors appeared on the master list.[99] But the 10 per cent not covered included many disadvantaged people. *The Jury Project*, the 1994 report of New York's Jury Project, stated: 'The fact that a disproportionate share of those who are not registered to vote are either poor or are members of minority groups or both is well-documented.'[100] As a result, steps have recently been taken to broaden the pool by including persons receiving unemployment compensation, medical assistance, or public assistance.[101]

Some provinces have also widened the jury pool – for example, Manitoba and Saskatchewan include members of the provincial health plan.[102] There have been numerous calls throughout Canada to increase the number of disadvantaged people who serve on juries,[103] but in Ontario, apart from Native people on reserves,[104] municipal voters' lists are the only source of the jury pool.

Challenges for cause also differ greatly in the two jurisdictions. In Ontario, a potential juror cannot be questioned unless the trial judge permits it. The Ontario Court of Appeal stated in a 1975 case[105] (upheld by the Supreme Court of Canada): 'The trial judge has to know what the reason is, in more than general words; otherwise he cannot properly direct and control the trial of the truth of the challenge. Counsel must be prepared to state the reason for his challenge, and if he refuses to do so, the trial Judge may refuse to permit the trial of its truth, because that trial cannot properly be had without some definition of the issue.'[106]

Counsel in Canada cannot simply ask questions to elicit possible reasons for a challenge. And because counsel has virtually no information about potential jurors, apart from name, address, and occupation,[107] it is difficult to challenge a juror for cause. Canadian courts are apparently worried about bringing in lengthy American practices. The Ontario Court of Appeal stated: 'We believe that from time to time, and in various parts of the Province, the process has been abused by counsel. The influence of American practices in some States has crossed the border – and sometimes not in the actual form of the prescribed practices, but as they are thought to be by Canadian imitators.'[108] Occasionally, however, the courts have permitted use of set questions, worked out in advance, in certain unique or high-profile cases.[109]

In New York, in contrast, counsel have very wide latitude in challenging jurors for cause.[110] Even if the juror is not excluded for cause, the questioning will help the lawyers to determine whether to use a peremptory challenge.[111] Moreover, in many cases – the practice is not mandatory – jurors will have filled out a questionnaire that can be used by counsel.[112] We asked judges in Niagara County in New York and Ontario to estimate the length of time it takes to choose a jury. The Canadians estimated that it might take about half an hour to an hour to choose a jury in the type of case that might take at least four or five hours in Niagara County, New York. Some estimates in the literature about the time generally taken to choose a U.S. jury are in fact much higher.[113] New York is concerned about the length of time taken and is taking steps to reduce it.[114] But it is still significantly easier to challenge for cause in New York than in Ontario.

Ontario has expanded the challenge for cause in one specific area. Questions about prejudice against Blacks can be asked when the accused is Black.[115] Such questions can obviously be asked in New York, but as one Niagara county court judge told us, jurors are rarely asked this question directly. Persons with racist attitudes will normally hesitate before admitting them publicly. Racist attitudes will instead be brought out through more subtle questioning, which cannot at present be done in Canada.

We come to the final issue to be discussed in jury selection – the peremptory challenge. In the past, New York's rules were clearly more favourable to the accused than were the Canadian rules. In Canada, the prosecutor, in addition to being able to use peremptory challenges, could 'stand aside' jurors, without giving any reason for doing so, until the jury panel was exhausted.[116] Even though peremptory challenges in the two jurisdictions may have been comparable in the past, the use of 'stand asides' by the prosecutor gave a distinct advantage to the prosecution side in Canada. The 'stand aside' procedure was, however, struck down by the Supreme Court of Canada in the *Bain* case[117] in 1992. Justice Cory stated for the court: 'Apart from challenges for cause the provisions of the Criminal Code provide the Crown with the ability to stand by 48 prospective jurors and to peremptorily challenge four jurors. The accused in this case has but 12 peremptory challenges. I do not suggest that the ideal of absolute equality is required by the Canadian Charter of Rights and Freedoms. However, a discrepancy of 4.25 to 1 in favour of the Crown seems to be so unbalanced that it gives an appearance of unfairness or bias against the accused. The impugned provisions permit the Crown to obtain a jury that would at the very least appear to be favourable to its position rather than an unbiased jury.'[118] No doubt the combination of the prosecutors' stand asides and the rule preventing questioning for cause discouraged many defence counsel from seeking a jury trial in Canada in the past.

As a result of the *Bain* case, the federal government introduced new legislation equalizing the peremptory challenges of the prosecutor and the defence.[119] There are now twenty challenges for each side for high treason and first-degree murder, twelve when the potential sentence is five years or more, and four in other cases. On balance, this is still not as generous as the system in New York.[120] It is not easy to compare the two schemes, however, because the classifications are different. New York provides twenty challenges for a class-A felony, fifteen for class B or C, and ten for other felonies. Class-C felonies 'comprise the vast majority of the commonly tried crimes'[121] and allow fifteen challenges. Such commonly tried cases in Canada have only twelve challenges, and in many serious cases, such as advocating genocide,[122] infanticide,[123] and assaulting a police officer,[124] only four. New York's number of peremptory challenges is amongst the highest in the United States.[125] New York's Jury Project report (1994) recommended that the numbers be reduced,[126] but this has not yet been done.

There is some control on the use of peremptory challenges in the United States as a result of the 1986 case of *Batson v. Kentucky*,[127] which held that the equal-protection clause of the Fourteenth Amendment prevents the prosecution from challenging prospective jurors solely on account of their race. New York has, of course, followed *Batson*[128] and has extended it to the use of peremptory challenges by the defence[129] and to gender issues.[130]A racially or gender-neutral explanation of peremptory challenges must be given when the composition of the jury is challenged when it ends up with disproportionate numbers. But this is often not difficult to give.[131]

Thus the ability of defence counsel to shape a jury through jury selection is an important difference between the two jurisdictions and a disincentive to the use of juries in Ontario. Whether this situation will change as the two systems become more compatible remains to be seen.

Case Assignment

One reason why an accused person may avoid a bench trial is because the trial judge may know too much about the accused and the case. This will be of particular concern to accused people who have criminal records, have indicated in plea discussions a willingness to plead guilty, or have had evidence such as a confession excluded. There are in fact significant differences in case-assignment systems for criminal trials in New York and Ontario, which could affect the extent to which juries are used.

Since 1986, New York state has been using what is called an individual calendaring system, whereby cases are assigned to a specific judge as soon as they enter the superior court.[132] That judge handles all the pre-trial proceedings, including bail applications, pre-trial suppression and other motions, and plea discussions. The judge therefore would normally, for example, know about the accused's prior record and about evidence that had been excluded in pre-trial motions and be aware of the accused's willingness to enter a plea of guilty. This is the system now used in Niagara County, New York. It contrasts with the master calendaring system, whereby judges are selected to hear the case only when it is ready to be heard.[133] It is more difficult to have such a system when there are only two judges hearing the cases, as in Niagara County, but one could work out a system whereby the judge who handled the pre-trial proceeding did not hear the case.

The individual calendaring system was supposed to cut down on delays.[134] Whether it has done so is still an open question. One can have efficiency with both types of systems or variations of the two systems,[135] such as individual calendaring with actual trials conducted on a master system.[136] New York's method may well have helped increase – or at least prevented a decrease – in the use of juries for trials.[137] Thus, though it may be more efficient, it probably results in more jury trials, which are usually longer than bench trials. One interesting hypothesis is that the states with more bench trials are also those with master calendaring systems. We leave it to others to test this hypothesis.

In Ontario, the superior courts use a master calendaring system. Pre-trial hearings are mandatory in all jury cases and may be held, with the consent of the prosecutor and the accused, in cases where the accused elects trial by a superior-court judge alone.[138] These pre-trial hearings, in which plea discussions usually take place, are dealt with by judges who do not then hear the cases.[139] Judges holding pre-trial hearings may, however, accept guilty pleas. The vast majority of individuals who elect to be tried in a superior court choose trial by jury, even though most re-elect to be tried by a judge alone.[140] The Ontario system means that a judge who eventually hears the case will not usually have prior knowledge of the case, and thus there is not the same incentive to choose trial by jury as there is in New York.

Rules of Evidence

Although the rules of evidence in Ontario and New York are fairly similar, there are some differences that might be a factor encouraging a New York accused, but not necessarily an Ontario accused, to choose a jury. The rules of evidence in New York are those that one finds in most common-law jurisdictions where there is widespread use of juries. Canada, in contrast, has eliminated a number of these rules, which are designed to prevent the jury from hearing certain evidence or require a special instruction by the judge, warning the jury to be careful about certain types of evidence. One probable reason why Canadian rules of evidence have been changed is that, as we saw above, most criminal trials are now conducted without a jury. The same is true for civil cases. Thus rules that protected the jury are not now needed to the extent that they are in the United States. Canada has not developed separate laws for juries as distinct from trials by judges. As far as we are aware, no jurisdiction has.[141] The relaxation of the rules of evidence has, however, made trial by jury less favourable to the accused in Canada than it was in the past. The change of rules because few cases are tried by jury thus may result in even fewer cases being tried by jury.

The rule relating to hearsay is a good example. Although Canada still has specific exceptions to the hearsay rule, as does New York, it will also allow in hearsay evidence if it is reliable and reasonably necessary – even if it does not fit within one of the exceptions.[142] In contrast, New York keeps out such evidence unless it fits into one of the exceptions.[143] Thus in New York a jury is less likely to be aware of hearsay evidence than a jury in Ontario.

Another example is the rule respecting circumstantial evidence, which in the past in both jurisdictions required a special warning to the jury to take extra care. The early English rule in *Hodge's Case*[144] required the trial judge to tell the jury that if the evidence was wholly or mainly circumstantial the jury 'must be satisfied, not only that the circumstantial evidence is consistent with the conclusion that the accused committed the offence with which he is charged, but also that the facts which have been proved are such as to be inconsistent with any other rational conclusion than that the accused is guilty of the offence with which he is charged.'[145] In 1977, however, the Supreme Court of Canada abolished the circumstantial-evidence rule.[146] Now, only a charge relating to reasonable doubt is required. In New York, in contrast, a special warning is required when the evidence is wholly circumstantial, to the effect that the jury 'must exclude to a moral certainty every other reasonable hypothesis.'[147] This is in addition to a charge relating to reasonable doubt.

The corroboration rule – to give one more example – still exists in its classic form in New York but has for the most part been abolished in Canada. Section 60.22 of the New York Criminal Procedure Law, for example, states that 'a defendant may not be convicted of any offense upon the testimony of an accomplice unsupported by corroborative evidence tending to connect the defendant with the commission of such offense.' Again, in contrast, the Supreme Court of Canada abolished the corroboration rule with respect to accomplices in 1982.[148] England, which still has a large number of jury trials in criminal cases, still has the rule.

A further difference in the two jurisdictions is with respect to comments on the accused's failure to testify. In Canada, neither the prosecutor nor the judge is entitled to comment on such an occurrence.[149] Juries and judges are, however, entitled to draw a natural inference against the accused.[150] In New York[151] and all other American jurisdictions,[152] however, the judge must tell the jury at the request of the accused that no inference may be drawn from a failure to testify. In New York, unlike other American jurisdictions,[153] such a specific charge may be given only if the accused requests it. Such a charge would not be requested, of course, unless the accused's lawyer thought that it would be helpful. It is probably asked for in the majority of cases.

One additional difference between Canada and the United States that may tend to encourage jury trials in the United States is the surprising American rule that inadmissible evidence that has been admitted by a judge sitting without a jury will not be a ground for reversal if there is competent evidence sufficient to support the conviction.[154] There is no such rule in the United States when the trial is with a jury. Because many, if not most, appeals are on evidentiary rulings, the scope for a successful appeal decreases considerably when there is a bench trial. In Canada, no legal distinction is made between a trial with or without a jury when the issue is the admissibility of evidence.

These small, but cumulatively important differences help make jury trials more attractive in New York state than in Ontario.

Previous Convictions

In both jurisdictions, an accused who enters the witness box may, at the discretion of the judge, be cross-examined on his or her previous convictions.[155] Whatever the trial judge may say with respect to the limited use that may be made of the accused's record, the jury is no doubt going to give it more weight than it deserves. It is not likely to limit its use to testing the accused's credibility. As one leading New York practitioner's text states, 'A defendant with a criminal record bears a heavy burden. Many jurors will cast aside the presumption of innocence.'[156] Both jurisdictions now have hearings to determine to what extent an accused's previous record is admissible.[157]

But there is a significant difference between the two jurisdictions in the timing of the motions. In Canada, the motion is made during the trial, after the prosecution's case. The Ontario Court of Appeal stated in a 1994 case: 'In most cases, however, an application with respect to the admissibility of evidence concerning an accused's criminal record should not be dealt with until the Crown's case has concluded.'[158] This means that accused in Ontario may not know whether their criminal record will be admissible until long after they have decided whether to have a jury or a bench trial. If they are averse to the risks of juries' being influenced by their past convictions, they will opt for trial by judge alone.

In New York, however, the hearing takes place before the trial. In the *Sandoval* case,[159] the New York Court of Appeals stated: 'In most cases ... but not necessarily in all cases, a pretrial motion will be preferable.'[160] The result of a so-called Sandoval hearing is that an accused in New York knows in advance whether and to what extent previous convictions can be used. If they are excluded, the accused will be more willing to have a trial by jury than if they are to be admitted. If they are admitted, the accused may try to strike a deal with the prosecutor or waive a jury trial on the assumption that the judge will probably not give as much weight to the previous convictions as would a jury.[161] So an accused in New York has a better idea where he or she stands than an accused in Canada, who has to wait until midway through the trial to find out. Under these circumstances, it is not surprising that in Ontario trial by a judge alone may seem more attractive.

Double Jeopardy

One important difference between Canadian and American law is that in the United States the prohibition against double jeopardy prevents appeals from acquittals, except in limited cases,[162] whereas in Canada such appeals are permitted on questions of law.[163] It is possible that this difference might have an effect – even though perhaps a minor one – on the extent to which juries are selected. In Canada, a judge must be careful in ruling on questions of law not to favour improperly one side or the other. To do so could invite an appeal by either side – by the accused from a conviction if the ruling was against the accused or by the prosecutor from an acquittal if the ruling was in favour of the accused. Judges in Canada therefore will attempt to rule according to the law as they understand it. In contrast, American judges might tend to favour the defence on close evidentiary and other calls to prevent an appeal by the accused if there is a conviction. Alan Dershowitz's book on the O.J. Simpson case specifically states that the defence team 'wanted Judge Ito to know that we were always thinking about a possible appeal so that he might be influenced in his trial rulings by a desire not to be reversed on appeal.'[164] New York Judge Harold Rothwax makes a similar point in his discussion of the serious sanctions imposed on the prosecution in the Simpson case for impropriety compared to the less severe sanction imposed on the defence for its conduct. He states: 'Why was the sanction against the defence violation a small fine, while the sanction against the prosecution was exclusion of reliable evidence? One reason might be fear of reversible error. A judge can't be reversed on appeal if he rules against the prosecution.'[165]

If the case is heard by the judge alone, the judge will have heard the evidence and may well take it into account, even if it is excluded. If the trial is with a jury, however, the jury will in many cases not be aware of incriminating evidence that the judge excluded in order to avoid an appeal by the accused. Thus an accused might be better off in such cases with a jury, and this might be one more reason for selecting juries in the United States that does not apply in Canada.

Conclusion

The above discussion sets out a number of specific factors that may influence the selection of juries in the two jurisdictions.[166] There are other, more general influences that are perhaps less easy to identify. One is the fact that the widespread use of jurors in the United States is consistent with a more populist, grassroots approach, which tends to distrust government, compared with the traditional respect for authority in Canada. One of the authors wrote some years ago in a study of gun control: 'Both countries came into existence as a result of the American Revolution. But whereas the United States was founded as a result of defiance of authority, Canada was the result of obedience to the Crown ... There is no right to revolution in Canada, no declaration of independence, no "right to bear arms," no tradition of civil disobedience, and no violent civil war. What we have, instead, is the simple phrase in the British North America Act, "Peace, Order and Good Government."'[167] As Kenneth McNaught has written,

'We have certainly shown deference to the concept of established authority and procedures and even to the legal idea that valid authority flows downward from the crown.'[168] Note that it is 'the People' who prosecute in the United States. In Canada it is the Queen. Accused in the United States regularly trust the People, as represented by the jury, with their fate. In Canada, this trust is most often placed in one of her majesty's judges.

Further, there is a clear assumption in many U.S. jurisdictions that jury trials for indictable offences are more desirable than bench trials. In *United States v. Martin*, the Federal Court of Appeals for the Sixth Circuit stated: 'Trial by jury is fundamental to American criminal jurisprudence ... The public interest in jury trials is so great that defendants cannot waive their right to trial by jury except under certain conditions ... The trial court bears a substantial responsibility for jealously preserving jury trials, the constitutionally preferred method of disposing of criminal cases ... A court, therefore, should not lightly approve the jury trial waivers.'[169] In Canada, in contrast, for most indictable cases the accused simply elects the mode of trial.[170] Waiver of jury trial is not an issue in Canada except for such serious offences as murder and treason.[171] Canada does not attach as much importance to jury trials as the United States does.

Another factor is that the failure to use juries in Canada in the past will have an effect on their future use. Because juries are not widely used in Canada in either civil or criminal cases, lawyers may be less comfortable in having jury trials than are lawyers in New York. This will affect the number of juries selected and cause a further decrease in experience in the use of juries in Canada. There are over 20,000 practising lawyers in Ontario. With only about 1,000 criminal jury cases a year, this works out to an average of one criminal jury case per lawyer every twenty years. There are juries in civil cases in Canada, particularly for libel and some personal-injury cases, but relatively few compared to the United States.[172] One very experienced civil litigator in Toronto told us that he had not had a jury case in over thirty years. Lawyers who specialize in murder cases have far more jury cases than other criminal lawyers, and so, based on the above statistics, the average lawyer has even less experience with juries. Many experienced criminal lawyers will not have had a jury case in the past year.

The purpose of this paper is to help explain differences in law and practice between the two jurisdictions. As stated at the outset, the two authors are not in agreement on whether more jury trials should be encouraged. We agree, however, on the role of local legal culture and the complex interplay of legal rules and practices that may influence the defendant's decision to select or waive a jury.

NOTES

Michael Code was involved in the early stages of the project and has continued to contribute ideas from his wide experience in government and the practice of criminal law. Donald Waters, a recent graduate of the Faculty of Law, University of Toronto, was an excellent summer research assistant. A number of knowledgeable people commented on an earlier draft. We are grateful to Justice Vincent Doyle of New York and Justices Archie Campbell and Victor Paisley of Ontario; prosecutors Diane LaVallee from New York and Peter Griffiths from Ontario; defence counsel Mark Mahoney from Buffalo and Michelle Fuerst from Toronto; and political scientists Carl Baar and Peter Russell. We would also like to thank the Social Sciences and Humanities Research Council of Canada and the Canadian Institute for Advanced Research for their support. The paper was competed in December 1996 and reflects the law and practice at that date.

1 A companion study on policing in the two Niagaras was published earlier: see Kent Roach and M.L. Friedland, 'Borderline Justice: A Comparison of Policing in the Two Niagaras,' *American Journal of Criminal Law* 23 (1996), 241. See also Michael A. Code, *Trial within a Reasonable Time* (Toronto: Carswell, 1992); Code, 'American Cadillacs or Canadian Compacts: What Is the Correct Criminal Procedure for S. 24 Applications under the Charter of Rights?' *Criminal Law Quarterly* 33 (1990–1), 298 and 407.

2 See, for example, Russell's pioneering writings on the effects of a constitutional bill of rights in increasing the role and power of courts in Canadian politics: Peter Russell, 'A Democratic Approach to Civil Liberties,' *University of Toronto Law Journal* 19 (1969), 109; 'Judicial Power in Canada's Political Culture' in M.L. Friedland, *Courts and Trials: A Multidisciplinary Approach* (Toronto: University of Toronto Press 1975); 'The Effect of a Charter of Rights on the Policy-Making Role of Canadian Courts,' *Canadian Public Administration* 25 (1982), 1; 'The Political Purposes of the Canadian Charter of Rights and Freedoms,' *Canadian Bar Review* 61 (1983), 30; 'The First Three Years in Charterland,' *Canadian Public Administration* 28 (1985), 367. See also F.L. Morton, Peter Russell, and Michael Withey, 'The Supreme Court's First Hundred Charter of Rights Decisions: A Statistical Analysis,' *Osgoode Hall Law Journal* 30 (1992), 22. See, generally, Peter Russell, *The Judiciary in Canada: The Third Branch* (Toronto: McGraw-Hill Ryerson 1987).

3 Russell, *The Judiciary in Canada*.

4 Criminal law and procedure are a federal responsibility in Canada, although their administration is a provincial responsibility: see the Constitution Act, 1867, ss. 91(27), 92(14) and (15), 30 and 31 Vict., c. 3 (UK); RSC 1970, App. II, No. 5. See, generally, M.L. Friedland, 'Criminal Justice and the Constitutional Division of Power in Canada,' in *A Century of Criminal Justice* (Toronto: Carswell 1984), chap.

2. In the United States, criminal law and procedure are mainly a state responsibility, although there is also a large measure of federal responsibility, and the U.S. Supreme Court has imposed minimum constitutional standards in many areas of criminal procedure. See, generally, Laurence H. Tribe, *American Constitutional Law*, 2nd ed. (New York: Foundation Press 1988).

5 See Roach and Friedland, 'Borderline Justice.' In New York, prosecutors and public defenders are subject to far less control from Albany than their counterparts in Ontario are from Toronto.

6 New York *Criminal Procedure Law*, Laws 1970, chap. 996, sec. 260.10: 'Except as otherwise provided in section 320.10 [the waiver section], every trial of an indictment must be a jury trial.' Article VI, section 18(a), of the Constitution of the State of New York also requires that 'crimes prosecuted by indictment shall be tried by a jury composed of twelve persons, unless a jury trial has been waived.'

7 New York *Penal Law*, Laws 1965, chap. 1030, sec. 10.00(5).

8 *Criminal Procedure Law*, sec. 340.40. See Peter Preiser, 'S.340.40, Practice Commentaries.' *McKinney's Consolidated Laws of New York, Annotated, Criminal Procedure Law*, 11A (St Paul, Minn.: West 1994), 119ff.

9 United States Constitution, Amendment VI, right to a jury trial, as applied to the states through the Fourteenth Amendment due-process clause: see *Duncan v. Louisiana*, 391 US 145 (1968).

10 *Baldwin v. New York*, 399 US 66 (1970); *Blanton v. City of North Las Vegas, Nev.*, 489 US 538 (1989).

11 Canadian Charter of Rights and Freedoms, sec. 11(f), set out in Part I of the Constitution Act, 1982, as enacted by the Canada Act 1982 (UK), c. 11. The subsection relating to trial by jury was added during the deliberations of the Special Joint Committee of the Senate and the House of Commons in 1991: see its minutes, 1 and 28 Dec. 1981.

12 Criminal Code, sec. 787(1), RSC 1985, c. C-46, sec. 787(1), as amended.

13 *R. v. Smythe* (1971), 3 CCC (2d) 366 (SCC).

14 The number of hybrid offences in the Criminal Code has been increasing. There were about fifty in 1970, seventy in 1986, and eighty in 1996. Moreover, in the current environment of fiscal constraint, the number will continue to grow as the government tries to stream more cases away from the more costly superior-court system and therefore avoid preliminary inquiries and the possibility of jury trials. See Kirk Makin, 'Overhaul of Prosecution Planned: Provinces Could Get Right to Ticket Minor Criminals, Limit Preliminary Inquiries, Jury Trials,' *Globe and Mail*, 1 June 1996. The use of preliminary inquiries is becoming less important in Canada because of the extensive disclosure required in all criminal cases by the *Stinchcombe* case: (1991) 68 CCC (3d) 1 (SCC). England has also moved to eliminate jury trials for certain offences: see S. Doran, J.D. Jackson, and M.L. Seigel, 'Rethinking

Adversariness in Nonjury Criminal Trials' *American Journal of Criminal Law* 23 (1995), 6.

15 *Criminal Code*, sec. 271(1); see Stat. Can. 1980–81–82–83, c. 125, sec. 19.

16 Ibid., sec. 270; see Stat. Can. 1972, c. 13, sec. 22.

17 Ibid., sec. 271(1)(b); Stat. Can. 1994, c. 44, sec. 19. A 1996 bill, the Human Reproductive and Genetic Technologies Act, provides for four years' imprisonment for a summary-conviction offence: see Toronto *Globe and Mail*, 15 June 1996.

18 Ibid., sec. 553.

19 Stat. Can. 1994, c. 44, sec. 57. The monetary limit for theft was fifty dollars in 1970, $200 in 1976, and $5,000 today. Fraud and mischief under $5,000 are on the list of offences in addition to theft. Counselling, attempt, conspiracy, and accessory after the fact to all of the offences listed in section 553 are also now within the absolute jurisdiction of the provincial court, rather than just attempted theft.

20 Criminal Code, sec. 469; subject to sec. 473, which permits trial without jury if both the accused and the attorney general consent to trial by a superior-court judge alone.

21 In 1970, for example, the list of offences within the exclusive jurisdiction of the superior courts (then section 413) included bribery of officers (the present section 120), death by criminal negligence (section 220), manslaughter (section 234) and attempted rape (now sexual assault, section 271). These offences are no longer in section 469.

22 Criminal Code, sec. 473(1): 'Notwithstanding anything in this Act, an accused charged with an offence listed in section 469 may, with the consent of the accused and the Attorney General, be tried without a jury by a judge of a superior court of criminal jurisdiction.' Although the Supreme Court of Canada has held that there is no constitutional right to a non-jury trial – (see *Turpin and Siddiqui v. The Queen* (1989) 48 CCC (3d) 8) – it has not yet dealt with the right of a crown prosecutor to object to a non-jury trial in these cases. The Ontario Court of Appeal has held in *R. v. E (L.)* (1994) 94 CCC (3d) 228 at p. 241, per Finlayson, JA, that although the crown does not have 'an unfettered right to withhold consent ... the court cannot review this exercise of statutory discretion relating to the mode of trial unless it has been demonstrated on the record that there has been an abuse of the court's process through oppressive proceedings on the part of the Crown ... There would have to be some showing before the trial judge that the Crown had exercised its discretion arbitrarily, capriciously or for some improper motive so as to invite an examination as to whether there was an abuse of process under s. 7 of the Charter.'

Other courts have adopted a less restrictive test. In *R. v. Cardinal* (1996) 107 CCC (3d) 186, Jones, J, of the Alberta Queen's Bench stated at 187 that 'it seems appropriate that against the background of the spirit of the Charter, an accused should have the right to trial by judge alone in respect of an offence referred to in s. 469 of the Criminal Code unless the Crown has a reason of substance to justify refusing consent, where the accused's request is made timely.' And in *R. v. Bird* (1996) 107 CCC (3d) 186. Berger, J, of the Alberta Queen's Bench held that it was improper to refuse consent because of the identity of the trial judge who would hear the case, stating at 192: 'Such a consideration constitutes, in all of the circumstances, an improperly motivated exercise of the Crown's discretion to withhold consent and an interference with the integrity of the process of the court.'

23 Criminal Code, sec. 536(2): 'Where an accused is before a justice charged with an offence, other than an offence listed in section 469, and the offence is not one over which a provincial court judge has absolute jurisdiction under section 553, the justice shall ... put the accused to his election in the following words: You have the option to elect to be tried by a provincial court judge without a jury and without having had a preliminary inquiry; or you may elect to have a preliminary inquiry and to be tried by a judge without a jury; or you may elect to have a preliminary inquiry and to be tried by a court composed of a judge and jury. How do you elect to be tried?'

24 *Criminal Procedure Law*, sec. 320.10.

25 *People v. Follette*, 282 NYS 2d 729 (CA, 1967); *People v. Davis*, 424 NYS 2d 372 (CA, 1979); *People v. Swan*, 519 NYS 2d 581 (App. Div., 1987); *People v. Diaz*, 198 NYS 2d 27 (App. Div., 1960). See also Peter Preiser, 'S.320.10, Practice Commentaries,' *McKinney's, Criminal Procedure Law*, 788–9. See also *People v. Fossett* 629 NYS 2d 21 (App. Div., 1995), where the waiver was subsequently set aside because it 'was not knowing and voluntary, and was induced by the Trial Justice's statement implying that the case would be disposed of in defendant's favor if he waived a jury.'

26 Article I, sec. 2.

27 See *People v. Cosmos*, 205 NY 91 (Ct App., 1912); Preiser, 'S. 320.10, Practice Commentaries,' 788–9.

28 *Federal Rules of Criminal Procedure*, Rule 23(a) requires that the waiver receive 'the approval of the court and the consent of the government'; see *Singer v. United States*, 380 US 24 (1965). There is no constitutional 'right' to have a bench trial in the U.S. federal courts. The same is true in Canada: see *Turpin and Siddiqui v. The Queen* (1989), 48 CCC (3d) 8 (SCC).

29 See C.H. Whitebread and C. Slobogin, *Criminal Procedure*, 3rd ed. (Westbury, New York: Foundation Press 1993), 670.

30 New York statistics were generously provided by Chester Mount and Gail Miller, Office of Court Administration, New York City, and Harold J. Brand, Jr, and Carol Evans of the Office of the Administrative Judge of the Eighth Judicial District. Ontario statistics were supplied by Dorothy Gonsalves Singh of the Ontario Attorney General's Department and by Grant Goldrich of the Office of the Chief Justice of the General Division.

31 The three city courts are in Niagara Falls, Lockport, and North Tonawanda. See Doris Marie Provine, *Judging Credentials: Nonlawyer Judges and the Politics of Profes-*

sionalism (Chicago: University of Chicago Press 1986). Provine, a lawyer and former town justice, interviewed lay and lawyer judges in lower courts in New York state (see 86–7) and states (94): 'No one I interviewed liked jury trials: they require more time, trouble, and stress than any other means of disposing of cases. The time problem can be acute if the part-time judge has a law practice or other full-time occupation because the proceedings can easily consume a whole evening or most of a weekend.'

32 See S.J. Schulhofer, 'Is Plea Bargaining Inevitable?' *Harvard Law Review* 97 (1984), 1062: 'Defenders uniformly pointed to sentencing expectations as the overriding consideration in the decision to waive the right to a jury. In general, they believe that defendants convicted in jury trials receive sentences substantially more severe than those imposed in bench trials.'

33 B. Ostrom and N. Kauder, *Examining the Work of State Courts, 1994: A National Perspective from the Court Statistics Project* (National Center for State Courts 1996), 56. See also S. Doran, J.D. Jackson, and M.L. Seigel, 'Rethinking Adversariness in Nonjury Criminal Trials,' *American Journal of Criminal Law* 23 (1995), 9, who state that the proportion of bench trials for criminal cases in the U.S. federal courts in 1993 was also 14 per cent.

34 See Canadian Centre for Justice Statistics, *Adult Criminal Court Statistics 1994*, (Ottawa: Statistics Canada 1996), which contains breakdowns for five provinces and two territories for 1993 and 1994. Ontario is unfortunately not included. According to statistics in other provinces, however, indictable offences (consisting of indictable offences and hybrid offences that are tried by indictment) comprise on average about 40 per cent of all Criminal Code charges. In 1995 there were about 250,000 persons charged with criminal offences in Ontario. Forty per cent of that figure would be about 100,000 persons. I have somewhat arbitrarily reduced that figure by 20,000 to take into account the absolute-jurisdiction cases, where the accused cannot elect to be tried by a superior court.

35 Officials in the Attorney General's Department often use the 10 per cent figure in planning documents.

36 The figure for 1995 for all of Ontario for jury trials was 1,105, and for non-jury superior-court trials, 1,282. For 1994, the figure was 1,022 for jury trials and 1,216 for non-jury trials. The number of people who initially elect trial by jury is much higher, but many of these eventually plead guilty or re-elect trial by superior-court judge alone. There were 2,354 re-elections from jury to judge in 1995, mostly for the purpose of pleading guilty. In Niagara South in 1995, 105 person initially chose trial by jury, but, as we saw above, only twenty-four jury trials actually took place.

37 See *Stinchcombe* (1991), 68 CCC (3d) 1 (SCC).

38 Harry Kalven, Jr, and Hans Zeisel, *The American Jury* (Toronto: Little, Brown 1966).

39 Ibid., 59.

40 Ibid., 29.

41 Ibid.

42 Michael Zander and Paul Henderson, *The Royal Commission on Criminal Justice: Crown Court Study*, Research Study No. 19 (London: HMSO 1993).

43 Ibid., 170. There were far fewer problematic convictions: ibid., 171.

44 *The Royal Commission on Criminal Justice: Report* (London: HMSO 1993), 86, relying on Julie Vennard, 'The Outcome of Contested Trials,' in David Moxon, ed., *Managing Criminal Justice* (London: HMSO 1985), 126ff.

45 *Royal Commission on Criminal Justice: Report*, 86. See also Sid Butler, 'Acquittal Rates,' in Moxon, *Managing Criminal Justice*, 152–3: from 1976 to 1980 the acquittal rates for contested cases were approximately 50 per cent and only in the crown court 25 per cent in magistrates' courts. However, about one-half of the acquittals in the crown court came by direction of the judge. See the high acquittal rates cited in Brian P. Block, Claire Corbett, and Jill Peay, *The Royal Commission on Criminal Justice: Ordered and Directed Acquittals in the Crown Court*, Research Study No. 15 (London: HMSO 1993), 11ff. Butler says (154) that the acquittal rate in the crown court is about one-third after acquittals by order or direction of the judge are taken out. Magistrates, courts include such cases, and so their acquittal rate is lower than the 25 per cent mentioned above.

46 *Royal Commission on Criminal Justice: Report*, 86, citing C. Hedderman and D. Moxon, *Magistrates' Court or Crown Court? Mode of Trial Decisions and Sentencing* (London: HMSO 1992). For the comparable encouragement of bench trials in the United States, see S. Doran, J.D. Jackson, and M.L Seigel, 'Rethinking Adversariness in Nonjury Criminal Trials,' *American Journal of Criminal Law* 23 (1995), 5.

47 *Royal Commission on Criminal Justice: Report*, 86.

48 Doran, Jackson, and Seigel, 'Rethinking Adversariness,' 9.

49 *McKinney's New York Criminal Law Pamphlet, 1991* (St Paul: West Publishing 1991), 1241ff; *Penal Law*, secs. 70.00–70.15, 70.30.

50 Material supplied by the State of New York, Office of Court Administration, shows that, for the year 1995, 61,821 out of 72,913 dispositions in the supreme and county courts were disposed of by plea.

51 Kathleen Maguire, Ann L. Pastore, and Timothy J. Flanagan, eds., *Sourcebook of Criminal Justice Statistics 1992*, U.S. Department of Justice, Bureau of Justice Statistics (Washington, DC: USGPO 1993), 528, and see also *Sourcebook* for 1994, containing 1992 statistics, 486.

52 There were 38,540 pleas out of 46,451 dispositions in 1995 in New York City and 23,781 out of 26,462 dispositions outside New York City.

53 See C.H. Whitebread and C. Slobogin, *Criminal Procedure*, 3rd ed. (Westbury, NY: Foundation Press 1993), 669. See also S.J. Schulhofer, 'Is Plea Bargaining Inevita-

ble?' *Harvard Law Review* 97 (1984), 1063, for other factors, including the fact that 'a defendant in custody may have to wait less time for a bench trial' and 'a district attorney has less time to prepare for a bench trial, and the defender therefore may have a better chance to exploit inconsistencies in the complainant's testimony.'

54 See *Smith v. The Queen* (1987), 34 CCC (3d) 97 (SCC).

55 O.E. Fitzgerald, *The Guilty Pleas and Summary Justice* (Toronto: Carswell 1990), 1. See also *Report of the Attorney General's Advisory Committee on Charge Screening, Disclosure, and Resolution Discussions*, Chair: G. Arthur Martin (Toronto: Queen's Printer for Ontario 1993), 15 note 6. In the early 1980s, the estimates were lower: see A. Brannigan and J.C. Levy, 'The Legal Framework of Plea Bargaining,' *Canadian Journal of Criminology* 25 (1983), 400. At that time, there was considerable ambivalence about the legitimacy of plea bargaining. The change in attitude can be seen in the different approaches taken by the Law Reform Commission of Canada in two working papers of 1975 and 1989. The earlier document, *Criminal Procedure: Control of the Process: Working Paper 15* (Ottawa: Law Reform Commission 1975), states (46) that plea bargaining is 'contrary to the entire notion of justice.' The later one, *Plea Discussions and Agreements: Working Paper 60* (Ottawa: Law Reform Commission 1989), concluded (8) that 'it would be a mistake to dismiss plea negotiation as a distasteful practice.'

Available Canadian statistics do not enable one to estimate the numbers accurately. Provincial statistics for the provincial courts deal with counts rather than individuals. The general division statistics show a much lower rate of guilty pleas – 34 per cent of the cases in 1995 – because most persons who are going to plead guilty do not elect trial in the higher court. Carl Baar's figures on guilty pleas in the mid-1980s in the then county and district courts in Ontario and British Columbia are also lower than what one would have found in all the courts. He found that the rate ranged from a low of 45 per cent in the County Court in Brampton, Ontario, to a high of 67 per cent in London, Ontario; Carl Baar, 'Trial Rates and Plea Rates in Canadian Criminal Cases: Local Legal Culture, Gender Politics and the Comparative Study of Trial Courts,' presented at the Meeting of the Research Committee on Comparative Judicial Studies at the World Congress of the International Political Science Association, Buenos Aires, Argentina, 22 July 1991, 3.

56 There were 651 acquittals out of a total of 1,282 dispositions (50.78 per cent) by the Ontario Court (General Division) for non-jury trials, and 527 acquittals out of a total of 1,105 dispositions (47.69 per cent) for jury trials. There was a total of 1,178 acquittals out of a total of 2,387 criminal dispositions (49.35 per cent) by the court: *Ontario Court (General Division): Caseload Statistics for 1995.*

57 *Caseload Statistics for 1995.*

58 Nine acquittals out of twenty-four cases with a jury (37 per cent) and seven cases out of thirteen without a jury (54 per cent).

59 Baar, *Trial Rates and Plea Rates.*

60 Ibid., 16.

61 Counsel nevertheless think that they may be better off with a jury in certain narcotics cases. One federal prosecutor in Canada told us that those prosecuted for importing narcotics at Pearson International Airport near Toronto usually choose a jury, which they think may be more sympathetic – or less cynical – than a judge to the defence that the accused did not know there were narcotics in the suitcase. Available statistics show that significantly more persons in that county who elect to be tried by a higher court choose trial by jury than in the province as a whole, but this is not broken down into offences.

62 See Harry P. Stumpf and John H. Culver, *The Politics of State Courts* (New York: Longman 1992), 40. See, generally, 'The Road to the Judiciary: Navigating the Judicial Selection Process,' *Albany Law Review* 57 (1994), 973.

63 Stumpf and Culver, *The Politics of State Courts*, 22.

64 Dershowitz, *Reasonable Doubts: The O.J. Simpson Case and the Criminal Justice System* (New York: Simon and Schuster 1996) 151; see also, 47.

65 Ibid., 151.

66 See, generally, Martin L. Friedland, *A Place Apart: Judicial Independence and Accountability in Canada* (Ottawa: Canadian Judicial Council 1995).

67 Ibid., chap. 3.

68 Brian J. Ostrom and Neal B. Kauder, *Examining the Work of State Courts, 1994: A National Perspective from the Court Statistics Project* (National Center for State Courts 1996), 56, 65; the method of selection is found on 16 and in Stumpf and Culver, *The Politics of State Courts*, 40.

69 For a discussion of the merit system, see Friedland, *A Place Apart*, 252–3.

70 See *Federal Rules of Criminal Procedure*, Rule 23(a); *Singer v. United States*, 380 US 24 (1965); Preiser, 'S.320.10,' 788–9.

71 See Ostrom and Kauder, *Examining the Work of State Courts, 1994*, 56.

72 Ibid., 65.

73 See Valerie P. Hans and Neil Vidmar, *Judging the Jury* (New York: Plenum Press 1986), 159–60; I.A. Horowitz, 'The Effect of Jury Nullification Instruction on Verdicts and Jury Functioning in Criminal Trials,' *Law and Human Behavior* 9 (1985), 25.

74 *Morgentaler, Smoling and Scott v. The Queen* (1988), 37 CCC (3d) 449 (SCC). See also *R. v. Swietlinski* (1994), 92 CCC (3d) 449 at 460 (SCC).

75 Ibid., 481.

76 Ibid., 483.

77 *Canadian Criminal Code*, sec. 676(1).

78 *People v. Croswell*, 3 Johns. 337, 366–8 (NY Sup. Ct, 1804); *Duffy v. People*, 26 NY 588, 592 (1863).

79 See, generally, *U.S. v. Dougherty*, 473 F. 2d 1113, 1130 (CA Dist. Col. 1972); Jeffrey Abramson, *We, the Jury: The Jury System and the Ideal of Democracy* (New York: Basic Books 1994), chap. 2.

80 *Sparf and Hansen v. U.S.*, 156 US 51 (1895).

81 *People v. Mussenden*, 127 NE 2d 551, 553 (Ct App., 1955). Two states allow the jury to determine the law: Maryland and Indiana. See Chaya Weinberg-Brodt, 'Jury Nullification and Jury-Control Procedures,' *New York University Law Review* 65 (1990), 847; cf. J.J. Duane, 'Jury Nullification: The Top Secret Constitutional Right' *Litigation* 22 (1996), 7.

82 *People v. Goetz*, 536 NYS 2d 45 (Ct App., 1988).

83 Ibid., 46.

84 *People v. Weinberg*, 609 NYS 2d 155 (Ct App., 1994).

85 Ibid., 158.

86 *U.S. v. Dougherty*, 473 F. 2d 1113 (CA Dist. Col., 1972).

87 Ibid., 1142; See also David C. Brody, '*Sparf* and *Dougherty* Revisited: Why the Court Should Instruct the Jury of its Nullification Right,' *American Criminal Law Review* 38 (1995), 89; Weinberg-Brodt, 'Jury Nullification,' 825.

88 *U.S. v. Dougherty*, 1144. The majority, however, stated that jurors already knew about their power to acquit. 'The jury,' the majority stated at 1135, 'knows well enough that its prerogative is not limited to the choices articulated in the formal instructions of the court. The jury gets its understanding as to the arrangements in the legal system from more than one voice ... The totality of input generally convey adequately enough the idea of prerogative, of freedom in an occasional case to depart from what the judge says.' Chief Justice Bazelon countered 1141: 'I simply do not understand the justification for relying on a haphazard process of informal communication whose effectiveness is likely to depend, to a large extent, on whether or not any of the jurors are so well-educated and astute that they are able to receive the message. If the jury should know of its power to disregard the law, then the power should be explicitly described by instruction of the court or argument of counsel.'

89 Harold J. Rothwax, *Guilty: The Collapse of Criminal Justice* (New York: Random House 1996), 218. See also Duane, 'Jury Nullification,' 14.

90 Seymour Martin Lipset, *Continental Divide: The Values and Institutions of the United States and Canada* (New York: Routledge 1990). Judges, according to a survey done for the Law Reform Commission of Canada, would prefer even greater deference. Only 5 per cent of the judges surveyed would permit jury nullification, whereas 75 per cent of lay persons would: A.N. Doob, *Studies on the Jury* (Ottawa: Law Reform Commission of Canada 1979), 1ff

91 See, generally, B.M. Dickens, 'The Morgentaler Case: Criminal Process and Abortion Law,' *Osgoode Hall Law Journal* 14 (1976), 229.

92 See R.P. Kerans, 'Two Nations under Law' in *Canada and the United States: Differences that Count* (Peterborough: Broadview Press 1993), 218 and 220; C. Granger et al., *Canadian Criminal Jury Trials* (Toronto: Carswell 1989) 273ff. See the Ontario Court of Appeal case of *R. v. Varcoe* (1996), 104 CCC (3d) 449 453, adopting an earlier Court of Appeal statement that 'generally speaking, the trial judge has a duty to review the evidence so as to assist the jury in understanding the factual issues in dispute, the competing positions of the parties, and the evidence relied on by the parties in relation to the issues.'

93 See, generally, M.L. Friedland, *Double Jeopardy* (Oxford: Clarendon Press 1969) 281ff.

94 As set out in Dershowitz, *Reasonable Doubts*, 119.

95 Comments of Marcia Clark and Judge Ito on defence closing argument, 1995 WL 704342 (Cal. Super. Trans.). After the verdict, California Governor Pete Wilson is reported to have called for the State Judicial Council to devise restrictions on lawyers' closing arguments: *Globe and Mail*, 5 October 1995.

96 *Municipal Elections Act*, RSO 1990, CM 53, s. 21. The sheriff must also select names of eligible persons inhabiting Indian reserves in the same manner as employed in a municipality, though from any records available: see Juries Act, RSO 1990, c. J.3, s. 6(8). See, generally, C. Granger, L. Charron, and P. Chumak, *Canadian Criminal Jury Trials* (Toronto: Carswell 1989), 120ff.

97 For U.S. voters lists, see *The Jury Project: Report to the Chief Judge of the State of New York*, 31 March 1994, 4. Although it is estimated that only 64 per cent of eligible Americans register to vote, voters' lists are the most commonly used source list for jury selection throughout the United States.

98 Ibid.

99 Ibid.

100 Ibid., 5.

101 Ibid., 6.; NYS, *Judiciary Law*, sec. 506. For a discussion of the New York Jury Project, see C. McMahon and D.L. Kornblau, 'Chief Judge Judith S. Kaye's Program of Jury Selection Reform in New York,' *St. John's Journal of Legal Commentary* 10 (1995), 263. In New York, the Niagara County Jury Commission currently uses electoral lists, tax rolls, records from the Department of Motor Vehicles and the Department of Labor, and social services lists; information provided by the Niagara County Jury Commission. The jury pool is also no longer a permanent list, as it was in the 1980s. At that time, the pool was updated with eligible jurors only as other persons were removed from the list because of ineligibility or death or as demand dictated. As a result, people who were on the list could be called for jury duty several times, while many potentially eligible jurors who were not yet on the list could not even be called regardless of whether they were fully qualified. This procedure not only created a stagnant pool that was more demanding on some citi-

zens but also naturally excluded younger persons: *The Jury Project* (New York), 10–14. Now the entire pool is randomly redrawn from the eligible returned questionnaires at frequent intervals. In addition, in 1996 New York completely eliminated its lengthy list of disqualifications (sec. 511) and exemptions (sec. 512) from jury service. See, generally, G.T. Munsterman, 'A Brief History of State Jury Reform Efforts' *Judicature* 79 (1996), 216.

Ontario continues to have several grounds for disqualification, covering, for example, medical practitioners, veterinary surgeons, and persons engaged in the enforcement of law: Juries Act, RSO 1990, c. J.3, ss. 2–4. However, Ontario has narrowed the list of disqualification somewhat by eliminating the exclusion of spouses of disqualified persons: Stat. Ont. 1994, c. 27, ss. 48(1) and (2).

102 As cited in the *Report of the Commission on Systemic Racism in the Ontario Criminal Justice System* (Toronto: Queen's Printer 1995), 253; see also Cynthia Petersen, 'Institutionalized Racism: The Need for Reform of the Criminal Jury Selection Process,' *McGill Law Journal* 38 (1993), 147.

103 See *Report of the Commission on Systemic Racism*, 252–3; *Report of the Aboriginal Justice Inquiry of Manitoba* (Winnipeg: Province of Manitoba 1991); Royal Commission on Aboriginal Peoples, *Bridging the Cultural Divide: A Report on Aboriginal People and Criminal Justice in Canada* (Ottawa 1996); David Pomerant, Minister's Reference: Jury Selection and Multicultural Issues (Jan. 1992), 16ff. Moreover, it is more difficult to challenge the entire jury panel in Canada than in New York. A challenge under section 629 of the Criminal Code will succeed only if the applicant proves the existence of a deliberate plan by the sheriff to exclude a group or class of jurors: *R. v. Chipesia* (1991), 3 CR (4th) 169 (BCSC). In New York, bad faith is not a requirement to challenge the panel: see *Criminal Procedure Law*, sec. 270.10; *People v. Guzman*, 469 NYS 2d 916 (Ct App., 1983); *U.S. v. Garces*, 849 F. Supp 852 (Dist. Ct, ED New York, 1994).

104 Juries Act, RSO 1990, c. J.3, s. 6 (8).

105 *R. v. Hubbert* (1975), 29 CCC (2d) 279 at 293 (Ont. CA).

106 *R. v. Hubbert* (1977), 33 CCC (2d) 207 (SCC). See also *R. v. Barrow* (1987), 38 CCC (3d) 193 (SCC); *R. v. Sherratt* (1991), 63 CCC (3d) 193 (SCC).

107 Juries Act, RSO 1990, c. J.3 s. 27.

108 *R. v. Hubbert* (1975), 291 (Ont. CA). See, generally, Neil Vidmar, 'Pretrial Prejudice in Canada: A Comparative Perspective on the Criminal Jury' *Judicature* 79 (1996), 253–4.

109 See, for example, *R. v. Zundel* (1987), 31 CCC (3d) 97 (Ont. CA); *R. v. Morgentaler*, 15 Oct. 1984 (unreported), cited in *Zundel*, 133. See, generally, F.L. Morton, *Morgentaler v. Borowski: Abortion, the Charter and the Courts* (Toronto: McClelland and Stewart 1992), chap. 16.

110 *Criminal Procedure Law*, ss. 270.15, 270.20. A leading New York practitioners'

text states: 'A judge may still allow considerable leeway to counsel depending upon the nature of the case, the stature of the attorneys and their persistence': Robert W. Vinal, *New York Criminal Practice Handbook* (Albany: New York State Bar Association 1991), 331. It is often the judge who does the questioning in New York: *The Jury Project* (New York), 46.

111 In both New York – *Criminal Procedure Law*, ss. 270.15(2), 270.20, 270.25) – and Ontario – Criminal Code, s. 634; see Stat. Can., 1992, c. 41, s. 2) – a peremptory challenge can be made after a challenge for cause has failed.

112 *Criminal Procedure Law*, s. 270.15(1); *The Jury Project* (New York), 47–8.

113 See Pomerant, *Jury Selection*, 48–9; H. Fukurai, E.W. Butler, and R. Krooth, *Race and the Jury* (New York: Plenum Press 1993), 68; V.P. Hans and N. Vidmar, *Judging the Jury* (New York: Plenum Press 1986), 67.

114 *The Jury Project* (New York), 60–2.

115 *R. v. Parks* (1993), 84 CCC (3d) 353 (Ont. CA); *R. v. Wilson* (1996), 107 CCC (3d) 86 (Ont. CA); *cf. R. v. Williams* (1994), 90 CCC (3d) 194 (BCSC), aff'd. BCCA (1996) 106 CCC (3d) 215; see, generally, Kent Roach, 'Challenges for Cause and Racial Discrimination,' *Criminal Law Quarterly* 37 (1995), 410. The Supreme Court of Canada granted leave to appeal in the *Williams* case: see *Globe and Mail*, 7 Oct. 1996 [subsequently reversed by The Supreme Court of Canada (1988), 124 CCC (3d) 48.] The Ontario Court of Appeal decided in *R. v. Alli* not to extend the *Parks* case to other racial minorities or gay accused persons (*Lawyers Weekly*, 11 Oct. 1996); cf. *R. v. Musson* (*Lawyers Weekly*, 8 Nov. 1996).

116 Criminal Code, RSC 1985, c. C-46, s. 634: 'The prosecutor ... may direct any number of jurors who are not challenged peremptorily by the accused to stand by until all the jurors have been called who are available for the purpose of trying the indictment.'

117 *R. v. Bain* (1992), 69 CCC (3d) 481 (SCC).

118 At p. 511. However, the court was divided four to three.

119 Stat. Can. 1992, c. 41, sec. 2, amending sec. 634.

120 *Criminal Procedure Law*, s. 270.25. In Canada, with multiple defendants, each defendant still receives the same number of peremptories as if the accused were tried alone, but the crown receives the same total number of peremptory challenges available to all the accused: Criminal Code, s. 634(4). This factor is particularly important in certain cases, since the crown will always have complete discretion over its use of peremptories, while the defendants may or may not have coinciding interests.

However, in New York, both the prosecutor and defendants have the same number of peremptories, regardless of the number of defendants, although the trial judge can grant additional peremptories to the defendants in appropriate cases. Defendants in New York cannot exercise their peremptory challenges unless a majority of the defendants support the challenge: *Criminal Procedure Law*, s. 270.25. In addition, New York does not allow the prosecution to use its remaining peremptories once the defence have exhausted theirs: s. 270.15(2).

121 *The Jury Project* (New York), 67. Only three peremptory challenges are granted for misdemeanours, which may help further explain why so few misdemeanours are tried by jury: *Criminal Procedure Law*, s. 360.30; Vinal, *New York Criminal Practice Handbook*, 338.

122 Canadian Criminal Code, sec. 318.

123 Ibid., s. 233.

124 Ibid., s. 270.

125 *The Jury Project* (New York), 66.

126 Ibid., 67.

127 *Batson v. Kentucky*, 106 S. Ct 1712 (1986).

128 *People v. Jenkins*, 555 NYS 2d 10 (Ct App., 1990), *People v. Scott*, 522 NYS 2d 94 (Ct App., 1987), *People v. Bolling*, 582 NYS 2d 950 (Ct App., 1992), *People v. Childress*, 598 NYS 2d 146 (Ct App., 1993), *People v. Smith*, 601 NYS 2d 142 (App. Div., 1993); *People v. Allen*, 629 NYS 2d 1003 (Ct App., 1995).

129 *Georgia v. McCollum*, 112 S. Ct 2348 (1992).

130 *People v. Blunt*, 561 NYS 2d 90 (App. Div., 1990).

131 In *Purkett v. Elem*, 115 S. Ct 1769 (1995), the U.S. Supreme Court held that long hair constituted a valid, racially neutral reason. Unless a court can conclude that the challenge was racially motivated, the peremptory challenge may be justified even if the basis given for the challenge may seem (see p. 1771) 'silly or superstitious.' See also *People v. Hernandez*, 553 NYS 2d 85 (Ct App., 1990); *People v. Miranda*, 631 NYS 2d 873 (App. Div., 1995); *People v. Hewitt*, 633 NYS 2d 58 (App. Div., 1995); *People v. Allen*, 629 NYS 2d 1003 (Ct App., 1995), citing *Purkett v. Elem.*

132 N. Gary Holten and Lawson L. Lamar, *The Criminal Courts: Structures, Personnel, and Processes* (New York: McGraw-Hill 1991), 332–3, citing Sam Roberts, 'State to Adopt One-Case, One-Judge System,' *New York Times*, 12 Oct. 1985, 1 and 30.

133 Holten and Lamar, *The Criminal Courts*, 332–3; Maureen Solomon and Douglas K. Somerlot, *Caseflow Management in the Trial Court: Now and for the Future* (Chicago: American Bar Association 1987), 33–44.

134 Holten and Lamar, *The Criminal Courts*, 333; Solomon and Somerlot, *Caseflow Management*, 38–40.

135 Solomon and Somerlot, *Caseflow Management*, 43–4.

136 Ibid.

137 We obtained statistics on bench trials before 1986 for New York state, expecting to find that they were higher for 1984 and 1985 than for 1986 and 1987. In fact, the

number of bench trials went up slightly in 1986 and 1987. Perhaps other factors played a role in those years.

138 Criminal Code, s. 625.1.

139 *Report of the Attorney General's Advisory Committee on Charge Screening, Disclosure, and Resolution Discussions* (Toronto: Queen's Printer for Ontario 1993), 378; *Ontario Court of Justice Criminal Proceedings Rules*, SI/92–99, 1992 *Canada Gazette* Part II, p. 2298, Rule 28 (specifically Rule 28.04).

140 In the General Division of the Ontario Court in 1995, there were 2,354 (39.14 per cent) re-elections from jury to non-jury trial. In Toronto, about 50 per cent of all accused who selected trial by jury re-elected trial by judge alone. Out of about 6,000 accused who originally selected trial by jury, less than 10 per cent (578, or 9.61 per cent) actually had jury trials. In contrast, only seventy-one (1.48 per cent) of the accused who had elected trial by judge alone re-elected jury trials, and a somewhat higher proportion (631, or 13.19 per cent) (631) of accused who originally opted for trial by judge alone did in fact go to trial: caseload statistics were provided by the Ontario Court, General Division.

141 See, generally, Doran, Jackson, and Seigel, 'Rethinking Adversariness,' 1.

142 *R. v. Khan* (1990), 59 CCC (3d) 92 (SCC); *R. v. Smith* (1992), 75 CCC (3d) 257 (SCC); *R. v. B. (K.G.)* (1993), 79 CCC (3d) 257 (SCC).

143 Jerome Prince, *Richardson on Evidence*, 10th ed. (New York: Brooklyn Law School 1973), 176–86.

144 *Hodge's Case* (1838), 2 Lewin 227, 168 ER 1136.

145 *R. v. Comba* (1938), 70 CCC 205 (SCC); John Sopinka, Sidney N. Lederman, and Alan W. Bryant *The Law of Evidence in Canada* (Toronto: Butterworths 1992), 40.

146 *R. v.* Cooper (1977), 34 CCC (2d) 18 (SCC).

147 *People v. Barnes*, 429 NYS 2d 178 (Ct App., 1980); *People v. Daddona*, 599 NYS 2d 530 (Ct App., 1993).

148 *R. v. Vetrovec* (1982), 67 CCC (2d) 1 (SCC). However, the corroboration rule was partially brought back in *Bevan and Griffith v. The Queen* (1993), 82 CCC (3d) 310 (SCC); see also Martin L. Friedland, *The Death of Old Man Rice* (Toronto: University of Toronto Press 1994), 112 note 4.

149 Section 4(6) of the Canada Evidence Act states: 'The failure of the person charged, or of the wife or husband of such person, to testify shall not be made the subject of comment by the judge or by counsel for the prosecution:' RSC 1985 c. C-5; see *R. v. Vezeau* (1976), 28 CCC (2d) 81 (SCC); *cf. R. v. Naglik* (1991), 65 CCC (3d) 272 (Ont. CA).

150 *R. v. Lepage* (1995), 95 CCC (3d) 385 (SCC); *R. v. Johnson* (1993), 79 CCC (3d) 42 (Ont. CA); *R. v. Boss* (1988), 46 CCC (3d) 523 (Ont. CA).

151 See New York's *Criminal Procedure Law*, s. 300.10(2).

152 See Rothwax, *Guilty*, 193: *Carter v. Kentucky*, 450 US 288 (1981).

153 The U.S. Supreme Court held in *Lakeside v. Oregon*, 435 US 333 (1978) that the accused cannot constitutionally prevent such a charge. New York specifically deals with the issue in section 300.10(2) of the *Criminal Procedure Law*.

154 See Doran, Jackson, and Seigel, 'Rethinking Adversariness,' 31–3. As stated in one federal case cited in Doran et al., the trial judge 'must be presumed to have exercised the proper discretion in distinguishing between the improper and proper evidence introduced at trial, and to have based his decision only on the latter, in the absence of a clear showing to the contrary by appellant'; *U.S. v. Menk*, 406 F. 2d 124 at p. 127 (7th Cir., 1968).

155 Section 12 of the Canada Evidence Act, RSC 1985, c. C-5, states that 'a witness may be questioned as to whether he has been convicted of any offence.' Prior to *R. v. Corbett* (1988), 41 CCC (3d) 385 (SCC), the court did not have any discretion to exclude prejudicial evidence of prior convictions. The admissibility of prior convictions of a witness in New York state is governed by section 60.40 of the *Criminal Procedure Law*. See Preiser, 'Section 60.40 Practice Commentaries,' in 691: 'It does *not* add to or detract from common law principles as to when and to what extent such impeaching questions may be asked.'

156 Vinal, ed., *New York Criminal Practice Handbook*, 605.

157 The following cases outline the procedure for determining the admissibility of prior convictions in Ontario: *R. v. Corbett, supra*; *R. v. Thompson* (1992), 83 CCC (3d) 273 (BCCA); *R. v. Trudel* (1994), 90 CCC (3d) 318 (Quebec CA); *R. v. Ramirez* (1995), 97 CCC (3d) 353 (BCCA). The procedure for determining the admissibility of accused's prior convictions in New York state is governed by the following cases: *People v. Sandoval*, 357 NYS 2d 849 (Ct. App., 1974); *People v. Bennett*, 573 NYS 2d 322 (App. Div., 1991); *People v. Smith*, 464 NYS 2d 399 (Ct App., 1983); and *People v. Duffy*, 367 NYS 2d 236 (Ct App., 1975).

158 *R. v. P. (G.F.)* (1994), 89 CCC (3d) 176 at 181 (Ont. CA).

159 *People v. Sandoval*.

160 Ibid., 854. On the general tendency of New York to employ more pre-trial motions than Ontario, see Code, 'American Cadillacs,' 407.

161 In *People v. Miller*, 630 NYS 2d 99 (App. Div., 1995), the accused waived the jury after previous convictions were admitted by the trial judge in a *Sandoval* hearing. The Appellate Division rejected the accused's claim that 'the *Sandoval* ruling unfairly coerced him into waiving his right to a jury trial and, thus, the waiver was not voluntarily made as constitutionally required.'

162 See the U.S. Fifth Amendment: no person shall be 'subject for the same offence to be twice put in jeopardy of life and limb'; New York Bill of Rights, article 1, section 6: 'No person shall be subject to be twice put in jeopardy for the same offence.' See also *Kepner v. United States*, 195 US 100 (1904); *People v. Brown*, 386 NYS 2d 848 (Ct App., 1976); cf. *Palko v. Connecticut*, 302 U.S. 319 (1937). See, gener-

ally, M.L. Friedland, *Double Jeopardy* (Oxford: Clarendon Press 1969), 281ff.; Preiser, 'Section 450.20 Practice Commentaries.' The limited right of appeal by the prosecutor is found in *Criminal Procedures Law*, sections 450.20, 450.40, 450.50 and 450.55.

163 See Criminal Code, s. 676(1)(a): 'The Attorney General or counsel instructed by him for the purpose may appeal to the court of appeal (a) against a judgment or verdict of acquittal of a trial court in proceedings by indictment on any ground of appeal that involves a question of law alone.' See also subsections (b) to (d). The Canadian position was held in *Regina v. Morgentaler* (1985), 22 CCC (3d) 353 (Ont. CA) not to violate the Charter's provision against double jeopardy, section 11(h), which provides: 'Any person charged with an offence has the right ... if finally acquitted of the offence, not to be tried for it again.' The court held 409–10 that the insertion of the word 'finally' was intended to preserve the right to appeal by the prosecution.

164 Dershowitz, *Reasonable Doubts*, 188–9.

165 Rothwax, *Guilty*, 182.

166 We have not discussed the effect of different systems of legal aid in the two jurisdictions, in part because the rules are changing in Ontario and in part because of uncertainty what impact the various schemes would have on the incentive to choose a trial by a judge or jury. Does the public-defender system in Niagara County, New York, result in proportionately more jury trials than the assigned-counsel system for felonies in Erie County, New York, with its relatively low hourly rates and its low cap on the total available unless there are 'extraordinary circumstances'? See *Criminal Procedure Law*, s. 180.10, and the County Law, s. 722, and the Ontario Legal Aid Act, RSO 1990, chap. L. 9, as amended.

167 M.L. Friedland, 'Gun Control in Canada: Politics and Impact,' in Friedland, *A Century of Criminal Justice: Perspectives in the Development of Canadian Law* (Toronto: Carswell 1984), 134–5.

168 See K. McNaught, 'Political Trials and the Canadian Political Tradition,' in M.L. Friedland, ed., *Courts and Trials: A Multidisciplinary Approach* (Toronto: University of Toronto Press 1975), 142.

169 *United States v. Martin*, 704 F. 2d 267 (1983) at 271–2 *per* Keith J.

170 See section 536(2) of the Criminal Code, which states simply, after setting out the various alternatives: 'How do you elect to be tried?'

171 Section 469 of the Criminal Code. For a discussion of waiver in Canada see Ron Levi's 'Towards a General Standard of Waiver in the Criminal Process,' LLM, Thesis, University of Toronto, 1996.

172 *Consultation Paper on the Use of Jury Trials in Civil Cases*, produced by the Ontario Law Reform Commission in 1994, showed that there are well under one thousand civil-jury cases in Ontario in any year, the majority of which involve

motor vehicles. Quebec abolished the civil jury in 1976 (p. 10 – SQ 1976, c. 9, s. 56). The Law Reform Commission recommended at 33 that 'the current presumption in Ontario law favouring the availability of juries in civil cases should be reversed, and that juries should be available, upon judicial order, only where the predominant issues in the action concern the values, attitudes or priorities of the community and the ends of justice will be best served if the findings of fact or assessment of damages are made by a jury.' If the recommendation is adopted, there will be even fewer civil juries.

14

South Africa's Constitutional Odyssey: Can the Law Be Trusted?

HUGH CORDER

If a constitution derives its legitimacy from the consent of the people, then those who share a constitution must first agree to be a people.[1]

Peter Russell, *Constitutional Odyssey*

In borrowing unashamedly from the title of Peter Russell's outstanding treatment of Canadian constitutional development, I seek to achieve two immediate objectives. Firstly, I wish to pay tribute to the man as a scholar, a writer, and a teacher who, in our all-too-brief contacts over the past five years, has helped to stimulate my own thinking about matters judicial,[2] and who has thus, indirectly and to a modest degree, influenced the structure and procedures for the appointment of judges in South Africa.[3] Second, I have replaced the reference to the sovereignty of the Canadian people in the subtitle of the original work[4] with a focus on the role of law in the constitutional transition in South Africa. The very notion of 'sovereignty' in the sense that Russell uses it is not relevant to South Africa, given the incredible divisions that exist among its people. Also, many lawyers who saw the rule of law defiled under segregation and apartheid[5] are astonished that the law (particularly in the form of a written constitution with a Bill of Rights) and the courts (especially a Constitutional Court empowered to review legislative action) should be the single most important and most trusted medium for the transfer of power from a minority to the majority. In fact, recent debates about the law and the constitution have begun a process whose end may be such sovereignty.

The role of law in social change has absorbed my attention for some time,[6] and it raises any number of profound jurisprudential and political questions. What is it about the law that makes it a basis for compromise between political factions that advocate and use violence against their opponents daily? How can a legal system undermined consistently over more than a century by governments using it to visit manifest injustice on the vast majority of people be transformed into a system that can undo that injustice? How can the law and the courts that suffered widespread perceptions of illegitimacy, because they were an instrument of injustice, become a trusted and effective mechanism to transform social relations in the direction of justice? How ought the accessibility of the law, and the practice and teaching of it, be altered in order to take account of its changed and elevated profile in government and affairs of the day? And so on.

While many will have instant reactions to such questions, they raise complex issues, to which there are no full and absolute answers. In this paper I wish to describe the process whereby the rule of law moved rapidly to centre stage from the wings of South African politics over the past ten years. Considerable debates have centred on the 'legalization of politics' in Canada since the early 1980s, and such an experience has been crucial in constitutional change in South Africa. These questions are therefore familiar to Canadian lawyers and political scientists.

Indeed, the themes into which sessions at our conference were divided resonated to a large extent with this type of question. Participants displayed considerable 'rights-scepticism' – an argument not unfamiliar to my ear, but emerging from a very different political agenda: most such proponents in South Africa espouse a relatively radical form of popular democracy as a means to achieve socialism. Discussion concerning the rights of Aboriginal peoples took a form that is not often seen in South Africa, where the focus tends to be on policies of equity and land restitution to correct the effects of more recent discrimination and denial of rights. As I hope to show, the adoption of a bill of rights was a necessary element in the negotiated revolution in South Africa; how effectively it will transform social relations and deliver social services is the crucial question. The first two sections of this paper set the historical context for the third and fourth, which describe the framing and implementation of a democratic constitution and speculate on its future.

Law in Decline

While the law has always been prominent in civil society in South Africa, and while its content represents a unique blend of much of the best of the common- and civil-law traditions, its role in government had, by the late 1980s, become increasingly attenuated and formalistic.[7] Establishment of the Union of South Africa in 1910 brought with it government according to Westminster, including many of the prerogatives and conventions. The South African constitution, however, differed from its colonial counterparts. At a formal level, the battle over the franchise for Black South Africans was translated in compromise terms into the South Africa Act – such rights as did exist, chiefly in the old Cape Colony, could not be eliminated except through parliamentary enactment, adopted unicamerally with a two-thirds majority.[8] At a substantive level, the 'rule of law' or the 'sense of fair play,' said to epitomize the Westminster way (but excluding women[9] and bedevilled by class antagonisms), had been only minimally observed in those governments that formed the Union, and its benefits were effectively limited to those represented in such governments. The pre-Union constitutions of the Orange Free State and the Transvaal limited the benefits of the law and civil rights to their white male citizens, and in the latter President Kruger described the attempted exercise of the judicial testing power in regard to legislation as the instrument of the devil.[10] Natal had an effectively white-male franchise, while Rhodes and his followers in the Cape Colony made extensive use of 'hut' and 'poll' taxes and land dispossession through the law to force the 'Natives' into the market economy and create a surplus of unskilled labour for the mines.

The fate of the sections that entrenched 'Native' and 'coloured' voting rights is notorious,[11] and the National Party government cynically undermined the constitutional guarantees in the mid-1950s, doing incalculable damage to the idea of government limited by constitution and regulated by an independent and impartial court system. The terms of the first Republican constitution of 1961[12] did not change the formal adherence to Westminster, although the power of the executive soon grew rapidly, to the detriment of Parliament. This process was taken further and formalized in the tricameral constitution of 1983,[13] which marked the break from Westminster and the apex of constitutional apartheid. This instrument combined the offices of head of executive government and head of state, divided the legislative authority into separate and unequally empowered houses for coloured, Asian, and white South Africans, and banished Black citizens to the cruel delights of 'self-determination' in the bleakness of the Bantustans, breeding grounds for pomp, corruption, and poverty. The popular outrage that greeted this further entrenchment of apartheid caused the rapid erosion of any pretence at South Africa's adhering to the strictures of the rule of law, as the executive responded with terror tactics, described as 'state lawlessness.'[14] It was at this low-point in the formal development of South Africa's constitution that the negotiations about transformation through the law were initiated.

What of the substantive level, the law in the relationship between the state and its subjects in the courts? There had been some notable examples of the pre-Union Cape Supreme Court upholding the rights of the subject, regardless of race or class, in the face of unlawful state action,[15] and the High Court of the Zuid-Afrikaansche Republiek (Transvaal) had done the same in its celebrated clash with the Volksraad.[16] The postUnion Supreme Court continued to insist on the observance of the basic principles of the rule of law and justice from time to time,[17] especially in its Appellate Division and Cape Division. These decisions became more exceptional by the 1930s, however, as strongly individualistic judges, with backgrounds in party politics, gave way to a judiciary drawn from the ranks of 'professional' legal practitioners and as the 'race question' (relations between English and Afrikaans-speaking white South Africans) gave way to a broad (white) South Africanism.[18] Apart from a brief flare-up of civil libertarian resistance to early social-apartheid measures in the early 1950s, the courts, led once more by the Appellate Division, retreated from any real questioning of executive action in apartheid and security and took safe refuge in the calmer waters of private and criminal law.[19] (These areas thus witnessed an intriguing battle for supremacy between the civil-law and common-law traditions, the so-called purist–pragmatist debate, redolent with nationalist and 'scientific' overtones.)[20]

One of the most graphic ways of demonstrating judicial politics is through an examination of the application of the maxim *audi alteram partem* by the courts in the face of the exercise of administrative discretion. Until the mid-1950s, the South African courts had insisted on the observance of audi as an inherent element of procedural lawfulness whenever an individual's 'liberty, property or existing rights' were negatively affected by such action.[21] Towards the end of that decade, however, the judicial approach began to show more tolerance towards the needs of the state administration for the 'unfettered' exercise of discretion, and consequently courts began only to require the application of the right to a hearing, when it could be implied positively from the legislative language that granted that discretion. In other words, the maxim was not 'there until excluded expressly or by necessary implication,' but rather 'not there unless its presence could be implied from the circumstances.'[22] This shift, while subtle, had devastating results, which once more demonstrates the enormous power in the hands of the interpreter of the written law.

There are signs of a judicial rethinking of this executive-sensitive approach and a return to the individual-first policy of former decades from the mid-1970s, accelerating in the early 1980s, but significantly only in 'non-security' administrative action.[23] Faced with extraordinary levels of discretionary power granted to officialdom in the successive states of emergency under which most of the population was ruled from mid-1985, the Appellate Division held a line consistently denying the need for procedural justice,[24] until the landmark decision of *Attorney General, Eastern Cape v. Blom* in 1988.[25] Here the court, in a judgment written by its leading liberal judge, emphatically rejected the 'implied incorporation' test for audi and returned to the 'inherent' approach of the pre-1950s. The following year witnessed a substantial extension of the availability of the right to a hearing when the courts included the doctrine of 'legitimate expectation' in the list of interests that, if affected negatively, trigger its application.[26]

Thus, by the time of State President F.W. de Klerk's remarkable address to Parliament on 2 February 1990,[27] there were clear signs that judicial policy was reverting at least to its former stance of greater concern for the individual and less for the practical difficulties faced by the state. Had this judicial meander down the road of executive-mindedness irreparably damaged public trust in the courts and the law as mechanisms for limiting the exercise of government power in the cause of justice and democracy? There were certainly signs during the 1980s, even before the first state of emergency was declared, that the legal system was under severe strain, particularly as a result of the criminal justice system in the magistrate's courts and the cynical abuse of judicial process in the enforcement of the pass laws, which sought to prevent the influx of Africans to urban areas.[28] Surprisingly, there had been only isolated objections to the jurisdiction of the courts by those on trial for political offences committed in opposition to apartheid, the most celebrated of which was uttered by Nelson Mandela in 1962.[29] It was only in the later 1980s that such accused refused to participate in court proceedings with greater frequency at the level of the trial court.

Perceptions of a 'crisis of legitimacy' in the law became widely accepted, even though the basis of such attitudes has been questioned subsequently.[30] However, for the overwhelming majority of those South Africans not classified 'white,' the law and the courts as experienced in reality were the blunt instruments of apartheid, doing injustice to their liberty, property, and dignity on an enormous scale. Only a small section of the entire population had access to legal assistance, primarily because of its great cost and the pathetic level of funding for state legal aid. It was only from 1979, with the foundation of the public-interest law movement through the universities' legal aid offices and of a handful of charitably funded firms of attorneys, that relief from state lawlessness could be pursued by those individuals and civic organizations that could typically not afford it.[31]

This last development was significant, as were the establishment of lawyers' groups pressing for human rights and for the abolition of the death penalty and the continued outspokenness of a number of academic lawyers and sections of the press.[32] Such efforts, however, could not sustain general belief in the capacity of the law to achieve justice.

Law on the Rise

Law's revival at the level of discourse about negotiating a transfer of power can be traced to at least two developments – one of long standing in the African National Congress (ANC) and one more recent, within the Afrikaner nationalist legal community – but both of which achieved particular prominence from about 1985. In stating this, I do not intend to minimize the role of the courageous proponents of limited government and basic rights-protection through the law who had consistently, but increasingly forlornly and then desperately, spoken out over the decades. Their efforts, perhaps, created and maintained sufficient public pressure to ease the passage into popular consciousness of the rule of law and judicial review after 1990.

The first and longer-running strand of support is to be found in the programs and politics of the African National Congress from its foundation in 1912. Early notice of its adherence to the importance of law and the courts came with promulgation of the African Bill of Rights in 1923. This document called on the South African and British governments to accord full recognition to the rights of Black South Africans, emphasizing land ownership. Some years later, in response to the Atlantic Charter of the Allied leaders in 1941, the ANC adopted the African Claims of 1943, which repeated the essence of the 1923 Bill of Rights but added strong demands for rights in industry and labour, commerce, education, and public health. The ANC and the Congress Alliance promulgated the Freedom Charter at the Congress of the People in Kliptown near Johannesburg in 1955. This document contains the seeds of much of what appears in the bills of rights included in the transitional and final constitutions. Though ultimately drafted by a small committee of activists, the Freedom Charter's content was shaped by a relatively widespread gathering of demands from ordinary people in towns and in the countryside, and it was endorsed by probably the largest representative political gathering in South Africa until this decade.

With the prohibition of the ANC and other resistance movements in 1960, and with the move to armed struggle as the chief means of dislodging white hegemony, the 'rights-protection' aspect of ANC policy tended to be submerged in the struggle to survive in exile and to prosecute the guerrilla war. By the 1980s, however, the regime was almost completely isolated, though relatively easily able to ward off armed attacks, and the ANC, increasingly accepted by many liberal democracies, turned again to constitutional plans. A process set in motion by the Kabwe Consultative Conference in 1985 culminated in the official adoption of its Constitutional Guidelines published by the

ANC in August 1988.[33] Earlier that year, a group of ANC leaders and legal experts had produced 'Towards a Bill of Rights in a Democratic South Africa.'

While purporting to be little more than a modern restatement of the Freedom Charter, the Constitutional Guidelines contained vital commitments to limits on official power, a multi-sector economy, and the protection of many basic rights, including that to property. They also envisaged a strongly centralized, unitary, and non-racial state. The document had been widely canvassed in the ranks of the ANC in exile, and they were much discussed inside South Africa, especially as the inevitability of a negotiated settlement began to take root. The effective endorsement of the document by the Organization of African Unity in the Harare Declaration of 1989 as the basis for talks about constitutional change in South Africa, and the support for this declaration at the massive Convention for a Democratic Future held near Johannesburg in December 1989, further entrenched the idea of written constitutional guarantees. It was essentially this vision that the ANC and its allies tabled as its bargaining position once serious negotiations began in December 1991 (at the Convention for a Democratic South Africa – CODESA).[34]

What of the other side? As was mentioned above, Afrikaner Nationalist history bore witness to a keen desire for freedom and a recognition of the part that a bill of rights could play in achieving this happy state, albeit within a strictly limited and homogeneous community.[35] A strong adherence to the idea of legalism, at least in the formal sense, helps explain the official outrage (and the response of the Department of Foreign Affairs) when an internationally respected observer of the first major trial under the Terrorism Act of 1967 wrote of the demise of the rule of law in South Africa.[36] Many Afrikaner leaders had been lawyers, although when the end – removal of coloured voters from the common roll in 1955 – justified it, the Nationalist government did not hesitate cynically to manipulate basic constitutional guarantees.

From this stage to 1985, however, the government relied increasingly on administrative discretion, with minimal opportunity to regulate it through law.[37] This began to change after the massive internal and external rejection of the 1983 bicameral constitution – it was as though the government was anxious nevertheless to display its good faith and adherence to the rule of law. Thus State President P.W. Botha pledged the government to the observance of the rule of law when he opened Parliament in 1985, and the minister of justice instructed the South African Law Commission in April 1986 to investigate the protection through the law of 'group and human rights.'[38] It has become clear that this stance formed part of a new strategy to preserve the status quo by invoking rights talk in the guise of 'group' rights, as defined essentially by race classification, after the tricameral initiative failed. To that point, the government had adamantly rejected repeated pleas for the entrenchment of basic rights.[39]

This rapid about-face caused many progressive lawyers to campaign against this initiative, but they reckoned without the political sensitivity of the Law Commission. After extensive research and consultation, the Law Commission surprised most by recommending a full list of protected rights to be granted to the individual, and effectively rejected group rights, in its Working Paper of March 1989. Of course, this took place against the background of the terror of the states of emergency, but it is clear now that constitutional guarantees of limited government and minimum rights were already central in such secret talks as were occurring between ANC and government leaders.

It became certain therefore, once serious negotiations were in prospect in 1990, that the law would be an essential part of any settlement and transfer of power.

Law as Process, 1990–93

The first two formal meetings between the ANC and the National Party (NP) government in 1990 were billed as 'talks about talks' and were in effect negotiations about how to cope with the legal difficulties created by the 'criminal' acts of the returning exiles and those recently released from prison. There were, of course, additional discussions about the logistics of ensuring the safe reintegration into South African society of thousands of such persons, but much of the work was done between meetings by 'technical' teams of lawyers.

The first public and inclusive negotiating session, CODESA, took place a few days before Christmas 1991 and allowed each grouping and party to describe its constitutional vision. The entrenchment of basic rights, judicial review of legislative action, and the separation of powers, both vertically and horizontally, figured large for many of the parties, and the prominence of the two judges who chaired the proceedings gave added emphasis to the law as the common discourse.[40]

The Declaration of Intent subscribed to by the vast majority of participants at the close of the first session of CODESA featured supremacy of the constitution; an independent, impartial, and non-racial judiciary; regular elections and universal adult suffrage; separation of powers; an entrenched and justiciable Bill of Rights; and a legal system guaranteeing equality before the law.[41] Unfortunately, these high-sounding statements could not be translated into agreements by the working groups set up to negotiate subsequently, so that the plenary gathering in May 1992 reached deadlock.

The eventual success of the enterprise, however, allows us to state with reasonable certainty that the main negotiating elements had not yet recognized that the process was unlikely to produce any real 'winners,' that compromise on closely drafted terms was to be the name of the game. The resistance movements once more pursued popular struggle in the streets, while the moribund forces of apartheid and their collaborators resorted to strong-arm tactics in response. The futility of both such movements became clear within a few months, when the ANC and NP once again acknowledged the need to return to bargaining. Perhaps it is one of the more significant qualities of law that it provides last-resort or lowest-common-denominator potential, which means that all sorts of other temptations (such as violence) have to be eliminated as options before it can act as a catalyst.

Whatever the situation, by the time that the Multi-Party Negotiating Process (MPNP) convened in early April 1993, it was widely accepted that the way forward would be through the medium of the law and the entrenchment of constitutionalism. So the delegates to the MPNP, representing a wider cross-section of political views than had participated in CODESA,[42] resolved to proceed on the basis of the Declaration of Intent. A second formality, expedient yet effective, was to refer potentially divisive issues to 'technical' committees (TCs), whose advice was mostly accepted after debate, in order to sustain the momentum of the talks. While these seven TCs[43] brought much technical know-how and some independent thought to bear on intractable political questions, their membership reflected the various political approaches present at the MPNP.

The TCs were composed overwhelmingly of lawyers, most of whom were known for their support for the basic premises of the rule of law. A further reason for their considerable influence was the manner in which the MPNP worked: areas or points of contention were referred to the TCs in a relatively open-ended fashion, allowing them a fair degree of room to determine the agenda for subsequent report to and debate in the Negotiating Council (the 'parliament' of the process). Also emphasizing the role of the TCs was their 'closed' deliberations and the fact that they had been instructed[44] neither to seek submissions and advice from outside the process nor to speak to the media. The notion of 'popular sovereignty' was somewhat obscured, probably to good effect at the time, as the absence of such public consultations facilitated compromise, but this led to a muted backlash against the role of the TCs (and lawyers) in the next constitutional round.

At a political level, the key concession by the opponents of apartheid in the MPNP proved to be their acknowledgment of a phased transfer of power, with a 'transitional period' – a 'Transitional Government of National Unity'; certain aspects of government (such as the public service) effectively continuing as before, subject to 'sunset clauses'; and a 'final' constitution drafted by a popularly elected Constitutional Assembly, subject to certain pre-conditions agreed to at the MPNP. This approach to the intractability of change had been one of the products of the stand-off after the breakdown of CODESA, and it proved to be critical. The most difficult issue was the length of the transitional period – should it be as short as six months (as the ANC suggested) or as long as ten years? Those at one end of the spectrum wanted an immediate handover of power or no transitional period at all – the MPNP should draft the full and final constitution. By early July 1993, this question was resolved in favour of a five-year term for the transitional government.

This approach relied on the law as a written instrument, in the shape of the transitional constitution[45] and subject to all the ambiguities of the written word, to express this contract of compromise. This realization in turn concentrated the negotiators' attention on identification of a mechanism for interpreting and reviewing it and on that body's composition. There was never really any doubt that the mechanism would be a court of some kind (the name 'tribunal' was proposed at one stage to emphasize the temporary nature of the transitional arrangements), so the debate centred on whether a new body should be created or the task entrusted to a part or all divisions of the old Supreme Court.[46] Because of the courts' record in human rights, and to create the opportunity to appoint a judicial bench largely representative of the population, it was agreed that a Constitutional Court should be established. This body would be the final arbiter in all constitutional matters,[47] including 'certification'[48] that the final constitution complied with the guarantees (in the form of the Constitutional Principles) agreed to by the MPNP and recorded in the transitional constitution.[49] The extent to which the existing courts were distrusted is to be seen in the very limited constitutional jurisdiction given to the provincial divisions[50] and the absolute exclusion of the Appellate Division from this sphere.[51]

Balancing political accountability with the independence of this powerful institution was the next challenge. The negotiators chose two means: a limited term of office[52] (seven years, which significantly exceeds the life of the transitional government) and a selection process that departed completely from the traditional Westminster approach.[53] A Judicial Service Commission (JSC) was proposed, which would oversee all facets of the working lives of all judges (not only the constitutional judges) and would determine (in the case of non-constitutional judges and the recommendation for dismissal of all judges) or recommend (in regard to constitutional judges and the chief justice) who should be appointed judges.[54] Arrangements made for similar judicial-appointment bodies in the Commonwealth (not least, the study by the Canadian Bar Association in the mid-1980s[55] and Peter Russell's pioneering work on this theme in Ontario)[56] clearly influenced the composition of the transitional JSC: a seventeen-person body, with non-lawyers as well as lawyers drawn from all sections of the legal profession. (The clear majority's being made up of lawyers would not have accorded with Russell's views, however!)

Further establishing constitutionalism, the MPNP entrenched a large number of rights, including certain socioeconomic rights, as 'fundamental,' subject only to limitation according to a general formula that stresses reasonableness, justifiability, openness, democracy, freedom, and equality.[57] As well, it compiled an unamendable list of thirty-four constitutional principles – a guaranteed agenda for drafting the 'final constitutional text.'[58]

What prospect is there that these radical changes in the structure and process of the constitutional body politic will find support and so endure? The fate of these provisions over the last few years provides hints about the answer to this question, which is so vital to the establishment and flourishing of democracy, as well as the future legitimacy of the legal process as a whole. The final section of this paper explores these issues.

Law in Ascendancy: For How Long?

'The great conceit of constitution-makers is to believe that the words they put in the constitution can with certainty and precision control a country's future. The great conceit of those who apply a written constitution is to believe that their interpretation captures perfectly the founders' intentions. Those who write constitutions are rarely singleminded in their long-term aspirations. They harbour conflicting hopes and fears about the constitution's evolution. The language of the constitution is inescapably general and latent with ambiguous possibilities. Written constitutions can establish the broad grooves in which a nation-state develops. But what happens within those grooves – the constitutional tilt favoured by history – is determined not by the constitutional text but by the political forces and events that shape the country's subsequent history.'[59]

The question at the head of this section is asked not with a sense of alarm or impending doom, but rather because of the harsh denial of the benefits of the rule of law for most South Africans until so recently and because of the very ambition that the new constitutional structure represents. In other words, how secure are the foundations and girders of the constitutional mansion that stands so proudly in South Africa today? I suggest that two lines of inquiry will assist us in reaching a solid prognosis. Both are issues of process, one relating to constitution-making mainly in the past, the second more narrowly to the law, now and in the future.

First, then, the making of the constitution. There was considerable disquiet about the MPNP's lack of openness. Coverage of the considerable portion of the proceedings held in open session was inadequate in quantity and quality. Some of the delegations failed to inform and consult with their constituencies. Most notably, COSATU, the largest trade-union federation, proposed a national strike over inclusion of a provision relating to the lockout as a fundamental right. This clause had been agreed to in June 1993, without objection from the federation's general secretary, who was a delegate of the South African Communist Party at that session, yet the constituent elements of COSATU raised their voices against this clause only in October.[60] Other examples turned on the dissatisfaction of the land-redistribution lobby in regard to the formulation of property rights[61] and the mutual disenchantment of both women's groups and traditional leaders with the various attempts at compromising the demands of customary law with those of gender equality.[62]

But much of the concern was well-founded, and some crucial activity occurred far from the glare of public accountability. While it could be argued that this degree of secrecy was not only justified by the successful outcome but also necessary to facilitate the compromises essential for the transitional pact, there was sufficient uneasiness to convince the Constitutional Assembly (CA) to do it otherwise. Other than some picket demonstrations at the entrance to the negotiating centre, and a dramatic forced invasion of the premises by several hundred mostly armed far-right-wingers, there was no direct popular involvement in the MPNP, no widespread consultation, no plebiscite.

As a result, the 'elitist accommodation' approach gave way, at least initially, to a drive for 'popular constitutionalism' by the CA when it formulated plans in the second half of 1994. For a start, six all-party Theme Committees were established, as well as a Constitutional Committee and a Management Committee, thus involving about half of the members of the CA directly in constitution-making. The Theme Committees were to solicit and assemble representations from the public on a wide range of constitutional questions, to identify points of agreement and points of contention, but not to negotiate. This function was to be entrusted to the forty-six-member Constitutional Committee.[63]

In order to publicize the CA's task and to gather the views of all sectors of society, a massive Public Participation Programme was launched in early 1995. Extensive media advertising, a series of 'town-hall'–type meetings attended by members of the CA throughout the nine new provinces, and public hearings conducted by the Theme Committees at Parliament in Cape Town encouraged South Africans to express their opinions on what should be included in 'their' constitution.

They responded with enthusiasm, millions of individual and collective submissions being forwarded to the CA from people in all walks of life and parts of the country. Certain issues predominated: language – particularly the future of Afrikaans; religion – a strong, though misconceived reaction to the notion of a 'secular state' and controversy over omission of a reference to 'Almighty God' in the preamble to the constitution; life – inevitably, constitutionality of the death penalty and abortion, as well as a further attempt to have the ownership of guns elevated to the status of constitutional right; and the 'capital city' – bids for the home of Parliament, were it to be decided to move it from Cape Town.

But perhaps the most constant refrain was heard at the socioeconomic level, there being many calls for bread, water, work, houses, and health services. These demands echoed those that preceded the drafting of the Freedom Charter forty years earlier, and their urgency was heard by the constitution-writers. With no resistance to the principle, and very little to the details of formulation, the final Bill of Rights grants such second-generation rights with greater generosity than had been the case in the transitional constitution.[64] They are cast in a slightly different way from the rest of the rights, as rights 'to have access to' adequate housing, health care services, sufficient food and water, and social services. In this respect, at least, the politicians gave expression to the voice of the masses.

This 'open' phase of the writing of the final constitution lasted until the hard negotiating in September 1995. At this point, a subcommittee of the Constitutional Committee was established to expedite the process (the two-year deadline for the writing of the final constitution looming ever closer), and this body, assisted by endless bilateral and multilateral meetings behind closed doors, became the engine-room that drove the CA ship. A month before the adoption date, all pretence at transparency disappeared as the negotiators and advisers spent a few days cloistered in meetings held in complete security on a missile-testing base controlled by the military. In the last few days of negotiations, crucial use was again made of bilateral talks behind closed doors, often through the night.

Outside, nevertheless, the media hype continued (under the slogan 'one law for one nation'), and several hundred representatives of civil society were invited to a sumptuous banquet in May 1996 to celebrate the 'birthday' of the nation on the evening after the formal vote in the CA confirming adoption of the final text. That the certification of that text by the Constitutional Court still had to be obtained (which, in the event, was not forthcoming, so that the CA had to reconvene in September) was of little consequence. It was important to mark the achievement of further levels of compromise and to impress on ordinary people their stake in that achievement.

The extent to which this publicity and participation campaign have persuaded the public of the legitimacy of the product is uncertain, although there is evidence that it has educated people widely. On the one hand, few would seriously argue that the popular voice as expressed in submissions was eternalized in the constitutional text, otherwise Afrikaans would have retained greater privileges as an official language, capital punishment and the carrying of guns would have been specifically sanctioned, South Africa would have become an official 'Christian' state, and Cape Town would have been named as the legislative capital in the constitution. On the other hand, many would say that South Africa has done well to be spared most of the above and that it was unrealistic to anticipate such a direct form of popular involvement.

The program was intended not as an opinion poll, but rather as a mechanism for raising awareness and encouraging involvement in the process. In this sense, it succeeded to an extent. Certainly, as opposed to the situation with the MPNP, no South African could claim ignorance about the process, the product, and the opportunity to 'have a say' on the matter. Whether this amounts to the level of credibility needed for the survival and flourishing of the constitutional regime is doubtful, although it probably assisted in this regard. What was clearly of greater significance was the popular mandate possessed by the members of the CA as the result of their election to office in the first free poll based on universal suffrage in April 1994. For this reason, the relative speed with which the CA acted to complete its task within the time allocated to it by the transitional constitution ensured that its product would be able to rely on a considerable degree of public goodwill towards the new Parliament.

Against this background generally sympathetic to, though not constitutive of, the rule of law in government practice, we need to look at the legal system and how it has adapted to the transition. Here, it is significant that the continuity of the law's *Grundnorm* was preserved in a formal sense, through the insistence of the apartheid regime that the transitional constitution be enacted by the tricameral Parliament in its dying days. Although it exercised no independent discretion in this matter, merely reacting to instruction from the MPNP through the National Party's majority in Parliament, its endorsement ensured that there was no procedural revolution in constitutional government – a step that many opponents of apartheid had wanted in order to emphasize the clear break from the tainted past.

Of greater significance, however, has been the new government's respect for the judgments of the Constitutional Court. This has been especially marked on three occasions: when the court decided that the death penalty was unconstitutional;[65] when the central government was found wanting, in its adherence to constitutional practice, by the (National Party–led) Western Cape provincial government, leading to the postponement of local government elections there;[66] and in the CA's acceptance of the court's decision on certification and its speedy remedying of the shortcomings identified.[67] In each case (and many others emanating from the divisions of the Supreme Court, in both constitutional and other disputes), the government, and particularly the ANC component led by President Nelson Mandela, has reacted swiftly and positively to shore up the authority of the law, the constitution, and the courts. This has been a vital and welcome policy, especially when the experience in neighbouring Zimbabwe is contrasted.[68]

In some other respects, however, the picture from government is less promising. The executive seems unable to stem the rapidly rising tide of crime and corruption evident in South Africa. Early in the life of the transitional constitution, the 'due process' aspects of fundamental rights in the criminal justice system were extensively used – for example, to gain limited access by an accused to the police investigative docket and to be released on bail.[69] This placed severe stress on the criminal investigative mechanisms of the police, unused to having to observe such legal safeguards, and the presiding officers in the lower courts had not been sufficiently well trained to handle these new responsibilities. Some spectacular examples of prisoners being released early on parole, through the fault of the correctional-service authorities, combined with the problems outlined above to produce in a frightened and vulnerable public the view that the government was 'soft on crime.' The outlawing of the death penalty by the Constitutional Court in May 1995 (there had been an effective moratorium on executions since November 1989) further stoked the fires of public opinion and focused it very firmly on the impact of the transitional Bill of Rights.

There has thus been a strong tendency to blame the constitution for aiding and abetting South Africa's major public evil, the escalation in crime. No matter how often it is pointed out that the chief causes lie in shocking socioeconomic conditions, disparities in wealth, and antiquated systems of policing and criminal justice, this perception seems widely held by the public. It has unfortunately been fuelled by the utterances of some politicians and senior public servants who, faced with their own inability to turn the ship around quickly enough and the resultant public wrath, have sought scapegoats in the constitution as interpreted by the courts.[70]

At the level of public opinion this situation clearly damages the constitutional enterprise, but it has also given rise to a potentially more destructive impetus. This has been seen in two forms: the passage of legislation by Parliament that limits the scope of the rights protected in the constitution[71] and the temptation to attenuate severely or even eliminate the 'troublesome' rights in the final constitution.[72] Although neither initiative has assumed great proportions, it has been a worrisome (though perhaps understandable) political reaction, potentially very damaging to the rule of law, and something to be monitored closely.

Invaluable in gauging the law's reaction in transition must be the approach of the judiciary, particularly in the Constitutional and Supreme courts, and the workings of the Judicial Service Commission (JSC). In the latter, the judicial appointment process has been remarkably open and accountable, even though the JSC had to be cajoled into such a stance. The public hearings that preceded appointment of the six remaining members of the Constitutional Court were marked by robust though responsible questioning of the candidates. The choice of nominees reflected a predictable and broad mix of political and personal characteristics, with preference for a liberal/social democratic mainstream. What is of great concern, however, was the minimal participation in the questioning by most of the members of the JSC and the clearly partisan approach of some.[73] Even more worrisome was the JSC's decision thereafter to hold subsequent interview sessions behind closed doors. This was indeed implemented for one round of appointments to the Supreme Court, but fortunately this experience caused wiser counsel to prevail, and the principle of openness has been observed in all cases since then. This transparency does not extend to the JSC's deliberations as to its choice of nominees, which approach some commentators find problematic.

How has the JSC changed the face of the judiciary since its word in the appointment process has effectively been final? Whereas the judiciary was almost entirely white and male in September 1994 (there being two Black and two female judges), the picture since then is as follows: forty-one judges appointed, of whom sixteen are Black and seven female (there is one Black woman judge). At the magistrates' court level, where departmental policy directly affects appointments, the number of Black magistrates has increased ten-fold (mainly because of 'reincorporation' of the homelands' Departments of Justice), while the prosecutorial staff has declined from being two-thirds to about 55 per cent white. The South African Department of Justice has a special team that works entirely on 'transformation' and has embarked on a pilot project for the extensive use of lay assessors (almost exclusively Black) to assist magistrates in their criminal trials.[74]

These practical steps will no doubt gradually begin to affect public perceptions of the legitimacy of the justice system and, it is hoped, inspire confidence in the constitutional system that underwrites it. The judgments of the Constitutional Court and the Supreme Court thus far show a commendable ability to engage with the new discourse and its basic premises, though there is perhaps undue caution and there have naturally been some aberrations.[75] Overall, however, while much remains to be done in this field, there is cause not to despair, indeed to be slightly optimistic.

Conclusion

This paper has attempted to depict the fluctuating fortunes of the law as an integral part of constitutional government in South Africa over the past hundred years. In particular, we have looked at the establishment and strengthening of the ideas of limited government/constitutionalism/the rule of law. In the process, I have emphasized certain aspects of the interaction of the law and political transition, which I hope will provide the basis for comparison and discussion. The future of the law in government in South Africa and those inherent qualities that make it a useful if not indispensable ally in the process of social change are matters that deserve particular attention.

NOTES

I gratefully acknowledge the constructive criticism of Dennis Davis and Christina Murray, who read an early draft of this paper, and the financial support of the Centre for Scientific Development (Pretoria) and the University of Cape Town, without which I would have been unable to attend the conference. None of what follows necessarily reflects the views of any of those just mentioned.

1 Peter H. Russell, *Constitutional Odyssey*, 2nd ed. (Toronto: University of Toronto Press 1993), 6.

2 See Hugh Corder, 'Judicial Service and Accountability: Some Questions and Suggestions,' *South African Public Law* 7 (1992),181, and 'The Appointment of Judges: Some Comparative Ideas,' *Stellenbosch Law Review* 3 (1992), 207, both of which were written soon after my first meeting with Russell.

3 During 1993, I was privileged to serve as a 'technical adviser' to the negotiating process that produced South Africa's transitional constitution, working particularly on the protection of fundamental rights and the administration of justice.

4 Which read 'Can Canadians become a sovereign people?'

5 This well-documented process gave rise to perceptions, by the 1980s at the latest, that the administration of justice was illegitimate in the eyes of most South Africans. See, for example, John Dugard, *Human Rights and the South African Legal Order* (Princeton, NJ: Princeton University Press 1978), and Stephen Ellmann, *In a Time of Trouble* (Oxford: Clarendon Press 1992).

6 See 'Establishing Legitimacy for the Administration of Justice in South Africa,' *Stellenbosch Law Review* 6 (1995), 202.

7 Dugard, *Human Rights*, passim.

8 9 Edw, VII c. 9 (1909), ss. 35 and 152.

9 White women were enfranchised by the Women's Enfranchisement Act, (Act No.) 18 of 1930.

10 For a description of the history of government in these territories, see L.M. Thompson, 'Constitutionalism in the South African Republics,' *Butterworths South African Law Review* (1954), 49.

11 The cases of *Ndlwana v. Hofmeyr. NO* 1937 AD 229, *Harris v. Minister of the Interior* 1952 (2) SA 428 (A), and *Collins v. Minister of the Interior* 1957 (1) SA 552 (A) are well-known to constitutional lawyers in the Commonwealth and demonstrate the ineffectiveness of guarantees-in-law in the face of a determined and duplicitous legislature acting with electoral support.

12 Republic of South Africa Constitution Act, 32 of 1961.

13 Republic of South Africa Constitution Act, 110 of 1983.

14 Geoff Budlender, 'On Practising Law,' in Hugh Corder, ed., *Essays on Law and Social Practice in South Africa* (Cape Town: Juta 1988), 321.

15 For example, *In re Willem Kok and Nathaniel Balie* (1879) 9 *Buch* 45, and *Sigcau v. The Queen* (1895) 12 *SC* 256.

16 See *Hess v. The State* (1895) 2 *Off Rep* 112 and *Brown v. Leyds. NO* (1897) 3 *Off* Rep 17.

17 For example, *Shidiack v. Union Government* 1912 AD 642 and *R. v. Detody* 1926 AD 198.

18 See, generally, Hugh Corder, *Judges at Work* (Cape Town: Juta 1984), chap. 9.

19 See C.F. Forsyth, *In Danger for Their Talents* (Cape Town: Juta 1985), passim.

20 Ibid.

21 *R. v. Ngwevela* 1954 (1) SA 123 (A).

22 *South African Defence and Aid Fund v. Minister of Justice* 1967 (1) SA 263 (A).

23 For example, *Tshabalala v. Minister of Health* 1987 (1) SA 513 (W), in which the court insisted on a right to a hearing before dismissal of workers after an unlawful strike.

24 See *Omar v. Minister of Law and Order* 1987 (3) SA 859 (A) – one of South Africa's delightful paradoxes is that Omar is the incumbent minister of justice!

25 1988 (4) SA 645 (A).

26 In the case of *Administrator, Transvaal v. Traub* 1989 (4) SA 731 (A).

27 In which the various opposition movements were legalized and the release of political prisoners announced.

28 See Commission of Inquiry into the Structure and Functioning of the Courts, *Final Report* (Hoexter Report) (Pretoria: Government Printer 1984).

29 Set out in *The Struggle Is My Life* (London 1978),125–6.

30 See Stephen Ellmann, 'Law and Legitimacy in South Africa,' *Law and Social Inquiry* 20 (1995), 407.

31 As described by Richard L. Abel, *Politics by Other Means* (New York: Routledge 1995), 20–1.

32 Ibid.

33 See Hugh Corder and Dennis Davis, 'The Constitutional Guidelines of the African National Congress: A Preliminary Assessment,' *South African Law Journal*, 106 (1989), 633.

34 For a general description of the negotiations and their precursors, see Hugh Corder, 'Towards a South African Constitution,' *Modern Law Review* 57 (1994), 491.

35 Thompson, 'Constitutionalism,' passim.

36 *South Africa and the Rule of Law* (Pretoria: Department of Foreign Affairs, South Africa, 1968), reacting to Richard Falk, *Erosion of the Rule of Law in South Africa* (Geneva: ICJ 1968).

37 See Hugh Corder, 'Crowbars and Cobwebs: Executive Autocracy and the Law in South Africa,' *South African Journal on Human Rights* 6 (1989), 1.

38 Project 58.

39 See President's Council of South Africa, *Second Report ... on the Adaptation of Constitutional Structures in South Africa* (Cape Town: Government Printer 1982), 71–8, and (Minister of Justice) H.J. Coetsee, 'Hoekom nie 'n Verklaring van Menseregte nie?' (Why Is a Bill of Rights Not Needed?) *Journal for Juridical Science* 9 (1984), 5, for officials views opposed to basic rights-protection.

40 The best and most extensive treatment of the negotiation process leading to the transitional constitution is in Steven Friedman, ed., *The Long Journey* (Johannesburg: Ravan 1993). See also Lourens du Plessis and Hugh Corder, *Understanding South Africa's Transitional Bill of Rights* (Cape Town: Juta 1994), chap. 1. These sources provide further details of what is summarized in this and succeeding paragraphs.

41 Further details of the declaration appear in Du Plessis and Corder, *Understanding*, 5.

42 Estimated at about 95 per cent of the population: David Welsh, 'Holding the Centre,' *Towards Democracy* 2 (1993), 2.

43 The seven issues dealt with by the TCs were violence; repeal of discriminatory legislation; an Independent Media Commission and Independent Broadcasting Authority; the Transitional Executive Committee; an Independent Electoral Commission; the protection of fundamental rights during the transition; and constitutional issues.

44 At the initial briefing on 11 May 1993.

45 Constitution of the Republic of South Africa Act, 200 of 1993.

46 The South African Supreme Court consists of six provincial divisions with an Appellate Division at its apex, staffed by about 150 judges.

47 Constitution 1993, s. 98(2) and (3).

48 Ibid., s. 71 (2).

49 Ibid., Schedule 6.

50 Ibid., s. 98(3) read with s. 101 (3).

51 Ibid., s. 101(5).

52 Ibid., s. 99(1).

53 Ibid., ss. 99 and 104.

54 Ibid., s. 105.

55 Canadian Bar Association Committee, *Appointment of Judges in Canada* (1985).

56 Through his design of and service on the Judicial Appointments Advisory Committee.

57 Constitution 1993, chap. 3.

58 Ibid., Schedule 6.

59 Russell, *Odyssey,* 34.

60 For further details of this fiasco, see Du Plessis and Corder, *Understanding*, 181–2.

61 Ibid., 182–3.

62 Ibid., 56–8 and 114–5.

63 Details of the constitution-making process in 1995–6 were not legislated, but they appear in the *Annual Report* of the Constitutional Assembly for 1995 and are in the experience of the writer.

64 Constitution of the Republic of South Africa 1996, ss. 26 and 27.

65 *S. v. Makwanyane and Ano* 1995 (3) SA 391 (CC).

66 *Executive Council, Western Cape Legislature v. President of the Republic of S.A.* 1995 (4) SA 877 (CC).

67 *Ex parte Chairperson of the Constitutional Assembly: In re Certification of the Constitution of the Republic of South Africa. 1996* 1996 (4) SA 744 (CC).

68 The Zimbabwean Parliament has on several occasions amended the constitution to counter the effect of judgments of the Supreme Court. For example, the decision in *Catholic Commission for Justice and Peace in Zimbabwe v. Attorney General, Zimbabwe* 1993 (4) SA 239 (ZC) was reversed by the Constitution of Zimbabwe (Amendment) Act, 9 of 1993.

69 *Shabalala v. Attorney-General. Transvaal* 1996 (1) SA 725 (CC).

70 For example, the right of access to bail in section 25(2)(d) of the 1993 constitution, though limitable in the 'interests of justice,' was so liberally granted in the Magistrates courts that the problem was seen to be the right itself.

71 The right of access to bail was substantially limited by the Criminal Procedure Second Amendment Act, 1995.

72 There were strong moves to eliminate the rights of access to information and to administrative justice from the text of the final constitution.

73 For a good review of the JSC's hearings, see Richard Calland, 'A Step in the Right Direction: An Analysis of the Interviews of the Nominees for Membership of South

Africa's First Constitutional Court,' draft dissertation for the LLM degree, University of Cape Town, 1995.

74 This information is contained in Roger Friedman, 'D-Day for New Chief Justice,' *Cape Times*, 4 Oct. 1996, 1.

75 For reviews of the jurisprudence thus far, see Hugh Corder and Dennis Davis, 'A Ringing and Decisive Break with the Past?' *Review of Constitutional Studies* 3 (1996), 141, and the special issue of *South African Journal on Human Rights* 12 no. 1 (1996).

Summary of Discussion on Law and the Courts

Mr Justice Robert Walmsley of the Ontario Court began a discussion of gender equality by mentioning a recent book entitled *Brain Sex*, which concluded that physiological differences in brain structure should make women better judges then men. Ian Greene commented that he found, in interviewing Canadian appellate-court judges for a recent project with Carl Barr and Peter McCormick, that the responses of women judges were qualitatively different from those of the male judges, particularly in Alberta.

Jacob Zeigel observed, on the basis of his many years as law professor at the University of Toronto, that there were no major differences between men and women as law students, lawyers, or judges. In his view, the political battle over gender equity has been largely won, in Canada at least, with major breakthroughs in judicial appointments, entries into law firms, and enrolments in law schools.

Madame Justice Rosalie Abella thought, however, that there was something of a backlash under way resulting in part from intellectual elites' having prematurely decided that the equity issues were resolved. As for differences between men and women as judges, she concluded that one of the accomplishments of Ontario's Advisory Committee on Judicial Appointments was demonstrating that quality was not dependent on gender, race, or religion; being a good adjudicator requires openness to what one hears and not knee-jerk thinking about people's gender or race.

Noting the developing research on transnational policing, Jean-Paul Brodeur queried Kent Roach about cooperation between the police forces of the two Niagaras. Roach replied that he and Martin Freidland were struck by how little knowledge or cooperation there was between the two forces, noting that they probably found out more about each other through having researchers sitting in the back of their squad cars than anything else.

Replying to Jennifer Nedelsky, Hugh Corder emphasized that while there clearly had been suspicion of the law and the courts in South Africa under apartheid, the excluded majority nevertheless often resorted to the courts in an effort to claw back basic rights and privileges. As examples, he cited the Harris and Collins cases responding to the removal of the African vote in 1936 and of the coloured vote in the 1950s, respectively. Corder also cited studies by Richard Abel and Steven Ellman suggesting that the lack of legitimacy of the courts and the law occurred largely at the level of rhetoric among leaders attacking the legitimacy of the government generally. For the people on the ground, turning to the courts remained common, as for example with the Black independent trade-union movement and various community organizations. He did admit, however, that he was uncertain about the law's capacity to accommodate the demands being placed on it today. His paper's subtitle, 'Can the Law Be Trusted?,' therefore remains an open question.

Peter Russell recalled that under apartheid the Blacks in South Africa had developed their own system of underground courts. Their quality varied, of course, with the worst receiving publicity for 'necklacing' people with burning rubber tires. Less well-known, however, were the many underground courts that succeeded in solving people's problems and binding their communities together, particularly in some of the newer suburban shanty towns in which many Blacks were forced to live. Advising the minister of justice in 1996, Peter opposed both benign neglect and regulation of those bodies – the two options then under consideration. He counselled official recognition, making the courts' decisions subject to appeal to the Human Rights and Gender commissions. Peter spoke of how he admired people's capacity to develop such spontaneous institutions, commenting finally on the irony of this development coming out of the horror of apartheid.

Hugh Corder concurred but reflected on the complexity of accommodating some of these practices, rooted in African and Islamic customary law, with the equality provisions of the recent Bill of Rights.

PART V:
RIGHTS AND THE CHARTER

Peter Russell long ago earned a reputation as a charter sceptic with his 1969 article 'A Democratic Approach to Civil Liberties,' published in the *University of Toronto Law Journal*. In the intervening years his position has perhaps softened somewhat, for by 1994 he described himself as a Charter agnostic, toting up the gains and losses for liberty under the Charter of Rights and Freedoms in 'The Political Purposes of the Charter: Have They Been Fulfilled?' in Philip Bryden, Steven Davis, and John Russell, eds., *Protecting Rights and Freedoms* (Toronto: University of Toronto Press). Whichever label one uses, and neither seems quite adequate, to describe Peter's reaction to the Charter, it is abundantly clear that he has never fully embraced the Charter or the political agenda behind it. Long concerned over Pierre Trudeau's setting aside of civil liberties in handling the October crisis, Peter also detected a fundamental ignorance about judicial review in the prime minister's push for a constitutional charter of rights. Thus he has persistently challenged the view that judicial enforcement of a constitutional charter or bill of rights is the best way of making decisions about basic rights and freedoms.

The core of his reservations about the Charter spring from the value that he places on democratic government. He was among the very first to recognize that entrenchment of the Charter in the constitution would alter the Canadian system of government by significantly expanding the policy-making role of the courts. His clear concern was that this transfer of decision-making power entailed a decisive step away from the democratic ideal of representative government. Ultimate responsibility for decisions about rights increasingly would become the province of the judiciary rather than of elected representatives. Rather than putting limits on legislative action to guarantee rights, he has consistently urged revitalizing the deliberative potential of representative institutions.

Given his reservations regarding the Charter, Peter was invited to Ottawa by the federal Progressive Conservatives to give expression and perhaps academic legitimacy to a position that they were not themselves willing to espouse publicly. His critique of the Charter did little, of course, to deflect Trudeau's drive to enact the document, but, along with the criticism of like-minded scholars, it may have helped encourage a distinctively Canadian approach to permitting legislative review of judicial review. The 'notwithstanding' or 'override' clause in the Charter permits the legislature to set aside, for five years at a time, judicial enforcement of key sections of the Charter – an innovation that he vigorously defended in a memorable exchange published in the 1991 *Alberta Law Review*. In the wake of the Charter, he wrote influential pieces on 'The Effect of the Charter on the Policy Making Role of Courts' in *Canadian Public Administration* (1982) and 'The Political Purposes of the Charter' (1983), offering a refreshingly original and dispassionate view of the already very popular Charter of Rights. By 1986 he noted how candid and realistic Canadian judges had become about their power to shape or block public policies.

With Canada in a constitutional muddle following the patriation of its constitution without the endorsement of Quebec, Peter began looking at constitutional politics comparatively. Returning to Australia for a sabbatical in the mid-1980s, he became a visiting fellow at the Australian National University's Federalism Research Centre. He explored the rich grounds of Canadian-Australian constitutional comparison in his essay 'The Politics of Frustration.' Noting both the similarities and the differences between the two countries, he particularly found the Australian elites committed to macro-constitutional reform, despite the studied indifference of the citizenry. Coming home to Canada, he embarked on a large-scale survey of public and elite attitudes towards the Charter of Rights. In 1997, he co-wrote *The Clash of Rights* based on that project. A central theme of that work is the elite's destruction of the consensus in support of the Charter among ordinary Canadians throughout Quebec and the rest of Canada.

Summary of Papers

The papers here stake out three very different positions on rights and the Charter. The first, by Madame Justice Rosalie Silberman Abella, reflects on 'The Judicial Role in the Development of Law.' Situating her comments within the social upheaval begun in the 1960s, Abella describes herself as a 'Charter romantic,' cherishing the constitutional guarantee of rights and freedoms. She explains the role of the judiciary and defends it against the charge that it has been politicized by the Charter. Recognizing a certain 'political' dimension in judges' interpreting the law, Abella argues that the Charter makes public a centuries-old partnership between courts and legislatures. Thus it does not alter basic judicial and legislative roles; instead it adds certain entrenched human rights to an already existing understanding of constitutional supremacy. This represents a willing subjugation on the part of legislatures to the supremacy of human rights. In her view, there is no better guarantee that human rights will not be unduly compromised than an independent judiciary, insulated from the whims of public opinion. The duty of courts remains that of synchronizing the law and principles of justice.

Rainer Knopff and F.L. Morton take a very different perspective in their essay, 'Does the Charter Hinder Canadians from Becoming a Sovereign People?' They endorse the view common in both the early American and the Westminster traditions that a judicially enforceable bill of rights does not promote rights. The best way to protect rights, they insist, is through representative government. They see bills of rights and the 'judicialized politics' following in their wake as an unwelcome development in liberal constitutionalism. According to Knopff and Morton, they lead to a dangerous inflation of ordinary policy claims and replacement of parliamentary debate with coercion by the courts. The authors trace the outline of these trends in the relations between Quebec and the rest of Canada by detailing the dispute over the language of outdoor signs in Quebec. They contend that recourse to the courts in this case distorted and derailed a democratic debate among Quebecers. More generally, they argue that judicial decision-making pre-empts the representative procedures and democratic discussion at the heart of liberal society, ultimately undermining the possibility of Canadians becoming a sovereign people.

As if in response to the point and counterpoint of the preceding contributions, Janet Heibert offers her Russellesque 'Legislative Scrutiny: An Alternative Approach for Protecting Rights.' In it she questions whether rights receive adequate consideration in existing executive, judicial, and legislative arrangements. Sharing Russell's concerns about the Charter, she pursues his suggestion of protecting rights through standing legislative review committees. With the goal of fostering greater public debate and a political culture in which government is more sensitive to its own tendency to infringe on rights, Hiebert turns to the Australian experience with legislative rights scrutiny, recommending it as a model for Canada. She tempers her approach by addressing tough questions about balancing such scrutiny with party discipline, the role of these committees vis-à-vis the courts and the Charter, and the democratic adequacy of yet another elite body as a means of securing the rights of citizens. Several of her concerns parallel those discussed above by Atkey, Whitaker, and Brodeur regarding effective oversight of security-intelligence services.

15

The Judicial Role in the Development of Law: The Impact of the Charter

JUSTICE ROSALIE SILBERMAN ABELLA

I went to the University of Toronto from 1964, when I entered an arts program, to 1970 when I graduated from the law school. It was a fertile environment for anyone who was young, enthusiastic, and eager for relevance. Tutored by the creative courage of people such as Peter Russell, we took it all in and learned to see society as necessarily fluid, and the institutions in it as not necessarily necessary. In other words, we learned to take the status quo as a starting point, not a rebuttal.

The social changes in those years were nothing short of breath-taking. The election of John F. Kennedy at the beginning of the 1960s sent a message of change and youth and difference all around the Western world. Later the riots in the U.S. ghettos, the civil disobedience spawned by the Vietnam War, the flower children who resisted everything but non-conformity, and the general impatience with everything that had gone before were all translated by the late 1960s and early 1970s into a demand for a revolutionary revision of all aspects of the social contract.

Children demanded both more and less from their parents, women demanded more from everyone, persons with disabilities demanded access, minorities demanded an end to discrimination, Aboriginal people demanded self-government, and Quebec demanded independence. It was very clear by the end of the 1960s that no institution would be untouched by performance appraisals from this new generation, and it was also clear that every appraisal would find every institution wanting. It was impossible not to respond to the demands for change, and it was impossible to ignore the cry that what appeared to work for some was no longer working for many.

When society reflected on its post-1960s mandate, it concluded that the laws by which it was governed were no less in need of revolution and revision than the social expectations that had emerged from the turbulence of the

1960s. So we set in motion a whirlwind of law reform, which continues to this day.

Look, for example, at how we have transformed the law of the family, in a neck-and-neck race between the law and society for mature understanding. We started to understand how the old law of the family had created subordinate roles and perceptions for women, which travelled with depressing but unsurprising portability into the workplace, and we tried equality as the remedy for this social undervaluing. The 1970s demanded equality for women, the 1980s gave them some, and the 1990s started to blame social upheavals on the role that we gave women in the 1970s and 1980s. We acknowledged that raising children was important, being a mother was important, being a father was important, making a living was important, and that equality and the economy were beginning to demand that every adult in the family be responsible for every responsibility in the family.

We have seen women's shelters, increased violence, the debate about 'recovered memories' and 'mommy tracks,' the spread of AIDS, multiculturalism, political correctness, deficit preoccupations, the rise of religious fundamentalism, the Charter of Rights and Freedoms, Quebec and western nationalism, free-trade agreements, global pressures, Nintendo, and the cultural trinity of Madonna, Michael Jackson, and O.J. Simpson.

It is quite a picture. Any art gallery would be proud to hang it in its postmodern section. But just one glance at the cluttered canvas, at the different textures and colours and shades, at the sharpness of some of the images and the haziness of others, and we instantly understand why people today are so confused about how they and their law are supposed to respond to all these realities in the social environment after our society has spent a century ignoring them.

In the tidal wave of law reform, it was inevitable that people would start to pay attention to the junior partner in law reform – the courts. And they did not always feel comfortable with what they saw. This transition generation – the generation ready to respond after the recuperative 1950s to the postwar world – was understandably anxious about much of what it had wrought. A lot was happening very quickly in the race to the millennium, but as society was looking over its shoulder to see whether social justice was keeping up, it noticed increasingly that a new referee was insisting on an active role in defining the terms of the race: judges. And just as the questions were starting to form about the judiciary in the public's mind about 'who,' and 'how,' and 'why,' the Charter came along. It was too late for the questions.

And in the frustration that followed, so much was said about the relationship between courts and law and society that seemed so alarmingly unformed and, worse, uninformed that insults, diatribes, epithets, and facile labels started to replace analysis. And so, as a Charter romantic who cherishes the constitutional guarantees donated by the Charter, I want in this paper to try to explain my understanding of the judicial role in lawmaking, and particularly to defend the Charter from the charge that it represents an aberrational judicial function.

The question in almost all judicial decision-making comes down to how you frame the issue and how you decide which of the available choices should receive more or less weight. The classic story of Max Brod, Franz Kafka's closest friend and lawyer, is frequently used by professors of jurisprudence to show how the framing of the issue can affect the outcome. Kafka's last request was that his unpublished manuscripts all be burned unread. Brod not only read them, he published them. That is how we came to have available to us, among other works, Kaflka's novel *The Trial.* Brod wrestled with what he called his 'conflict of conscience' and decided that the works were literary treasures worthy of public access and therefore worthy of publication, in defiance of Kafka's last wishes.

Was Brod right? Whose perspective decides: Kakfa's as testator, or Brod's as literary executor? Did it matter that Brod was a lawyer? Was he entitled to decide the literary merit of the work? Does it matter whether he was right or wrong about its quality? Did Brod do the public a favour publishing the book? Is the public interest even relevant to this issue? In other words, in interpreting the relevant language, law, and human behaviour, can there be any doubt that there is often more than one valid, principled judgment available?

It is unrealistic to say that judges should not make law, that they should only interpret it. Almost every time judges interpret, they make law and implicitly weigh competing values. Long before we had a Charter, we had judges obviously taking existing values into account when they interpreted statutes or phrases or legal entitlements – the judge who in 1873 said 'the paramount destiny and mission of women are to fulfill the noble and benign office of wife and mother'; the judge who in 1915 thought that admitting women to the legal profession would be a 'manifest violation of the law of ... public decency'; the judge who said in 1905 that fault-based support laws were desirable because wives 'ought to be preserved from imminent temptation'; the House of Lords, which said in 1959 that privative clauses ousting the jurisdiction of the courts were to be disregarded; the courts that said in 1949 that sanctity of the contract and restrictive covenants took precedence over the rights of Jews to purchase property; and the court that said in 1939 that freedom of commerce took precedence over the rights of Blacks to be served beer. Not to mention the entire history of common law. That was all lawmaking, it was all weighing and applying values and policy, and it was all before the Charter.

Values and social realities change over time. Judges cannot be shy about acknowledging this. In 1776, when the U.S. Declaration of Independence pronounced that all men were created equal, many of the framers of the document had slaves, and women could not vote. In 1633, Galileo was forced to apologize publicly for spreading news of the evidence revealed by his telescope – that the earth revolved around the sun, not the other way around, as the church had taught for centuries. And, in 1938, the then editor of *Saturday Night* magazine said: 'The business of women is to keep house and keep quiet.' Truths change over time, and judges cannot be hesitant to acknowledge these changes.

The following two cases are illustrative of how values evolve and how courts evolve with them. In 1896, the U.S. Supreme Court in *Plessy v. Ferguson* enunciated 'separate but equal' as emanating from the Thirteenth and Fourteenth amendments, which abolished slavery and guaranteed equality respectively. The resulting judgment permitted separate railway cars for whites and non-whites.

Sixty years later, in 1954, Chief Justice Warren, in *Brown v. Board of Education,* struck down school segregation in a mere six pages, directly repudiating the policy in *Plessy v. Ferguson*: 'Separate [is] inherently unequal ... We must consider public education in the light of its full development and its present place in American life throughout the Nation.'

In revisiting the territory abandoned since *Plessy,* the court filled a vacuum created by decades of legislative rigor mortis, notwithstanding powerful indictments to the contrary, such as those found in Gunnar Myrdal's 1944 book, *An American Dilemma.* Earl Warren, newly appointed chief justice of the U.S. Supreme Court, was convinced that it was time to end legal segregation. The challenge, according to his colleague Justice Jackson, was 'how to make a judicial decision out of a political conclusion.' Another colleague, Justice Clarke, worried about the vulnerability of the court as an instrument of social policy: 'We don't have money at the court for an army and we can't take ads in the newspapers, and we don't want to go out on a picket line in our robes. We have to convince the nation by force of our opinion.' Values changed, and the courts changed with them.

Sometimes the change can be dramatic. In Canada, for example, the family property laws confirmed by the Supreme Court of Canada in 1973 in *Murdoch v. Murdoch* were completely revised in 1978 by the same court, without benefit of legislative reform – or of the Charter – in *Rathwell v. Rathwell.*

Nothing about the institutional role of the courts has changed with the introduction of the Charter of Rights except the extent to which people notice what it is that courts do. We now call them activist because they intervene on behalf of the expansion of rights in the political process. But to show the elasticity of the labels it is worth remembering that we used to call courts activist when they intervened on behalf of the prevention of the expansion of rights.

In the nineteenth century, for example, the British prime minister Lord Salisbury felt sufficiently moved to rebuke Lord Halsbury as follows for the House of Lords' routine declawing of social welfare and labour legislation: 'The Judicial Salad requires both legal oil and political vinegar, but disastrous effects will follow if due proportion is not observed.' And in the 1930s President Franklin Roosevelt was so incensed by the U.S. Supreme Court's striking down of his New Deal legislation that in 1937, just two weeks after his second inauguration, he introduced his court-packing Judicial Reform Bill, only to withdraw it six weeks later when Justice Owen Roberts switched sides to help form a pro–New Deal majority.

Though deemed activist, courts preventing rights were rarely dismissed as 'politicized,' even though they were no less active than later courts that expanded them. If expanding rights is political, so is restricting them. The selective, pejorative application of the term to courts only when they expand rights is both inaccurate and mischievous. 'Politicization' did not start with the judicial expansion of human rights, but the use of the word did. When people suggest that the courts are being political, what they are really suggesting is that courts are dealing with something they ought not to be dealing with. Yet if it is appropriate for courts to deal with the interpretation of rights, as it clearly is, it seems odd to call them 'politicized' only when they interpret them expansively.

Laws flow from the politics of the legislature; courts interpret those laws. This does not make courts 'political,' but it does mean that there is a 'political' aspect to judicial review of legislation. In addition, in so far as laws reflect values, and values can be said to have 'political' veins, a 'political' dimension flows through the interpretation of all law.

This is, however, very different from saying that the courts are becoming politicized. They are becoming nothing that they have not always been – namely, reviewers and interpreters of the rules to which society has proclaimed itself subject – through the legislature. The Charter is the flashlight that exposed this judicial reality; it is not the instrument of a new judicial norm. The relationship between courts and legislatures in the interpretation of public values has not changed; only the public's interest has.

What the Charter did was to allow public policy to come out of the judicial closet and participate more openly in the policy partnership to which courts and legislatures have in reality been parties for centuries. Since 1867, Canada has lived with the concept that the legislature, though supreme, is itself subject to the constitution. In Chief Justice Dickson's words, the 'judiciary is the guardian of the constitution.' The Charter does not therefore introduce the novel concept of constitutional supremacy. What it does is add the concept of constitutionally entrenched human rights to the content of that supremacy.

The Charter is about human rights, not about judicial versus legislative roles, or about judicial activism versus restraint, or about the politicization of the judiciary. The Charter, introduced after all by the accountable legislature, represents the willing subjugation by the legislature of its conduct to the scrutiny and supremacy of certain principles of human rights – as interpreted by the judiciary. The morality of any law is now subject to the supreme morality of civil and human rights. The debate as to whether this is an appropriate role for the judiciary was held and resolved in favour of the judiciary or, at the very least, in favour of declaring the reach of human rights and the values that they represent to be beyond simple legislative grasp.

Both legislatures and courts enunciate and apply values, law, and public policy, but they do so in very different ways and for very different constituencies. The legislature's basic function is to determine which values will be translated into statutory law, based on its perception of public opinion, the importuning of constituents, the prevailing partisan ideology, collegial input, and perceived electoral risk. In this legislative blender, the application of public policy is purely a political judgment. But this in no way detracts from its fundamental character as originating from values. It means rather that the values that inspired the statute are subject to political realities and may not emerge intact. The final legislative product is still called public policy, but it is public policy as political compromise. It is political in the purest sense of the word: an accountable institution – the legislature – assesses how best to balance societal values with the prospect of re-election. Essentially, the application of public policy is an exercise in the promulgation, as law, of selected perceived majority wishes.

The courts, vis-à-vis public policy, are also involved in an evaluative process. The process, however, is interpretive and not blatantly political. It is impervious to electoral judgment, unrestricted by the constraints of partisan ideologies, and relatively immune to compromise. The public policy values that the Supreme Court of Canada is therefore free to evaluate are related to, but independent from, the political values that motivated the existence or absence of a statute. Parliament passes laws, courts decide what the law means, and in so doing courts react, at least to some extent, either consciously or unconsciously, positively or negatively, to what they feel are the public policy values that underlie the statute.

If one feels that this interpretative role has the potential for interfering with the parliamentary supremacy that emerged triumphant from the Glorious Revolution of 1688–9, overthrowing the obstructive Stuart kings, it was ever thus. The interpretive judicial function, whether of statute or of common law, has always necessarily involved the sifting of normative considerations, not only because laws derive from and operate in a social system and culture of values, but because judges do too. In so far as the sifting of legal choices is the sifting of policy values, judges, in interpreting law, do consider and always have considered, in addition to logic and precedent, the values of the policy implications that their legal conclusions represent.

Antonin Scalia admits that it is 'foolish to deny the relevance of moral perceptions to law'; Lon Fuller talks about law's 'inner morality,' Oliver Wendell Holmes implicitly acknowledges that values are the inarticulate major premise of judicial reasoning; Emmett Hall explains every decision as a 'court's decision about how competing interests and values ought to be reconciled'; and Lord MacMillan once said that 'in almost every case it would be possible to decide the issue either way with reasonable legal justification.'

In response to the argument that it is anti-democratic for unaccountable persons to impose their will on the majority, there is the belief that there should be an institution in society that can independently and fairly and without fear of consequence a safeguard against what Lord Scarman called 'the modern menace of unbridled majority power.' Human rights essentially concern the protection of minority rights from arbitrary erosion or violation by the majority. The legislature that relies on majority support cannot be expected routinely to risk political self-destruction by promulgating minority causes; however, the courts, which do not rely on any constituency, risk nothing in protecting them. What body can better attenuate the impact of majoritarian expectations when they may unfairly circumscribe minority ones than one that does not depend for its survival on an appeal to popularity with the majority?

In a country as heterogeneous as Canada, it is in any event an illusory task to attempt to ascertain or define consensus, but to the extent that this task is necessary, it is one that the legislature must undertake in deciding whether to ignore, implement, or redirect consensus statutorily. In interpreting human rights, the consensus may not only be ineffable, in so far as it represents a majority view, it also may also be irrelevant, involving as it may the protection of rights from the majority's views.

As Lord Scarman observed, human rights may be so fundamental that civilized people cannot survive without them, but they are 'more conspicuous in the mouths of men than in their practice.' As concerned, therefore, as one might be about an individual judge's skill in interpreting and allocating human rights, institutionally there is no better guarantee that human rights will not be unduly compromised than entrusting their protection to the 'unaccountable' judiciary.

This task exposes the judiciary's role to controversy – inevitably and unavoidably. The judiciary, after all, is in the business either of taking stands that the legislature has refused to take, for fear of antagonizing a majority of the electorate, or of restricting stands that the legislature has decided to take to attract the same majority. Either way, the majority of the public will feel tampered with by the judiciary and may vociferously insist on explanations as to why its demands were not met. Judicial discretion may well be, according to the public's opinion, judicial *in*discretion.

And here we come to the role of public opinion. Society is horizontal and vertical, and it is practically impossible to know at which point a consensus emerges. Until we know who the public is and how it forms opinions, courts deciding cases are entitled scrupulously to regard public opinion as the responsibility of the legislature and generally as immaterial to judicial determination. In Edith Wharton's *The Age of Innocence,* the van der Luydens and Mrs Manson Mingott were the custodians and interpreters of social norms in old New York. They were the self-appointed and accepted arbiters of what passed for public opinion at the time. Judges have available no such omniscient oracles of prevailing social opinions. Nor should they.

Public opinion, in its splendid indeterminacy, is not evidence. It is a fluctuating, idiosyncratic behemoth, incapable of being cross-examined about the basis of its opinion, susceptible to wild mood swings, and reliably unreliable. Part of the judiciary's task, in fact, may be to reach a conclusion *despite* perceived, prevailing public opinions. When we speak of an independent judiciary, we are talking about one free from precisely this kind of influence. Whatever evidentiary tool the legislature uses to gauge public acceptance, judges use a totally different measurement of evidentiary relevance and reliability, because the object of *their* task is completely different. In framing its opinions, the public is not expected to weigh all relevant information, or to be impartial, or to be right. The same cannot be said of judges.

But although judges are not accountable to the public in the same way as are elected officials, this does not mean that they are not accountable. While they may not be accountable to public *opinion,* they are none the less accountable to the public *interest* for independent decision-making based on discernible principles rooted in integrity.

Courts, and the societies in which they function, will continue to evolve, as will the values that judges are called on to enunciate and apply. Despite the inevitability of that evolution, however, certain values can and should endure. The most defining of them is the pursuit of justice. It is a polycentric pursuit, and many are charged with its protection. But only the justice system exists exclusively on its behalf.

The interpretation of justice as the most enduring of values involves a complex balancing of legal principle and public interest. Law and justice are or should be related concepts, and courts have an ongoing duty to try to synchronize the two. Performing the task properly may invoke controversy and criticism. But better to court controversy than irrelevance, and better to seek criticism than injustice.

This is an ideologically polarized and cynical age, which treats the status quo as the least detrimental alternative; generosity as a barrier to gratification; tolerance as an expendable amenity; fairness as a figment of philosophy; civility as an expedient negotiating tactic; and empathy as a passing trend. All of this, it seems to me, argues for a system devoted exclusively and unreservedly to the passionate and impartial defence of justice. This is what the justice system tries to be. For what is justice if not the compendium of all of these values: the appropriate application of reform, generosity, tolerance, fairness, civility, and empathy – regardless of public opinion, but not of a duty to the public; regardless of accusations of politicization, but not of the values of the polity.

16

Does the Charter Hinder Canadians from Becoming a Sovereign People?

RAINER KNOPFF AND F.L. MORTON

This paper draws together and elaborates two of the central themes of Peter Russell's work – one from his analysis of Canada's mega-constitutional politics, the other from his reflections on judicial policy-making. First, in *Constitutional Odyssey*, Russell infers from our constitutional history, especially from the mega-constitutional politics of recent decades, that 'not all Canadians have consented to form a single people in which a majority or some special majority have, to use John Locke's phrase, "a right to set and conclude the rest."'[1] This willingness to be 'concluded' by the majority is what defines a 'sovereign people,' at least one that wishes to govern itself democratically. Although a sovereign democratic people will certainly exhibit partisan political division, such division remains subordinate to an overarching agreement to remain a 'single people.' As a member of a sovereign people, in other words, one must agree to treat one's partisan opponents as fellow citizens, whose rule, should they form the majority, one is willing to accept. Because 'not all Canadians' have agreed to treat each other in this way – because, in other words, what divides us often outweighs our common citizenship – we are not, in Russell's view, a sovereign people; the subtitle of his book asks whether we can become one.

Second, in an oft-quoted passage from an early article on the Charter of Rights and Freedoms, Russell worries about the 'negative side' of 'transferring the policy-making focus from the legislative to the judicial arena.' This transfer, he says, 'represents a further flight from politics, a deepening disillusionment with the procedures of representative government and government by discussion as means of resolving fundamental questions of political justice.'[2] This second concern is connected to the first inasmuch as it suggests that the Charter, which was intended to help Canadians become a sovereign people, may in fact hinder us from becoming one – indeed, it may make us even less of a sovereign people than we currently are. A people prepared to treat political opponents as legitimate surely needs to make 'government by discussion' a leading means of settling political differences. To the extent that the Charter represents a 'flight' from this kind of politics, it can be understood as threatening rather than promoting the unity necessary to a sovereign people. This paper argues that the Charter does indeed intensify our failure 'to form a single people.'

There is a sense, of course, in which this conclusion is already a truism. As many commentators have noted, the Charter has done little to remedy the division that most obviously reflects the failure of Canadians to become a sovereign people – namely, that between Quebec and the rest of Canada (ROC). As Russell was the first to point out, the Charter's main political purpose was to bridge territorially based divisions between Canadians, including that between Quebec and the ROC.[3] The 'father' of the Charter, Pierre Trudeau, saw it as a way to emphasize what Canadians had in common, what made them a single people despite their regional differences. However, this strategy obviously has not ameliorated the tensions between Quebec and the ROC – indeed, it appears to have intensified them.[4]

The exacerbation of Quebec–ROC tensions is far from the only way in which the Charter threatens the capacity of Canadians to act as a sovereign people. While the Charter has clearly taken deeper root in the ROC, it is questionable even in this context whether it fortifies or threatens the existence of a single people. Canadians in the ROC may indeed be more united by Charterphilia,[5] but the resulting flight from 'the procedures of representative government and government by discussion' does little to maintain or strengthen the inclination to allow the majority 'to set and conclude the rest.' The Quebec–ROC divide, in other words, is not the only deepening gulf between Canadians. Contemporary identity politics and inflated political rhetoric are making ordinary majoritarian politics more difficult in many other respects. Even in the ROC, Canadians are arguably becoming less of a single people – and the Charter-induced flight from representative government is at least partly to blame.[6]

Many of liberal democracy's early constitutionalists in Britain and the United States, as we see below, might have predicted the corrosive effects of the Charter. They understood what we appear to have forgotten: that even a regime dedicated to the protection of rights does not necessarily benefit from institutionalizing 'rights talk' too prominently in public life. These pioneers put little faith in judicially enforceable bills of rights – and for good reason. Peter Russell follows in the footsteps of these explorers when he worries about the 'flight' from representative government embodied in the Charter. Like his predecessors, Russell believes that representative government, not judicialized politics, is mainly how a sovereign people should protect rights.

How Representative Government Protects Rights

Although one would never guess it from the current infatuation with bills of rights, the tradition of constitutionalism that Russell invokes is not historically distant. Indeed, it is remarkable just how recently bills of rights have become prominent features of modern constitutionalism. The protection of rights was certainly the chief end of early liberal theorists and statesmen, but constitutionally and judicially enforceable bills of rights as we know them were not their preferred means to this end. The first major bill of this kind is to be found not in the recommendations of Locke or Blackstone, but in the U.S. Constitution.[7] And there it appears as a series of amendments, insisted on by the 'anti-federalists' as a way of constraining only the national government, not their preferred state governments. Although the federalist proponents of the constitution were willing to concede the bill of rights, they obviously did not think that it was necessary – not because they did not respect rights, but because they thought (and said) that the main constitution, the pre–bill-of-rights constitution, was itself the true and most effective bill of rights.[8]

Rights, in this view, were best protected by preventing the emergence of oppressive majority 'factions,' not by preaching moral rectitude to majorities through such 'parchment barriers' as bills of rights. Oppressive factions would be prevented by the so-called new science of politics. At the heart of this new science was representative government, organized in a system of institutional checks and balances, and superimposed on a society sufficiently diverse to require the moderating aggregation of many factions into decent governing majorities.[9] For the American founders, in short, the surest protection against majority tyranny was to destroy – that is, fragment – the possibility of natural majorities. Properly structured representative government (as opposed to 'pure democracy') was to replace 'majority rule' with 'minorities rule' – that is, majority coalitions of diverse minorities.[10]

Representation facilitated this strategy by permitting a territory large and diverse enough to forestall the emergence of natural majorities. But representation did more than extend the size and diversity of a republic; it also served 'to refine and to enlarge the public views by passing them through the medium of a chosen body of citizens.'[11] Members of the proposed new Congress, a 'select and stable body,' would have the opportunity to acquire a 'due sense of national character,' as opposed to being mere spokesmen for the parochial concerns of their constituents.[12] Thus deliberation or 'government by discussion' – not just representation of interests – was also considered a vital safeguard for rights.

It would be a mistake to exclude the courts from the ambit of the 'new science of politics.' When Alexander Hamilton listed the components of that science in Federalist Paper No. 9, he explicitly included 'the institution of courts composed of judges holding their offices during good behavior.' But Hamilton was interested primarily in adjudicative independence, not in judicial enforcement of entrenched rights. True, he did believe that the judiciary would sometimes have to declare laws unconstitutional and thus 'void,' but he saw this as a limited power to invalidate only 'acts contrary to the manifest tenor of the Constitution'[13] – that is, absolutely clear contraventions of the constitution. This is made clear by his only example: the passage of bills of attainder or *ex post facto* laws, which are explicitly prohibited by the constitution.

There is nothing in Hamilton's defence of judicial review that suggests that he would have supported modern 'purposive analysis,' which contemplates the invalidation of legislation that contravenes no explicit textual prohibition, so long as it contravenes the deeper 'purposes' of the text, as discovered between its lines by judges.[14] In fact, in Federalist Paper No. 81, Hamilton suggests that such 'noninterpretivist' rulings would be 'usurpations on the authority of the legislature' and grounds for impeachment.' More to our point, his limited defence of judicial review was part of his attempt to urge the ratification of a constitution that *did not* include a bill of rights. Indeed, it was Hamilton who in Federalist Paper No. 84 insisted that the proposed constitution – the pre–bill-of-rights version – 'is itself, in every rational sense, and to every useful purpose, A BILL OF RIGHTS.'

According to recent scholarship, the most prominent theorists of the Westminster parliamentary tradition – Lord Durham and A.V. Dicey, for example – thought along similar lines. Thus Janet Ajzenstat argues that Durham saw responsible government as contributing to constitutional 'balance,' which for him, as for other Whigs, meant just what 'checks and balances' did to the Americans, and served precisely the same function.[15]

Ajzenstat comes to similar conclusions about Dicey. Dicey believed that 'the Westminster system's two great principles, parliamentary sovereignty and the rule of law, are ... mutually reinforcing.'[16] To be sure, Dicey believed that the security of rights depended primarily on judge-made law (that is, the common law and judicial interpretation of statutes) and thus required independent and impartial courts. Still, Ajzenstat argues, he thought that 'in the absence of parliamentary sovereignty efforts by the judiciary will come to nothing.'[17]

For Dicey, as for Durham, parliamentary sovereignty was the key to protecting rights – rather than the main threat to rights, as is now generally assumed – because the sovereign parliament embodied the principle of checks and balances. Parliamentary checks and balances were certainly different, and perhaps less elaborate, than those of the U.S. congressional system, but they were no less effective for that. Their essence lay in the freedom of the opposition parties to criticize and expose government violations of the people's rights. Anticipation of such criticism – and the prospect of being punished at the polls – was expected to pre-empt any governmental proclivity to invade the rights of its citizens.[18] Dicey and his generation had great confidence in the efficacy of 'partisan debate' and public deliberation in producing sound public policy – i.e., policy that respects rights. Part of this confidence came from the Whig embrace of the natural-right tradition and of the power of reasoned debate to apply this tradition to the affairs of state.[19] Ajzenstat laments that, with the advent of the Charter (and probably before), Canadians' 'confidence in the power of public debate to resolve issues for the common good has taken a beating.' If we lose it altogether, she warns, 'we lose the essence of constitutional democracy.'[20]

In sum, early constitutionalists in both the American and English systems sought to protect rights more through representative government and checks and balances than through bills of rights. If these devices of the 'new science of politics' were in good working order, a bill of rights would not be necessary; if they were not working well, the constitutional pronouncements of robed judges, wielding the power of neither sword nor purse, would make little difference.

As these early theorists would have predicted, the U.S. Bill of Rights did in fact make *very* little difference, at least for most of U.S. constitutional history. During the nineteenth century, only nine federal laws were voided for violating the Bill of Rights. As recently as 1925, the total was only fifteen.[21] The most prominent judicial invalidation, moreover, was *Dred Scott v. Sanford*, 'scarcely a monument to liberty.'[22] As for the states, we have seen that the original Bill of Rights did not even apply to them. The origins of the modern emphasis on the Bill of Rights by Americans – and then quickly by all us copycats – can be traced back *at best* to the *Gitlow* case in 1925, when the U.S. Supreme Court began incorporating the Bill of Rights into the Fourteenth Amendment, thus making it applicable to the states. In fact, the modern infatuation with bills of rights is probably most accurately traced to *Brown v. Board of Education* in 1954 – less than fifty years ago. For most of its history, liberal-democratic constitutionalism has depended for the protection of rights mainly on properly constructed representative institutions and the 'government by discussion' that they promote.

The Challenge to Representative Government

Recent decades, however, have witnessed a sustained challenge to representative institutions. As Robert Vipond's contribution (chapter 2) to this volume makes clear, the challenge is two-fold. In Canada, as elsewhere, it is manifested by the growing popularity of both populism and constitutionally entrenched rights. To adapt Russell's formulation slightly, if populism reflects a 'flight' from 'representative government and government by discussion,' the Charter represents 'a further flight' in the same direction.

Although they are different in many obvious ways,[23] populism and the rights movement pose similar challenges to representative government. Thus if populists do not like what representatives have done, they generally do not wish to wait until a general election to 'throw the rascals out'; they want to be able to be able to 'recall' them *now*. Similarly, if rights advocates do not like legislative policies, they increasingly want courts, not elections, to reverse those policies. By the same token, populists advocate the use of initiatives and referenda to force their agenda on reluctant legislatures, just as rights advocates increasingly ask the courts to force their agenda on the legislature through such devices of 'positive activism' as 'reading in.' The growth of both populism and the rights movement reveals the extent to which confidence in representative institutions has indeed 'taken a beating.'

Just how bad a beating is being inflicted by the rights movement is illustrated by a 1996 decision by an Ontario divisional court judge. In *M and H*,[24] Judge Gloria Epstein was faced with a homosexual challenge to a provision in the Ontario Family Law Act that defined 'spouse' as a member of the opposite sex. Less than two years earlier, the Ontario government had tried to amend this provision to delete reference to the opposite sex and thus open up the Family Law Act to homosexual couples. After a lengthy and heavily publicized debate, which included many appeals to the principle of equality and the Charter of Rights, the government's amendment was defeated in a free vote in the legislature. What was the judge's assessment of this rather clear statement of legislative preference? Rather than defer, she observed: 'Other than in a narrow technical sense, it is virtually impossible to attribute clear legislative intent to the defeat of that bill.' Perhaps sensing the weakness of this assertion, she added: 'The defeat was strongly affected by perceived gains and losses in the then pending election.'[25] In other words, legislators are no longer to be trusted if their arguments and votes are influenced by the prospect of electoral reward or punishment! We have come full circle from the perspective of Dicey. Rather than legitimate the exercise of legislative power, free elections are now deemed to corrupt it. (We cannot resist asking why judges have spent so much effort using the Charter to extend the right to vote to convicted prisoners, if this is the value that they attach to the results of elections.)

Russell clearly worries that the loss of confidence in representative institutions poses a threat to liberal-democratic constitutionalism. We agree. It is an unhealthy development because it simultaneously leads to a dangerous moral inflation of ordinary policy claims and substitutes the coercion of court orders for the persuasion of parliamentary (and public) debate. Taken together, these features of judicialized politics threaten the capacity of even Canadians in the ROC to form a single people prepared to be 'concluded' by the majority.

Inflationary Rhetoric

Because the other rights-protecting features of Canadian constitutionalism are in reasonably good repair, policies that have been challenged under the Charter cannot be honestly described as truly tyrannical deprivations of rights. As Russell observed in 1969, it is simply not reasonable to claim that constitutionally entrenched rights prevent real tyranny and oppression by democratic majorities: 'Do you feel menaced by the prospect of the great Canadian majority, acting through its elected representatives in Ottawa, steam-rolling over your basic rights and liberties in pursuit of its own interests? Are you comforted by [entrenched rights that enable] our judiciary to veto these strident majoritarian demands and secure your liberty? If you ask yourself these questions and can honestly answer them in the affirmative, what you surely need is a psychiatrist not a bill of rights.'[26]

On a sane view of our legislative process, the pros and cons of the kinds of policies that actually issue from that process, and that come to be challenged under the Charter, are almost always matters of reasonable disagreement among reasonable people – as shown by the fact that they generally arouse disagreement even among judges. In Russell's terms, Charter cases tend not to turn on the 'central core' of the values enshrined in the Charter – i.e., on matters of such widespread agreement that constitutional entrenchment seems appropriate – but on issues at some distance from that 'core.'[27] Indeed, if the core meaning of a right were to be violated by government policy, judicial review would almost never be effective. Concerted government attack on the core meaning of a fundamental right is the very definition of tyranny, and courts are normally too weak to oppose either the tyranny of the majority[28] or the tyranny of a single despot.[29] The real effect of the Charter is thus not to protect rights in any fundamental sense, but to encourage what we call 'rights-claiming.'

Rights-claiming is typically a partisan exercise, whose objective is not to protect the fundamental core of existing rights but to change public policy through the judicial creation of new rights. As the founding document of the Legal Education and Action Fund (LEAF) declared, we Canadians, with the adoption of the Charter, 'find ourselves at the opportune moment to stress litigation as a vehicle for social change.' The same sentiments animate the other interest groups and lawyers who have been most active in Charter litigation. 'Rights-claiming' becomes possible because while the core meaning of a right may be widely agreed on, its outer limits are always contestable and often contested. The practical scope and contents of a right thus change over time, and those changes are driven by partisan interests' attempts to infuse their policy claims with a higher moral status by identifying their policy goal as within the indeterminate periphery of that right.

A generation ago Canadians understood the distinction between truly fundamental rights and 'rights-claiming.' Speaking against Pierre Trudeau's proposal for an entrenched charter, Donald Smiley warned: 'When we are engaged in analysis rather than rhetoric we should perhaps do better to use the expression "preferred human claims" ... rather than "human rights."'[30] Even the late Chief Justice Bora Laskin, celebrated for his early defence of civil liberties, saw the difference: 'Claims of interests which are labelled "civil liberties" differ from other claims or interests that are the product of our society in the weight that is attached to them. Indeed, association of the label with a particular demand is a recognized technique for focusing attention upon it and for surrounding it with substance and respectability.'[31]

More 'substance and respectability,' one must add, than the demand would otherwise have had. Indeed, 'substance and respectability' are terms much too tame to describe the 'weight' that is added to a political demand by translating it into 'rights talk.' Mary Ann Glendon has most clearly set out the ways in which rights talk acts as an uncompromising language of trumps that does not brook reasonable disagreement.[32] Rights-claiming, in other words, inflates issues well beyond their true significance.

The inflationary character of rights-claiming is crystal clear in a case reported on the CBC 'National.' A woman in Toronto had, for environmental reasons, replaced her lawn with a garden of weeds – a project likely to arouse the sympathy of anyone who, like us, hates the weekend chore of mowing lawns. Apparently the local by-law officers displayed no such sympathy. Instead of obeying the law, however, the woman went to court, arguing that the by-law infringed her freedom of expression – and she won! No doubt a higher court would be more sensible, but that is beside the present point. The point is that the Charter allowed an environmental activist to claim a 'fundamental right' to grow weeds, a right that would trump the majority's desire for manicured lawns and its fear that unkempt 'weed gardens' lower neighbouring property values. Perhaps the majority is misguided in these concerns, but to claim that its will is trumped by a fundamental right to grow weeds is an inflated policy claim if ever there was one.

Now, there are obviously many claims brought under the Charter that are not as trivial as this. But we would contend that, however important and controversial the issues raised by Charter jurisprudence might be, they almost always turn out to be matters of reasonable disagreement that are unnecessarily inflated through courtroom rights talk. Courtroom rights talk, in other words, is encouraging in Canadians the same bad political instinct that Alexander Bickel criticized the U.S. Supreme Court for fostering in American society in the 1960s: moral oversensitivity. For a democracy, being morally oversensitive is as dangerous as being morally undersensitive. It unduly lowers the threshhold at which citizens feel justified in abandoning the democratic process – be it through civil disobedience, appeal to the courts, or (in the extreme case) revolt and secession. Canada would do well to heed Bickel's plea that the 'morality of rights' be balanced with the 'morality of consent.'[33]

Judicial Coercion

The moral inflation of rights-claiming entails an institutional transfer of power. As a logical corollary of translating reasonable disagreements into uncompromising rights talk, in other words, the responsibility for 'concluding' these agreements moves from legislatures to courts. Because opposition to the rights claim is presented as 'beyond the pale,' it cannot be left to the decision of representative institutions, where opposition to virtually any policy able to make it onto the agenda is a fact of life. In other words, the policy issue cannot be left to be 'concluded' by legislative majorities, because the 'wrong' side may form the majority.

Shifting power from the legislative to the judicial arena, in short, is a way of substituting coercion for 'government by discussion.' To be sure, we should not exaggerate the distinction between the two institutional contexts. On the one hand, much debate takes place in the courtroom. On the other hand, no one should romanticize the nature of parliamentary (and public) debate. We all know that there is as much posturing and inflation of claims in legislative politics as there is in the courtroom. The symbolism of having legislative partisans separated by two swords' lengths underscores the intensity and uncompromising intransigence of much of their debate. Still, important differences between legislative and judicial 'debate' must be kept in view.

For all its sound and fury, for all its raucous and uncompromising posturing, everything about legislative debate implies the sine qua non of a sovereign people: the willingness to abide by the rule of majorities with which one disagrees. Thus the rules of legislative debate require its participants to use civil and decorous language even as they insult their opponents. Insults are hurled not at that

'SOB' over there, but at the honourable member opposite. Indeed, it is not even permitted to address a member directly or by name. Debate must not be personalized and ad hominem, so representatives address the Speaker and use the name of other members' constituencies or offices.

Such rules are suggested by the very nature of political debate among a sovereign people. As Walter Berns has said, democratic debate 'implies on the part of those participating in it a capacity and willingness to be persuaded, persuaded by another with an equal right to form the majority or to be part of it, with an equally legitimate interest, and, perhaps, with a superior argument. And it implies, and even encourages, the willingness to abide by the vote of the majority assembled. The importance of this cannot be exaggerated. Those who participate in this process are not permitted to overlook, because the rules require them to recognize, the right of every representative to be part of the majority, or to overlook the fact that the purpose of forming a majority is to govern.'[34]

Judicialized politics, especially when it concerns constitutionally entrenched rights, carries a quite different set of implications. It has a much more closed and intolerant character. True, rules of decorum also govern courtroom combat. Nevertheless, the point of the formalized courtroom combat about constitutional rights is to determine which side holds uncompromisable trumps. Courts do not always issue the trumps requested by rights claimants, of course. Sometimes, as in the *Morgentaler* case, for example, courts are much more moderate than the litigants. Thus, the majority of Supreme Court justices struck down Canada's abortion law in *Morgentaler* not by explicitly siding with the prochoice position but by emphasizing the procedural defects of the law. But this qualification is somewhat beside the point. The point is that the judicial arena encouraged extremists to claim constitutional trumps rather than to engage in 'government by discussion.' Moreover, the subtlety of the judicial reasons for invalidating the law were lost on the media and the public, allowing the prochoice side to claim that the constitution was more unambiguously on their side than it actually was. Inevitably, the winners in courtroom battles are publicly presented (or present themselves) as having absolute right – or 'rights' – on their side; the logical corollary, of course – and it is a corollary that winners typically go out of their way to emphasize – is that the losers are not only wrong but legally illegitimate. The losers, in other words, are 'beyond the pale'; theirs is not an eligible policy position, and if they form the majority, it is not a majority that can be allowed to 'set and conclude' the rest.

A sovereign people's willingness to be concluded by the majority is implied by legislative politics, and undermined by judicialized politics, in yet another way. The assumption of legislative politics is that there are no permanent winners and losers. A majority that 'sets and concludes' an issue is nevertheless not 'conclusive' in its victory. As Janet Ajzenstat has written, the 'boast' of liberal democracy 'is that it does nothing to limit complaint and debate and nothing to prevent opposition groups and parties from organizing to plot the overthrow of particular laws and policies. As decrees of the executive branch, laws must be obeyed, but as measures emanating from the legislature, they may be endlessly contested. The fact of debate and popular participation does not undermine the requirement to obey; and the fact that obedience is required enables continuing debate. No political loss is entirely without remedy. If interests remain unaggregated and the players retain their energy, the game can be virtually endless. Those who fall rise to fight again.'[35] This 'boast' is logically entailed in liberal democracy's attempt to replace natural majorities with shifting coalitions of minorities. And it is essential to the agreement that forms a sovereign people – the agreement to abide by the will of the majority – that neither majorities nor minorities be permanent, that today's majority can become tomorrow's minority, and vice versa.

No such 'boast' of policy flux issues from the realm of judicialized politics. To the contrary. Victory in a courtroom rights battle carries the implication of permanence. The victor's policy is constitutionally entrenched, and the whole point of entrenchment is to guarantee a degree of permanence not possible in legislative politics.

Again, actual practice sometimes belies institutional symbolism. Thus, while the policy outcomes of legislatures are in principle easier to change and reverse than the constitutional rulings of courts, they tend to display a robust resistance to opposition. As Thomas Flanagan has demonstrated, legislative rules are biased in favour of the status quo, giving it a remarkable 'staying power.'[36] Similarly, although constitutional rulings are in principle more permanent than legislation, we know that they can and do change because of 'court bashing,' 'court packing,' or simply the generational changing of the judicial guard. Nevertheless, while the actual difference between the staying power of legislation and that of judicial rulings is not as stark as the formal distinctions suggest, the symbolism of those distinctions remains important. Even if constitutional victories are not as permanent as they appear, those who seek them want, and are encouraged to claim, such permanence. Even if constitutional trumps cannot be made to stick in perpetuity, political partisans are nevertheless urged to speak and act as if they could, instead of being forced to live with the sobering thought that their policy preferences reflect no more than the will of a transient majority.

In brief, to entrench rights and thereby transfer the resolution of reasonable disagreements from legislatures to courts not only inflates rhetoric to unwarranted levels but also grants the policy preferences of courtroom victors an aura of coercive force and permanence that they do not deserve. Issues that should be subject to the ongoing flux of 'government by discussion' are presented as beyond legitimate debate, with the partisans claiming the right to permanent victory. The result is to embitter politics and decrease the inclination of political opponents to treat each other as fellow citizens – that is, as members of a sovereign people.

Dissolving a Sovereign People

Russell claims that '*not all* Canadians have consented to form a single people.' The opening words of this formulation imply, of course, that *some* Canadians *have* so consented. Given the progression of Canada's constitutional politics, one can conclude only that such consent is less and less common. We maintain that courtroom Charter politics contributes in major ways to the erosion of a sovereign Canadian people.

This is most obvious, of course, with respect to the Quebec–ROC divide, which has clearly been widened not only by the Charter's symbolic role in the macro-constitutional politics of formal amendment, but also by the inflationary rhetoric and judicial coercion encouraged by the politics of Charter litigation. Indeed, the corrosive effects of amendment and litigation politics have interacted to make our mega-constitutional politics even more intensely 'mega.' In other words, Quebec's Charterphobia is fed not only by the perception that the Charter was imposed on Quebec without its consent, but also by the province's relatively poor track record in Charter litigation.[37]

The paradigmatic case is surely the Quebec signs case. Now, we were not fans of the restrictive law at stake in that case. We believe it to have been a foolish and misguided law. So did a significant segment of Quebec opinion – including Québécois opinion – in the period preceding the litigation. Indeed, the Bourassa government had gone so far as to promise during the 1985 election to relax the law. This proved to be a highly controversial promise, and thus not one easy to keep. Nevertheless, there was an ongoing debate about the matter in Quebec and no reason to suppose that the moderates could never carry the day.[38]

Unfortunately, opponents of the law were unwilling to continue the process of 'government by discussion' and endure the rule of existing majorities in the meantime. The Charter encouraged them to think and act as if the existing policy was not only misguided, but wholly illegitimate, and thus 'beyond the pale' of ordinary democratic politics. They went to court, and by doing so they distorted and derailed the political debate among Quebecers about signs policy.

The debate was well and truly derailed when the Supreme Court of Canada ruled in 1988 that the law violated the 'fundamental right' of freedom of expression and could not be 'demonstrably justified' as a 'reasonable limit' on that right. This ruling entailed a serious and regrettable inflation of the issue. However misguided one considers the law to be, it is going considerably 'over the top' to characterize it as a tyrannical suppression of fundamental rights. Are people's lives put in danger when octagonal red signs at intersections say only 'Arret'? Is it anything more than a minor inconvenience or irritation for an anglophone Montrealer to see well-known English establishments sporting French-only signs? Are we really to believe that anglophone visitors from elsewhere cannot recognize restaurants and department stores or find ones that will serve them in English. 'Get real,' one is inclined to say!

What is even more important, the Supreme Court ruling sent the following message to members of the Quebec community: 'The issue you have been debating is not one you are entitled to debate, and thus decide, for yourselves. In important respects, the issue has already been decided by the Charter. Those of you who have thus far been winning the political debate have done so illegitimately. Your opponents have been right all along.' Paradoxically, this implicit message put Québécois opponents of the signs law in a difficult position. They had to choose between their opposition to the law and the right of the Quebec community to govern itself in this matter. Not surprisingly, the Bourassa government chose self-government, a choice it could make effective only by re-enacting the law with a 'notwithstanding' clause. The ironic result was that a government that was on record as wanting to relax the law was put in a position of reinvigorating it.

By uniting the Québécois behind the signs law, moreover, the Supreme Court's ruling intensified tensions between Quebec and the ROC. As Russell aptly put it, the reaction in English Canada 'was severe and equally tribal.'[39] Coming at a crucial point in the debate about the Meech Lake Accord, the ruling helped undermine the accord's ratification. English Canadians were not about to agree to the status of 'distinct society' for a province that would trample the 'fundamental rights' of fellow anglophones. We were not supporters of the Meech Lake Accord, but neither do we wish to celebrate the inflated rights rhetoric that helped defeat it. If the failure of Meech is the event of our recent mega-constitutional politics that has most severely undermined the capacity of citizens of Quebec and the ROC to become a single, sovereign people, Charter litigation contributed significantly to this result.

Although its contribution to the possible separation of Quebec is the most obvious way in which the rhetorical inflation and judicial coercion of Charter litigation hinders Canadians from becoming a sovereign people, it is far from the only way. In the ROC, the issues raised in Charter politics tend not to divide people as much, or as intensely, along territorial lines; indeed, to some extent, they may help to ameliorate territorialism by dividing people in non-territorial ways, as Trudeau appears to have intended. Thus Charter politics in the ROC is not likely to contribute to the geographic break-up of the ROC (although, if Quebec separates, there are plenty of other forces that will promote further fragmentation).[40] But the mere fact of continuing geographical unity does not signify the existence of a single, sovereign people.

The key to the existence of a sovereign people is its agreement to allow the 'majority to set and conclude the rest.' The Charter does little to promote such agreement. To the contrary! The inflationary rhetoric and coercive methods of Charter litigation undermine the conditions of common citizenship even where territorial division is not an option. Political opponents do not become common citizens by virtue simply of their inability to escape each other. They may become more like scorpions in a bottle than like the moderate opponents envisioned, and promoted, by 'representative government and government by discussion.' The Charter has helped to turn Quebec and the ROC into something not unlike two scorpions in a bottle, though in this case the bottle is open and these scorpions *can* escape each other. Canadians within the ROC are still more of a sovereign people than this, but the Charter does less to keep them this way than its founding intention might suggest.

Conclusion

Far from being the cornerstone of liberal constitutionalism, the inflationary rhetoric and coercive methods encouraged by the Charter threaten its foundations. Liberal-democratic constitutionalism requires the willingness of political losers gracefully to accept the rule of majorities they do not like, until they can themselves garner enough support to form the next majority. This is what it means to be a single people willing to be concluded by the majority. Not only do representative institutions and government by discussion imply the existence of such agreement but their processes and procedures may also promote (or at least help maintain) the agreement that they imply.[41]

Judicialized rights talk, in contrast, is hostile to 'the procedures of representative government and government by discussion' and thus to the agreement to form a sovereign people implied by those procedures. Rights talk is hostile to liberal-democratic constitutionalism unless truly serious violations of rights are at stake. And if rights are being violated in such a truly serious way, armed resistance is likely to be the only appropriate and effective response. Bills and charters of rights promote rights talk when it is not needed and when it is likely to prove destructive. When uncompromising rights talk is really needed, robes and parchment barriers will prove useless. The reluctance of most of the founders of liberalism to emphasize (or in some cases even to mention) judicially enforced bills of rights turns out to be well founded, not just an oversight on their part. As Peter Russell has argued, there is a 'democratic approach to civil liberties,' one that we ignore, or abandon, at our peril.[42]

NOTES

1 Peter H. Russell, *Constitutional Odyssey: Can Canadians Be a Sovereign People?* (Toronto: University of Toronto Press 1992), 5.
2 Peter H. Russell, 'The Effect of a Charter of Rights on the Policy-Making Role of Canadian Courts,' *Canadian Public Administration* 25 no. 1(1982), 32.
3 Peter H. Russell, 'The Political Purposes of the Canadian Charter of Rights and Freedoms,' *Canadian Bar Review* 61 (1983). Cf. Rainer Knopff and F.L. Morton, 'Nation-Building and the Charter of Rights and Freedoms,' in A. Cairns and C. Williams, eds., *Constitutionalism, Citizenship and Society in Canada* (Toronto: University of Toronto Press 1985), 98–114.
4 Peter H. Russell, 'The Political Purposes of the Charter: Have They Been Fulfilled? An Agnostic's Report Card,' in Philip Bryden, Steven Davis, and John Russell, eds., *Protecting Rights and Freedoms: Essays on the Charter's Place in Canada's Political, Legal, and Intellectual Life* (Toronto: University of Toronto Press 1994) 33–44.
5 Charterphilia should be distinguished from rights consciousness. As Russell and many other commentators have pointed out, Quebecers are just as rights conscious as other Canadians. It is the 'imposed' Charter, not rights, that they do not like.
6 See F.L. Morton, 'The Charter and Canada outside Quebec,' in Kenneth McRoberts, ed., *Beyond Quebec: Taking Stock of Canada* (Montreal: McGill-Queen's University Press 1995), 98–114.
7 Some of the original thirteen states had bills of rights prior to the present U.S. constitution. However, by comparison with the U.S. Bill of Rights, which has become the model for modern bills of rights generally, they were quite limited in scope. Only two, for example, guaranteed freedom of speech. Many permitted religious establishments. And protections now considered routine, such as freedom of assembly, right to counsel, and protection against double jeopardy, were far from common. See Michael J. Sandel, *Democracy's Discontent* (Cambridge Mass.: Harvard University Press, 1996), 35.
8 See Walter Berns, 'The Constitution as a Bill of Rights,' in Robert A. Goldwin and William A. Schambra, eds., *How Does the Constitution Secure Rights?* (Washington, DC: American Enterprise Institute 1985), 50–73; Herbert Storing, 'The Consti-

tution and the Bill of Rights,' in ibid., 15–35; Thomas L. Pangle, *The Spirit of Modern Republicanism: The Moral Vision of the American Founders and the Philosophy of Locke* (Chicago: University of Chicago Press 1988), 71–2, 125; Judith A. Best, 'Fundamental Rights and the Structure of Government,' in Robert A. Licht, ed., *The Framers and Fundamental Rights* (Washington, DC: AEI Press 1993), 35–56; Robert A. Goldwin, 'Congressman Madison Proposes Amendments to the Constitution,' in ibid., 57–85; Rainer Knopff and F.L. Morton, *Charter Politics* (Scarborough: Nelson Canada 1992), 173–5; Joseph M. Bessette, 'Guarding the Constitution from Legislative Tyranny,' in Robert A. Licht, ed., *Is the Supreme Court the Guardian of the Constitution?* (Washington, DC: AEI Press, 1993), 46–58; Christopher P. Manfredi, *Judicial Power and the Charter: Canada and the Paradox of Liberal Constitutionalism* (Toronto: McClelland and Stewart 1993), 23–5; Bradley C.S. Watson, 'The Language of Rights and the Crisis of the Liberal Imagination,' in Anthony A. Peacock. ed., *Rethinking the Constitution: Perspectives on Canadian Constitutional Reform, Interpretation, and Theory* (Don Mills: Oxford University Press 1996), 88–91; Michael J. Sandel, *Democracy's Discontent: America in Search of a Public Philosophy* (Cambridge Mass.: Harvard University Press, 1996), 33–9.

9 See *Federalist Papers*, Nos. 9, 10, and 51.

10 See especially ibid., Nos. 10 and 51.

11 Ibid., No. 10.

12 Ibid., No. 63. These terms were used in reference to the Senate but apply with lesser force to the House as well.

13 Ibid., No. 78.

14 See Knopff and Morton, *Charter Politics*, chap. 5.

15 Janet Ajzenstat, *The Political Thought of Lord Durham* (Montreal: McGill-Queen's University Press 1988), 71.

16 Janet Ajzenstat, 'Reconciling Parliament and Rights: A.V. Dicey Reads the Canadian Charter of Rights and Freedoms,' paper presented to the annual meeting of the Canadian Political Science Association, June 1996, 1.

17 Ibid., 2.

18 Ibid., 16–17, 23–4.

19 Ibid., 8, 18, 19, 24.

20 Ibid., 25.

21 Walter Berns, *Taking the Constitution Seriously* (New York: Madison Books 1987), 127.

22 Ibid.

23 See H.D. Forbes, 'Trudeau's Moral Vision,' in Peacock, *Rethinking the Constitution*, 23.

24 M. v. H., [1996] OJ. No. 365.

25 Ibid.

26 Peter H. Russell, 'A Democratic Approach to Civil Liberties,' *University of Toronto Law Journal* (1969), 107.

27 Peter H. Russell, 'The Political Purposes of the Canadian Charter of Rights and Freedoms,' *Canadian Bar Review* 61 (1983), 43–5.

28 In the United States, consider the Supreme Court's unwillingness to oppose Japanese-American relocations during the Second World War.

29 In Uganda, when the Supreme Court began to intervene to stop Idi Amin's persecution of his political opponents, he ordered his secret police to shoot the judges. They did.

30 Donald Smiley, 'The Case Against the Canadian Charter of Human Rights,' *Canadian Journal of Political Science* 2 (1969), 277–91.

31 Bora Laskin, 'An Inquiry into the Diefenbaker Bill of Rights,' *Canadian Bar Review* 37 (1959), 79.

32 Mary Ann Glendon, *Rights Talk: The Impoverishment of Political Discourse* (New York: Free Press, 1991).

33 Alexander Bickel, *The Morality of Consent* (New Haven, Conn.: Yale University Press 1974).

34 Berns, *Taking the Constitution Seriously*, 143.

35 Janet Ajzenstat, 'The Decline of Procedural Liberalism,' in Joseph H. Carens, ed., *Is Quebec Nationalism Just?* (Montreal: McGill-Queen's University Press 1995), 130.

36 Thomas E. Flanagan, 'The Staying Power of the Status Quo: Collective Choice in Canada's Parliament after Morgentaler,' *Canadian Journal of Political Science* 30 (1997), 31–53.

37 See F.L. Morton, 'The Effect of the Charter of Rights on Canadian Federalism,' *Publius: The Journal of Federalism* 25 no. 3 (1995), 173–88.

38 Eventually moderates did carry the day. See Scott Reid, 'Penumbras for the People: Placing Judicial Supremacy Under Popular Control,' in Peacock, *Rethinking the Constitution*, 208. Nevertheless, the victory of moderation in this policy area was almost certainly delayed by the signs case.

39 Russell, *Constitutional Odyssey*, 146.

40 Charles F. Doran, 'Will Canada Unravel?' *Foreign Affairs* 75 (1996), 97–109.

41 See George Kateb, 'The Moral Distinctiveness of Representative Democracy,' *Ethics* 91 (1981), 357–74; and Robert D. Putnam, *Making Democracy Work* (Princeton, NJ: Princeton University Press 1993).

42 Russell, 'A Democratic Approach to Civil Liberties.'

17

Legislative Scrutiny: An Alternative Approach for Protecting Rights

JANET L. HIEBERT

The inspiration for this paper comes from musing about two of Peter Russell's observations about the political significance of entrenched rights. The first is that the main effect of the Charter is not to guarantee rights but to change the way in which decisions are made on how to establish limits on the extent to which rights and freedoms can be enjoyed. As we move away from those values that reflect ideals common to all contemporary liberal democracies (political freedom, religious toleration, due process of law, and social equality), we incur considerable dilemmas in determining what limits are appropriate for less universal and more contested values.[1] His second observation is that one of the liabilities of a system of entrenched rights is that it may discourage political participation in resolving contentious issues. Any society that aspires to be democratic should resolve the most important of its social and political conflicts through its elected legislatures rather than through the courts, because the legislative rather than the judicial process is more likely to facilitate the kind of discussion and reflection desirable in making difficult social and political choices.[2]

Together, these observations suggest that we need to reassess the way we look at rights by moving away from the idea of viewing them as primarily legal concepts that are assumed to be both preferable to and distinct from public policy concerns. Rather we should conceptualize the issue in terms of how best to evaluate conflicting values and determine what priority should be attached to each. We might ask several questions. Does one particular institution have a unique capacity or particular expertise that would recommend it as the best venue for reconciling rights claims with public policy? Does the judiciary face obstacles that make it inherently difficult for it to perform this task? Would institutional reforms better prepare and enable Parliament to undertake greater responsibility for ensuring that public policy is justified where serious rights concerns are raised?

The initial response to these questions, at least in the Canadian context, might be to dismiss them as being entirely academic or, worse, irrelevant. After all, the entrenchment of rights in the constitution would appear to have resolved the issue of which institution will ultimately determine the justification of policies that conflict with rights. Courts have been given an authoritative role to interpret the Charter of Rights and Freedoms, provide remedies, and declare offending legislation invalid. Yet these questions remain important, even after entrenchment. While the Charter may have rendered futile any further debate about whether Canada should or should not give courts an authoritative role in determining whether legislation duly respects rights, the Charter has not foreclosed on the need to consider how best to evaluate and reconcile conflicting values. The veracity of this latter claim may not be readily apparent. Let me now make the arguments about why this debate is both relevant and important. In this paper, I look at judicial review under the Charter, at Parliament as a possible arbiter, at Australian answers to this type of problem, and at their possible relevance to Canada.

Judicial Review under the Charter

The structure of the Charter has had a decisive influence on judicial review. The inclusion of an explicit limitation clause in section 1 has encouraged the Supreme Court of Canada to adopt a two-stage approach to judicial review. The court has decided to distinguish questions about whether a right has been infringed from inquiries into whether a legislatively imposed limit on a protected right is reasonable. But in doing so, the court has decided to interpret rights initially in broad and generous terms, subject to subsequent case-by-case assessments of whether the government's reasons for limiting rights are demonstrably justified and consistent with a free and democratic society. This initial broad interpretation has implicated a far greater range of legislative activities than if the court had adopted a more restrictive interpretation of rights. Take, for example, free speech. The court has decided that the issue of whether a particular form of expressive activity is protected under the Charter will not depend on the content of speech. Thus constitutional protection for speech embraces 'all content of expression, irrespective of the meaning or message sought to be conveyed'[3] and includes solicitation for prostitution, obscenity, hate literature, and commercial advertising, including the advertisement of tobacco products.[4] This expansive approach has meant that a broader range of legislative activities are found to conflict with protected rights than had the court defined protected speech on the basis of qualitative assessments about the content, nature, or importance of the message. This is not to say that governments cannot justify restrictions on expression, but the court will assess them case by case, and the government bears the burden for demonstrating the justification of its actions.

Not only has the court's broad approach to interpreting rights increased the frequency with which legislation will be found to conflict with protected rights, but the criterion that the Charter establishes for evaluating the justification of impugned legislation – a free and democratic society – is sufficiently broad that it has expanded the range of policy objectives that governments may claim to represent reasonable limits on protected rights. Together, this combination of an expansive approach to defining rights and a vague criterion for evaluating the justification of legislation has guaranteed that the court will regularly have to assess the reasonableness of legislation.

But this responsibility is troublesome. The standard that the Charter lays down for evaluating the reasonableness of legislation is sufficiently contested that it invites philosophical debates about what kinds of policies are important enough to justify limiting rights. Should rights be limited only to protect other enumerated rights? Is it acceptable to limit rights to promote community or collective values? Are concerns about the polity's general welfare sufficient justification? Or should apprehension of harm be replaced by empirical evidence of actual harm? The Charter provides little in the way of guidelines for how courts should determine whether policies are sufficiently important to justify limiting rights. In its attempt to resolve competing social values, the court has decided that the section-1 standard for justifying limits on protected rights is not a universal one but one that can 'accentuate a uniquely Canadian vision of a free and democratic society.'[5] But this domestication of reasonableness does not define which values are integral to Canadian conceptions of freedom and democracy.

When assessing the importance of legislation, the court has been extremely reluctant to disagree outright with governmental claims that the policies they promote are important enough to justify limiting rights. Because governments generally enact policies for good reasons, it is not surprising that the court rarely disagrees with claims that impugned policies are justified. A more cynical view is that because judicial review is prone to democratic criticisms, the court does not go out of its way to invite accusations that it is frustrating the will of democratically elected representatives when it can do indirectly what it is unwilling to do directly. It can rule that legislation is unjustified without actually criticizing the objective by deciding that the legislation has not been carefully enough designed or drafted.

Regardless of what motivates its approach, the court rarely presents governments with a ruling that under no circumstances can the legislative objective be enacted. The principal emphasis in section-1 evaluations has been on whether legislation has been carefully enough designed to constitute a reasonable limit on protected rights: does it meet judicially imposed criteria of proportionality,[6] the most important element of which is whether it restricts rights as little as possible.

This raises a second, more serious reason why judicial review of the reasonableness of legislation is troublesome. Assessments of reasonableness pose particular challenges for the court because they presume an evaluation of the merits of impugned legislation in terms of how the policy was conceptualized and drafted. In making policy, those responsible often must address multiple objectives, make distinctions about who will benefit or be affected by policy, and anticipate circumstances that may undermine or influence the realization of objectives. Policy development is of necessity subject to discretionary judgments based on a combination of relevant expertise, comparative experience, and informed best estimates.

This lack of precision in the making of policy sits incongruously with the seemingly objective standard asked of the court: does the legislation impair rights as little as possible? The objective quality of this standard arises from the implication that to restrict rights as little as possible there must be a preferred and apparent policy alternative – indeed a correct one: preferred, because it imposes a less severe restriction on rights; apparent, because it is readily identifiable; and correct, because it is the optimum policy option – the one with the least restrictive implications for protected rights. Policy-making, however, is not some precise science amenable to correct/incorrect, good/bad evaluations that would allow policy-makers, or those scrutinizing their decisions, to home in on the perfect solution to complex social problems (from a rights perspective, as well as from a practical one).

Over time, the court has shown greater appreciation for the complexity of policy development, especially where the evaluation of conflicting social science data is required.[7] While the court earlier stated that rights can be limited only where legislation constitutes the least intrusive infringement on a right, its test has softened considerably to a requirement that a policy be 'reasonable' under the circumstances.[8] In choosing from a range of means, Parliament need not select the perfect or best possible legislative scheme,[9] but rather one tailored in the context of the infringed right.[10]

Nevertheless, despite its evolving approach, the court continues to interpret rights in an unqualified and uncritical manner that implicates a broad and sweeping range of legislation. This way of interpreting rights, when combined with the fact that the court is still not prepared to disagree openly with Parliament or the provincial legislatures about the importance of their objectives, means that judges have systematically to scrutinize policy not in the context of whether the objective is justified in rights-based terms but on the basis of the quality of how the policy initiative was translated into legislation. Such an inquiry presumes analysis both of how policy is conceptualized and drafted and of the utility and effects of alternative schemes.

The court's jurisprudence on the rights/limits nexus leads to the following observation. Since the court places emphasis deciding not on whether policy objectives themselves are acceptable, in rights-based terms, but instead on whether the ways and means of a policy are carefully enough designed, the judicial task cannot be distinguished conceptually from the kind of subjective and discretionary considerations that originally shaped the policy decision. In viewing the court's task in this manner, one may ask:

- Do judges bring any particular expertise to this task?
- If a constitutional text is of limited guidance to this aspect of judicial review, how should the court assess the justification of impugned legislation?
- If the exercise rests on anything less than applying apparent and accepted constitutional values or standards, is there any justification for discretionary judicial opinions to be given primacy over discretionary political ones?
- Would it be preferable for courts to rely more heavily on the views of Parliament on how best to reconcile conflicting values?

While at one level it may be too late to be worried about this issue because the Charter has given judges the responsibility to determine the constitutionality of legislation, these questions remain important and relevant for two reasons. The court's approach to judicial review is still developing, and how it decides to evaluate the reasonableness of impugned legislation will probably continue to evolve for some time. Thus the court may revise over time both how it interprets rights and how it decides whether legislation is reasonable. Second, judicial difficulties with reviewing reasonableness have created new pressures and incentives for parliamentary reforms to ensure that the Charter's values are meaningful, without imposing undue obstacles on responsible policy-making.

Is Parliament a Better Arbiter?

Notwithstanding the difficulties that the court faces in evaluating reasonableness, it does not necessarily follow that Parliament is a better institutional choice for rights-based scrutiny. Although the minister of justice is statutorily obliged to report to Parliament when proposed legislation does not to comply with the Charter, this has not occurred to date. Two explanations are possible.

One is that the Charter's existence has encouraged the federal government to adopt an internal process of scrutiny[11] and that this process has been so effective that ministers respond to Charter concerns and revise bills accordingly (at least to the extent that the minister of justice feels that there is a reasonable chance that the legislation will pass the court's section-1 test).

The other explanation is more sceptical. A system of executive-based internal scrutiny within a parliamentary system is inherently weak: the Canadian model lacks the independence necessary for systems of scrutiny that operate beyond the direct control of the executive.[12] The requirement that the justice minister report to Parliament where proposed legislation does not comply with the Charter is similar to a provision in the Canadian Bill of Rights of 1960 that the minister of justice submit all draft bills and regulations to the clerk of the Privy Council to ascertain whether they conflict with the Bill of Rights and report any inconsistencies to the House of Commons. Peter Russell, writing in 1969, believed that this concept was a step in the right direction to facilitate more robust parliamentary debate. However, the process 'entrusts the Government itself with the responsibility of testing its own proposals against a Bill of Rights' and lacks the teeth to ensure proper scrutiny.[13] Russell argued that a standing committee of the House of Commons ought to be established to review the possible effects of legislative and executive initiatives on fundamental rights and freedoms.[14]

Little is known about how proposed bills are scrutinized. One account suggests that rather than 'Charter proofing,' the process is more akin to risk assessment, in which government lawyers give advice on the likelihood of a Charter challenge and probable difficulties in justifying the legislation under the charter. Usually the advice comes with the recognition that a legislative objective is important but with suggestions for how to make the policy more sensitive to the adversely affected rights and therefore reduce the risk of a successful Charter challenge. Departments are then left to decide how much risk they are prepared to accept.[15] However, empirical research is lacking on what role Department of Justice lawyers play, the nature of their advice, and its influence on policy decisions. Whatever scrutiny takes place within the executive, the information is not shared with Parliament. Parliamentary committees, if they take the initiative, can require that lawyers from the Department of Justice appear in committee hearings to address questions about the Charter. But the executive does not disclose the specific Charter concerns that have influenced the content and design of legislation. Specifically, it does not provide Parliament with a statement about why the legislative objective was considered important enough to restrict protected rights or why alternative and less restrictive legislative means were not adopted.

Parliamentary debate has not generally compelled governments to explain or justify their choices where rights are implicated. The combination of an ineffective upper house, strict party discipline, and a single-member plurality electoral system that overrepresents the winning party has resulted in executive dominance, in which Parliament has little influence on policy choices. The relative failure of representative institutions to require that governments explain to Parliament their policy choices in terms of the Charter shields, from public and judicial purview, evidence of what assumptions have influenced these policies, how rigorously they have been scrutinized, and whether less restrictive measures have been contemplated.

This failure of the executive to disclose charter considerations is unfortunate. As I argue elsewhere, the court's difficulty in evaluating whether alternative legislative means are available has encouraged judges to relax considerably the threshhold for establishing that legislation has been carefully enough designed, particularly in social policy. This devolution of the court's application of reasonableness criteria, when combined with its reluctance to disallow specific policy objectives, has meant that governments have been able to exert considerable influence in determining the scope of justifiable limits on protected rights. They have helped define the very constraints that the Charter was intended to impose on them.[16] With few exceptions,[17] judicial review of the Charter has not generally resulted in priority being given to a significantly different range of values than those espoused by federal or provincial governments.

Australian Bills Committees

In the last part of the paper, I propose that Parliament and the provincial legislatures establish standing legislative committees to evaluate bills in terms of their implications for protected rights. The existence of such a process might compel the government to explain and justify infringements on rights and explain the legislative or administrative means chosen.

If Parliament is to press the government to justify policy choices involving fundamental rights, its operations must change. Parliament is not a forum where independent members engage in philosophical debate in a principled, nonpartisan manner. Rather, it is a weak institution, where the structure of power gives members a subordinate role, disciplined along party lines and dealing with issues in an adversarial format which assumes that multifaceted conflicts can be reduced to two viewpoints – in favour or opposed.[18]

However, this incongruence between how Parliament operates and my suggestion for a greater role for it vis-à-vis rights does not mean that it cannot press governments to justify legislation in terms of its effects on rights. British experience shows that party discipline need not be as onerous as in Canada and that parliamentary committees can have more autonomy, without undermining responsible government.[19] The Canadian Parliament has shown itself capable of principled debate about government's obligations under the Charter in the context of refugee-determination policy and revised rape-shield legislation after a negative judicial decision.[20] Parliamentary committees in Australia, which face many of the constraints of their Canadian counterparts, scrutinize the implications of governmental initiatives for rights.

This proposal for standing legislative committees is influenced by initiatives in Australia, where three jurisdictions have established such committees. These multi-partisan bodies examine proposed legislation, report possible rights concerns, ask for ministerial clarifications and explanations, and publish their observations for MPs to use in debate.

The Senate Standing Committee of the commonwealth Parliament was established in Canberra in 1981, in 1992 Victoria set up a Scrutiny of Acts and Regulations Committee, and in 1995 a Scrutiny of Legislation Committee was created in Queensland. The first two have similar terms of reference. Neither has a codified statements of rights, and both refer to rights generically. Canberra's committee considers whether bills or acts 'trespass unduly on personal rights and liberties,' whereas Victoria's looks at whether a provision 'trespasses unduly on rights or freedoms.' Other criteria include whether a bill or act makes rights, liberties, and/or obligations unduly dependent on insufficiently defined administrative powers or on non-reviewable administrative decisions.[21] The Queensland committee's terms of reference are more specific. They include whether bills and subordinate legislation are consistent with fundamental legislative principles, which require that legislation:

(a) makes rights or liberties, or obligations, dependent on administrative power only if the power is sufficiently defined and subject to appropriate review; and
(b) is consistent with the principles of natural justice; and
(c) allows the delegation of administrative power only in appropriate cases and to appropriate persons; and
(d) does not reverse the onus of proof in criminal proceedings without adequate justification; and
(e) confers power to enter premises, and search for or seize documents or other property, only with a warrant issued by a judge or other judicial officer; and
(f) provides appropriate protection against self-incrimination; and
(g) does not adversely affect rights and liberties, or impose obligations, retrospectively; and

(h) does not confer immunity from proceeding or prosecution without adequate justification; and
(i) provides for the compulsory acquisition of property only with fair compensation; and
(j) has sufficient regard to Aboriginal tradition and Island custom;
(k) is unambiguous and drafted in a sufficiently clear and precise manner.[22]

Role of Bills Committees

The hope of civil libertarians is that these committees, by evaluating proposed legislation in a systematic manner and reporting to Parliament about possible rights concerns, will facilitate debate about the justification of policies, which in turn will put pressure on governments to explain, justify, and, where warranted, amend their bills. The Australian committees publish an *Alert Digest*, which provides a brief background of a bill, describes its major provisions, and raises rights concerns and relates these to specific clauses. The Victoria committee also has held public hearings to garner broader or different perspectives on controversial issues.

Perhaps the greatest challenge that committee members face is to reconcile the conflict between their statutory obligations and their loyalty to party. As in Canada, the parliamentary system in Australia is intensely partisan, and parties operate and act in a cohesive manner. Strict party discipline makes it difficult for members to vote against their party's position, which makes life very difficult for government members of a legislative scrutiny committee. They may have a strong sense of the policy history of a proposed bill and be sensitive to the government's intents and objectives, yet they are part of a multi-partisan committee that scrutinizes that very policy.

The most important element in managing this inherent conflict is that committee members distinguish the task of identifying possible rights violations from that of making qualitative or partisan judgments about the merits of the policy. Members from all three committees insist that in evaluating bills they do not, and will not, pass judgment on whether the policy is warranted. Not only is this a fundamental characteristic of the committees but members suggest that the system would break down if the committee ever crossed this conceptual line: 'I think it's a good thing that we've managed to take a lofty approach and stay above politics. We stick to our terms of reference and look only at potential infringements on basic rights, not at the policy objectives behind the legislation. Once you get into policy you also get into politics, and if we got bogged down by our political persuasions, the committee probably wouldn't be able to raise many of the problems it has raised.'[23]

Members and legal advisers suggest that if the committees proffered political assessments of policies, they would cease to be effective. They would simply mirror partisan divisions within Parliament, and they would frequently produce minority or dissenting reports, which would diminish their influence on the government. This ability to press governments, through correspondence with ministers or parliamentary debate, would decrease in the face of conflicting opinions, because these multiple and competing perspectives would suggest that the dispute is not so much about principles as about policy preferences. Thus differing opinions would provide a ready excuse for the government to maintain its original position.

The pressure to avoid partisan divisions has encouraged committees to look at two separate issues: does a policy restrict a right, and, if so, is the infringement undue? Further, they tend to concentrate on the first issue and leave resolution of the second, where it is controversial, for Parliament. This conceptual distinction has not only allowed them to avoid partisan divisions but has enabled them to take a consensual approach. They vote rarely and tend to couch their analysis in qualified language. While they at times report unequivocally that a bill imposes an undue restriction on a right, where members differ, the committees couch their report in more qualified terms. For example, the Senate committee often reports that a provision may unduly trespass on rights and freedoms, whereas Victoria's frequently reports that a provision diminishes rights but refers to Parliament the question of whether the reduction is undue. This more qualified language helps overcomes differences of opinion, particularly when members are either unsure or unwilling to make a firm pronouncement.

This reporting style fits with many members' view that an undue restriction on a right often involves a policy issue. Because they often see rights issues as inextricably intertwined with policy considerations, many believe that the collective judgment of Parliament should decide. What a committee can do is to solicit and gather information, raise the spectre that a right may have been unduly infringed, present this to Parliament, and facilitate debate.

Not everyone agrees that a consensual approach is always best. A committee may not go as far as it otherwise might in terms of pointing out conflicts. Compromises exist to satisfy internal conflicts, and therefore a committee's emphasis on consensus may leave it less vigilant. While its multi-partisan nature may prevent it from making firm pronouncements on the merits of a bill, some believe that a bills committee could opt for a middle ground. Instead of simply alerting Parliament about possible rights violations, a committee could recommend specific ways of making a policy more sensitive to rights concerns. It could be more vigorous when evaluating the ways and means of policy, without actually assessing the merits of the policy goal itself. The Queensland committee's reporting style is more consistent with this approach. The committee is less prone to adopt qualified language in its reports. Although it often refers to Parliament the question of whether a bill has sufficient regard to rights, it also frequently makes recommendations on how to improve a particular bill – for example, by removing a worrisome word, section, or clause. Once members resume their parliamentary role, they engage freely in partisan debate. Members do not, and will not, cross a party line, even when the party position is insensitive to the committee's concerns. This seems to contradict members' commitment to protect rights, but members insist that this is not the reality. They argue that they can, and must, be loyal to their party position – that the survival of a parliamentary system requires cohesive parties and that members must support their party. Indeed, analysis of Hansard verifies the fact that committee members act and vote along party lines, even when the committee has raised issues that have not been addressed by the relevant minister.

If government members vote against the government, this action may attract attention for a particular issue, but in the end it will be a less effective way of compelling governments to take rights issues seriously. Both Labor and Liberal members agree that their futures with their parties would be hurt, perhaps irreparably, if they voted against the party in Parliament. So too might the credibility and standing of the committee. Legislative scrutiny committees are in a vulnerable position. Governments do not like to face barriers to the implementation of their programs. If these committees are seen as particularly obstructive, they may jeopardize their ability to influence policy decisions and, perhaps, their continued existence.

Bills Committees and Policy

To date little empirical research has been conducted to assess what effects these committees are having on policy; in particular, whether protection of rights and freedoms has been improved by the systematic scrutiny of bills. Research has not addressed the extent to which Parliament is making use of this valuable resource and, where serious rights concerns are raised, whether parliamentary debate is putting pressure on the government to justify or revise proposed legislation. What has been written about these committees is largely anecdotal and usually flattering. For example, the Senate Bills Committee in Canberra has been acclaimed as 'a model for all Parliaments,'[24] in that it has made a 'substantial contribution to the output of legislation.'[25] The committee's *Alert Digest* has enabled the Senate to consider problematic clauses that otherwise might not have been drawn to its attention and has 'undoubtedly precipitated a considerable number of amendments to government bills.'[26] Furthermore, its systematic review of bills may have encouraged more careful drafting of legislation. Thus 'while it may not be possible to relate, conclusively, the work of the Scrutiny of Bills Committee to the final form of legislation, there can be no doubt that it has contributed significantly to the legislative process, filling a gap that was manifestly open, and ensuring that "debate has been an informed debate and that the Parliament has legislated with open eyes."'[27] One report suggests that the Victoria committee has led to improvements in drafting procedures and to changes in bills, particularly vis-à-vis issuance of warrants and appeal rights. However, 'departments are obviously not going to admit that they were going to infringe on rights but did not because of the Committee's presence.'[28]

Political scientist John Uhr is not as convinced about the Senate committee, particularly in the absence of empirical evidence. Uhr, who has served as secretary to the committee, describes one of its goals as being process-oriented – to provide information so that the Senate can properly deliberate and pass the proposed legislation 'with open eyes.' Its second role is to effect a preferred outcome – in short, 'to fix things up.'[29] Unfortunately, from his perspective, the committee does not take the second task as seriously as it should; it 'has not developed an agenda or policy of its own related to social justice ... One manifestation of this is seen in the Scrutiny reports with that kind of anchorless drift of observations on possibly defective provisions which attract the routine response from government that, of course, they are required for reasons of policy, to which the Committee succumbs with a mild protest and then incorporates the Government's response.'[30]

Uhr would like to see the committee adopt a more corporate approach to its job, determining issues for which it can and should go out on a limb. He expresses doubts about whether the current approach produces better outcomes: 'It is a process activity which tells the community very little about how seriously the Committee is prepared to protect it against threats to social justice, through denials of rights and access.'[31]

Models for Canada?

Clearly, empirical research on how bills committees contribute to the policy process is required before any confident predictions can be made that adoption of such committees would improve rights scrutiny in Canadian governments. These committees would face similar constraints in Canada because of our shared parliamentary heritage and tradition of party discipline. However, even in the absence of comprehensive analysis of these committees and their influence, it is reasonable to expect that a similar structure would improve practice.

Two of the three Australian jurisdictions with scrutiny committees have an elected upper house, which provides more effective checks and balances on governmental authority than Canada has.[32] However, in Canada the judiciary has a clear mandate to nullify laws that are inconsistent with the Charter. The possibility of judicial nullification, which may increase where serious rights concerns have been identified by a bills committee but not addressed by the executive, should augment the influence of a Canadian committee on parliamentary debate.

Rights considerations do influence public and policy debates in Australia, reinforced by recent High Court decisions that have interpreted the constitution as including certain implied rights as the basis for striking down legislation and by Australia's participation in international rights treaties. Indeed, the establishing of bills committees to examine the implications of policies from a rights perspective confirms this interest in protecting rights. Nevertheless, the lack of a Bill of Rights has meant that the language of rights has arguably not had the same prominence as it has in Canada since 1982. Although the globalization of rights discourse would inevitably have given more ascendancy to rights considerations in Canada, introduction of the Charter of Rights and Freedoms in 1982 can be thought of as a dynamic force that has ensured greater prominence to rights considerations in judicial and public assessments of state actions.

Despite controversy over the value of judicial review, and the systematic focus on the rights dimensions of social and constitutional policy, the Charter has increased the frequency of rights talk in judicial, public policy, and constitutional debates. This increased focus on rights has manifest itself in pressures to reassess existing ideas about what particular rights mean, and the nature of state obligations, whether in equality claims or in procedural protections offered to those suspected of breaking the law. Together, the symbolic aspects of the Charter (for example, its claim to 'guarantee' rights), the new ability of citizens to challenge legislation in rights-based terms and obtain remedial redress, and the distinct possibility that legislation can be nullified if the courts deem it inconsistent with the Charter's fundamental values have increased the political costs for governments insensitive to rights considerations. Notwithstanding party cohesion and discipline, the Charter will probably make it more difficult for government parties to admonish and punish committee members who, in performing their statutory duty, are not only trying to protect rights, but to uphold fundamental constitutional principles.

A Canadian scrutiny of bills committee would face many of the constraints that Australian committees face, particularly those that arise because of the existence of strict and cohesive political parties. A Canadian committee would likely want to follow the Australian lead and distinguish between scrutinizing rights violations and evaluating the justification for the legislation.

A parallel exists between how Australian committees conceptualize their task and the Supreme Court of Canada's two-stage approach to the Charter, which distinguishes analytically the question of whether a right has been violated from the inquiry into whether the legislation is reasonable. These distinctions can blur because an implication of concluding that legislation does 'unduly trespass' on a right, or that it is 'not a reasonable limit' on a right, is that it imposes too great a burden on a right to be justified. In other words, the policy does not warrant restricting rights, at least to the degree that it has.

Nevertheless, this distinction may be a prudent one for a parliamentary bills committee to maintain. Its blurry nature is less problematic for a bills committee than for a court. The role of courts is not to facilitate debate about whether a policy decision is appropriate from a rights perspective. Courts are asked, under a system of entrenched rights, to pronounce on whether a policy is or is not constitutional. As was argued above, the Supreme Court's two-stage approach, when combined with its reluctance to say that policy objectives are not important enough to justify limiting rights, has caused the court considerable difficulty. Its primary emphasis has been on whether the legislation has been carefully enough designed. But this emphasis is often a thinly disguised way of asking whether the policy is important enough to warrant the deprivation of rights that it imposes.

However, the role of a bills committee is different. This conceptual distinction is troublesome only if one views the committee's role in terms of deciding whether a policy is justified in rights-based terms. But this would be to assign to these committees a different role than that for which they are best suited. It is better to view their role as facilitating and giving structure to parliamentary and public debate about the merits of and worthiness of policy.

Partisan considerations may transcend attempts to evaluate the merits of policies, and the possibility that such a small number of individuals would effectively define the bounds of what is acceptable, from a rights perspective, is troubling. As Victor Perton, former chair of the Victoria committee, suggests, to expect such a body to determine whether a policy is or is not justified in rights-based terms does little to address a principal concern that many have about giving to courts this task. The resolution to many rights disputes is not always obvious or uncontested. Thus to give an elite body an authoritative voice to make this decision raises a serious democratic concern, regardless of whether it is composed of judges or parliamentarians.[33]

A Canadian committee might structure its inquiry around these questions: 1/What is the nature of the rights infringement? 2/What is the policy objective, and what goals does it serve? 3/Can it be accomplished by less restrictive means?

The purpose of this legislative debate, as I see it, is not to turn parliamentarians into arm-chair judges but to evaluate government's policies from a principled perspective: in terms of the public interest but with regard to the values and principles in the Charter. In this sense, a Canadian committee would operate similarly to the Australian committees, which exist without a bill of rights. Such committees, through principled and multi-party scrutiny of legislation and identification of rights concerns, should place pressure on governments to justify and, where necessary, revise policy decisions to be more sensitive to rights concerns.

The Charter scrutiny that Parliament could engage in differs from the kind that takes place within the executive. Clearly, a system of executive-based rights scrutiny is welcome. For public officials in departments and agencies and for ministers who bear ultimate accountability, it provides them information about some of the specific legal difficulties that can be anticipated and enables ministers to revisit policy objectives, assess alternative means, and ultimately make more responsible decisions about whether to recommend that the policy be enacted.

However, its existence does not placate concerns about whether, in the face of judicial deference, rights considerations are being taken seriously by representative institutions. More important, to assume that an executive-led Charter evaluation process diminishes the need for parliamentary scrutiny would be to accept the propositions that resolution to rights-based conflicts involves exclusively legal issues (in that the scrutiny is done by government lawyers); that the Charter provides clear and authoritative answers to constitutional questions (to the extent that the Supreme Court jurisprudence provides the basis to make exact or clear pronouncements on the desirability or constitutionality of legislative actions); and that representative institutions do not have the political responsibility to challenge and contest legal assumptions about the scope of their responsibilities or the importance that should be attached to conflicting values.[34]

Conclusions

The Supreme Court's decision to interpret the Charter in a manner that places considerable emphasis on whether policies have been carefully enough designed, as opposed to assessing whether the policy objectives themselves are warranted in rights-based terms, raises the question of whether the court's task can be distinguished conceptually from the kinds of discretionary policy considerations undertaken by policy drafters. It also raises the question of whether other institutions, such as Parliament, would be better situated to scrutinize the merits of policies in rights-based terms.

Although conventional criticisms of judicial review often emphasize the superiority of representative institutions in determining the priorities that should be attached to conflicting values, the Canadian Parliament does not live up to these expectations. Provincial and federal legislatures should think seriously of following Australia's lead of establishing a standing parliamentary committee to scrutinize bills in terms of their consistency with rights. If Parliament were to become a place for discussing the justification for policies and their effects on protected rights, this public record would, through media coverage and observation by interested individuals and groups, stimulate broader public debate on the merits of policies that raise rights issues. This would put pressure on the government to explain, justify, and, where warranted, revise its policy decisions – which is perhaps the most important contribution that the Charter can make to the policy process.

The existence of systematic legislative scrutiny would also benefit judicial review. Because judges are poorly situated to assess the reasonableness of complex policy choices, the greatest contribution to rights protection that they can provide does not arise from the expertise they bring to the task of determining whether alternative, preferable legislative means were available. Rather, what judges can and should do is to hold parliamentarians to account by ensuring that they have scrutinized and justified their legislative decisions where these impose limits on protected rights. Where legislative records reveal that a policy has been the product of meaningful and deliberative debate about the worthiness of its objective and has been sensitively drafted, little justification exists for judges to nullify these decisions unless the court is relatively certain that shortcomings identified in debate had not been adequately rectified or that the legislation restricts a core right or imposes a limit that is obviously excessive or unreasonable. Conversely, where legislative decisions have not been the product of careful deliberation about why the policy is justified in light of its effects on rights, or of alternative and less restrictive means, judicial deference may be inappropriate. By refusing to accept the justification of impugned policies where rights concerns have not been fully considered, the court will provide an incentive for representative institutions to pay more attention to the effects of policy choices on protected rights.[35]

NOTES

I would like to acknowledge financial assistance provided by a grant from Queen's University's Advisory Research Committee, which has facilitated research on Australian legislative-scrutiny committees. I would like to thank members, legal advisers, and past and present secretaries of the Senate Standing Bills Committee for the Scrutiny of Bills in Canberra, the Scrutiny of Acts and Regulations Committee of Victoria, and the Scrutiny of Legislation Committee in Queensland for their generosity and time in meeting with me in Canberra, Melbourne, and Brisbane, respectively, in June and July 1996. A variant of this paper appears as 'A Hybird-Approach to Protect Rights? An Argument in Favour of Supplementaring Canadian Judicial Review with Australia's Model of Parliamentary Scrutiny,' *Federal Law Review* 25 (1998), 115–38.

1 Peter H. Russell, 'Political Purposes of the Canadian Charter,' *Canadian Bar Review* 61 (1983), 30–54.
2 Peter H. Russell, 'A Democratic Approach to Civil Liberties,' *University of Toronto Law Journal* 19 (1969), 109–31.
3 *Reference re Sections 193 & 195.1(1)(c) of the Criminal Code, (Canada)*, [1990] 1 SCR 1123 at 1181.
4 The court has indicated that protected speech will not probably include threats or acts of violence.
5 *R. v. Keegstra*, [1990] 3 SCR 697 at 743.
6 The court's general approach to assessing the reasonableness of legislation under section 1 was provided for in *R. v. Oakes*, [1986] 1 SCR 103.
7 *Irwin Toy Ltd. v. A.G. Quebec*, [1989] 1 SCR 927 at 989–90.
8 Chief Justice Lamer stated, on the issue of whether Parliament should be required to choose the perfect or the best possible legislative scheme, that the Charter 'does not require Parliament to "roll the dice" in its effort to achieve "pressing and substantial" objectives in order to adopt the absolutely *least* intrusive provision.' *R. v. Chaulk*, [1990] 3 SCR 1303 at 1343.
9 Ibid. at 1343.
10 *Reference re ss. 193 and 195.1(1)(c) of the Criminal Code (Man.)*, [1990] 1 SCR 1123 at 1138.
11 Patrick Monahan and Marie Finkelstein suggest that the common interest of Canadian governments to consider rights issues early in the policy process has increased the role and status of attorneys general and their legal advisers to the point that, in many governments, they now constitute a new central agency. Patrick J. Monahan and Marie Finkelstein, 'The Charter of Rights and Public Policy in Canada,' in Monahan and Finkelstein, eds., *The Impact of the Charter on the Public Policy Process* (North York 1993), 42.
12 David Kinley, *The European Convention on Human Rights: Compliance without Incorporation* (Aldershot, England, 1993), 103.
13 Russell, 'Democratic Approach to Civil Liberties,' 125–6.
14 Ibid., 126.

15 Stephen Zaluski, Department of Justice, Guest Lecture, School of Policy Studies 810, 4 Oct. 1996.

16 Janet L. Hiebert, *Limiting Rights: The Dilemma of Judicial Review*, (Montreal 1996), 152.

17 A particularly notable exception was the narrow majority in *RJR-MacDonald Inc. v. Canada (Attorney General)*, [1995] 3 SCR 199.

18 C.E.S. Franks, *The Parliament of Canada* (Toronto 1989), 14–15, 31.

19 Ibid., 31.

20 For a discussion of the role that rights played in structuring particular political debates, see the following articles by the author: 'Debating Policy: The Effects of Rights Talk,' in F. Leslie Seidle, *Equity and Community: The Charter, Interest Advocacy and Representation* (Montreal 1993); and 'Political Approach to Reasonable Limits,' in Patrick Monahan and Marie Finkelstein, *The Impact of the Charter on the Public Policy Process* (North York 1993), 000.

21 The commonwealth committee's reference here does not include the word 'administrative' but instead refers only to 'non-reviewable decisions.' In addition, the terms of reference for both committees include inappropriately delegating legislative power and insufficiently subjecting the exercise of legislative power to parliamentary scrutiny. The Victoria committee has additional responsibilities relating to its own constitution and to the jurisdiction of the Supreme Court. It also is charged with scrutinizing subordinate legislation or to review any act referred to it. In Canberra, a separate committee, established in 1931, scrutinizes subordinate legislation.

22 Fundamental legislative principles are described as 'the principles relating to legislation that underlie a parliamentary democracy based on the rule of law.' The principles include requiring that legislation has sufficient regard to rights and liberties of individuals and the institution of Parliament. Legislative Standard Act 1992, sec. 4(1), Queensland.

23 Senator Judith Troeth, member and former chair of the Senate Standing Committee on the Scrutiny of Bills, Canberra, as cited by Melissa McKerihan, 'Unknown Watchdog,' *Australian Lawyer* 30 (July 1995), 000–00.

24 G.S. Reid and Martyn Forrest, *Australia's Commonwealth Parliament 1901–1988: Ten Perspectives* (Melbourne), 177.

25 Ibid., 190.

26 Ibid., 217.

27 Ibid., 218.

28 Maree Henwood, 'The Scrutiny of Acts and Regulations Committee: It's [*sic*] Role in and Impact on the Parliamentary Process since November 1992,' paper prepared for parliamentary internship project, (Melbourne, 7 Nov. 1994), 6.

29 John Uhr, Proceedings of *Ten Years of Scrutiny*, Parliament House, Canberra, 25 Nov. 1991, 76–86.

30 Ibid., 84.

31 Ibid., 86.

32 Queensland is the exception, with its unicameral system.

33 Interview with Victor Perton, 4 July 1996, Melbourne.

34 Hiebert, *Limiting Rights*, 118–25.

35 Ibid., 150–7.

Summary of Discussion on Rights and the Charter

In the discussion following the session, Leslie Seidle said that he would like to share in the optimism of some of the panelists for parliamentary reforms, but past reforms, such as those following the McGraw Report, have changed the climate of public debate very little, partly because of the effectiveness of party discipline. In response, Janet Hiebert noted that Parliaments in both Canada and Australia have been able to transcend party lines and act in a principled manner on contentious rights debates. She sees legislative rights scrutiny committees as such an instance. From what she has observed in Australia, committee members are able to act in a non- or multi-partisan fashion by focusing on whether rights may be infringed by an act, not on the ends of the policies involved. She did comment, however, that serving on these committees did nothing to further a member's legislative career and that some thought that taking a role in legislative scrutiny foreclosed any realistic aspiration to a ministerial role.

Rainer Knopff and Ted Morton endorsed Hiebert's recommendations to bring the rights debate out of the courts and into the legislature. In their view, the committees would lower the temperature of rights claims and lead to the more balanced democracy that Canada lost under the Charter.

Paul Chartrand questioned Knopff and Morton about their characterization of rights talk in courts as coercive, noting that an essential function of the courts was to maintain social harmony. He also thought that there is often a cooler temperature in courts than in parliaments for the determination of the merits of new claims. Knopff agreed that there is a certain coolness in the courtroom that does not exist in legislatures, but he argued that the battle for rights in the courtroom is more coercive in that it takes the flux out of legislative politics, where whatever is done today can be undone tomorrow. Morton chimed in, recognizing a coercive aspect to both courts and parliaments, but arguing that under the Charter the coercive power of judicial order has been used to conclude many peripheral issues, not only core issues fundamental to the proper working of a political society.

Lorraine Weinrib challenged Knopff and Morton's characterization of both the Quebec signs and Morgentaler decisions. She thought that the Meech Lake Accord failed not because of the court's decision but because Premier Robert Bourassa reversed his own language policy, and, as other premiers and the prime minister had warned, his use of the override cost him Meech Lake. As to Morgentaler, she had several points. First, the case arose in the context of a prosecution of a doctor, not through the efforts of public interest groups, as Knopff and Morton contend. Second, the Supreme Court decision said that Parliament had known that the administration of the statute was contrary to what had been set down as the rule for access to therapeutic abortion since at least the 1976 Badgley Report and had done nothing about it. Third, in the aftermath of the decision, the Senate's consideration of the Mulroney abortion bill recognized the court's analysis of the unfairness of the statute as a better way to think about women's lives. Pursuing a comment by Kent Roach to the effect that Knopff and Morton were overly legalistic in looking only at the court decisions and not at the legislative replies, Weinrib argued that we are now getting much better analyses of rights in the legislative arena. She concluded by saying that we need the strength of healthy analysis in both our courts and our legislatures, so that they can work in a proper discursive arrangement.

Knopff replied regarding the signs case. He said that the important point was that there was a debate going on in Quebec among Québécois about the desirability of the signs law, and there were some indications that in time the government might relax or do away with the law. When the issue went to court, the debate in the political arena was short-circuited in ways that were not helpful.

Regarding Morgentaler, Morton quipped that to say that the case arose out of an individual prosecution and not out of an interest group is to reverse the charge of being rather legalistic. More substantively, he argued that Parliament well understood that the abortion law would be applied differently in different parts of the country, because that was part of the 1969 legislative accommodation and compromise. The courts chose to ignore this. And at trial, not one witness was called who could say that she was denied an abortion. What happened in Morgentaler, according to Morton, was a change from a legislative to a court venue, enabling one group to override what satisfied the majority. He concluded that when courts make decisions on clearly contestable issues of public policy, democracy takes a beating.

Contributors

Madame Justice Rosalie Silberman Abella
Court of Appeal for Ontario

Hon. Ronald G. Atkey, PC
Osler, Hoskin and Harcourt Barristers and Solicitors

Professor Carl Baar
Department of Political Science
Brock University

Professor Jean-Paul Brodeur
Centre International de Criminologie Comparée
Université de Montréal

Paul Chartrand
Victoria, BC
formerly at Department of Native Studies, University of Manitoba, and Royal Commission on Aboriginal Peoples

Professor Hugh Corder
Faculty of Law
University of Cape Town

Hon. Stéphane Dion, PC
President of the Queen's Privy Council for Canada and Minister of Intergovernmental Affairs

Georges Erasmus
Aboriginal Healing Foundation, Ottawa
formerly co-chair, Royal Commission on Aboriginal Peoples

Professor Christine Fletcher
North Australia Research Unit
Australian National University, Casuarina

Professor Martin L. Friedland
Faculty of Law
University of Toronto

Professor Janet L. Hiebert
Department of Political Studies
Queen's University

Professor Rainer Knopff
Department of Political Science
University of Calgary

Professor F.L. Morton
Department of Political Science
University of Calgary

Madame Justice Maryka Omatsu
Ontario Court of Justice
(Provincial Division)

Professor Kent Roach
Faculty of Law
University of Toronto

Madame Justice Katherine Swinton
Ontario Court of Justice (General Division)
formerly at
Faculty of Law
University of Toronto

Professor James Tully
Department of Political Science
University of Victoria

Professor Robert C. Vipond
Department of Political Science
University of Toronto

Professor Reg Whitaker
Department of Political Science
York University